THE
INVENTION
OF THE
RENAISSANCE
WOMAN

Pamela Joseph Benson

THE INVENTION
OF THE
RENAISSANCE WOMAN

The Challenge of
Female Independence
in the Literature and Thought
of Italy and England

The Pennsylvania State University Press

University Park, Pennsylvania

Library of Congress Cataloging-in-Publication Data

Benson, Pamela.
    The invention of the Renaissance woman : the challenge of female independence in
the literature and thought of Italy and England / Pamela Joseph Benson.
        p.   cm.
    Includes bibliographical references and index.
    ISBN 0-271-00812-1.—ISBN 0-271-00814-8 (pbk.)
    1. English literature—Early modern, 1500–1700—History and
criticism.   2. Women and literature—England—History—16th century.
3. Italian literature—15th century—History and criticism.
4. Italian literature—16th century—History and criticism.
5. Feminism and literature—England—History—16th century.
6. Women—England—History—Renaissance, 1450–1600.   7. Literature,
Comparative—English and Italian.   8. Literature, Comparative
—Italian and English.   9. Women—Italy—History—Renaissance,
1450–1600.   10. Feminism and literature—Italy—History.   11. Women
and literature—Italy—History.   I. Title.
PR418.W65B46 1992
820.9'352042'09031—dc20   91-22934
                                                                                          CIP

It is the policy of The Pennsylvania State University Press to use acid-free paper for the first
printing of all clothbound books. Publications on uncoated stock satisfy the minimum
requirements of American National Standard for Information Sciences—Permanence of
Paper for Printed Library Materials, ANSI Z39.48–1984.

*To my mother
and in memory of my father*

CONTENTS

Acknowledgments

This book began as a seminar paper in my first year of graduate school, and thus there was ample time for me to incur numerous debts to colleagues and friends while I reshaped that simple effort into this long book. Louise George Clubb, the instructor of the seminar for which I wrote the paper, and James V. Mirollo, the director of my dissertation, both helped me to define the lines of inquiry and encouraged me to continue my work with their skillful and generous instruction. Robert Hanning's and Daniel Javitch's extensive written comments on the thesis helped me begin the long process of developing the topic into a book. Many colleagues and friends read and commented on parts of the text: Donald Cheney, Thelma Fenster, and the members of the New England Seminar on Women in the Renaissance and Reformation all gave encouraging but sharp criticism. Mary Purnell Frederick helped me establish a methodology for the presentation of the texts, and Robert Grudin, from his extensive knowledge of Renaissance culture, asked careful and detailed questions. The comments of the two readers for Penn State Press, Constance Jordan and Elizabeth Hageman, assisted me enormously in my revisions. I have benefited from letters of recommendation, information, conversation, and practical advice of many others: Barbara K. Lewalski, Carolyn Swift, Heather Dubrow, Elizabeth Robertson, Guido Ruggiero, Thomas P. Roche, Jr., Elissa Weaver, James Nohrnberg, Richard Neuse, David Wallace, Maureen Quilligan, Margaret Ferguson, and Steve Shelburne knowingly and unknowingly were of great help. The Pepys Library, Magdalen College, Cambridge, kindly allowed me to read the Howard manuscript at odd hours. The National Endowment for the Humanities gave me a year to work intensively and to travel to collections, and Rhode Island College has generously supported my work with research grants and research assistants.

And finally, the most personal debts: to my mother, whose unstinting generosity gives me the time to write every summer; to my children, Michael,

John, and Thomas; and to my husband, David, whose faith, encouragement, and careful scholarly criticism have helped me to think clearly and to bring this book to an end.

Material from Chapters 4 and 5 and 10 and 11 appeared in issues of *Quaderni d'italianistica* and *English Literary Renaissance,* respectively. All translations from Italian are my own; translations from *De mulieribus claris* are by Guido A. Guarino (Rutgers, 1963) with his permission. All other translations from Latin are acknowledged in the notes.

INTRODUCTION

Late in his life Giovanni Boccaccio, author of many works dedicated to his "dearest ladies" and of *Il Corbaccio*, a scurrilous antifeminist satire, produced the *De mulieribus claris*, a collection of biographies of over one hundred famous secular women. This work was different from any other work about women in Boccaccio's opus and, as he says in his Proem, different from any known postclassical work by any author. It praised many women for acting with strength, valor, fortitude, and intelligence, that is, for exercising "manly" virtues in traditionally male fields (xxxvii).

Enthusiastic as the author represents himself to be about his literary endeavor, however, the text is shadowed by fear. Writing praise of women for such actions might have real political consequences; it might lead a reader to the conclusion that the traditional powerless and inferior position of woman cannot be reconciled with her capacity for political action and that, therefore, social and political institutions ought to be modified in order to accommodate this new woman. Such a radical political conclusion is forestalled by the frequent assertion that the famous women were miraculously endowed with the qualities that enabled them to succeed, and, thus, cannot be models for ordinary women, and by the drawing of ethical rather than political morals from the exemplary lives. By these means the tension between the content of the lives and existing political and social structures is resolved in favor of the status quo.

In its reluctance to follow its own evidence that women are capable of performing like men to its logical political conclusion, the *De mulieribus claris* forecast the attitude of the works that followed in its wake. First, in collections of biographical sketches of famous women written in imitation of Boccaccio's, then, in a variety of documents about the education of women, in encomia and defenses of womankind, in dialogues on the nature of woman and her place, and in narratives such as the *Orlando furioso* and *The Faerie Queene*, Renaissance authors confronted the problem faced by Boccaccio: how to contain the political implications of evidence that women are capable of acting with prudence, fortitude, justice, and temperance. These numerous profeminist texts produced in the fifteenth century through the 1530s in Italy and in the sixteenth century in England are the subject matter of my book. I suggest that, although most of them do explicitly offer a new notion of what woman is, as Boccaccio's does not, they share his reluctance to initiate political reform. For this reason I have used the term profeminist rather than feminist to refer to them. They use genre, characterization, comedy, contrasting levels of style, and other literary means to short-circuit the logical political consequences of their praise. I argue that in defending woman in the particular ways they do, they defend their society and their own literary voices against new womankind, and I suggest that this self-defense succeeded. The male remains the authoritative author of literary texts and the governor of social institutions. By permitting genuinely profeminist content to exist without a feminist political program, the works in praise of women contributed to the phenomenon noted by Ian Maclean in his authoritative study of the fate of the Aristotelian notion of women; "at the end of the Renaissance, there is a greater discrepancy between social realities and the current notion of woman than at the beginning" (*Renaissance Notion* 1).

When I speak of "invention" in my title, I am invoking both the Renaissance and the modern senses of the term. Renaissance writers thought of invention as the recovery of a notion or object, the finding of something that had been lost. Like St. Helena's "invention" of the cross, the texts that I discuss find a woman who has always existed, yet has not been recognized in recent times. Moderns, however, think of invention scientifically, the making of something original and never before possible. Like Edison's "invention" of the electric light, the texts I discuss create an ideal woman suited to the anxieties and expectations of their time and place. The "Renaissance Woman" is both a recovery of the old and a construction of the new.

The first challenge that I face in proving my assertions about these works is to demonstrate that the texts in defense and praise of womankind are at all serious. The majority of them are extreme in style. They veer from high to low and back again. They flirt with the ladies and address themselves to male readers behind the ladies' backs. They indulge in antimasculine invective. Even if they appear sober, they attempt to slander the character of their opponents and ostentatiously suppress evidence that might contradict their case. They are exercises in paradox: women, like folly, baldness, and the ass, have not traditionally been valued, and the proof that they ought to be is an essay in proving the unprovable. Examples of the Renaissance delight in "serio ludere"; they demand to be appreciated for the skill with which they manipulate rhetoric in the service of an absurd topic.

Because of their stylistic and logical pyrotechnics, these works were long dismissed as merely playing games with the topic and their readers and of having no genuine profeminist content, but I suggest that the choice of genre brings with it a significant ability to disrupt readers' comfortable certainties. Because woman's inferiority to man was assumed, a text that proposed to defend her and praise her excellence or superiority was attempting to defend the indefensible and praise the unpraisable. If, however, the text succeeded in its mission and discovered reasonable topics of defense and praise, then the societal assumption that woman was inferior was undermined. As Rosalie Colie observed, "the paradox is always somehow involved in dialectic: challenging some orthodoxy, the paradox is an oblique criticism of absolute judgment or absolute convention" (10). The orthodoxy being challenged is literally present in the comments of the antagonist in dialogues, but in the formal paradox, the judicial defense, and the encomium it is there by implication; most authors represent their works as having arisen out of an animated discussion of the topic, and they frequently refer to the points they are refuting in detail.

I shall show that the presence of the voice of conventional opinion, even if only implied, is one factor in the inhibition of political consequences because it prevents the reader from aligning himself with the extreme position advocated by the authorial voice. The author is not the authority any more than his opponents. Because all absolute and fixed forms are attacked by the mode of paradox, such texts, in their purest form, disrupt the absolute notion of woman's inferiority without dictating a new orthodoxy of superiority, no matter what they may claim to do. Most of the works end without coming to closure, and they would be likely to prompt the debate that initiated them to continue after the voices of the text had ceased to speak.

In reading these texts as open-ended and part of an ongoing debate rather than as closed statements of position, I differ from Joan Kelly, the scholar who initiated the modern study of them with her famous essay, "Did Women Have a Renaissance?" Kelly defined her job to be the discovery of historical and social information about "sex role conceptions" (21). In the interest of discovering information about social conditions she, like Ruth Kelso before her, read these highly inventive literary texts as "doctrine," that is, more as conduct books than as paradoxes, and did not notice the conflict that, I postulate, lies at the heart of them. She was not a literary scholar and her literal reading of the *Cortegiano,* for example, assumes that the text has only one voice and means only one thing and that the articulation between literature and life is literal and direct.[1] By reading in this way she can conclude that the "dialogue . . . is not only developed by men but directed toward their interests" (35) as though men's interests were unitary and uniformly repressive of women's. I will argue that, for the most part, the dialogues, defenses, and encomia of womankind are dynamic and conflicted rather than being static representatives of fixed attitudes. I hope to show that they are more subtle, more provocative, and less comfortably patriarchal than Kelly and others who have accepted her readings have recognized.

The central orthodoxy that these paradoxical texts challenge is the notion that the kind of intellectual, ethical, and physical strength with which woman is naturally endowed is inferior in kind to that with which man is endowed or, to put it another way, woman's capacity for the cardinal virtues is partial, if it exists at all. As a direct consequence of this inequity, she is assigned an inferior position in political and economic hierarchies and is governed by men in both her private and public life. Renaissance defenses offer two very different positive models of women's virtue and physical and mental strength to counter this assumption.

According to the first model, women can be expected to be capable in just the same ways men are because they are endowed with the cardinal virtues as men are and because they suffer no special disabilities because of their reproductive function. Even though it is shared in by both sexes and would logically seem to be gender-neutral, virtue continues to be conceived of as masculine by the proponents of this model, and, thus, physiological gender is separated from the attributes that are indicated by the adjective of gender. A virtuous woman is masculine without violating nature and, in the most extreme versions of the theory, can compete on equal terms with men.

The second model transforms qualities traditionally considered liabilities into assets. Women can be expected to be capable in a particularly female fashion because they are endowed with specifically female virtues, and they can be strong in a feminine way because of their reproductive function. Virtue can be either masculine or feminine, but a person must display the virtue appropriate to his or her gender; physiological gender and gender attributes are

---

1. For an example of a literal reading, see the discussion of his "aestheticizing of the lady's role" (33). Even when Kelly mentions the presence of two points of view in the text, she chooses one. "Thus, Castiglione gave both sides of the debate. . . . Using a bourgeois spokesman to voice the misogynous part of the dialogue on the Lady, he appears to favor the "gentle" (aristocratic) pro-woman side" (75).

united. A woman who is masculine violates nature, with one exception: if this violation of nature is socially beneficial, it may be described as miraculous rather than as unnatural; the woman might be described as temporarily containing a male soul within her female body. Usually, however, those who employ this theory praise women's feminine virtue as superior in kind to men's masculine virtue.

Both models would produce political consequences if followed to their logical conclusions. Conventional Renaissance thought defines the cardinal virtues as essential for good political action, so woman's right to participate in the political life of the community follows logically from the first model, which sustains female moral and physical equality with the male sex. Given the education and opportunity, women can play all the roles men can with equal skill, wisdom, and virtue. Because of their capacity to be free from dependence on men for moral and political governance, I have called women as defined in the first model "independent." By rejecting conventional political theory and preferring feminine nurturing virtues over the cardinal virtues, however, an exponent of the second model could suggest that the nature of government itself ought to be redefined in order to take advantage of superior female virtue. In society as it then existed, however, feminine virtue and strength did not apply to the political sphere. Care for family and spirituality, for example, would motivate such women, who were fully virtuous, to restrict their activities to traditional female fields except in crises when the boundary between the political and the domestic broke down and male spirit miraculously entered them. Because of their capacity for self-government but not for public government, I have called woman as defined in the second model "interdependent."[2]

These two attitudes toward female virtue produced different strategies of male self-defense within the very texts that proposed them and praised women. Equality could be defended against by suggesting that attributing the same kind of virtue to each sex did not necessarily mean attributing the same quantity of virtue to each. Women could have the same virtue but to a lesser extent, and, thus, be excluded from politics. Superiority could be defended against by asserting that male political systems are necessary to govern the corrupt world and protect good women. Woman rule could be shown to be appropriate only to a Golden Age.

In practice, distinctions were not nearly so clear as I have made them here,

2. Eva Feder Kittay and Diana T. Meyers identify these two positions as the "justice tradition" and the "care perspective" (3). Their discussion of the history of these two traditions and their definition of autonomy were of great use to me in formulating this concise statement of the philosophical positions in the debate.

and, most frequently, both approaches were invoked at different times in the same work at strategic moments. As I have said, only a very few authors sustained women's capacity for the cardinal virtues consistently, endorsed independence in its pure form, and argued for change in contemporary political structures. Examples of two who did are the Italian humanist Agostino Strozzi (in one manuscript out of the three that exist of his work) and the English Catholic Henry Howard (discussed in Chapters 2 and 9, respectively). The superior because different argument was slightly more common; it was used by Bartolomeo Goggio, an Italian humanist contemporary with Strozzi (Chapter 2), and by many English popular defenders of womankind (Chapter 8). Most frequent of all was a mixed defense; it appears in Castiglione's *Cortegiano*, Elyot's *Defence*, Ariosto's *Orlando furioso*, and Spenser's *Faerie Queene*. I argue that recognition of the model of womankind being invoked helps to reveal the kinds of ethical, social, and political argument being made by each text and that advocacy of each model produces a different kind of defensive strategy.

In discussing the paradoxical nature of these texts, I pointed out that many of them represent themselves as part of an ongoing discussion; they do not exist as separate entities and are hard to interpret when read in isolation, yet that is what has happened to them in the years since they were written. Except for the obvious canonical texts by Castiglione, Ariosto, and Spenser, these works were always marginal literature, and now many of them have become obscure and rare. The defenses by Goggio and Strozzi, the biographical collections by Cornazzano, Vespasiano da Bisticci, and Sabadino degli Arienti, and the defense of female regiment by Henry Howard were not published in their own day; some exist in a single manuscript, none appears complete in more than three; none has been edited in modern times.[3] Critical work on these manuscript texts is scant, though often excellent. Goggio has been discussed at length by Werner Gundersheimer, Goggio and Strozzi have been summarized and briefly analyzed by Conor Fahy, Howard has been considered within the context of Elizabethan politics, and the rest have received no substantial attention in the last fifty years.

The Italian and English defenses that were printed in the sixteenth century are better known. They still exist in numerous copies—they seem to have been popular—and several have been issued in modern editions. Both Ian Maclean and Constance Jordan included many of these texts among the sources that they used for their respective works, *The Renaissance Notion of Woman* and

---

3. There are modern editions of partial versions of Vespasiano, Sabadino, and Strozzi's texts, but as I shall explain when I reach them, each is inadequate for an understanding of the methods of defense.

Renaissance Feminism, each of which breaks important new ground in the field of gender ideology in the period. Linda Woodbridge's *Women and the English Renaissance* called attention to many texts that had been neglected for years, and many of the texts specific to the English problem of female rule have benefited from the current interest in cultural studies. Yet, despite the recent critical discussion of these printed texts, there still is no thorough analysis of their diverse literary strategies for dealing with the new notion of woman that they create. In addition to providing the first substantial discussion of the majority of these texts, I hope that by bringing all of them into relationship with each other I shall make it possible for readers of any single text to appreciate its position within its larger context, its novelties, and its conventional strategies.

This brings me to the last, and, perhaps, most radical premise of my study. I have asserted that the *Orlando furioso* and *The Faerie Queene* belong in this group of controversial works. They can be differentiated from the other texts because they are narrative fiction, include a great many other topics within them, and are written with extraordinary skill; however, when looked at from the point of view of the controversy about women, these grand poems display many of the characteristics of their more humble companions. Both make their connection with the contemporary praise and defense of women explicit, and, like the other books both debate with the attitudes toward women expressed by their contemporaries. Their narrators employ the defensive strategies and evidence of the "real" participants in the controversy. The *Furioso* includes an extensive three-part debate about womankind, and *The Faerie Queene* includes an allegorization of the contributions that female virtue makes to justice. The good lady knights—Bradamante, Marfisa, Britomart, and Queen Elizabeth (to stretch a point)—exemplify the energy and force of female virtue.

The *Furioso* and *The Faerie Queene* are deeply connected to each other because the *Furioso* is one of the most important authorities on woman with which *The Faerie Queene* debates. I shall argue that Spenser's text is not just an imitation, a reworking, or a borrowing but a careful and conspicuous refutation of Ariosto's handling of the woman problem. Nearly every scene that Spenser borrows that touches on the topic of womankind points to the opposite conclusion from the parent scene in the *Furioso*. Although the technical details of the debt (canto and stanza) have long been on record along with Spenser's other debts to Ariosto, the nature of the intertextuality on the topic of womankind has barely been explored. In essence, the *Furioso* exemplifies the defense of the notion of woman's virtue as equal to man's and *The Faerie*

Queene represents the paradoxical argument in favor of the superiority of feminine virtue.

Finally, the *Orlando furioso* and *The Faerie Queene* appeared at parallel moments in their national discussions about women. Each text was written at a turning point. The third edition of the *Furioso* was published on the eve of the Counter-Reformation, and *The Faerie Queene* appeared shortly before the death of Elizabeth. Because of these events, the tone and terms in which the topic was discussed changed significantly in each country; thus, these major, popular, fictional texts make appropriate closing points for the Italian and English halves of my study.

1

BOCCACCIO'S *DE MULIERIBUS CLARIS:* AN AMBIGUOUS BEGINNING

De mulieribus claris is the foundation text of Renaissance profeminism. All the texts discussed in this book are directly or indirectly indebted to it because it establishes the issues and many of the rhetorical methods of the defense, collects evidence useful for demonstrating the political, social, and personal virtue of women, offers the example of a man daring to speak out in favor of womankind, yet never directly advocates social change. Indeed, its method of presenting the evidence defends society against the feminist conclusions that seem to be implicit in this evidence. The key to Boccaccio's success in writing a profeminist text without political consequences is a technique that he mentions frequently: intermixing. He mixes together contradictory kinds of women, differing interpretations of the value of their actions, and both social and ethical methods of imitating them.

In the Proem Boccaccio explains that all kinds of women are mixed together, "immixtas," in this text (xxxvii; 24).[1] Conventionally heroic, chaste women like Penelope and Lucrece appear alongside ruling queens and Amazons like Semiramis and Penthesalia and alongside wicked women like Medea and Flora. All are united by the simple fact of being renowned for whatever it is that they have done; they are "claris." This presentation of women for what they were in a domestic, social, and political context rather than in a moral or an amorous one offers a new way of looking at women and their place in history. Where before there were blank pages or absent paragraphs, there now is a female presence in the historical record.

---

1. All references to and quotations from the *De mulieribus claris* cite the edition edited by Zaccaria. All translations are by Guarino. In all citations of *De mulieribus*, the first number refers to the translation, the second to the Latin text.

A reader might infer from this restoration of women to the past that they might have a more public role in contemporary society, but the *De mulieribus claris* is not just a collection of historical biographies; it is a collection of exemplary lives, and the old view of women as inferior and necessarily private is intermixed with the new view. Boccaccio is a moral counselor in addition to a recorder of events; he thus often evaluates the heroines' conduct according to traditional gender and moral expectations and produces opinions incompatible with his praise of their deeds. In addition, in order to apply the lessons of the lives to modern life, he must try to discover how women, whom common knowledge asserts to be weak, find the inner resources to perform these deeds. At times he seems to advocate a new understanding of the sex as strong and capable and to suggest social remedies for the perceived weakness of women; often, however, he asserts the contradictory opinion that positive nontraditional female behavior is extraordinary and miraculous and, thus, not indicative of the usefulness of reform. Even the two pieces of prefatory material—the dedicatory letter to Andrea Acciaiuoli and the Proem addressed to all readers—offer contrasting guidance for applying the lives to one's own life.

As a result of Boccaccio's intermixing of good and bad, social and ethical, practical and miraculous, historiographer and moralist, the text urges two different views of itself and of womankind. It may be dangerous and subversive of established social order; it may be safe and supportive of existing gender roles. In this chapter I study the tensions produced by the intermixing in the text of contradictory notions of woman and of what the relation of the *De mulieribus claris* to the reader's private life and to public institutions ought to be; I then speculate on how the Renaissance reader might resolve these dilemmas and choose the new view of woman.

Dangers of Praise: The Dedicatory Letter

One of the major problems that Boccaccio faced in writing about famous women was the possibility that praise of their virtue by a male author would be counterproductive. Their very dependence on the male to tell their story might make them seem weak, and, as Lucrece's sad history shows, in a traditional culture public recognition for virtue exposes women to risk. Boccaccio shields his famous women against the risks that male authorship brings by placing the text in the control of a woman; the dedicatee is Andrea Acciaiuoli, the sister of the seneschal of the Court of Naples.

The dedicatory letter begins the defense of the work by creating the impression that the text is feminine. Boccaccio alludes to the genesis of this book in a period of his life when he had withdrawn from public affairs, and describes it as having a private purpose: "Some time ago, illustrious lady, while away from the crude multitudes and almost free of other concerns, I wrote a little book in praise of women, more for the pleasure of my friends than as a service to the state" (xxxiii; 18). Rather than fulfilling the masculine office of serving the state, it will fulfill the feminine one of giving pleasure (or comfort) to friends, unless, as Boccaccio immediately goes on to say, it can be escorted into public by a female patron who will provide it with safety.

This reference to the need for safety further feminizes the text by suggesting that it needs protection from those who would pollute it in their thoughts. Their masculine readings of it would in some way denigrate the women represented in it, as a male observer may degrade a woman with his gaze. The female dedicatee would protect the text by means of her ability to read it purely and by means of her personal virtue: she would translate the ancient deeds into their modern, less aggressive equivalents. This application of the trope that the text needs a patron to defend it to a female patron violates gender expectations; the shy feminine text of the praise of women is being brought out of privacy by a woman. The strategy obscures the fact that the female patron has not written in her own defense but merely is being asked to accept the responsibility of using her status to add credibility to the author. With regard to the text, she plays a masculine role.[2]

It is also possible, however, that the threat to safety comes not from the male gaze but from the feminine text. The act of praising women may simply comfort friends when it occurs in private, but when brought to public attention it may do something that will put it in danger. Rather than being passively "not useful" to the state, the text would be actively inconvenient for the state if the image of woman found in its pages threatened political or domestic stability by rewriting gender roles, as, of course, it does at times. Such a work might well need a sponsor who could provide a buffer between it and outraged society. Andrea Acciaiuoli's virtue and conventional feminine conduct, then, provide a disguise for the radical potential of the text, even as the text's attribution of patronage to her creates a masculine active role for her that is unfounded in her own actual actions.

2. Jordan points out that Boccaccio's discussion of her name "compliments her by suppressing her actual gender and by rhetorically reconstituting her as male through an act of language" ("Boccaccio's Infamous Women" 28).

Boccaccio's life provides yet another possible, though unverifiable, reading of this opening that reinforces the interpretation of the text as actively defiant of conventional gender expectations. The reference to the writing of the work away from the crowd calls attention to its initial composition in the period of the author's life when he had moved out of Florence because of difficulties with his brother over their patrimony (Zaccaria, ed. 481). Boccaccio seems to have felt himself an enemy to "rei publice" at that time, and it is possible to see the text as a sort of vengeance on that patriarchal system that has made his life so difficult. Once again, that it is not written to the advantage of the state may mean that it is written to its disadvantage. By this reading, the profeminism of the text would have its source in Boccaccio's animus against the patriarchal forces that pushed him into a feminine position of retirement and weakness, and his praise of women in the moments when they rise above the limits imposed on them by nature and society may arise from his desire to escape the limits imposed on him, an escape that he may see himself as having effected when he elicited the invitation to the Neapolitan court, which was governed by a woman.

Whether or not readers can legitimately be expected to notice the animosity to Florence and the patriarchal abuse that has feminized the author, the appreciation for the matriarchal alternative of Naples cannot go unnoticed. Boccaccio reports that he had initially intended to dedicate the book to Queen Giovanna, but that the queen as dedicatee might have outshown his book by displaying so effectively in her person the virtues that he was trying to demonstrate in the text. Her activity would make his efforts at literary mediation between women and society unnecessary. The image of shining so brightly as to obscure suggests that masculine Giovanna would throw the feminine text back into the obscurity of privacy. She belongs where Boccaccio placed her, among the famous women celebrated in the text; there, she is firmly under the author's control. He can choose what sort of image of her to bring before the public, whereas as patron she would have remained in control.

Boccaccio's retraction of his dedication to Queen Giovanna reveals the paradox that lies at the heart of any male author's attempts to praise female independence. By definition, the need for praise indicates present or past weakness, and women as a group in need of praise must, therefore, be weak and the author of praise must foster their dependence on him even as he celebrates their capacities for greatness. A living, independent woman like Giovanna endangers the virility of the author because she is fully masculine on her own. She has no need of praise to bring her to the attention of the public; she has no need to read the praise of other women to receive instruction in virtue, because she is already fully versed in the subject, and, consequently, she might feel no reciprocal obligation to the author. Because Giovanna is not weak, the most Boccaccio can do is freely offer her his intention to dedicate the book to her, praise that in no way puts her into his debt. Although he must appear to approve of matriarchy and may genuinely admire it, in fact, it serves his personal interests no better than patriarchy. Part of the reason that Boccaccio does not seem fully committed to his undertaking may be that it is essentially contradictory: the author of praise of women *must* undercut his own efforts to represent women as self-sufficient if he is to succeed in promoting his own personal interest in fame and fortune.

The replacement dedicatee, Andrea Acciaiuoli, a member of this new society governed by a female monarch, does not threaten the author. Unlike the great queen, who is within the normal range of woman's nature and is open to emulation, Andrea is miraculously infused with masculinity: "when I saw that what Nature has taken from the weaker sex God in His liberality has granted to you, instilling marvelous virtues within your breast, and that He willed you to be known by the name you bear (since in Greek *andres* means 'men'), I felt that you should be set equal to the worthiest of men, even among the ancients" (xxxiii–xxxiv; 18 and 20). This description suggests that the conversion of ordinary women into "men" can be achieved only by God, not by the efforts of ambitious women themselves.[3] Acciaiuoli's extraordinary masculinity provides a means of retreating from the radical implications of the *De mulieribus claris* and protects society from the danger that modern women will literally emulate political deeds.

Similarly, her virtuous reading of the lives defends the author against accusations that the text is masculine, aggressive, and subversive of the interests of the patriarchal state. The letter explains to Acciaiuoli in some detail how she should go about reading the biographies and what she should hope to get out of them.

> Nor will the reading have been in vain, I believe, if by emulating the deeds of ancient women you spur your spirit to loftier things. . . . Whenever you read of a pagan woman having qualities which are worthy of those who profess to be Christians, if you feel that you do

---

3. Maclean explains how this trope works. "The separation of sexual characteristics from gender . . . ('a manly soul in a weak female body') seems to result in a pursuit of paradox and a provocation of wonderment in the reader or listener, and not in the development of a new paradigm of psychological characteristics. The paradox strengthens the presumption of female weakness, and acts as a conservative force on language and ideas" (*Renaissance Notion* 26).

not have them, blush a little and reproach yourself that although marked by the baptism of Christ you have let yourself be surpassed by a pagan in integrity, chastity, or virtue. (xxxiv; 20 and 22).

The result of her emulation of the ancients will be fame in this life and a warm welcome from God in the next. The accent here is on moral imitation and the moral effects of reading. Boccaccio suggests that the spiritual attitude that makes the deeds possible, rather than the deeds themselves, is to be imitated.[4] Boccaccio does not suggest that Andrea transform herself into a great queen or warrior, but that she spur herself to practice those virtues that pagan and Christian women share.

Because her virtue expresses itself ethically and not politically, Andrea does not threaten to outshine Boccaccio's achievement. She will "give the book courage to appear in public" but will also receive a benefit from it; the book "will make you and your virtues known to our age and will render you eternal for posterity" (xxxv; 23). This woman who will perform the masculine function of defending the book from the public gaze will do so not by means of speech, political power, or even money, but by means of her virtue. She will provide the shield that is needed for the book's entry into the world, and it in turn will provide a shield for her private virtue by suggesting its magnificence without exposing it to view in a detailed portrait in a biographical sketch. The book, the author, and the patron are entwined in each other's success.

Women and History: The Proem

Acciaiuoli's ability to translate accounts of actions into ethics makes her a better dedicatee than Queen Giovanna, but once we pass from the dedicatory

---

4. Petrarch expresses a similar goal for his reader in the Proemio of his De viris, the immediate model for the De mulieribus claris. Petrarch says the goal of a historian is to "esporre quelle cose che i lettori debbono seguire o fuggire" [expose those things that readers must follow or flee] and that he will include details only if they will draw the reader toward virtue or turn him from vice (224). In this passage Boccaccio treats his female reader just as Petrarch treated his, presumably, male reader. He assumes that she will be able to dispassionately reject all the lascivious material he has included for historical accuracy and concentrate on the deeds of good women, which will improve her spiritually. As the capacity of women to read the deeper moral content of superficially immoral works would soon be a point of debate among humanist educators, Boccaccio's easy assumption that Andrea Acciaiuoli will be able to read "like a man" suggests either that the education of women had not yet been differentiated from the education of men or that Boccaccio did indeed have substantial respect for female intelligence.

letter to the Proem, which is located within the formal boundary of the text of the *De mulieribus claris*, women like Giovanna are not excluded either as subjects or as readers. In the Proem Boccaccio is not concerned with the danger praise poses to a woman's reputation, and he does not represent himself as the least bit timid about his endeavor to make their deeds public. He does not speak modestly of his little book ("libellum") but speaks of a major undertaking; he is deliberately setting out to rewrite the history of women. He represents the *De mulieribus claris* as breaking with medieval literature in the seriousness with which it takes women's actions. Several well-known works dealing with famous men include a few women, he says, but not one deals exclusively with women; he intends to make up for this lack because women have done many great deeds and are worthy of a book in their own right (xxxvii; 24).

The notion that the author of a work in praise or defense of women is making up for the neglect of previous male authors has the same potential to undermine the very praise it offers that the suggestion that women need praise has. Just as the need of praise suggests weakness, so does having been left out of the historical record. Boccaccio's approach to this problem is rudimentary; I would even say that he does not perceive it as a problem. He gives no reason for the male neglect of women's deeds, and he does not seek any benefit for himself as the restorer of women's reputation. Unlike Boccaccio, all other Renaissance encomiasts of women develop this topic extensively to defend against the possibility that some failure on the part of women has led to their present inferior social position. The absence of such a defense leaves open the possibility that a reader will respond by blaming women (women themselves might have kept records and did not), although it is more likely that, here at the very beginning of discussion of the topic, one would simply respond with surprise at the neglect and admiration for Boccaccio for his heroism in attempting to restore glory to women and to undo the damage done to their reputation by ancient and modern male writers.[5]

The theme of the natural weakness of women runs through the Proem as it did through the dedication, but it is not clear here that great women owe all their success to God's special grace.

5. In telling of the wife of Orgiagonte, Boccaccio is troubled that he does not know her name. Because her name is unknown, he says, honor and fame have been withheld from her. His sense that her own particular name, as distinct from her husband's, is important shows Boccaccio's desire to separate her from her husband and to see her distinctly on her own. Her chastity, her honor, her name are at issue here. Again, although Boccaccio assigns no blame to male historians, later defenders of women blame the namelessness of female heroes on male intention: troubled by female fame, men conspire to exclude women from history.

> If men should be praised whenever they perform great deeds (with
> strength which Nature has given them), how much more should women
> be extolled (almost all of whom are endowed with tenderness, frail
> bodies, and sluggish minds by Nature), if they have acquired a manly
> spirit and if with keen intelligence and remarkable fortitude they have
> dared undertake and have accomplished even the most difficult deeds?
> (xxxvii; 24)

This is not a pure example of the trope of the extraordinary woman, despite
Boccaccio's use of the term "manly" ("virilem") to describe the spirit needed
to produce powerful public action and his description of ordinary women as
weak in mind and body, because it is not clear how the women "acquire" the
masculine attribute. The verb "acquired" ("evaserint") suggests action on their
part as does "dared" ("audeant"), and, thus, the courage to act counter to
tradition and nature seems to come from within the women and not from God.
The ordinary woman seems to be present not as an indication of the fixed
limits of women's natural abilities, but as an indication of the average above
which the great woman rises through her own skills. Similarly, the choice to
include spectacularly bad women works against the notion of the "extraordinary
woman," for no benign external force can be credited with their strength.

Boccaccio shows respect for modern women throughout the Proem. They
are singled out as the intended audience for the book, as Acciaiuoli was in the
dedicatory letter, but they are not represented as translators of deeds into
ethical principles. The author expects that they will be interested in the book's
historical content and states that the leisurely expository method of the book
was dictated by their needs as a group that has traditionally been excluded
from the reading of history (xxxviii; 26). The exact use to which these female
readers will put their new knowledge of history is left open. In contrast to the
extensive and limiting development of the topic in the letter to Acciaiuoli, the
Proem merely explains that the author hopes that a "sacra utilitas" will be
"inmixta" with delight (xxxviii; 26).

This usefulness does not seem to be specifically Christian, despite the
adjective "sacra."[6] Boccaccio explicitly excludes martyrs and saints from his
collection, not only because they are the only kind of woman consistently
remembered by historians, but because the kind of virtue that they exhibit is
irrelevant to his concern.

6. See Cerbo for a contrary argument.

In order to attain true and eternal glory Hebrew and Christian women did indeed steel themselves to endure human adversities, imitating the sacred commandments and examples of their teachers. But these pagans through some natural gift or instinct, or rather spurred by desire for this fleeting glory, reached their goal not without great strength of mind and often in spite of the assaults of Fortune, and they endured numerous troubles. (xxxviii–xxxix; 26)

Once again, the naturalness of these virtues to women conflicts with the extraordinary woman theory introduced elsewhere. Boccaccio makes it clear that he is talking about classical virtues—strengths, one might say—as distinct from the Christian ethical virtues usually recommended to women. The natural ability and natural ambition for temporal fame that distinguish these pagan women from their Christian sisters make them attractive.

The radical content whose presence was suggested obliquely in the dedicatory letter is emphasized here with no effort to shield it from view. Because the Proem is addressed to all readers and the dedicatory letter only speaks directly to Acciaiuoli (even though its inclusion makes it available to all), it seems reasonable to assume that the directions for reading given in the Proem would be more likely to influence the reader setting out to experience the text than those in the letter. Having read this Proem, a woman might even be disposed to pay more heed to the novel tales of ability and ambition than to the conventional moralizing that accompanies some, but not all, of them and be moved to be ambitious to put her natural abilities to work to achieve secular glory. She might experience the text as distinctly profeminist.

Thus far, I have spoken of the reader as a woman, but the presence of male readers is indicated by the author's frequent addresses to them in the morals to the lives.[7] This is consistent with the defensive dedicatory letter and with the Proem. If male historians have ignored women, they must be made to read about them, so that the author's stated goal of changing the historical record may be met. The inclusion of men in the audience shows that, although the method of presentation may have been adapted to give women access to the

---

7. Many of the lessons are directed to both sexes together without differentiation. The stories of Arachne and Niobe exemplify the foolishness of the desire to outshine everyone else. The story of Medea condemns lascivious looking; the stories of Medusa and Procris condemn greed for gold. Ceres' story is followed by a very long disquisition on the disadvantages of agriculture and a nostalgic lament for the Golden Age that might inspire readers of either sex to emulate its simplicity. The story of Virginia is rare, perhaps unique, in the *De mulieribus* because the moral is based on the actions of Appias rather than those of Virginia.

work, Boccaccio did not consider the book to be women's literature or marginal in any way. Men as well as women are expected to be interested in women's history, to be susceptible to having their notion of woman changed, and to be able to discover their own image in women's actions.

Quid est mulier? The Lives

The exact relationship between the reading woman and the famous women whose lives Boccaccio recounts is an ever-present question in the biographies, as it was in the dedicatory letter and the Proem. The lives of the heroines are punctuated by comparisons between them and ordinary women, to the disadvantage of the ordinary woman, and the origin of the strength of will or body that produced heroic acts is often attributed to miraculous intervention. On the other hand, society is often blamed for having deprived women of moral education, thus indirectly causing their bad deeds, and their heroic acts are attributed to natural female abilities. Finally, I shall argue, the latter view dominates. A persuasive and sensitive profeminist voice emerges from the text, a voice that admires female political, moral, and physical strength although it does not endorse a change in the contemporary political status of women.

Many lives suggest that the undisciplined conduct of the ordinary woman is not her fault, but the fault of society, which denies her education and treats her as an object. When Boccaccio gives advice about bringing up young girls, for example, he insists that parents or guardians recognize their daughters as people whose desires must be taken seriously, and he attacks the common notion that women are property to be disposed of as parents or siblings wish. He urges that young women's sexual feelings be considered. The story of Rhea Ilia, a woman who prostituted herself after having been forced to become a vestal virgin at a young age, yields the lesson that parents ought not to consecrate their daughters to God when they are young but instead ought to allow their mature daughters free choice of marriage or the cloister.

This is not to say that Boccaccio entirely abandons the notion that women naturally tend in the direction of *luxuria*. Rather, he abandons the idea that nothing can be done about this tendency. For example, the prostitute Leena, who valiantly refused to reveal the names of her revolutionary accomplices under torture, is said to have ended up in her profession not because she naturally inclined that way, but because her parents indulged her (109; 204).

Similarly, the Roman Sempronia, whom Boccaccio praises for her learning but condemns for her lasciviousness, shows parents the importance of discipline:[8]

> I shall not condemn Nature, for no matter how strong its powers may be, at the beginning they are so flexible that with a little effort they can be guided almost at will. But if you disregard this evil when it begins, it will always grow worse. I believe that often the indulgence of parents towards adolescent girls spoils their character. (173–74; 316)

If one accepts Boccaccio's assumption that promiscuity is a vice, there is nothing antifeminist about this advice. The mother as well as the father is expected to impose restrictions on the daughter, and the girl herself is assumed to be completely capable of chastity if taught the virtue early in life.[9] Moral education produces the independence of spirit that enables a woman to triumph over vice on her own.

The education of which Boccaccio speaks here is not intellectual, and, oddly enough, nowhere in the *De mulieribus* does he directly advocate the instruction of women in any specific field other than basic morals. I say that this is odd because, although the writing of the text in Latin suggests that the female audience to whom he was addressing himself was very limited, in the Proem Boccaccio disapproves of his society's failure to educate women about history and suggests this very book as a remedy. Boccaccio takes the education of women for granted in the dedicatory letter, in the Proem, and throughout the text whenever he addresses a female reader. Without a good deal of education, his female reader would not exist.

Highly educated women writers are among the most positive and least ambiguous examples offered for imitation. For example, Proba and Cornificia, two early Christian women, are praised for their excellence in scholarship and literary pursuits. In speaking of both these women Boccaccio makes it clear that their talents were natural. Neither of them is spoken of as exhibiting the

8. Similarly, Boccaccio uses the story to suggest the dangers of seduction rather than rape: Europa followed the words of a pander and exposed herself to danger. The parents of a modern young woman would do well to prevent contact with foreigners because it may result in lifelong dishonor. This is not a particularly antifeminist rendition of the story; women are not condemned as particularly given to lasciviousness, and youth rather than her sex would seem to have been the cause of Europa's ruin.

9. Boccaccio is also severe on the subject of male inchastity, although he does praise Tertia Aemilia, the wife of Scipio Africanus, for tolerating it and even putting a good face on it to save her husband's reputation. Most women would not have cared that they were ruining the fame of a great man. This seems to be an example of the fidelity to marital family interests over personal desires that Boccaccio frequently praises. Tertia is like Portia.

action of a man's soul in a female body. Neither is manly. They arouse no feelings of inadequacy in the male reader; indeed, although Cornificia is compared with her brother, there seems room enough for both of them in the history of poetry. They win additional praise because they refused to play the slothful, self-indulgent roles society would have permitted them because of their sex. The morals at the ends of their stories reproach other women's low definition of themselves. [10]

> Let slothful women be ashamed, and those who wretchedly have no confidence in themselves, who, as if they were born for idleness and for the marriage bed, convince themselves that they are good only for the embraces of men, giving birth, and raising children, while they have in common with men the ability to do those things which make men famous, if only they are willing to work with perseverance. (188; 338)

This passage could be mistaken for the pronouncement of a twentieth-century feminist in its rejection of the notion that women are merely sex objects and household drudges. [11] Here, to rise above her sex means simply that her willingness to use her talents was unusual. All women can aspire to be what these women were, though like many men, they may not be so successful. According to these two lives, learning and writing and the glory to be gained by their practice are entirely open to women with no restrictions at all. The female reader is encouraged to see the compatibility of literary activity, virtue, and glory, and, as her act of reading this text indicates an adequate level of education, she might even feel honor-bound to exert herself to work to achieve fame.

The text's assertion that women should become responsible for their own conduct does not mean, however, that women should have equal authority and responsibility with men. For example, the decline of civilization from its proper order and rigor is clearly attributed to the male error of indulging women, of being soft like women, in the story of Veturia, the mother of Coriolanus. [12] We

10. There is a similar moral at the end of the history of the Sibyl Amalthea, but it is directed at men and invokes a feeling of shame that women have done better than they have.

11. Jordan reads this passage to support the statement "her art, which is seen as effacing or utterly subduing her sexuality, is termed a good thing, since her sexuality is debilitating and without it she can become a 'man' " ("Boccaccio's Infamous Women" 31–32). I understand this passage does not say that women must reject sexuality entirely, but that they ought to define themselves as worthy of an existence that includes more than sexuality.

12. The ill-judged bestowal of male rights on women and the social chaos consequent upon the action provides an opportunity for humor shared with the male audience in the biography of Soaemias,

are told that the women would have been satisfied with the dedication of a temple to Fortuna Muliebris, but the men, in their gratitude for Veturia's peacemaking, also ordered that men ought to rise when women entered the room and that women ought to be allowed to wear earrings, royal purple, and golden jewelry, and to receive inheritances from anyone. The narrator moralizes: "I cannot praise the excessive generosity of the Senate and the harmful custom which has lasted for so many centuries. . . . The world belongs to women, and men are womanish" (121; 226). The moral independence of individual women does not upset the conventional hierarchy of society, and, thus, the *De mulieribus* can be said to be conservative although not antifeminist.

In the biography of Veturia the different readings that Boccaccio offers female and male readers work in harmony to produce the same moral. There is nothing but praise in the biographical description of Veturia's heroic action, her speech is quoted at length, and the female sex is not blamed for having been granted privileges; the moral does not withdraw the praise given in the biography but rather focuses on a problem that arose because of male conduct.[13] Women are now corrupt, and the female reader, though not directly addressed, is offered the lesson that parents were told to teach their daughters: be modest in dress and use the family's wealth responsibly. None of this undercuts the example of Veturia's inspiring independent action, which remains open for imitation. The male reader, however, is advised to refashion his identity.[14] The notion that "the world belongs to women, and men are womanish" is a version of the "male spirit in a female body" trope; it appears again in the story of the wives of the Minyans, who changed clothes with their husbands and remained behind in prison to await execution.[15] A female spirit in a male body is the cause of the problem, and this passage and others like it seem designed to cause male readers to discover that their self-interest and duty lie in restoring

a prostitute who was given a seat as a senator. Boccaccio presents as ridiculous the creation of a women's senate at which matters of female dress and precedence were debated. He does not make this story into a myth of origin, however. With the death of the major parties involved, society returned to normal.

13. See Jordan's very different reading of Veturia's story ("Boccaccio's Infamous Women" 36–37). "As Boccaccio represents her, Veturia is chiefly memorable not as a woman whose powerful eloquence saves the state but rather as one whose sexuality nearly brings about its ruin" (37).

14. In the story of Epicharis the author reproaches men in a similar fashion. "I think men should be ashamed to be surpassed by a woman who was lewd but also very constant in the endurance of difficulties. For if we are stronger because of our sex, why is it not proper that we be stronger in bravery? If this is not done, we rightly seem to have exchanged characters with them and become effeminate" (210–11; 378 and 380).

15. "I dare affirm that these wives were true and tried men, while the young Minyans whom they impersonated were but women" (64; 134).

discipline to society by becoming less "womanish" and by eradicating the luxurious "prerogatives of women."[16]

Telling as it is against men, however, the male spirit in a female body trope is not used as a reproach to women who would attempt great deeds. In the case of Artemisia, for example, Boccaccio invites the reader to look at her brilliant strategic abilities and courage and to conclude that "[w]hile we admire the deeds of Artemisia, what can we think except that it was an error of Nature to give female sex to a body which had been endowed by God with a magnificent and virile spirit?" (127; 236). Two comparisons are at work here. Artemisia is being compared with the average woman and with men. The author resolves the conflict between Artemisia's clearly demonstrated abilities and the conventional understanding of the natural endowments of her sex by attributing the discrepancy to God's overriding of nature. Boccaccio, thus, is able to praise this individual woman very highly without reforming his appraisal of the abilities of the ordinary woman. As a result, women such as Artemisia do not threaten the established social order. Most women could not do what she did. She was extraordinary.

If Boccaccio consistently used the male soul in a female body trope to explain the actions of military and regal women, then it might be possible to assert that finally the De mulieribus confirms traditional gender categories by strengthening "the presumption of female weakness" (Maclean, Renaissance Notion, 26). However, the notion that women are naturally capable, which we first saw in the Proem, often offers a competing explanation of female valor. In telling the story of the Amazon queen Penthesilea, for example, Boccaccio abandons the male spirit–female body paradox altogether and suggests that female military strength can come from practice that develops abilities that occur naturally in women. After describing Penthesilea's accomplishments and intelligence (she invented the battle-ax), the narrator addresses the problem of the reader's surprise at her skill:

> Some may be surprised by the fact that women, no matter how armed, dared to fight against men. However, surprise will cease if we think of the fact that custom had changed their nature, so that Penthesilea and women like her were much more manly in arms than those who were made men by Nature but were then changed into women or helmeted hares by idleness and love of pleasure. (66; 136)

16. The Florentine sumptuary statutes of 1355 and 1356 printed by Cassell in an appendix to his translation of the Corbaccio seem a good example of a male attempt to do away with the prerogatives of women and suggest that Boccaccio in the life of Veturia was voicing a common attitude.

Here Boccaccio gives full credit to the heroine herself for her deeds. Practice, not a divine infusion of male spirit, has made her capable; lack of practice has made men weak.[17] Although the male reader still finds that indulgence in idleness and pleasure will make him "womanly," the female reader finds here a model of what women can become if they decide to be masculine.[18]

This passage suggests that the qualities of "masculine" and "feminine" that are conventionally tied to biological gender are actually socially induced. Both sexes can achieve glory for heroic "masculine" action and infamy for "feminine" timidity. This is not to say that Boccaccio advocates a change in custom that will turn the young ladies of his day into Amazons. He makes no explicit connection between Penthesilea's conduct and that of modern young women; he merely explains how such conduct could occur within the bounds of nature and leaves it to the reader to apply the knowledge to the modern world.

When, in the biography of the Volscian Amazon Camilla, he takes the further step of drawing a moral application for modern life from such activity, he ignores the radical independence of the Amazonian life.[19] The biography breaks into two distinct parts with two very different points of view.[20] The account of her life is heroic and praise of her virginity and admiration of her military skill and determination are equally fervent. Boccaccio follows this obviously legendary biography with a lengthy moral that develops its point from the moral virtues she displayed in her life, not from her social role as queen and soldier. It reads in part:

> I wish that the girls of our time would look at Camilla and, seeing that
> virgin already adult and free amusing herself by running through fields,

17. No critics of *De mulieribus* of whom I am aware recognize the distinction that I am making here. Most assume that if the trope of the male soul in a female body is invoked in some lives, it can be assumed to be present in all lives, even when it is not mentioned. I am suggesting that a reader might note its absence as a sign that there is an alternate way to explain a woman's "masculine" behavior. The danger of reading each biography as though it were written in the same terms as the others is that it makes Boccaccio far more decisive on the subject than he was and also that it deprives the reader of liberty to read the lives independently from one another.

18. In *The War Against the Amazons* Abby Wettan Kleinbaum says, "Boccaccio's main goal in writing about Penthesilea is to exhort men to manliness, not to praise and honor brave women" (62). She gives no evidence for this assertion that the passage must be read as really only about men.

19. Jordan notes that "Boccaccio's histories of women who attain *claritas* through purely heroic activity are generally typified by his accounts of Amazon warriors who are by nature chaste" ("Boccaccio's Infamous Women" 38).

20. The story of Semiramis is handled in much the same way. We are told of her military and political accomplishments, then of the one deed that blotted all the rest. One is first led to develop enthusiasm, then to feel disappointment that she failed to control her personal vices. The biography could inspire imitation or rivalry with Semiramis as a public figure even as it inspired aversion for her sexual corruption.

forests and the dens of animals with her quiver, curbing the pleasures
of lascivious desires with work, . . . would learn from her example what
is proper for them in their parents' home, in churches, and in theaters
where most onlookers and harsh judges of behavior congregate. (80;
160)

While we do not normally think of churches, theaters, and parents' homes as
being the equivalent of fields, forests, and battlefields, the moral does provide
a way of finding some practical connection between the strengths of these
ancient women and the challenges that contemporary society actually presents
to young women. The physical dangers of wild places are equivalent to the
moral dangers social interaction offers to the young ladies of Boccaccio's time.

This is a good example of the kind of reading that the dedicatory letter
encouraged. By means of the moral, a reader like Andrea Acciaiuoli could find
in Camilla's life, so different from her own, "ancient deeds" to emulate; if she
flirted at the theater, reading of the pagan woman's rejection of young men
might lead her to blush. Although the difference between the freedom of
movement of one life and the restriction of the other and between the kinds of
valor each setting permits a woman to display are likely to bother a modern
reader, it is possible that for an early Renaissance woman to find any connection at all between Camilla's life and hers might be exciting and liberating.
She has no opportunity to rove the woods with her quiver, but she does attend
the theater. Boccaccio makes conventional morality seem like a heroic adventure.[21]

Although this moral is disappointing if one thinks of the expanded realms
of glory that the Proem and biographies such as that of Penthesilea suggest, it
is like the Proem in its location of control over the young woman's actions in
her consent and judgment rather than in parental authority. Ancient freedom
of action translates into modern ethical freedom. This in itself would seem to
be liberating; however, while a variety of military choices existed, there is only
one wise moral choice to be made, and, thus, the very capacities that she
shares with Camilla bind the woman reader. Willing and responsible confor-

---

21. The moral drawn from the biography of Orgiagonte's wife, a queen and a victim of rape, is
similar to that at the end of Camilla's story in that it places control of her reputation in the hands of
the woman. Boccaccio praises her aggression against the perpetrator and, comparing it with Lucrece's
self-destruction, finds it at least equal in political and moral force. This praise introduces the explosive
notion that revenge, which one might expect to be the duty of a male member of the family, belongs
to the woman. See Jordan ("Boccaccio's Infamous Women" 34–35) for a more critical reading of the
episode.

mity substitutes for the enforced obedience of the traditional inferior woman. This strategic redefinition of the field of action as moral, capturing the energy of the independent woman and turning it to society's conservative purposes, recurs frequently in Renaissance texts in defense of women.

By contrast, some morals advise modern women to act exactly as their ancient sisters did and assert themselves against authority, for the most part, by boldly acting in the interest of the family. Similar to the moral applied to actions of Camilla, yet suggestive of active possibilities to the modern woman, is the moral at the end of the account of the life of Sulpicia, the wife of Truscellione. Sulpicia voluntarily disguised herself in order to escape from Rome and join her husband in exile. Boccaccio says that her belief that a wife ought to share her husband's hardships as well as his pleasures "is characteristic of a noble mind and savors more of a wise man than of a woman."[22] He goes on to say that women ought not always to indulge their taste for easy living, but

> when the blows of Fortune demand it, they must endure toil, go into exile, bear poverty, and face danger bravely with their husbands. This is the admirable service of women; these are their battles and their victories. Their striking triumphs are to overcome ease and luxury, as well as domestic difficulties, by means of their virtue, steadfastness, and purity of mind. (186–87; 336)

As in so many of the lives, feminine taste for self-indulgence is the enemy over which women must triumph, but here the action of overcoming it involves actual physical courage, not merely abstinence as the moral based on Camilla's life would suggest.[23] Sulpicia's flight to her husband led her to cross stormy seas and mountains, and Boccaccio suggests that a modern woman who went into exile with her husband might have to suffer similar hardships.

The virtue of the dedicatory letter and the valor of the Proem come together

22. The story of Hypsicratea does not offer a moral, but it is similar to Sulpitia's in its praise for the friendship of wife to husband. The stories of Portia and Turia praise the political solidarity of wives with husbands.

23. Jordan suggests that Boccaccio undermines the reality of Sulpicia's trials by the use of the metaphor of "woman's war." "Her important battles no longer take place on actual ground and over real conflicts but rather in her mind and against aspects of her own nature" ("Boccaccio's Infamous Women" 41). I suggest that the triumph over one's own reluctant nature is the essence of all heroism and that Sulpicia has not been "denied a real part in her own story"; rather, by means of the description of this inner conflict, other women are given access to heroic territory within themselves through which they may win real parts in their own stories.

in this biography and others like it. Given the reality of political exile in Boccaccio's Italy, this is advice that a woman might put to use in exactly the circumstances described in the biography. It is true that the praise is of a type that is frequently discounted by modern scholars because it demands that a woman act in the interests of her family, and, thus, is harmonious with her traditional social role, but it also can be considered as a serious challenge to the conventional way of playing that role because it considers women to have the capacity to discover ways to act publicly on their devotion to family. The text suggests that the fact that Sulpicia's act, which was "masculine" in its heroism, was motivated by love rather than self-interest will cause admiration and, even, imitation by the reading woman.

Because chastity and fidelity, the most traditional virtues expected of women, reappear so frequently in this text, it might seem that they are necessary for fame and that their lack might override all other considerations, but, just as we have seen that chastity does not always paralyze the adventurous spirit, so it is not always the supreme value. The prostitute Leena, whom I discussed as an example of advice to parents on the upbringing of their daughters, is included in the text because she bit off her tongue to avoid divulging the names of her fellow conspirators in a plot against a tyrant.[24] With Leena, Boccaccio poses a radical challenge to his society. He argues sternly in defense of her inclusion in the historical record because conformity to conventional codes of female behavior and high social status must not be the only qualifications a woman can offer to achieve fame. Her low and immoral profession ought not to rob her of her glory, and even her silence defies convention because the reasons for it go counter to the normal reasons that silence is expected of women. Her silence is a direct challenge to authority whereas normally female silence is considered a virtue because it signals obedience and submission. Leena's example does not teach women to be silent. A noble woman reading this text might be led to shame for her own sexual conduct, if it resembled Leena's, but the primary lesson available to her is political: she can see the potential that women of all classes have to gain fame for their courage in political causes.[25]

24. The story of Epicharis is very similar to that of Leena.
25. I disagree emphatically with Jordan's discovery in this episode of a repressive lesson against educated eloquence in women. "This art of keeping silent is achieved by women who have not been instructed in how to be 'eloquent.' Therefore a wholly natural act, it suggests that an educated eloquence in a woman is destructive and to be discouraged" ("Boccaccio's Infamous Women" 32). I cannot see that it is necessary to conclude that if a woman naturally has the capacity to act politically by holding her peace we need conclude that women would not benefit from the education of their

Despite Boccaccio's emphatic celebration of the radical political implications of Leena's story, however, he never suggests that the sexual immorality of women who had access to moral education can be overlooked, no matter what their other claims to fame. In Leena's case the ethical reading method of the dedicatory letter can be dominated by the profeminist historical-political method of the Proem without detriment to conventional sexual mores because the prostitute's development of ethical codes was stunted by her parents. In the biographies of women who should have known better, the method of reading proposed in the letter exists in open conflict with the method of the Proem.

The case of Semiramis is exemplary of this problem. Her monstrous lack of chastity and her valorous and independent spirit each provide a motive for including her in the book, and Boccaccio does not attempt to make a comprehensive judgment on her. Like the statue of her with her hair braided on one side and loose on the other, as it was when she rose from her dressing table to go into battle to quell a rebellion in Babylon, Boccaccio's account of her life clearly divides in two halves. In the first, her powers of mind and courage receive great praise, and we see her triumph over her "feminine" side as the story of the partly done hairdo illustrates. In the second, incest is said to stain her reputation. Boccaccio offers both visions of Semiramis as valid, unless one assumes that what is described last cancels out what has come before in the reader's experience.[26] If we read as Andrea was instructed to do in the letter, we recoil in horror from Semiramis's incest. If we read as instructed in the Proem, we are astonished by her military and governmental prowess.[27] Like his inclusion of the story of Leena, Boccaccio's telling of Semiramis's story challenges his society to see women in other than sexual terms, but her social rank and her education make her sexual vices much more troubling.

---

political capacities by instruction in eloquence. Boccaccio repeatedly makes the point that the male tendency not to educate women to the extent of their capacity causes problems. Boccaccio's praise of female eloquence elsewhere, as in the story of Veturia, shows that he is not anxious about female speech.

26. An aphorism from the story of Leena illuminates Boccaccio's use of the notion of a stained reputation here. "For virtue is valuable everywhere and is not stained by the blots of vice. . . . Therefore, if at times we see virtue fixed in the breast of someone given to detestable practices, we must condemn those practices, but not lessen the praise of that virtue" (107; 202).

27. Anthony Grafton and Lisa Jardine use Boccaccio's treatment of Semiramis to illustrate their contention that "[w]hen a woman becomes socially visible—visible within the power structure—Renaissance literary convention makes her a sexual predator" (41). This interpretation does not do justice to Boccaccio's division of the account of Semiramis into two halves, which permits the reader to give dominance to her private or public life or leads the reader to feel the waste of her political skill at the end of her life, but does not lead the reader to conclude that sexual corruption is inevitable in queens.

Living Women

A female reader might logically be expected to identify with and be inspired by the conduct of women of her own period more than with women of classical times, but when, in the final biography, Boccaccio finally tells the story of a living woman, the relationship of the female reader to the text is ignored. Giovanna, Queen of Sicily and Jerusalem, overpowers the biographical and didactic form that Boccaccio established for all the other women. The account of her life is written entirely in superlatives; details of her ancestors, her territories, and generalized accounts of her accomplishments stand instead of realistic details of her conduct; there is no moral appended to the life.[28] That her realm is mighty and "not usually ruled by women" (249; 446) makes her seem grand, but that she inherited it rather than acquiring it by heroic methods as did so many of the pagan women means that no amount of talent can raise a modern woman to Giovanna's position. The man's soul in a female body trope is absent, and, thus, Giovanna's accomplishments seem natural to her as a woman, but, again, unless Boccaccio's female readers also have inherited a kingdom, this naturalness will not advance them. Suddenly even the lessons of modesty and restraint that followed the biography of Camilla seem attractive because they led all good women to see themselves in a heroic figure. Nothing leads the reader to compare herself with Giovanna. The balance that Boccaccio achieved with Andrea Acciaiuoli in the dedicatory letter and between himself and his female subjects in the rest of the book is undone here. Giovanna is truly the master, and he is the subject.

Because of its encomiastic purpose, the biography of Giovanna seems part of the framing material rather than part of the collection of lives, and, indeed, in the Conclusion, Boccaccio suggests that Queen Giovanna exercised tyrannical force over the contents of the book: "As can be clearly seen, I have reached the women of our time, in which the number of illustrious ones is so small that I think it more suitable to come to an end here rather than proceed farther with the women of today, especially since this work, which began with our first mother Eve, concludes with so great a queen" (251; 448). Boccaccio's state-

---

28. For example, she "is more renowned than other women of our time for her nobility, power, and goodness" (248) [regina preter ceteras mulieres origine potentia et moribus evo nostro illustris est femina (442)]. "In our days and in those of our fathers no family in the whole world has been more famous than this for its nobility" (248) [et sic nulla diebus patrum nostrorum nec nostris orbe effulsit nobilior (444)]. "She is noble and of splendid fame, . . . an eminent glory of Italy such as has never before been seen by any nation" (250) [Quibus agentibus, ego non solum illam reor egregiam et splendida claritate conspicuam, sed singulare decus ytalicum, nullis hactenus nationibus simile visum (448)].

ment that "we have reached the women of our own time" suggests more to come. If we have reached them, the women exist. It is possible, of course, that Boccaccio simply does not know of any modern women other than Giovanna who are worthy of inclusion, but such an opinion of modern women hardly seems reasonable in an author who has repeatedly encouraged his contemporaries to seek glory and who has vowed to restore women to their proper place in history.[29]

It seems more likely that he is denigrating and excluding modern women as a compliment to Giovanna and that the real cause of modern women's absence is the power of Giovanna.[30] She holds not only the last place in the book, but the historical and ethical place in opposition to Eve that is traditionally held by the Virgin. Any modern woman whom Boccaccio praised would obviously be in competition with Giovanna. To threaten her position at the top could not possibly benefit Boccaccio, and so he falls silent despite his own admission that there are at least some other modern women who might have been described. Giovanna's presence has forced closure on an open text.

Two strategies of praise that we have already seen in conflict in the *De mulieribus* are at work here. Inasmuch as his goal is to flatter women, Boccaccio wants to give the impression that there are many great women and that any woman he praises represents her sisters; this is the strategy that Boccaccio adopts in the Proem and that guides the overall presentation of the lives. Even though he often says these women are extraordinary, the sheer weight of numbers tells in favor of the naturalness of their accomplishments. Inasmuch as his goal is to flatter one particular woman, however, he wants to give the impression that the woman he praises is somehow outside the category. This is the strategy that Boccaccio adopts in the dedicatory letter, in the biography of Giovanna, and here in the Conclusion. He makes it seem that no other women are worth praising.

Boccaccio's situation with regard to Giovanna is exemplary of an odd paradox that will reappear in the defenses of Elizabeth of England. When present as objects of encomia in literary works, living female monarchs who hold power in their own right tend to exclude contemporary women from glory

---

29. Although the paucity of great modern women could be seen as part of the decay of the world theme, it does not sit well with the encouragement to seek glory that Boccaccio has offered modern women up to this point.

30. We will see Ariosto, in a similar situation, say that there are so many modern women that he cannot include them all, so he will include only one, Vittoria Colunna, who will stand for all (*Orlando furioso*, canto 37). The tropes are related, but Ariosto's is complimentary to all women, Boccaccio's only to Giovanna.

rather than opening the way for them as one might expect. Instead of standing as an example of the capacity of womankind, the textually tyrannical queen demands all attention for herself. I would suggest the following explanation for this phenomenon. A queen is vulnerable because her inheritance of a throne is unusual; it is never the first choice and it only occurs because of a lack, a failure in the male line. All comparisons and all competition are potentially equalizing, and the queen's real political security might be threatened by the statement that her accomplishments make her the best of many candidates. Theoretically, another woman could arrive on the scene with equal or superior accomplishments and depose her in real life as well as in the literary work. Therefore, a wise encomiast, a Boccaccio, a Spenser, isolates the queen from her contemporaries. By allowing Giovanna into the contents of his work rather than keeping her firmly in the framing material, Boccaccio necessarily excluded all other women of his time and left himself no recourse but to say that it was the women's own fault that they were not included.

The exclusion of modern women partially defeats the purpose of the book as announced in the Proem and as reiterated in the morals that encourage modern women to action. Boccaccio has illuminated the past and brought many women out from the shadows of history, but he has kept no records of his own day and refuses to acknowledge any need for them. He cuts his contemporaries off from the past just when he seemed to be connecting them with it. If the women of the fourteenth century are to enter the pages of history, it is not by means of the pen of Boccaccio.

The rest of the Conclusion offers a possible means of their entrance. In an extended entertainment of hypothetical objections to his book, Boccaccio makes it clear that the text, so firmly circumscribed by Eve and Giovanna, is open to insertions and deletions. Readers may say he wrongly included or excluded particular women. Boccaccio defends himself, saying that he could not include all the ancient women he knew of—there were too many and the facts of some lives were irretrievably lost—but that his reader should make whatever corrections he or she deems necessary:[31] "And if anyone has a charitable soul, let him correct what has been improperly written by adding to it or deleting and improve it so that the work will flourish for someone's benefit, rather than perish torn by the jaws of the malicious without being of

---

31. An alternate version of the Conclusion appears in the manuscript called "L." It is titled "De feminis nostri temporis" (about women of our time), but it begins by excluding modern women just as the standard conclusion does. Its difference lies in its replacement of the extended development of the hypothetical objections with a list of the names of some women Boccaccio left out. They are all ancient women. See Zaccaria, note to "Conclusio" (556).

service to anyone" (251; 450). Boccaccio frequently uses the trope of the request for correction, but rarely, I would say, with such effect.[32] Boccaccio is not just suggesting mental corrections for personal use here or even rewriting of the material he has presented; rather, he is opening his text up to substantial additions of new lives. Thus, he makes his reader more than an audience; he makes him or her a collaborator in the very process of production and dissemination. The book that seemed firmly closed by Giovanna's presence has been opened again because, whatever Boccaccio's expectation, lives could be added after Giovanna's as well as before and modern women could join the ranks of the great.

This is exactly what happened. Those who came after found the *De mulieribus* weak in modern lives, and this is where the most extensive development took place. The works of the many continuers, plagiarists, translators, and imitators of the *De mulieribus*, the subject of the following chapters, are readings, corrections, and emendations of Boccaccio's text that attempt to make it live for the good of the new authors, their patrons, and, sometimes, womankind. Far as these works may go from the form and contents of the *De mulieribus*, they all have to deal with the essential problems that Boccaccio raised for the first time. They must somehow solve the problem of the relationship of a male author to a female subject and patron. They must decide whether they believe that the female sex is naturally capable of great deeds, and, if so, why women are absent from history and why contemporary women are excluded from almost all positions of authority and opportunities for glory. They must consider what the consequences of change would be and who would benefit from it. And, of course, they have to do all this in a literary form that will persuade an audience of the importance of the topic and the justice of the author's solution.

---

32. See his *L'Ameto*, *De genealogia deorum gentilium*, *Vita di Dante*, and *De casibus*. He asks for correction by patrons and by Petrarch.

2

FROM PRAISE TO PARADOX:
THE FIRST ITALIAN DEFENSES OF WOMEN

The *De mulieribus claris* was an anomaly in its time because of the importance it attributed to women and because of the evidence it presented that women had often demonstrated skill in areas of behavior previously considered to be exclusively male. It was soon translated into Italian, but no original works in the genre were written in Italian until 1467, when Antonio Cornazzano wrote his *De mulieribus admirandis;* this was followed by Vespasiano da Bisticci's *Il Libro delle lode e commendazione delle donne* (c. 1480) and Giovanni Sabadino degli Arienti's *Gynevera de le clare donne* (1483).[1]

These three works share certain superficial characteristics: all are dedicated to female patrons; all include only praiseworthy women. Cornazzano praises only women of the past; Vespasiano and Sabadino praise contemporary women extensively. All three books, however, do not praise the same kinds of activity. The works of Cornazzano and Vespasiano share little but the genre of biography with the *De mulieribus claris.* They praise conventionally good women whose actions do not go beyond those traditionally defined as feminine. Sabadino's work is very different. Like Boccaccio's text, it celebrates women for their accomplishments in male fields of endeavor, but without the extraordinary woman theory. Famous women are represented as using talents that are natural to all women. They have the capacity to do great deeds without male guidance and governance and without an infusion of male spirit.

Sabadino's work was not alone in praising this new ideal of womanhood. It forms a group with Bartolomeo Goggio's *De laudibus mulierum* (1487) and

---

1. Jacobus Phillippus Bergomas (Foresti) wrote a Latin continuation of Boccaccio's *De mulieribus*, *De claris mulieribus*, dedicated to Beatrice of Aragon. He included biographies of contemporary women in the collection.

Agostino Strozzi's *Defensio mulierum* (c. 1501), Italian language texts despite their titles.[2] These works develop and defend the theoretical ideal that lies behind Sabadino's heroines by incorporating the biographies of famous ancient women within a larger structure of defense and praise. They both use reason, experience, and classical authorities to disprove the beliefs of the years that intervene between themselves and classical times and to discover the original role of women in society and in creation. To make their point they confront traditional classical authorities previously used to establish the inferiority of women with newly discovered or newly favored classical authorities well disposed toward women; they reinterpret crucial passages in classical and biblical texts; they use logic to break down traditional assumptions about woman's nature and place in society; and they reexamine crucial moments in history and discover that the importance of women in them has been over-looked. Together Sabadino, Strozzi, and Goggio represent an extremely signif-icant change in the notion of what constitutes positive and socially valuable female behavior. They all represent woman as capable of moral and intellectual autonomy, and, therefore, capable of competing with men on equal terms.

The primary cause of the notion of woman presented in these works and of its difference from that in Cornazzano and Vespasiano is geographical and temporal.[3] Sabadino, Strozzi, and Goggio were all writing for Northern Italian courts, and one of the dominant characteristics of these courts was the high level of education among the women of the ruling families, the Este, Gonzaga, and Sforza, among others.[4] This was a group of women remarkable for their education, their patronage of art and literature, and their political wisdom. In other words, the early defenses, panegyrics, and collections of biographies were addressed to a society in which accomplished women already existed.[5] These women served as dedicatees, audience, and, in Sabadino's work, examples of the possibilities of the female sex.[6]

2. Mario Equicola's brief Latin defense also belongs in this group. See Fahy.

3. Cornazzano dedicated his work to Bianca Maria Visconti, duchess of Milan in 1467. The early date rather than geography may account for its difference.

4. To cite one example, the Estes of Ferrara married educated women and educated their daughters. The most famous members of the family are: Eleanora d'Aragona, wife of Ercole I of Ferrara (m. 1473); their daughters, Isabella (1474–1539), who married Francesco Gonzaga of Mantua, and Beatrice (1475–1497), who married Ludovico Sforza of Milan; Lucrezia Borgia, wife of Alfonso I of Ferrara (m. 1502); Renée of France, wife of Ercole II of Ferrara (m. 1528). Beatrice and Isabella spread the influence outward from Ferrara, and their courts in turn became cultural centers.

5. For the view that the existence of these women most likely was the cause of the flowering of laudatory literature about women because men aware of these women could not help but question the traditional derogatory definition of woman, see Gundersheimer, "Bartolommeo Goggio."

6. Joan Kelly in "Did Women Have a Renaissance?" criticizes the Este, Sforza, Gonzaga, and

Positive as these texts are about the capacities of women, however, none of the three promotes social reform.[7] Neither Strozzi nor Goggio offers a plan by which contemporary women can recapture the privileges that their ancient counterparts possessed or cites contemporary examples of independent women. Sabadino gives no theoretical framework; he too, thus, provides no means for the ambitious late fifteenth-century woman to justify a change in her way of life.

In this failure Strozzi, Goggio, and Sabadino resemble the humanist educators, especially Leonardo Bruni, whose program for women students omitted the politically important study of oratory.[8] Grafton and Jardine put the problem in economic terms.

> Within the humanist confraternity [sic] the accomplishment of the educated woman (the 'learned lady') is an end itself, like fine needlepoint or the ability to perform ably on lute or virginals. It is not viewed as a training for anything, perhaps not even for virtue (except insofar as all these activities keep their idle hands and minds busy). As signs of *cultivation* all such accomplishments satisfactorily connote a leisured life, a background which regards the decorative as adding lustre to rank and social standing, and the ability to purchase the services of the best available teachers for such comparatively useless skills. (56–57)

Although this interpretation seems to suggest that there is little difference between the Italian choice to give a daughter a humanist education and the Chinese choice to bind her feet, from the daughter's point of view, at least, there was a great difference, because knowledge could be put to use. Men with

---

Montefeltro women because their patronage does not "show any consistent correspondence to their concerns as women" (Kelly 36), but Eleanora of Aragon, wife of Ercole I d'Este, was the dedicatee of Bartolomeo Goggio's *De laudibus*, Margherita Cantelma, friend of Isabella d'Este, of Strozzi's *Defensio*, and Beatrice of Aragon of Foresti's Latin collection.

7. Gundersheimer asserts: "That the writings in which these views were expressed seem to have had no immediate, large-scale influence merely echoes the transitory impact of the women who inspired them. It was to take far more sweeping changes in ideology and socioeconomic development to produce a major reassessment of the destiny of 'the second sex' " (*Italian Renaissance* 57). See also "Bartolommeo Goggio" (177).

8. Bruni defends education for women by arguing against the possibility that education will make the role of his female charges more public. Eugenio Garin thought that Bruni's work was "one of the most notable, perhaps the most notable, affirmations of education for women for several centuries" (135); feminist critics recently have focused on the strains caused in women by the limitation on subject matter and have, perhaps, obscured its great importance as a first step. On the importance of oratory in humanist training, see Gray (202). For the view that even for men, who were taught oratory, a humanist education was not necessarily professional, see Grafton and Jardine (57).

the same knowledge held responsible jobs and received public praise, and Grafton and Jardine as well as Margaret Leah King chronicle cases of women who suffered from the misapprehension that their learning provided an entrée into public life.

The genres in which Strozzi and Goggio worked were especially well adapted to the omission of a program for action. We will see that the rhetorical methods of defense and paradoxical encomium undermine the profeminist theory and evidence that make up the matter of their books. These texts are in conflict with themselves. The choice of such inconclusive genres is in itself a symptom of a deep ambivalence about the new notion of woman. Without the suggestion of means by which women could come to play a more public role, the genres leave modern women in a dilemma: Should they imitate their ancient sisters and risk censure according to modern standards or should they apply themselves to conventional duties? This unanswered question is central to the failure of these texts to be feminist in any modern political sense.

Vespasiano da Bisticci and Antonio Cornazzano

Before discussing the works that praise "masculine" accomplishments in women, it will be useful to examine the two collections of female biographies that do not do so. Both Antonio Cornazzano's *De mulieribus admirandis* (c. 1467) and Vespasiano da Bisticci's *Il Libro delle lode e commendazione delle donne* (c. 1480) defend women against antifeminist charges by praising them for conventional virtues—beauty and chastity in the former and chastity, constancy, spirituality, and devotion to family interests in the latter. Although they show that they are aware of women's capacities for government (Cornazzano) and learning (Vespasiano), this knowledge prods neither into making these capacities the central feature of any of the biographies that make up his collection. Together, these books demonstrate that, even when dedicated to a female patron, the genre of biography was not in itself necessarily directed to the redefinition of woman but could offer a defense of her ability to live up to the virtues conventionally expected of her; thus, Sabadino, Strozzi, and Goggio made a choice when they used it to redefine.

Cornazzano represents his work as taking up a task that Petrarch and Boccaccio began, and he addresses it to Bianca Maria Visconti (Sforza), duchess of Milan. He was born her subject, he says, and so has observed a "monarchia di donne." Despite his awareness of Boccaccio's *De mulieribus* and his experience of female monarchy, Cornazzano's main goal is to use virtuous examples to defend women against misogynist slander of their capacity for chastity. He divides women into two categories: the beautiful and the chaste. The women whose lives he presents are almost all ancient, and he includes no great women of his own time: Eve, Venus, Medusa, Judith, Camma, and Virginia are typical examples, and his descriptions of them are superficial. Finally, there is nothing humanist about this work.

Vespasiano da Bisticci was in the Florentine humanist circle. He includes Hebrew, Christian, contemporary, and pagan women in *Il Libro delle lode e commendazione delle donne,* the latter group being used to demonstrate that the virtues prized in modern times were also valued by the ancients. The contemporary women are held up to the reader as models for behavior; what they do is natural to women, he says, though difficult to achieve. In the introduction Vespasiano explains that what he is doing is controversial. He describes himself as offering rational praise of women in opposition to irrational antifeminism (which makes no distinctions among women) and states that he has written this book in praise and commendation of women at the request of "a few worthy women" who were offended by the antifeminist attack that had been made on his encomiastic biography of Alessandra de' Bardi. He thus assumes that the kind of praise he is writing will please a female audience and will persuade both female and male readers that "in ogni istato sono istate le donne ripiene di tante virtù" (292) [in every nation there have been women full of many virtues].[9]

The conservative nature of Vespasiano's praise is immediately apparent in the defense of Eve with which the book begins (14r–18v). Eve is excused on the grounds that Adam was supposed to be her head because she had less reason and that God's actions as recorded in the Old Testament have repeatedly shown that he blames man more than woman (14r).[10] While this does absolve woman of responsibility, it does not gain respect for her. We will see that Northern court writers replace this particular defense of Eve with others or omit the topic altogether.

9. References to page numbers refer to the modern printed text of the lives; references to folio numbers refer to the manuscript, which I have cited when the necessary passage was omitted from the printed text.

10. This is a partial and false rendition of a Thomistic argument. Aquinas's handling of this question is very complex. In Part 2.2, Q. 163, he states, "the gravity of a sin depends on the species rather than on a circumstance of that sin. Accordingly we must assert that, if we consider the condition attaching to these persons, the man's sin is the more grievous, because he was more perfect than the woman.

As regards the genus itself of the sin, the sin of each is considered to be equal, for each sinned by pride. . . . But as regards the species of pride, the woman sinned more grievously" (1865).

In the biographies Vespasiano's standards are far more limited than Boccaccio's. He is not filled with admiration for those acts by which women seem men, but rather each woman whose life he records displays

> quelle condizioni che debbe avere una donna singulare: grave, di poche parole, modesta, temperata, liberale dove bisognava, volta tutta al divino culto, religiosa. (302)

> [those qualities that an outstanding woman must have: serious, of few words, modest, temperate, liberal where it was appropriate, entirely directed toward divine worship, religious.]

Although for some of the pagan women some elements of this pattern are omitted—the sibyls could hardly be praised for being sparing in their speech, but they are examples of constancy and freely willed virginity—all ten modern women exemplify these virtues.

Even women whose acts might be perceived as political are described so as to make their virtue strictly domestic. Vespasiano praises Francesca Acciaiuoli for her use of her wits to save the property of her husband's house for his descendants, but the condensation of the account and the absence of details make it impossible to figure out what she did.

> Tutto si fe' col senno e colla bontà di questa donna; e per suo mezzo si conservò la casa sua, che ebbe molti ostacoli. (300)

> [All was done by means of the wits and the goodness of this woman; and by her skill her house was saved despite many obstacles.]

Acciaiuoli's deeds may have been public; they may have been brave; we are not told. The focus is not on her cleverness in its own right nor on the value of her activity as an example of women's moral strength, as Boccaccio's was in the story of Sulpicia, but on the result: the house was saved. Thus, the point that women can contribute to the welfare of the family is communicated without the radical implication that the same capacities that make them able to help the family might make them able to act in a larger political arena.

Vespasiano's portrayal of his great women as domestic heroines continues even when he writes about women who were famous in their own day for their learning. The outstanding example of the narrow scope of his praise is Battista da Montefeltro Malatesta, the recipient of Bruni's "De studiis et litteris" and the author of secular and religious works.[11] Although Vespasiano speaks of her relationship with Bruni, he does not clearly connect it to her learning.

> Fu di tanta fama e di singulari virtù, che messer Lionardo, iscrivendole una orazione, dice nel suo principio che fu mosso da romore e fama delle sua virtù. (295)

> [She was so famous and so unusually virtuous that Lionardo, writing an oration to her, says at the beginning of it that he was moved to write by the fame of her virtues.]

Correspondence with a humanist was a sign of great prestige for a man or a woman because it indicated respect for the person's learning; it was a sort of badge of membership in an exclusive club.[12] Yet Vespasiano's use of the term *virtù* rather than a word referring to her accomplishments makes the compliment unclear. He turns evidence that could have been used to demonstrate the lady's "masculine" intellectual ability into praise for a generalized quality compatible with a "feminine" ideal.

Similarly, when he refers to the ways Battista da Montefeltro Malatesta used her learning, Vespasiano plays down radical deeds and plays up piety. One of Battista's most celebrated acts was the making of a Latin oration to the Emperor Sigismund, but Vespasiano describes her eloquence as persuasive speech to other women, not public speaking.

> . . . fu tanta la fama delle sua virtù, che moltissime volte al mondo, per lo suo esempio mutorono la vita sua . . . e potè assai non solo con lo esempio, ma colle parole; chè fu eloquentissima (295–96).

> [The fame of her virtues was so great that many worldly women changed their way of life because of her example . . . she had a great effect, not only by her example, but with words; for she was very eloquent.]

By describing speaking in this way, Vespasiano constructs Battista's life to fit his notion of what a woman ought to be. He mentions those abilities for which she was famous, but he makes them serve socially conservative functions.

11. For references to these works, see Kristeller (93). For an English translation of her Latin oration to the Emperor Sigismund, see King and Rabil (36–38).

12. On the subject of the correspondence between learned women and humanists see Grafton and Jardine (29–57 passim).

In this biography and in all others, learning is presented exclusively as an aid to piety and to the education of children.[13] Although Vespasiano clearly respects women and thinks that acquiring an education is worthwhile, he perceives it as in no way expanding their social or intellectual opportunities. He nowhere shows Bruni's sense that education is important as an end in itself or that the reading of even pagan literature can be of use to a woman.[14] His attitude toward the education of women as well as the piety and domestic virtues for which he praises them are excellent evidence that, in the late fifteenth century, defense of women and, even, of education for them, was not at all necessarily linked with the questioning of gender roles.

Sabadino degli Arienti

Vespasiano's biographies are constructed on a moral framework; he assumes that what constitutes proof of the worth of the women is examples of their dedication to God and to their families, and he offers his collection as a means of moral education for readers female and male (293). In *Gynevera de le clare donne* Sabadino degli Arienti is not trying to prove to a skeptical reader that women are worthy; the assumption that women are worthy is the basis of his praise. He is not offering moral education; he makes no suggestion that female readers can learn from the biographies. Instead, he states his goal to be to praise and to please Gynevera Sforza di Bentivogli. The book begins with the

13. Vespasiano praises Paola Malatesti Gonzaga for hiring Vittorino da Feltro to teach her male and female children, and he praises Cecilia, her daughter, for having learned Latin well (297), but the only use he envisions for their knowledge is uninventive piety. Paola "aveva buona notizia delle lettere; ella diceva del continovo ogni dì tutto l'uficio come i sacerdoti" (296–97). [She had a good knowledge of letters; she said the entire divine office continually every day like a priest.]

14. In the biography of Alessandra de' Bardi, not contained with the *Lodi*, Vespasiano makes his attitude toward the education of women clear: mothers should learn from the life "a non fare loro leggere nè il Cento Novelle, nè i libri del Boccaccio, nè i Sonetti del Petrarca, che, benchè e' siano costumati, non è bene che le pure mente delle fanciulle imparino ad altro che Iddio e i loro proprii mariti. Fare loro leggere cose sacre: vite de' santi Padri, o istorie, o simili cose, acciò che imparino a temperare la loro vita e i loro costumi; e vòltinsi a cose gravi e non leggieri. Essendo loro di loro natura vòlte alla leggerezza, . . ." (288) [not to make them read the *Hundred Tales*, nor the books of Boccaccio, nor the sonnets of Petrarch, because, although these are refined, it is not good that the pure minds of girls should learn about anything other than God and their own husbands. Make them read holy things: lives of the holy Fathers, or histories, or similar things, so that they learn to temper their lives and their customs; and they turn to serious things rather than light ones. Being by their nature disposed to lightness . . .]. That he has to give this advice suggests that many mothers permitted such light reading to their daughters.

biography of Gynevera and then offers every subsequent biography as a tribute
to her with variations on the following refrain: "la cui memoria . . . habiamo
ne la Gynevera opera recordata per ornare bene de fronde del nostro amato
Gynevero, che tanto letifica per sua virtù ciascuno" (16) [whose memory we
have recorded in the work *Gynevera* in order to decorate it well with the fronds
of our beloved juniper that so cheers everyone with its virtue]. There is no
profeminist framework, only pro-Gynevera. The work is designed unabashedly
to praise and to turn a blind eye to faults, even grievous ones, yet because of
the qualities that Sabadino chooses to praise and because of the genre in which
it is written, the *Gynevera* is an important example of humanist profeminism.[15]

Sabadino's use of the genre of the biography of famous women for propagandistic and selfish purposes suggests a real difference between the way women
were perceived in the society he was addressing and that addressed by Vespasiano.[16] To use biographies of women to praise and not defend, to use them to
entertain and not educate suggests a confidence in the subject matter. This
confidence is confirmed by the large number (thirty-two) of modern women
included and, especially, by the terms in which Sabadino writes about them.
He does not attempt pure historical research aimed at telling the facts any
more than Vespasiano did, but rather presents the elements of each woman's
personality and actions that best fit the notion of good womanhood that he is
trying to express.

As he represents them, they are a publicly active group. They all display the
virtues of chastity, charity, and devotion to family that formed the entirety of
the character of Vespasiano's modern women; however, few of the biographies
stop with praise of such traditional female virtues. According to Sabadino's
accounts seven of the women were successful rulers; five actually fought battles;
others accompanied their husbands in the camps to encourage them and to
participate in the excitement. At least three schemed to keep their families in
power. Many were educated and active scholars. Even their piety was political
and conspicuous; they demonstrated it by endowing churches and convents
more often than by retiring into them.

15. See, by contrast, Laura Torretta's assertion that Sabadino's book is typical of Renaissance
"historians . . . [who became] as ardent and exaggerated in their glorification of the female sex as the
previous writers had been vehement and unjust accusers" (40: 65).

16. Sabadino sent a copy of the *Gynevera* to Isabella d'Este. In her letter of thanks to him she said,
"Essa opera, e per esser cum summa elegantia compilata, et per essere de utile matheria, c'è stata ultra
modo grata. Legeremola cum attentione et sforzeremose imitare le vestigie de quelle ill.me matrone"
(Luzio and Renier 51). [This work was extremely pleasing to us because it was compiled with the
highest elegance and because it contains useful material. We will read it attentively, and we will
attempt to follow in the footsteps of those illustrious ladies.] Isabella takes the ladies described as
examples for conduct even though Sabadino does not state that these are exemplary lives.

Sabadino assumes that it is normal to educate girls. He often emphasizes that public display is a natural consequence of education, as in his biographies of the serious scholars Isota and Agnola da Nugarola, but he also praises a far more humble woman for her learning: his own wife, Francesca. "Havea piacere assai in audire legere li versi de Virgilio; legea lei voluntiera Plinio de naturali hystoria, posto in materna lingua, et de li libri spirituali et sancti" (365). [She took a good deal of pleasure in hearing verses of Virgil read; she willingly read Pliny's natural history, put into her mother tongue, and spiritual and holy books.] Sabadino's praise of Francesca, who otherwise resembles the women in Vespasiano's *Lode* far more than does any other woman in the collection, suggests that learning in a woman is prestigious (it makes a humble woman worthy to be in the company of great women) and that interest in secular subjects is praiseworthy even in a domestic woman. Like the great ladies, Francesca wins glory for herself and her family through her learning.

The substantial difference in the values applied to the women whose lives are described can best be seen by a comparison of the sketches of a woman whom both Vespasiano and Sabadino include. Battista da Montefeltro Mala-testa appears in Vespasiano's book as an intensely devout woman whose learning served a moral function and whose withdrawal into a convent with a very strict regime during her husband's lifetime was the central action of her life. Sabadino's representation of her is entirely different. According to his account, Battista was admirable for her skillful government of Pesaro, her learning, and her public eloquence. She was pious, but her piety was not the dominant feature of her character. Her entry into the convent was simply the last of many great actions in her life: five years *after* the death of her husband, she entered a convent "per più secura sanctitate viduile" (135) [in order to observe holy widowhood more securely].[17]

Unlike Vespasiano, who refers only to her private speech with women, Sabadino praises Battista's public eloquence extensively. "Fu de ornato et facondo eloquio, materno et latino, in lo quale fu erudita per modo, che traheva in admiratione qualuncha l'audiva" (133). [Her eloquence was deco-rated and copious in her mother tongue and in Latin, in which she was so learned that she led all who heard her to admire her.] He gives two examples of her public eloquence addressed to male audiences. Pope Martin praised one speech for its "ornato e ciceroniano stile et sentimento" [ornamented and

17. Modern feminist historical research follows Sabadino and emphasizes Battista's learning. See the biographical sketch in King and Rabil in which her piety is reduced to a lone line of fact: "she died as a Sister of the Franciscan order of Saint Claire" (16). They also do not mention her political activity, although they print her highly political speech to Sigismund.

ciceronian style and feeling], and she gave a "luculente oratione" [brilliant oration] (133) to His Majesty Sigismund and to the cardinals.

Sabadino represents Battista as actively engaged in the humanist life.

> Se lege de lei molti argomenti de' comentarii de philosophia et de sacre questione de summi homini. Scripse anchora non poco de la conditione de la vita humana et de la religione eruditamente. (133)

> [One reads many discussions that she wrote about philosophical commentaries and holy questions by great men. She also wrote eruditely and not just a little about the human condition and about religion.]

She also wrote secular "epistole, sonetti et cantilene morale" (134). She was a generous patron of those who wrote in praise of her, and she carried on a correspondence with "molti excellenti ingegni de quel tempo" (134) [many excellent intellects of that time]. Although Sabadino does not mention Bruni as one of these correspondents, the omission of this prestigious fact is outweighed by the representation of her as engaged in exchanges of letters with humanists rather than merely as the passive receiver of one.

Sabadino presents Battista's political skill as entirely natural to her. "Gubernava meglio il stato, per testimonio de nostri magiori, che il marito; per la qual cosa fu molto cara et in summa veneratione a li subditi suoi" (135). [Testimony of our elders attests that she governed the state better than her husband; for which she was held very dear and greatly venerated by her subjects.] As Battista's husband was an extremely cruel ruler who was assassinated, Battista was not competing against a high standard; nonetheless, the matter-of-fact manner in which Sabadino speaks of her rule and of the population's respect for her makes her entry into government seem a normal action.

Despite his assumption that an active political and intellectual life is proper for women, Sabadino suggests that their physiological gender keeps them from being a complete success, as the following description of Zanna di Bentivogli shows:

> Se existimava per suo naturale ascendente et sopra ciò in tal modo se infiamava, deponendo la timidità feminile, che spesse volte disse, che non li manchava altro che 'l segno virile per dare stato et reputatione a la casa Bentivoglia ad confusione de' suoi inimici. (120–21)

[She estimated herself to hold power naturally and got so animated on this subject that, putting aside her feminine timidity, she often said that the only thing she lacked to give a state and a reputation to the Bentivogli family and confusion to its enemies was the virile sign.]

Sabadino's mention of Bentivogli's own sense that her female sex, signified by her lack of a virile member, prevented her complete success argues that from the viewpoint of that society a woman could not establish the reputation of her house as a man could. The lack lies in the woman, but the fault lies in the organization of society.

Finally, what is most surprising about these biographies is the easy accep-tance of the openness of male social roles to all women. Female timidity is something that can be "put aside" by an act of will, and so Zanna is different from the average timid woman, but in degree, not in kind.[18] Sabadino is very far from Boccaccio's theory of the extraordinary woman and from Vespasiano's example of female political action, Francesca Acciaiuoli, whose deed was described as part of her domestic role. His work shows a real change in the way of looking at women. He represents them as autonomous to a significant degree. They have ambitions and accomplishments that do not have to do with family and religion. They are praised for activities that give them public exposure and gain fame for them as individuals. The limitations of their sex only rarely come up as a standard to which they are compared, and never as a control on their own activities.

Sabadino's lack of a sense of the need to justify himself for his perception of women as great leaders, scholars, and so forth makes his book one of the most radically profeminist books of the Renaissance. He assumes that his audience will be impressed by active, astute women who take opportunities to improve their own interests as well as their families'. He expects that his audience will not be surprised to find these qualities of perseverence, constancy, intelligence, piety, continence, and aggression in women. He attempts neither to educate nor to persuade his audience.

18. Some misogyny remains in the *Gynevera*. Avarice is innate in woman's "picolo animo" [little soul]. Biancha Maria and Zanna Bentivogli are generous "oltra il costume natural del sexo femineo" (117) [beyond the natural habit of the female sex]. Zanna speaks of "timidità feminile" [feminine timidity]. This suggests that Sabadino is adopting a way of talking about women that is not entirely natural to him. Generally, however, the assumption is that women do not necessarily fall into the sins traditionally associated with them.

Agostino Strozzi and Bartolomeo Goggio

The works of Agostino Strozzi and Bartolomeo Goggio bring out into the open the assumptions about womankind that lie behind the *Gynevera*. Their main topic is the defense of the natural capacity of the sex to perform virtuous actions and, in both of them, biography is moved to a subordinate position. The two works are nearly contemporary. Goggio's *De laudibus mulierum* was written in 1487; Strozzi's *Defensio mulierum* seems to have been in progress in 1501.[19] Goggio addressed his text to Eleanora of Aragon, wife of Ercole I d'Este of Ferrara; and Strozzi dedicated his to Margherita Cantelma, friend of Eleanora's daughter, Isabella d'Este, and longtime resident in Ferrara. Neither work was printed in its own day, yet they seem to have started the trend of integrating biographies of famous women with proof that they represented the natural capacity of womankind.

Goggio's and Strozzi's texts are motivated by an ambition that Hanna Gray noted as characteristic of humanist writings in the vernacular—the ambition to make difficult philosophical problems accessible to the understanding of a lay audience through rhetoric, which would lead them to understand and move them toward virtuous conduct (Aristotle, *Rhetoric* 1.2.1357a, and Gray 209). In other words, the authors of these works are popularizers who are attempting to bring to the attention of the larger society certain ideas that were already current in erudite humanist circles. To do so, they use Italian rather than Latin, and they attempt to entertain by means of extreme genres, but the purpose of the entertainment is not to give frivolous delight but to move the readers to accept the new ideas and to reformulate their own ethical system to accommodate a more positive notion of woman.

The *Defensio mulierum*, the *De laudibus mulierum*, and almost all the prose works that I will be discussing in the rest of this book participate in two large generic categories: panegyric (laud, encomium) and defense. The defense is contentious. It employs, at least to some extent, the places of forensic rhetoric: it attacks the character of the accuser, and it defends the accused on the grounds of place of birth, character, and so forth. The panegyric is less controversial. It demonstrates the positive attributes of women, whereas de-

---

19. Conor Fahy demonstrated quite conclusively that this work, published in 1876 as *La defensione delle donne d'autore anonimo*, is by Agostino Strozzi, a member of the order of Augustinian Canons and cousin of Margherita Cantelma, who may have commissioned the work (41–42). A reference to it in a brief Latin defense of women by Mario Equicola, itself of uncertain date, suggests that it was in progress in 1501. I am relying on Fahy's dating of the text (37 and 40) as I have not read Equicola's *De mulieribus* or the correspondence that suggests this date.

fenses alternate positive assertions about women with negative assertions about their detractors. As a consequence, the two forms have distinct tones: the defense is involved, snide, and extreme, while the panegyric is secure, detached, and informative. This separation of the genres is artificial, however; most works combine the two.

The genres of encomium and defense that the humanist-courtiers use to present their arguments about women are ostentatiously rhetorical; that is, they are attempts to persuade an audience of a point of view, and they are not neutral expositions of facts. This is not to say that they necessarily are sophistical; we do not find in them "the specious manipulation of language and argument for purposes of deception." Rather, they are attempts at "true eloquence, [which,] according to the humanists, could arise only out of a harmonious union between wisdom and style; its aim was to guide men toward virtue and worthwhile goals, not to mislead them for vicious or trivial purposes" (Gray 200).

The eloquence of the controversy about women is especially complex because its genres require the reader to discover the harmony produced by apparently discordant voices within the text. The genres of defense and encomia both push to extremes to counter doubts that may exist in the reader and, at times, in the writer.[20] Like a lawyer for the defense in a trial at law, the author defending women cites only the positive interpretation of each piece of evidence he introduces, yet the prosecution's case is implicit in the defense case, and the defense appeals to the reader as judge and jury. The work is only complete when it is read by a reader who is careful to listen to the explicit and implicit arguments and who sifts the evidence from its inflated presentation. In a trial, the defense lawyer is entirely on the side of the defendant. In a literary defense, the author stands somewhere behind the voice of the defender and at least suggests the case for the prosecution as well. The reader must judge the entire case, not just accept the loudest voice.[21]

There is an even greater difficulty in reading the wisdom of these texts, however, than the need to reserve judgment and weigh all the evidence. At the same time that they are seriously eloquent, all these works are also, to some extent, self-serving in two senses. Most obviously, the defenses, panegyr-

---

20. See Margaret Ferguson (8–11) on this topic.
21. The argument that I am making about defenses is similar to Gray's about dialogues. "In dialogue, a humanist could state a clear position or refuse to take one. Some dialogues were left deliberately without explicit conclusion, either because the author wished to point out what could be said on different sides of doubtful or complex matters, not to assert one final decision, or with the purpose of allowing the reader to render his own judgment" (214–15).

ics, and eulogistic collections of female biographies are encomiastic genres that cater to the interests of their audience in hope of praise and patronage. Less obviously, these are genres of self-defense, and this self-defensiveness, which is a natural part of the genre of defense, causes the difficulties. Self-defense does not appear as the conventional antifeminist slander by which men have perennially defended themselves from the feminine; rather, it appears as a subtext of restraint that results in the taming of the independent woman who is created in the explicit defense. It is the compromise by means of which authors seek to establish for themselves and their society a livable relationship with the threatening notion that women are equal to men.

Each text defends differently, but the works of Sabadino degli Arienti, Strozzi, and Goggio, the first Italian-language texts, share a few elements. I posit that they are serious challenges to the traditional notion of woman, but they do not conceive of any practical consequences being a necessary result of their argument. They neither offer means for women of their own time to enter the public arena nor do they offer means for society to exclude them. These early authors suggest that women are as capable as men, or nearly so, but they do not imagine that the equality they have discovered might make the hierarchical structure of society untenable.

I have used the words "do not conceive of" and "do not imagine" advisedly, because I think this first generation of defenders of women may have employed this self-defense unawares. The genre left them the opportunity to escape the consequences of their argument, and they did so, but from an unconscious desire to set limits rather than from an awareness of society's need to restrain a dangerous force, as the authors to be considered in Chapter 3 do. There exists in all three cases a paradoxical relationship between the author's understanding of women's capacity and the inferior role assigned to women by society, and each author ignores this issue and does not use the resources of the genre in which he writes to call his reader's attention to it. They do not make full use of the potential of the genre to control the subject.[22]

Strozzi's *Defensio mulierum* is particularly interesting because its manuscript history gives a sense of how controversial arguments for the equality of the

22. The sincerity of these tracts, or at least their fidelity to their thesis, is suggested by the presentation of the works in their proems or dedicatory letters, which address themselves to a particular woman who has commissioned the work or who will find special satisfaction in seeing herself mirrored in the work. If the work were truly paradoxical, it would assume that the lady's pleasure would not be direct (i.e., in reading praise and defense of her sex) but indirect (i.e., in seeing the categories by which the sexes are judged broken down). The separation of defense and laud in these early works, thus, increases the reader's sense of their sincerity and lets them focus attention on the contest between the sexes.

sexes were. It exists in three versions: a manuscript at the Biblioteca Nazionale at Florence, a modern printed edition from a manuscript that now is lost, and a Latin manuscript that would seem to be the original from which the lost manuscript was translated. The Latin and the lost manuscripts are anonymous. The Florentine manuscript carries Strozzi's name as author; it contains a dedicatory letter to Margherita Cantelma that states that Cantelma commissioned the work from him (2v); most suggestive of all, it includes a very long, intensely profeminist passage that is very different from the passage that occurs at the same place in the others.[23]

Strozzi's text is divided into a prologue in which the author explains why his book is needed and justifies his appropriateness as the author of such a work, a long and energetic first book that is structured as a series of defensive responses to major and minor calumnies raised against women, and, finally, a second book that contains very brief biographical sketches of ancient women that are offered in praise of women. In each of these sections Strozzi establishes strategies that become staples of the Renaissance defense of women.

The prologue reveals the impediment that ingrained literary habits could pose to the creation of a consistent program of defense. In it Strozzi carries out the first step of defense, the attack on the character of the opposition. Vespasiano merely called attacks on women presumptuous and irrational; Strozzi creates a myth. He represents antifeminism as a sign of the degeneration of the world from its original state and as part of an attempt by the "bad and depraved" to detract from everything that is "excellent and holy" (3). He describes the profeminist opponents of these wicked slanderers as knights who must use the sword of eloquence to defend the good "against their envious and evil speaking detractors" (5) and his writing in defense of the innocent as an example of charity, the original good from which the world has fallen. This is gallant of him, but self-defeating. The clichéd metaphor equating eloquent male speech with the valor of knighthood prevents female equality just as effectively as slander because it represents women as weak and helpless. The male writer rides on with pen in hand, ready to defeat the enemy whom she is too weak to take on. Strozzi's chivalrous language reveals how superficially he has examined his own attitudes and betrays him into unconscious repression of those whom he would free.

Once he begins the formal defense, Strozzi is much more effective. In answering the first calumny, that women have little intelligence, he first

---

23. Page numbers refer to the printed text; folio numbers to the manuscript in the Biblioteca Nazionale in Florence.

attempts to establish a profeminist reading of the scriptural notion of woman and of her relationship to man. To demonstrate that woman is rational, he discovers positive implications in God's creation of her in His image, and in order to define her proper relation to man, he limits the social implications of a series of fundamental Pauline texts. He attempts to use reason to reconcile biblical passages with each other when they appear contradictory.

At this point the texts diverge from each other. Folios 16r through 26r of the Florentine manuscript make a radical new argument: the sexes are physically equal as well as mentally equal and, thus, according to nature, women ought to play the same roles in society as men. Citing Gallen, Strozzi finds that women's more temperate nature makes them more reliable than men and is an advantage (18r) and that women actively contribute to conception and do not merely provide the matter onto which men print form and, thus, he reclaims their reproductive function as an asset rather than a liability (23r). Denying that women are naturally cold and humid of complexion, he cites Avicenna as proof that this condition is caused by lack of exercise and argues that if women began to exercise as children and continued to do so as adults, they would become more robust, whereas if men were raised the way women are, they would be as weak as women.[24]

As this last point suggests, Strozzi focuses attention on cultural causes for the apparent inferiority of contemporary women. He concludes,

> Possiamo cognoscere che non e la conditione de le Donne in commoda ne inepta a tutte le altre occupatione officii & pensieri quali pare che siano propriamente solo de li homini se cum exercitio e studio ad essi se assuefacesseno. . . . Percio che cotale occupatione non ha negate la natura ne interditte a le donne ma la usancia e consuetudine che se mutando cotal consuetudine come piu volte havemo letto e udito che gia e sta fatto, cominciaseno le Donne di exercitare quello che fano li homi. . . . E poi che per longo uso cotal costume si fosse confromato cessaria poi la admiratione cessando la novita . . . e cessaria insieme la stolta accusatione. (23v–24r)

24. ". . . non puo essere argumento di naturale imbecillitate se la complexione de le donne sia forsi piu humida e fredda ch non doveria: poi ch se cognosce ch non adviene cio da natura ma da occasione accidentale . . . si come potria anch acadere ne li homini se fosseno nutriti & alenati in cotal studii et exercitii quali sono loro" (21v). [if women's makeup is more wet and cold than it ought to be, that cannot be an argument for their natural stupidity as one knows that that does not happen by nature but by accident . . . as it could also happen in men if they were nourished and raised in the same studies and exercises as women are.]

[We may know that the condition of women is neither inconvenient nor ill suited for all the other occupations, offices, and thoughts which seem to belong properly only to men, if women were to get used to them with practice and study. . . . Because nature has neither forbidden nor denied such occupations to women but . . . custom so that if this custom is changed, as we have several times read and heard has already happened, women will begin to apply themselves to the things that men do. . . . And then, such custom being confirmed through long use, astonishment could cease with the cessation of the novelty . . . and at the same time foolish accusations would cease.]

Strozzi turns to history for support of these assertions. He argues that in the past women fought wars and governed republics and, thus, their lack of power and restricted role in contemporary society cannot be said to be natural. Plato was right, he says, to divide all work between the sexes in the *Republic*.

Thus far, Strozzi's arguments provocatively challenge his readers to rethink all the premises on which they have based their assumption that woman is inferior to man and ought to play an inferior and sheltered role. When he attempts to find a historical cause for the "custom" of female domesticity, however, he paradoxically reveals himself to be committed to the conventional notion of woman's physical weakness. He argues that the decline from the Golden Age of equality occurred because male daring or strength prevailed and women stayed home (24v):

Li quali (uomini) essendo piu potenti di forcie e anche di audatia facilmente restrinsero li pacifici animi de le donne a logette e ocio familiare. che molto non li fecero contrasto o resistentia. (26r)

[who (men) being stronger in physical strength and in daring easily restrained the peaceful souls of the women to the objects and ease of family life. They did not argue or resist much.]

This explanation contradicts his previous point. If the state of equality that he imagined had existed, then the sexes would have been equally or nearly equally daring and violent, even given women's greater temperance, and women would not have lost out. This logical inconsistency serves no rational purpose in the argument. As in the dedicatory letter when he used the chivalric metaphor, Strozzi represses female authority. It would seem that, for a man in this period, consistently imagining women as political and social equals was extremely difficult.

The radical nature of the defense of female physical strength in the Florentine manuscript is apparent when it is compared with the other manuscripts, which declare that woman's reproductive function makes her body weak and that her intellect is weaker than man's because it has to operate through her inferior body (33–40). Strozzi acknowledges that in making this statement he is accepting an assertion antifeminists traditionally make about women, but he insists that the reader recognize that this does not make women imbeciles:

> Anzi non si può negare, che non siano bona et onorevole parte della natura razionale, per divina grazia, non solamente con li uomini, ma ancora con li angieli, fatte degne del consorzio della celeste beatitudine ornata dalla opifice natura di sommo e precipuo ingegno e discorso di ragione, secondo la umana condizione, in questo solamente inferiore a la eccellenzia dell'uomo, che per la necessaria distinzione dell'ordine naturale, et a procreare li figlioli e nutrirli sostiene certa ragionevole differenzia di corpo più fragile et imbecille. (37–38)

> [Rather, one cannot deny that they are a good and honorable part of rational nature, by divine grace, not only with men but also with the angels, made worthy of the society of celestial beatitude ornamented by workmanlike nature with the highest and most important intelligence and reasonable discourse, appropriate to the human condition, in this only inferior to the excellence of man in order to maintain the necessary distinction of the natural order and to procreate and nourish children she is different to a reasonable degree, in that her body is more delicate and weak-minded.]

While it may seem of slight importance that this manuscript argues that women are nearly as intelligent as men whereas the other argues that the sexes are equal, the difference is very important in its cause and in its results. Here biology is destiny: women are less intelligent because their reproductive function diminishes their intellectual capacity. As a result of this biological determinism, the manuscript presents no challenge to conventional sex roles. There is no talk of the influence of custom on society's expectations of women because no evidence has been quoted that could provide a basis for questioning contemporary custom.

Although it is tempting to find the more liberal manuscript to be the more authoritative one, the radical pages are exceptional in the *Defensio*.[25] In the rest of the text, which is common to all the manuscripts, the author regularly assumes the inferiority of wives to their husbands both in moral capacity and in authority. Immediately before the variant passage, for example, the author says Scripture teaches that woman is subject to man (32). Later when answering the second and third calumnies—that women are unchaste and that they are ill-disposed to doing good and ready for every evil ["impudiche tutte e disonestissime," "al ben fare difficili et inettissime, ma ad ogni male, inganni, fraudi, insidie, tutte siano attissime et accomodate" (15)]—he does not consider women responsible for their own actions, but blames their misbehavior on the negligence of the men who have authority over them. If the wife is too flashy a dresser, the fault lies with her husband's carelessness ["poca cura e diligenzia" (76)]. The strongest defense that Strozzi offers for women in this section is that whatever the evil or immoral deeds of women, men have done at least as much and probably more (46). Even in wickedness, women are inferior.

Finally, it is impossible to establish any manuscript as a definitive version of the text, but the variant passage makes it clear that revision occurred and the conflicting readings suggest controversy. If we postulate the more liberal Florentine manuscript as representing the "true" text, then the conservative variant represents a scribe/reader's response to the text or an authorial revision of it away from radical profeminism. On the other hand, if we postulate the lost manuscript as the "true" text, then we see the author or the transcriber/ reader transforming a lukewarm profeminism into a far-reaching challenge to his society. Perhaps he had only begun his revisions. It is interesting that the Florentine text is the one directly addressed to a woman patron. Did the author expect that this text would please her and write another for some other audience? The dedicatory letter states that Cantelma commissioned him to write this book (2v); was this argument inserted in obedience to her wishes? It is, of course, impossible to know. What we can know is that it was possible for a writer in the late fifteenth century to conceive of the determinism of culture

25. In his description of the various manuscripts of Strozzi's treatise, Conor Fahy favors the Florentine as the best text, although he says one cannot be sure. He calls it "the best available text of this work at the moment" (45). He speaks of the manuscript as "forestalling the objection that women occupy a position inferior to men in society, the author reminds his readers of the influence of environment and the importance of convention in determining the activities to which the sexes devote themselves" (44). While this is an accurate description of the passage in question, it is important to note that not all the manuscripts question the assumption that women's social position should be inferior.

on behavior and to imagine the new society that would develop if the existing gender assumptions were overturned and women freed to participate in "occupations, offices, and thoughts which seem to belong properly only to men," that is, freed to be independent.

The second book of the *Defensio* is made up of a collection of lives of famous women. In its preface Strozzi moves from defense of women to praise of them, and his claims are once again in keeping with the more radical part of Book 1. The change in genre is made apparent by the way he speaks of his role; he represents himself as paying tribute to women rather than brandishing a naked sword of eloquence in their defense. The battle is won, and it seems that the women have won it for themselves. He states that he is writing praise of women

> acciò che venga in luce la loro gloria oscurata et oppressa alquanto per malivolenzia di alcuni uomini; e per lo avvenire siano chiuse e serrate le bocche maligne delli iniqui maldicenti. (92–93)

> [so that their glory, which has been obscured and oppressed by the spite of some men, will come to light; and so that in the future the malicious mouths of the unjust slanderers will be closed and locked.]

There are two extremely important profeminist points in this passage. First, Strozzi speaks of women's glory as being obscured by men, but not created by them; he, a male author, is simply restoring to women something that is already theirs. Women have acted independently, and glory, like the noise in the deserted forest, exists whether or not anyone is there to perceive it. Second, that the malevolence of males has kept women's deeds secret takes from women the blame for the comparative scarcity of great women and puts it on men; women have acted, but men have actively prevented us from knowing about it. Women are capable and are in charge of their lives, but not in control of the history books.

Strozzi begins with the assertion that the two sexes are equally able to achieve praiseworthy great deeds:

> è la loro mente et animo facile et espedito a pigliare qualunque cosa ardua e difficile da fare, et eseguire fortemente ogni grande impresa, che nella mente abbiano proposito di abbracciare. (93)

> [their mind and soul are ready and prompt to undertake any hard and difficult thing, and to energetically carry out every big enterprise that they have thought of embracing.]

Like the Florentine variant, this passage assumes the natural strength of women. The glory of great women illuminates womankind as a whole because they are of the same kind, though more gifted; these women are not exceptions to their sex as Boccaccio would have it. Because this claim is made in the mode of praise rather than defense, however, it presents less of a challenge to conventional social order. The author does not need to present a theory that will account for the difference between the past and the present conduct of women; he needs only to celebrate whatever examples he wishes.

The organization of the biographies that form the body of Book 2 is aggressively profeminist. Many of the lives are grouped by profession, a system typical of books of male biographies; Vespasiano used it for his famous men but not for his famous women. We read chapters about women excellent in letters, administration of states and armed deeds, and painting and sculpture, although these stand side by side with chapters filled with examples of women who excelled at preserving their virginity and whose deeds offer admirable signs of their love of their husbands. To conceive of women being various and defined at least in part by profession rather than by sexual state (virgin, married, widow) is nontraditional.

Strozzi weakens the profeminist effect by naming no individual living women in any of the categories, although he several times praises them as a group. At the end of his section on women who excelled in letters, for example, Strozzi mentions that many women of his own day have given excellent public speeches and have written learned poetry ["in questa nostra etade molte anche ne sono, delle quali noi stessi molte fiate avemo lette ornatissime orazioni avute in publico, e versi dottissimi" (99)]. The reader of the *Gynevera de le clare donne* can imagine that he may be referring to Battista da Montefeltro Malatesta or Isota and Agnola da Nugarola, but the absence of specific examples in this passage stands out in comparison with the dull but specific accounts of ancient women.

When Strozzi explains why he has omitted the names of his contemporaries, he betrays a lack of confidence in the success of his own defense. He says that he chose not to praise deserving contemporary women by name because envy would damage their reputations. "La loro virtù di continuo combatte con la pestilente rabbia di invidia, da quale non può essere che sempre non sia in parte guasta e corrosa" (180). [Their virtue continually has to combat the pestilential anger of envy by which it cannot always remain unspoiled and unimpaired.] We saw that Boccaccio anticipated a similar problem and made elaborate use of it to flatter his patron in the dedicatory letter, but Strozzi allows it to stand in the way of praising any contemporary at all. His efforts can recover fame for women of the ancient past, but can do nothing to gain it for women of his own time. It seems that they will have to wait for a Strozzi of some long-distant generation to receive their due (King and Rabil, perhaps), yet the example of Sabadino degli Arienti and, even, Vespasiano da Bisticci suggests that public praise was a desirable commodity in the community that they all were addressing.

Strozzi seems to be unsure that he wants to encourage modern women to free themselves from convention and seek public fame. Even his praise of deceased moderns is so general that it makes very little impression. For example, from Vespasiano we know that Paula Gonzaga was known for her interest in humanist education, and so we might have expected to find her among the women famed for letters instead of classified as miscellaneous, but Strozzi merely says that she is remembered with great praise in the city of Mantua and in the surrounding country ["con tituli immensi di laude" (179)]. As we saw in the examination of Vespasiano's and Sabadino's texts, the inclusion of modern women provides important evidence of continuity between past and present while the praise of them for "masculine" actions challenges conventional sex roles in just the way that Strozzi seemed to be doing in the Florentine variant. Their absence weakens the text's power to persuade the reader that modern women can compete.

Strozzi's conclusion encourages this reading of him as drawing back from the implied conclusions of his argument. It is directly addressed to husbands, so that, suddenly, women, who have been represented as men's equals and as the performers of great deeds, are reduced to dependents in the domestic sphere. Strozzi advises men to keep in mind all that he has said in women's defense when they are dealing with their wives, and, he says, should they still feel moved to blame them for being the weaker sex ["incolparle di fragile e debile sesso"], reverence for the Virgin should hold them back from doing them any physical harm (183). Indeed, he says, Mary alone would be enough to redeem the reputation of womankind even if all other women were what the most spiteful misogynist says they are. While the evocation of Mary is an appropriate ending to a book by an Augustinian Canon, the effect of the reference to her is similar to the effect of his offer to defend women with his pen. He seems to lack confidence not only in the evidence he has presented, but in women themselves. Mary's extraordinary virtue makes their ordinary virtue irrelevant to their own defense.

Despite these repeated lapses into an unconsciously misogynist rhetoric, the overall impression that Strozzi's text makes is rationally profeminist. With reason and examples he undermines the reader's notion of woman as foolish,

unchaste, exclusively domestic, and essentially different from man. By demonstrating that woman is endowed with the same virtues as man, he wins
respect for women. Yet, because he concedes that women are weaker in their
virtue and vulnerable to slander, he achieves this profeminist purpose without
leveling the existing social hierarchy.

In the *De laudibus mulierum* Bartolomeo Goggio does not merely assert that
women are capable of the same deeds as men as Strozzi does. Like Erasmus
when he praises folly, Goggio proposes to prove the superiority of a creature
always assumed to be inferior: woman.

> intendo demostrare la dona in cossa havere superato lhomo. Et essere
> piu et de piu laude digna como quella da cui tute le cosse mirabile et
> maravegliosi facti al mondo sono provenuti. (6r)

> [I intend to demonstrate women to have gone beyond man in some
> things. And to be more and more worthy of praise like the one from
> whom all the amazing and marvelous deeds in the world have come.]

As the terms of the reference to the Virgin reveal, Goggio's principal thesis is
that women are naturally superior to men. Mary is exemplary of the capacities
of her sisters, rather than an extraordinary exception who shields them from
criticism.

Goggio's praise takes two very different forms, both of which entail a
rewriting of history. On the one hand he presents a paradoxical proof that the
very qualities in woman that men usually disparage make her better than man,
on the other he uses catalogues of great female poets, rulers, and warriors to
prove that women are as good as men at doing masculine things. The latter
evidence writes women into conventional history. Goggio expects his male
reader to be surprised to discover the important role that women have played
in what he thought was a male production.[26] With the paradox, which gives a
privileged position to neglected feminine virtues, however, Goggio writes a
new kind of history in which great men are denigrated and previously obscure
women are celebrated.

---

26. "Dico chel non é da dubitare che essendo glhomini tuti esbigotiti . . . per la precedente
novitade . . ." (62v). [I say that it cannot be doubted that all the men being astonished by the
preceding novelty (or news) . . .]. I take this to refer to what he has said about women, but it could
refer to his discussion of the diversity of languages.

These two programs are contradictory. Logically, women cannot be superior because they are different and equal because they are the same. Goggio commits himself to two different kinds of feminism, and they result in an ambiguity in the text and a dilemma for the female reader and for the society as a whole.[27] Like French essentialist feminist theory, the paradoxical proof that feminine virtues are more valuable than male requires the reader to come to see that the values by which society usually determines worth are misguided and to accept that women are better than men because of the very qualities that previously made them inferior. This reasoning can affect the appreciation of women and, perhaps, encourage men to behave in a feminine manner, but it cannot sponsor any change in woman's social role because it is based in virtues for which her present one gives full scope. By contrast, the straightforward proof that women can achieve in male fields of endeavor reinforces the conventional valuing of the masculine and suggests that women are valuable only insofar as they can compete with men. The recovery of women from historical obscurity is the first step, but, for the strategy to be successful, a plan for reform to break the pattern of history must be offered. This Goggio does not do.

The dominant form of the work is encomia, as the title suggests, and Books 2, 3, and 5 through 7 are entirely devoted to topics of praise. Book 1 combines features of the judicial oration on behalf of an accused client with the paradoxical encomium, and Book 4 is a digression, a structure typical of the genre of judicial defense. Because of the intertwining of praise and defense in Book 1, the praise of women presented in the later books forms part of the case for the defense.[28]

Book 1 is the center of Goggio's paradoxical proof that women are superior. It puts the debate onto feminine territory and makes men compete for laurels in fields that they do not generally recognize as valid for themselves. It consistently takes qualities that are conventionally seen as signs of woman's inferiority and finds advantages in them. Chapters 3, 4, and 9 answer standard medieval arguments against women with standard medieval arguments in their favor. They argue that God's creation of woman after man makes her better,

27. Gundersheimer speaks of the text as "radically feminist. For Goggio sets out to prove that in all ways women are superior to men" ("Bartolommeo Goggio" 180). His essay is not aimed at discovering Goggio's exact position in Renaissance feminist thought, however, and so he does not identify the use of paradox in the text or the two conflicting kinds of feminism at work. He does not note that Goggio speaks of women as superior to men because the "feminine" is superior to the "masculine."

28. Margaret Ferguson discusses the frequent interconnection of the defense with the mock-encomium (11).

not an afterthought as antifeminists would have it, and that the place of this second creation, Paradise, and the material of it, Adam's rib, both indicate woman's superiority. Chapter 5 confronts woman's weakness with man's strength and cites Aristotle's statement that soft flesh is an indicator of intelligence to prove that women are more intelligent than men (12).

Chapters 6 and 7 form a pair and are among Goggio's most radical because they judge men by feminine standards. Chapter 6 gives examples of great men who were ruined because they gave in to their lust (Samson, Solomon, Plato) and concludes that the strength of soul ("forteza danimo") of all those men who have been most glorious in the world cannot compare with the women whose constancy and courage will be praised in Chapter 7 (15r). These women are the opposites of the great men of Chapter 6 in every way, and their brief biographies constitute one of the major rewritings of history in the *De laudibus*. They are not women who displayed valor in response to the same kind of challenges that traditionally lead men to valor—female warriors, great queens, or forceful women, such as Jael and Judith. Nor are they heroically constant wives. Goggio will not speak of

> quelle matrone la fama de lequale abrana tuto el mondo como fu Lucretia Portia Vetruria et tali che tuto el mondo honora Ma dela forteza et constantia dele fanzule in resistere ad quello in che tuti li piu famosi et eccelenti sono cascati et che dovevano dare lesempro ad tuto el mondo. (15v)

> [those matrons whose fame illuminates all the world such as Lucrece, Portia, Vetruria and those whom all the world honors but of the strength and constancy of girls in resisting that into which all the most famous and excellent men, who should have been an example for all the world, have fallen.]

Instead of Lucrece and the other women whom the male tradition had hitherto chosen to remember because their constancy to men made them fit the patriarchal system of values, we are to be shown women who are constant to virtue itself.

Goggio's heroines are worthy because of their autonomous sense of virtue. They are virgins martyred for their commitment to virginity—women like

> Serafia virginella de Anthiochia ne la sua piu fresca etade Data nele mane a dui governi che la contaminassero et pecasse con lei Aspecta

essere flagelada batuda et nel fine decapitada piu presto che consentire
ad una sola desonestad. (16r)

[Serafia, a virgin of Antioch, who was given to two guardians when she
was in her freshest youth; they wished to contaminate her and sin with
her. She chose to be whipped, beaten, and, finally, decapitated rather
than consent to a single dishonest action.]

In his discussion of the moral failings of male heroes in Chapter 6, Goggio
establishes that, as a test of strength, commitment to virtue is more important
than intelligence, wisdom, and aggressive physical power. Goggio uses examples of virgins like Serafia to show that women acting in the interests of virtues
that have always been considered feminine demonstrate constancy and valor.
Thus, women win the battle for superiority by fully realizing the potential of
their sex.

Similarly, in Chapter 10 Goggio creates grounds for admiration out of what
had previously been denigrated as irrelevant women's territory by reinterpreting
woman's role in generation. He admits that women do not contribute seed but
argues that the male seed is not active but passive, while the action of the
woman's body on the seed is active because it transforms the passive seed into
a generated thing, a child. Thus, woman is superior to man because of a quality
that she has always possessed but that has never before been interpreted
correctly. Goggio's stress on the opposition of active and passive shows that
there are limits on how far he will go in the reversals demanded by his
paradoxical praise of women. He does not identify activity with masculinity
and passivity with femininity and thus put himself in the position of praising
passivity (surely a difficult task). He discovers that female actions that appear
passive are in fact active and that, therefore, when we see clearly we perceive
the superiority of the female gender.

The absence of women from history is as strong an argument on the
misogynist side as are the voices of ancient philosophy and theology that
Goggio answers by means of paradox in Book 1. Books 2 and 4 write woman
into history in order to represent her as man's equal. In them Goggio leads his
readers to reexamine a field they thought they knew very well, a field that was
stable and certain, and to discover the presence of women in the foreground.
That women have invented the arts and sciences and displayed military valor
is not surprising to a reader of Boccaccio's De mulieribus, the source for much
of Goggio's information, but the claim that they founded Egypt, Germany,
Bohemia, Libya, Assyria, and other nations is. Of course, frequently the

founders of nations are the same queens and generals whom Boccaccio celebrated for political acuity—Semiramis, for example. Others are famous women celebrated for an accomplishment that is generally known but not emphasized: Dido is included as the founder of Carthage. Many are obscure, however, and twist the definition of "founding."

One of the examples to which Goggio calls most attention is one of the most surprising: Rome. It seems that Romulus did not found the city; he enlarged it. Goggio offers three possible explanations for the founding of Rome. Nicostrata (Carmenta), the creator of the Roman alphabet and mother of Evander, told her son to build on the Palatine Hill. Or, according to Heraclitus, when some wandering Greeks happened on the Tiber, Roma, a Trojan noblewoman who was their prisoner, counseled them to build there. Or, according to the historian Agathoche, Roma was the daughter of Ascanius, and she founded the city. In the latter cases the city was named for Roma.

Goggio's handling of the founding of Rome is typical of his representation of the founding of many countries. An obscure minor legend attributing the founding to a woman, reported in a respectable source, is given precedence over the standard story in which the foundation of the state is attributed to a man. Goggio cleverly does not ask the reader to discard his old historical knowledge completely—who could give up believing in Romulus and Remus, legendary founders in whom we believe even today, even though if questioned our proof is literary and suspect, just as Goggio's evidence for Roma is? The accepted version is not denied but is found to be compatible with the rediscovered story, and woman is restored to her place in history.[29] Although one may dispute individual entries, one comes away from the lengthy book knowing the names and deeds of many more women than one knew when starting to read. As a result, one receives the impression that women have been far more active and important than one had previously believed.

In addition to providing evidence of women's neglected glory, the story of

29. Goggio's dedication of such a substantial portion of his work to extensively developed historical examples is significant for another reason unrelated to the argument I am making. It shows that one of the pleasurable functions of this work, as with many of the books on women, is as a repository of interesting and unusual information. This view is confirmed by the dedication of Book 4 to a discussion of the origins of languages. The entire book is a digression and has nothing to do with the subject at hand, but Goggio says he includes it because the subject is interesting. Within his discussion of women Goggio also sometimes notes that he is going on at length, is digressing, because the material itself is so interesting that it warrants inclusion even though it is not necessary for the proof. This suggests that Goggio's standards for choosing his material were not rigorously rational; he did not demand verisimilitude, but only some degree of plausibility; unusualness made information more attractive. The book caters to the period's delight in curiosities.

the founding of Rome serves to suggest very indirectly a cause for the absence of women from history texts. Goggio jokingly says that he fears that praising women will do him harm because in ancient Rome it was a capital offense to reveal that Rome was founded by women, and he gives the example of Valerio Sovano, who was put to death for revealing this secret. The indirectness of the suggestion that male authorities have repressed female history is typical of Goggio's method. Boccaccio laments that women have been neglected by historians despite their worthiness, but he does not analyze the cause and blame men. Strozzi directly addresses the topic and shifts the blame for woman's absence from historical records from women to men; women have acted, but we have remained in ignorance because men did not want us to know. Goggio does not explicitly draw the obvious conclusion from his example, though an alert reader can. He praises without defending and so does not provide a clear basis for social critique.

In the last three books Goggio returns to paradox and the exaltation of feminine virtue in the person of Mary, whom he asserts to be the greatest founder of a realm—the kingdom of Heaven. The reader, who might quibble that secular power and Mary's power cannot be compared and that she is not a queen at all in the ordinary sense of the word, is answered by a long contrast of the extent and durability of her realm and that of earthly realms. Goggio does not deny that she is different in kind from the heroines of Book 4:

> [Non] como alcuna de quelle valorose done che fundatrice sono di regni mondani ma con pace povertade humilitade et obedienza et virginitade fusse de quello fundatrice. (94v)

> [Not like any of those valorous women who are founders of worldly realms but she was founder of that one with peace, poverty, humility, and obedience and virginity.]

These are the conventional ideals for women and Christians, so once again Goggio is asserting the superiority of the feminine over the masculine. The Virgin is intensely feminine and better than any man or manlike woman. She bests the more practical strain of thought represented by the "gloriosi gesti" and directs the reader's attention away from the political implications of the secular argument.

After offering the Virgin as his greatest piece of evidence for the superiority of feminine virtues, Goggio shows how daring he is willing to be in his attempt to overturn old prejudices against the feminine by revealing that Eve is a positive figure in universal history. He does not merely say that Eve was good because she prepared the way for Mary and for Christ; he offers his reader the delight of finding positive value in someone who has always been seen as bad. He points out the many benefits that came because of her sin. [". . . ad me pare tuto el mondo dovere essere obligato ad madona eva del suo peccato considerando li molti beni da quello provenuti" (139v).] For example, she opened the eyes of the intellect for mankind. He also demonstrates that Eve cannot be considered responsible for many of the evils for which she is blamed because they arise naturally from the composition of human bodies and not from the eating of the apple.

The profeminism of Goggio's treatment of Eve and Mary becomes clear when compared with Strozzi's citation of the Virgin. He did not include her as a woman but as an exception, and her existence outside the categories of discussion threatened to invalidate them. Goggio treats Mary and Eve as women who confirm the arguments he has made up to this point. They help his case, although it could have been made without them.[30]

In sum, the independent woman is strongly present in this work. Whether carrying their children or founding empires by means of military action, the women Goggio praises are active and autonomous; they act because of internal promptings and the innate capacities of their bodies, not because of the urging of male members of their families or the transforming action of male spirit. But the independent woman in Goggio's text is really of two kinds, the politically independent woman and the ethically independent woman; despite her presence as an important piece of evidence for the excellence of women, the politically independent woman is not the chosen ideal. The rhetoric of paradox that gives shape to the entire argument favors the ethical woman because it glorifies the feminine and shows that the "other" is a more significant force for social cohesion than the male.

The paradox is ideally suited to a society that has recognized that women have previously unacknowledged talents but that cannot permit the claims of inferiors to positions of power because it is rigidly hierarchical. By leading the society to see as positive what it previously saw as negative, the paradoxical encomium encourages it to feel richer without changing its structure. When he imagines his book being read by women, Goggio stresses the autonomy of female virtue, which he has proved by paradox, and does not follow through

30. That Goggio devotes one book to Mary and two entire books to the topic of Eve and original sin may have had to do with his immediate audience, as Eleanora was a very pious woman; it may also have had to do with his own piety. His only other humanistic work is a meditation on the immortality of the soul, occasioned by the death of Eleanora.

on the politically radical potential of his evidence for the female presence in history. He speaks of the text as stimulating and praising conventional moral behavior, as did Boccaccio in the dedicatory letter to the *De mulieribus*. The female reader who admired his examples of active women would find instruction and encouragement to follow their example in none of the places where he explicitly speaks to the problem of the use to which his society will put his book.

Even Eleanora d'Este, the dedicatee, is not treated as exemplary of either the potential for feminine virtue to reform society or the ability of women to equal men, although from historical evidence it is clear that she was worthy of praise in the fields of letters and politics. Goggio's dedicatory letter to her is thin on detailed praise. He assumes that she is the same kind of woman as the great ones he uses for his examples, but he does not identify any particular qualities she shares with them; he merely says that she will be able to look into the mirror of magnanimity and virtue of the women described in the book and see herself. Later in the book, at the end of the chapter in defense of the female role in generation, Goggio downplays Eleanora's intelligence; he assumes that she is not interested in philosophical disputation, apologizes to her for having entered into it, and suggests that the rest of his work will be more delightful (24v). This trope of apology to the female reader for complex material reappears frequently in later defenses (as in the *Cortegiano*); here it implies a notion of woman that Goggio would have seemed to be trying to escape. It suggests either a conflict between the ideal he is creating and his practical understanding of what women are like or his own inability to consistently think of women as being intelligent.[31]

In the first chapter of Book 1, the exordium, Goggio establishes moral and personal grounds for his work's quarrel with misogyny; this also undercuts the political radicalism of the text. The author offers his work as a refutation of the notion of woman and female psychology in the *Corbaccio*, Boccaccio's compendium of medieval antifeminism. Like Boccaccio, the deserving Goggio has been rejected and mocked by a woman he loved, but instead of writing an invective against all women because one was bad, he is going to write praise of women in the hope that this woman will feel shame that she has fallen away from what she might have been. Whereas Boccaccio wanted to devalue women and love in order to free men for more important activities, Goggio hopes to recall the woman to her higher self. He assumes the best of women and

---

31. The difference could also be attributed to professional versus amateur humanist. Perhaps no lay reader, male or female, could be expected to find such dry material interesting.

considers bad women to be a falling away from the good rather than considering bad women to be the norm and good women to be extraordinary. The implied advantage to be gained from accepting the text's arguments as true, however, is personal. Sexual relations between the sexes may improve. The larger social implications of the proof of women's virtuous capacities are not mentioned.

At the end of the book, when Goggio again turns to his female readers, he does not urge them to imitate the heroines, just to enjoy knowing about them. He enjoins Eleanora and other ladies to rejoice ("iubilati ed alegrativi") in the "gloriosi gesti" that they have learned that women have done, but above all "ad quella gloriosa vergine che fu figliola et madre del suo figliolo" (169r) [in that glorious virgin who was daughter and mother of her son]. Although Goggio still seems to be encouraging women to think of themselves as of the same kind as the Virgin by virtue of their gender, their response to her example, to that of the other women who performed great deeds, and, indeed, to this very long and complex argument in praise of women's activity is expected to be pride in their sex, but not active imitation of their deeds.

The lack of an active connection between the women of the audience and the women of the text makes *De laudibus mulierum* very similar to Strozzi's *Defensio* in its effect. Each work in its own way raises its readers' esteem for women, yet both omit a program by which modern women might achieve the deeds of their ancient sisters. Strozzi contains their actions within the bounds of their traditional social role by admitting that women are of the same kind as men, but often not so effectively virtuous; Goggio does so through paradoxical praise of the feminine. Neither achieves a political feminism. The similar results of the two most radical Italian texts in defense of women written at the very end of the fifteenth century, rhetorically diverse as they are, suggest that the anxiety they display about the independent woman is a characteristic of their society rather than their single authors, as the works discussed in the next three chapters will confirm.

3

The Literary Containment of the Independent Woman: Capella and Castiglione

During the first third of the sixteenth century, the defense of womankind moved from manuscript to printed book and became a popular topos among authors connected with the Northern court circle to which all the works in the last chapter (except Vespasiano's *Lode*) were addressed. Castiglione devoted an entire book of his *Cortegiano* to it, and a good number of less well known authors published defenses of women or integrated the topic into larger works. Although the authors of these defenses were themselves members of the court humanist society, they wrote for a wider audience than the court and its powerful female patrons. Their works show the effects of the change in audience in the diverse levels of their styles and in the more conservative nature of their defense.

Readers over the years have complained about a lack of sincerity in the majority of these texts. Vittorio Cian spoke for the critical tradition when he described these works as

> tedious, cold, and monotonous reworkings of old themes, written more to demonstrate wit and cleverness, or to satisfy the curiosity of the public or the greed of the popular press, than as a free and high-minded manifestation of pure and spontaneous feeling: and because of this they do not have any value except a historical one. (*Le Rime* clxxxv)

Cian is right. These works lack originality in their choice of material, they frequently are paradoxical and aim to be witty, and they are not written from the heart, but these qualities point to the texts' goals: they attempt to disrupt assumptions, not to demonstrate their authors' pure feelings.

From the defenses of women published by members of Northern court circles in the first third of the sixteenth century, I have chosen for analysis in this chapter two works that differ in genre, fame, and skill. *Della Eccellenza et dignità della donna* by Galeazzo Flavio Capella (a pseudonym; his real surname was Capra) was the first defense of women to be published in the Italian language.[1] It appeared on its own in 1525 and 1526 and then was republished with Capella's treatises on the excellence of men and on the execrable character of the human race. In method and contents it is representative of a good number of defenses that came out at that time—Agrippa von Nettesheim's *De Nobilitate et Praecellentia Foemenei Sexus*, for example. It is surely one of the works that Cian had in mind. Castiglione's *Il Cortegiano* is not. Although it is no more innovative in its arguments in favor of women than the *Della Eccellenza*, *Il Cortegiano* makes the routine delightful by the eloquence of its interlocutors and by skillful use of the dramatic aspects of the dialogue form. Together these works illustrate the self-defensive nature of the genre of defense in early sixteenth-century practice. Both aim to improve the moral status of woman without creating a new role for her that gives her the opportunity to follow through on the intellectual, moral, and physical strengths attributed to her.

Della Eccellenza et dignità della donna

Capella's *Della Eccellenza et dignità della donna* attacks society's assumption that woman is inferior morally, socially, and physically. The author represents himself as a gallant, disinterested defender of ladies, who is moved to speak by the irrationality of other men's attacks on women, but his text vacillates between rational and ad hominem modes of defense. Serious development of profeminist points is mixed with antimasculine satire of no more substance than traditional antifeminism, and no distinction is made between the validity of these two kinds of argument. The level of style is middle at best; the choice of words is often rough, even indelicate; and the arguments are generally not philosophically sophisticated. The result is an amusing and unsettling presentation that attacks the reader's antifeminism and makes some radical claims about the abilities of women but does not present a clear, rational definition of woman to replace the old negative one.

The *proemio* (preface) of the *Della Eccellenza* gives no indication that the

---

1. For Capella's fame as a defender of women in his own day, see my "Unrecognized Defender." Capra was ambassador to Venice for Duke Francesco Sforza II. For details of his life, see Capra, *Della Eccellenza*, ed. Doglio.

argument to follow will be seriously profeminist. It does not assume that the reader is naturally interested in political or philosophical issues about women but attempts to arouse interest by representing the defense of womankind as an entertaining literary activity. The friars are attacked for writing their antifeminist sophistries in a style so rough that Capella hesitates to dignify it by the name of Latin, and other profeminist works are described as so badly written that no one but their authors will read them.[2] This attack on the style of his opponents and competitors suggests that victory in this debate will be achieved by style; it does not suggest that the arguments presented will be definitive or even significant in themselves.

The same lack of emphasis on the importance of content for itself is evident when Capella describes the benefits that male readers will derive from reading his book. Misogynist texts, he says, are the bitter ravings of lovers whose disreputable approaches have been rejected; his book will instruct men in how worthy women are of love so that the service women expect of them will be less irritating (3r/63).[3] When Goggio made a similar point about the motivation of misogynists, he turned his attention from a male audience to a female one; he explained that he was holding up an ideal for women to follow. For Capella, it would seem, as for antifeminists, woman is of interest only as an object of desire, not as a member of the audience. This is hardly a profeminist approach.

The focus on the entertaining nature of the book's contents and the grounding of the text in the experience of love in the preface do not necessarily indicate that Capella has no interest in a genuine defense of women, however; they may serve as a lure to the reader and indicate that Capella feels his audience needs to be stirred up to an interest in the topic. In the preliminary exposition of the issues in the body of the defense, his tone is much more serious. He disclaims any emotional involvement in the question and states that he intends to demonstrate women's superiority on "the calm plane of reason." He will answer those who have misunderstood the "profound intellect of the philosophers" and have used the results of their literary studies to prove man more worthy and noble than woman (3v/64). He will prove woman is as worthy or more worthy than man.

2. "[O]pera . . . in sì rozzo stile scritta, che per auentura se non è dal suo autore, non sarà da alcuno altro tocca mai" (2v/62). All quotations from *Della Eccellenza* are spelled and punctuated as in the 1526 edition. For the convenience of the reader who may have Doglio's edition, I have included the page numbers on which the passages appear.

3. [Q]uanto da la Natura et da ì Cieli siano le Donne priuilegiate gli sarà più piacere il seruirle, & molto men'noia il correre ogni periglio & patire ogni tormento & danno per acquistare il loro amore" (3r/63).

The organization of the tract suits this serious ambition. Capella lists the charges against womankind; then he defends her capacity for the Christian virtues of faith, hope, and charity and for the four cardinal virtues; then, using examples drawn from history, he celebrates deeds exemplary for their magnanimity, self-sacrificing love, learning, and good fortune; he discourses on the superiority of female beauty and the composition of the female body; and he presents a general defense that touches on many topics. In this manner, he attempts to refute the philosophical and scientific basis of antifeminism.

Despite this serious framework, the reader who had been drawn in by the satiric delights of the first few pages would not be disappointed by the style of what follows. Capella's most frequent method of argument, especially in the sections devoted to the Christian and cardinal virtues, is to make the sophisticated, abstract arguments of the philosophers look foolish by confronting them with the evidence of everyday experience. For example, he cites the traditional axioms that women are imperfect and desire men as matter desires form and that women love the first man with whom they make love because they assume perfection from contact with a more perfect being, whereas men hate their first woman because they lose perfection to her. Instead of refuting these claims by entering into a medical and philosophical discussion of conception as Goggio and Strozzi do, Capella draws on everyday sexual experience: men would soon hate their wives if they constantly lost perfection to them, and, as men love their wives more as time passes, they clearly are not losing perfection to them, and the argument that women are less perfect is untrue. By appealing to the good sense of the common reader addressed in the introductory remarks, this method of argument undercuts the philosophical basis of antifeminism without providing a foundation for the construction of a new notion of woman.

The defense of women's capacity for the cardinal virtues has the potential to advance the debate onto political territory, but Capella considers the virtues of justice, strength, prudence, and temperance in their conventional feminine manifestations. Justice is discussed as generosity and is said to result in such virtues as innocence, religion, piety, friendship, affection, and humanity. The illustrious examples of strength demonstrate the ability of the soul to force the body to suffer pain, rather than the ability of the body to accomplish great feats. Prudence and temperance are illustrated by reference to domestic science and to chastity. The result is a defense of woman's ability to play her traditional role responsibly that puts no pressure on the reader to conceive of a new role for her.

Capella frequently uses antimasculine satire to discredit men and their slander of women. In the discussion of charity, we are told that both pro- and antifeminists admit that women go to church more often than men, but that while men claim that women go so frequently only to be admired, in fact, women are pious and men are the lascivious ones. According to Capella, men go to church and sit around girl-watching. We are even privy to a bit of conversation in which a speaker suggests that his reverent friends look at "quelle poppe" [those tits] (68). This scene does not prove anything about women's piety. It leads men to acknowledge their own flaws and reduces them to a level slightly lower than that which they assign to women. Everyday experience once again defeats the antifeminist point of view and demonstrates women's virtue in a field conventionally dedicated to them.

It is typical of Capella that he does not quarrel with the antifeminist notion of what woman is but rather looks to her actions to show how she controls her essential nature. On the topic of chastity, which is considered under the rubric of temperance, he admits that women suffer from cupidity more than men, but asserts that they act on this passion far less often so that "a nearly infinite number of women exist who, happy with one man, come to their last years without any more, whereas such men are extremely rare" (12r/79). By dividing desire from action Capella paradoxically turns the traditional misogynist assertion that women are oversexed to women's advantage. Yes, they are strongly moved by desire, but they deserve extra praise for conquering this desire so consistently. Similarly, Capella makes contemporary laws against adultery tell in women's favor. There is no punishment for male adulterers, he says, because everyone is guilty, but severe punishment is the rule for women because they so rarely commit the sin. Once again, he invites the reader to recognize that his own experience of women, in this case, his attempts to seduce them, offers proof of their temperance. "It seems that most often our desires are scorned even when we employ all of the arts of arms, jousting, speaking well, dressing elegantly, and the thousand other things we do to please them" (13r/80).[4]

This use of evidence from the reader's own life confirms the underlying seriousness of Capella's text. His argument about adultery may seem sophistical, but experience, so confidently called on, confirms the truth of what has come before. The double standard becomes a tribute to women's moral capacity rather than an indication of the need to impose social limits on her otherwise unrestrainable nature. By this means the text reinforces conventional expectations of women while making a profeminist point—women are naturally chaste.

---

4. [P]are il piu de le uolte con tutte nostre arte d'armeggiare, giostrare, ben parlare, andare ornati, et mille altri studii per piu piacergli, restiamo de nostri desiderii scherniti" (13r; 80).

Capella restrains woman within her traditional domestic role in his proof of her capacity for the cardinal virtue of prudence by citing the division of labor established in the pseudo-Aristotelian *Economics* and in Xenophon's *Oeconomicus*—men gather and women safeguard the fruits. He attempts to prove the value of woman's role by showing the chaos that results from her absence.

> How many houses of magnates and princes are there in which one lives with such disorder that one would be more comfortable at the biggest hospital in Milan and all because there is no woman to govern the place as there ought to be. . . . How many such places are seen to go from bad to worse every day and become nothing for the same reason? In contrast, how many are there that have always grown and grow every day because their government is in the hands of a woman? which results not in damage but in great utility and profit. . . .⁵ (10rv/76–77)

To a reader fresh from the most radical arguments in Strozzi and the examples in Goggio, this assertion of women's skill in domestic organization is not an earth-shaking claim; we might expect the author to work outward from this proof to discover other applications for women's capacity for prudence, but Capella does not. He assures his reader that entrusting household affairs entirely to his wife will result in great comfort and peace of mind for him and will not lead the wife to desire to run him as well as the household (10v/77). He clearly expects resistance even to his defense of the skill of household management.

Despite his overall commitment to the accepted notion of the virtues and skills appropriate to women, Capella does at times venture into radical territory. He asserts that custom, not nature, makes women appear inferior. When speaking of women's intelligence, Capella resembles the Florentine manuscript of Strozzi's *Defensio mulierum*. He seriously challenges his society's restriction of education to men, blames male discrediting of learned women with sexual slurs on their envy of the women's accomplishments, and asserts that woman is man's intellectual equal. "Just because they don't engage in it, you can't deny that they would profit as well or better than men (assuming that they were to spend their time in studying, as men do)" (16v/89).⁶ Capella does

---

5. "Quante case sono de' magnati e principi, ne' quali, per non essergli gouerno di donne a cui la cura appartenga, si uiue con tanto desordine, che piu commodamente se staria al spedale magior de Milano. . . . Quante si uedono andare ogni giorno di male in peggio, & a l'estremo annihilarsi per la medesima cagione? Quante sono quelle pel contrario, che sempre sono cresciute, & crescono ogni giorno per esser il gouerno in mano di donna? che non dia danno, ma utilità & profitto grandissimo" (10rv/76–77). See Aristotle, *Oeconomica* 1.2 [1343b–1344a]. See Xenophon, *Oeconomicus* 7.22–30.

6. "[P]er che non si essercitano, non mi si tole (posto che spendessero il loro tempo nei studii, como fanno gli huomini) non facessero quello profitto & piu che essi facciano" (16v/89).

not, however, go on to imagine exactly what women would do with learning if they were permitted to gain it.[7] Thus, he defends women's intelligence and their right to education without considering the positive or negative social and personal consequences of what he has asserted.

Capella again challenges the authority of patriarchal custom to define woman without objecting to present social structures when he attempts to account for the origin of women's political powerlessness. Like Strozzi, he asserts that the sexes originally were equal and that the social inferiority of women is due to the increasing "malvagità" (wickedness) of men, but he goes much farther than Strozzi, who simply attributes the oppression of women to male brute force or cleverness and women's passivity (24v and 26r). Capella creates a myth of a Golden Age of gender equality and its fall.

> In ancient times, civil offices were held by women as well as by men, and then women made many laws. . . . But because the wickedness of men grew in time and because they did not abstain from saying harmful and dirty words among themselves at trials in front of women, they removed women from trials so that the female sex would not hear such ugliness and filth. (26v–27r/108)[8]

In this theory Capella shows an inability to imagine women really holding power and equal to men. If the initial situation of complete equality he describes had been true, then the men would not have had the power to remove women from positions of judgment. If women were equal to men, then they would not need protecting from impolite language. Perhaps this failure of imagination accounts for Capella's not taking the logical next step and using this historical point to advocate a change in the contemporary social order.

Capella's explanation of woman's nonaggressive role in contemporary society

7. He mentions the study of law, but he seems to do so to mock the idea that professional education is the only measure of knowledge and wisdom, rather than to suggest that women be given the opportunity to prepare for careers: ". . . alcuni huomini inuidiosi . . . persuadendosi perche le donne non uadano è Pavia a studiare leggi, che nulla sappiano, & che da nulla sia loro ingegno & consiglio" (16v/89).

8. "[A]ntichamente li Ciuili officii cosi da le donne come da glihuomini erano trattati, & gia le donne fecero molte Leggi. . . . Ma crescendo poi in processo di tempo la maluagità de glihuomini, et non astenendosi tra loro nei giudicii (come aduiene) al conspetto de le donne de dire parole ingiuriose et petulanti, aciò che il muliebre sesso non udisse tali brutezze & spurcitie, fù da ì Iudicii rimosto. & da indi in qua gli officii de giudicare sono ne gli huomini rimasi" (26v–27r; 108).

also locates the cause in custom but does not advocate any change in their role. In ancient times, he says, the Amazons used force because in those days force could overcome tyrants, but now, in the Iron Age, arms only hurt, and women wisely refrain from using them. This at once cleverly asserts women's equal physical ability and reaffirms the status quo. Women are given credit for choosing passivity. They cannot be called inferior because they do not take part in war, but the only power they gain from this victory is moral.

This is Capella's solution to the challenge of the independent woman. Each time he proves that women have demonstrated themselves to be as brave, strong, or intelligent as men, he discovers a reason why this strength is no longer appropriate to their social role or to his age. He consistently approaches the verge of political feminism and retreats from it. He comes closer to imagining a new role for women than Goggio or Strozzi, but each time he offers woman's virtue as the barrier. Woman's very goodness is what holds her back. The antimasculine satire, which seems like an entertaining digression, creates a background of social corruption against which woman is shown to be superior, but her moral superiority condemns her to a social inferiority in the Iron Age.

In the conclusion to the *Della Eccellenza*, Capella reestablishes an erotic context for his work. Like Strozzi, he describes the debate as a battle between the sexes in which the ladies are dependent on their male friends for defense.

> These are the arguments, these are the reasons cited above with which men persuade themselves that they can win the skirmish; and certainly, I suspect that, because women are somewhat inferior in their physical strength, they would lose, if male friends ("amici") did not follow after their mercy ("mercé") so that in their every need, in every danger these men were equipped and ready to take arms in their defense. (111)[9]

The reference to the desire of "mercé" as the motivation for male engagement on women's behalf contradicts the author's insistence on women's autonomous worth throughout the tract, and, as the battle of which he speaks is a battle of words, the reference to women's physical weakness (a point he had not been willing to concede earlier) is irrelevant; according to everything he has said, women ought to be able to write in self-defense.

9. "Questi sono li argomenti, questi sono le ragioni sopradette con le quali gli uomini si persuadeno vincere la schermaglia; e certo dubito, per esser le donne ne le corporali forze alquanto inferiori, non la perdessero, se le loro mercé non seguitassero degli amici che in ogni loro bisogna, in ogni periglio fossero apparrechiati e pronti a prendere l'arme per loro difesa" (111).

This conclusion is not merely another example of a failure of imagination, like the inability to imagine that women could listen to impolite language. It is part of Capella's placement of his book outside the bounds of practical political discourse. He consistently avoids assigning women a social role commensurate with their abilities, and here the use of the suggestively salacious language of chivalric love diffuses the air of serious discussion that immediately precedes it and makes it possible for the male reader to leave the work and praise women without considering the social and political consequences. At the same time, however, the use of the metaphor suggests the success of the book: women now have "amici" ready to defend them, and the profeminist author, who was isolated at the beginning, now has companions, thanks to his persuasive efforts. A significant attack on the antifeminist notion of woman has been made.

Il Libro del Cortegiano

Unlike all the other works discussed thus far, Baldesar Castiglione's *Il Libro del cortegiano* sets the problem of the independent woman in a larger social and literary context.[10] Indeed, it does not even appear to be a participant in the controversy; the discussion about women appears only in Book 3 (after a brief introduction in Book 2) and is presented as incidental to the whole; the "real" subject of the book, as many of the male interlocutors repeat frequently with impatience, is the courtier and not the palace lady. Yet, as Lanham and others have pointed out, what Castiglione's characters say they are doing and what Castiglione is doing, consciously and even unconsciously, are very different. Whatever the participants may think, *Il Cortegiano* is one of the main documents of the Italian Renaissance controversy about women.[11] Throughout the text, though most obviously in Book 3, where the topic of discussion is the nature of woman and the role of the "donna di palazzo" [palace lady], Castiglione represents dramatically the attempt of the next generation of the Northern court audience to whom Sabadino, Strozzi, and Goggio addressed themselves to grapple with the new notion of woman advanced by the earlier writers.

10. Although published in 1528, three years after Capella's *Della Eccellenza*, Castiglione's *Il Libro del cortegiano* was in process for a good many years before it finally was published and is parallel to *Della Eccellenza* rather than derivative.

11. Ghino Ghinassi suggests that the entire work began as a defense of women.

The ideal woman who emerges from this dramatization is not politically or socially independent; she voluntarily submits to limited public liberty in order to retain control of her virtue and to forward the interests of court society. This is not to say that the autonomous or independent woman does not exist in *Il Cortegiano*. She is frequently present in the examples of virtuous women, and she hovers as a possibility behind the "donna di palazzo" as the Magnifico Giuliano de' Medici, the principal profeminist spokesman, creates her, but because he consistently chooses to repress her rather than bring her forward and because the "donne di palazzo" who are present at the discussion decline to accept any opportunity for independent action, she is not the ideal. It is my thesis that, far from being a celebration of the independent woman and a first step to the creation of a social role for her (Floriani, *Bembo e Castiglione* 149–50), *Il Cortegiano* uses literary means to contain her within an already existing social role.

The nature of the world that Castiglione creates in the *Cortegiano* is one of the reasons that the independent woman is a problematic figure in the text. It is a fragile world set off geographically, temporally, and spiritually from the harsh real world in which he and his readers live. Conclusively translated into the realm of the ideal by the death of many of its denizens, this society, as Castiglione portrays it, was remarkable even in its prime for its capacity to disarm and turn to advantage all the forces that threatened it. Geography, which would have made the site of Urbino seem unpropitious, provides a stunning isolated locale, a sort of Shangri-La, where the ravages of the world are felt less acutely. The "universal calamity of the wars" that were destroying Italy but that had, as yet, spared Urbino set the city off as an island of perfect civilization even as they threaten its continued real existence. The illness of Duke Guidubaldo, which imperils the physical existence of the state, makes him leave the government of the court's intellectual life to his wife and permits an atmosphere of reflection and retreat to prevail at the court.

This atmosphere is threatened with violation by the forces of real politics, not only in the person of men and outside commitments as one might expect, but also in the person of the independent woman. She holds it in her power to destroy this perfectly balanced society by an act of will. If she refuses to accommodate herself to the community's definition of her role, the nurturing privacy of the society will be ruptured and the courtiers will have no retreat from the pressures of the real world. The representation of women's willing suspension of their authority is a literary solution to a specific problem; it enables civilized society to exist. Just as time, war, and disease are enemies that are defeated by *virtù*, independent women in *Il Libro del cortegiano* are defeated by *virtù*, the *virtù* of the author.

Castiglione uses a variety of strategies to contain the autonomous woman while praising her. He creates female personae who foster discussion without themselves being interested in exercising the power of speech that is rightly theirs; he attributes a method of defense that resembles Goggio's rather than Strozzi's to the Magnifico Giuliano, the major profeminist spokesman; and he focuses on the differences between the sexes and includes radical arguments for equality only in an "irrelevant" digression on queens. Finally, in Books 3 and 4 the author handles sexuality and love, which would seem to be two very positive contributions that women can make to society, as threats that must be carefully restrained so that they generate no challenges to the social order in the form of illegitimate babies. The result of Castiglione's labors is a powerful defense of his sheltered society against the disruptive force of the independent woman who might choose to act and break the carefully created boundaries between the court and the real world of politics and the nursery.

Women's willingness to cooperate and play a fostering and nondisruptive role is exemplified by the Duchess Elisabetta Gonzaga, the most important woman within the closed society of the Urbino court in *Il Cortegiano* and the keystone of the entire Urbinese culture whose loss Castiglione regrets. Because her husband's illness leads him to go to sleep early, she reigns after dinner, so, although not a queen in her own right by day, she is so by night. As Castiglione represents it, her regal power derives from her virtue, in which are combined the qualities of an ideal prince and those of a mother. Her ill-fortune has revealed that "prudence and strength of spirit and all those virtues that are rare even in stern men may reside along with singular beauty in the tender breast of a woman" (86).[12] The reference to prudence and strength of spirit ("fortezza d'animo"), qualities necessary for a prince's success, put her directly in the tradition of famous women who govern well because virtues conventionally defined as masculine occur naturally in them. According to this description, Elisabetta balances benign maternal qualities with "masculine" severity; as a result, her court is "the very hostel of happiness" (85). She joins it together "in amor" more securely than if its members were brothers and sisters, and the desire to please her acts as a brake on the behavior of the two sexes; they mingle freely yet are so regulated by her presence and example that they are "onestissimi" [most honest].[13]

12. Citations refer to the edition edited by Bruno Maier.
13. ". . . mai non fu concordia di voluntà o amore cordiale tra fratelli maggior di quello, che quivi tra tutti era. Il medesimo era tra le donne" (86). [there never was a concord of will or heartfelt love between brothers greater than that which was between all men. The same was between the ladies.]

Thomas Greene has drawn a useful analogy between the feminine shelter of this court and the "maternal space" that allows a child to develop:

> as the experience of trust is confirmed, the area of creativity widens. This widening leaves the maternal space behind for a broader, agonistic public space. But in the *Cortegiano* the trust in a broader scope of activity is weak; the role of the soldier has become vestigial; each of the four prefaces bespeaks a helpless consciousness of mutability, loss, and death. Here the play-space has failed to expand; the area for creation has remained constricted, dominated by a benevolent but authoritative woman. ("*Il Cortegiano*" 185)

Greene seems to see this space as negative and wounded. An adult male must leave maternal space behind; Castiglione's work takes place entirely in this play-space; therefore, we are witnessing a failure, an inability to expand. Submission to women, even those who use their authority benevolently, is childish. The assumption is that expansion and escape from maternal rule would be for the best, and, of course, psychologically speaking, it would.

But *Il Cortegiano* is not a human psyche, and the protected situation that Castiglione has created is a comment on the world, not a representation of the real court at Urbino as the phrase "remained constricted" suggests. The "area for creation" does not preexist the text and therefore "remain"; it is cleared out from amidst the ruins of war, death, time, and the written word by the energy of the characters represented. The descriptions of negative external events, such as the deaths of particular people and the losses of particular military campaigns, heighten the value of the artistic construct that is the sheltered Urbino court, but so does the description of positive creative acts in the real world: Castiglione represents himself as regretting the publication of the text we are reading, *Il Libro del cortegiano*. For the male members of the court, the creative space could and did expand from spoken word to printed dialogue, from Urbino to all of the reading world. The isolation of the Urbinese court under its female governor is a fiction. It is also Castiglione's triumph. He makes us feel that we are witnesses to the moments of creative energy before publication, before spoken words are fixed in print and open to misinterpretation, judgment, and sentencing.

This freedom is made possible only by female government; it offers an absolute alternative to male government. Like the Virgin in Goggio's text, the Duchess Elisabetta and her lieutenant Emilia Pia govern by means of qualities that time-bound political scientists would perceive as weaknesses. They exercise benevolent authority. The Duchess's benignity gives the male courtiers the freedom to engage in their creative work without the harsh penalties they might suffer for speaking freely in the "agonistic public space" governed by her husband and by practical necessity.[14] In a fallen world where men have to grow up and temper their ideals with practicality, Castiglione creates by literary means a space where they can speak freely, temporarily step out of time, and experience liberties unknown in the real world.

The Duchess Elisabetta, the female ruler whom Castiglione has placed in the position of controller of this space, exhibits her benignity primarily by being silent and not exercising her authority. She very rarely speaks, and when she does she often voices a refusal to take charge. Of course, since her authority inheres naturally in her, the Duchess cannot really give it up; her example still controls the group and her power still makes space for their game, but she refuses to make decisions and actively govern; to the extent that she can, she voluntarily renounces her authority. This distinguishes her from the queens of medieval courts of love, those represented by Boccaccio, for example, where the noblewomen actively govern and render decisions on cases brought before them.[15] She abdicates to men the verbal authority that is natural to her in such a literary situation, even when the topic is love.[16] She offers the women of the court an example of womanhood cooperative with the needs of the larger society rather than dedicated to her own pleasures and power. She is not an independent woman.

Castiglione goes to a great deal of trouble to withdraw women from a game in which everyone, both characters within the dialogue and readers of it who are familiar with courts of love, expects them to participate actively. The scene (Book 1, section 6) in which Elisabetta resigns her actual practical authority in favor of Emilia Pia, her lieutenant, establishes a secondary role for all women

14. See, for example, Ottaviano's assertion that he would lose his prince's confidence if he were to express his whole mind to him (Book 4, section 26) as opposed to Emilia's and the Duchess's tolerance of antifeminist comments. "Poiché non ci costa altro che parole" (486) suggests that speech to his prince could cost him more than words. Even the Magnifico's attack on friars is tolerated without punishment, although it is silenced. Castiglione's correspondence with his mother suggests the very real danger that unguarded speech posed to a courtier.

15. On the similarity, see Greene ("*Il Cortegiano*"), Floriani (*Bembo*), and Kelly. Greene points out the relationship of the four games originally proposed to their medieval antecedents and discusses the difference of the game finally selected from the first proposals (175–76).

16. Joan Kelly discusses this difference at length in "Did Women Have a Renaissance?" She speaks of "the contradiction between the professed parity of noblewomen and men in *The Courtier* and the merely decorative role Castiglione unwittingly assigned the lady" (35). I push the argument a step farther: noblewomen and men are not even theoretical social and political equals in the *Cortegiano*, and Castiglione was not unaware of the kind of role he assigned his female interlocutors.

in the dialogue. Pia begins the female withdrawal from active participation when she obeys the Duchess's order to choose the evening's game by making a proposal that will bring her "little blame and less effort": each person present should suggest a game and the company will choose the most worthy. Her companions joke about her laziness—a female privilege to be exempted from work, antifeminist Gaspare Pallavicino says—and accept her game as really being a game only when the Duchess intervenes and assigns her authority to Pia, thus sanctioning her choice of a passive role. She confirms her interest in keeping women in passive roles when she silences Constanza Fregosa, whom Emilia has called on to propose a game, saying,

> Since Lady Emilia does not want to tire herself by finding a game, it would be reasonable for all the other ladies to take part in this leisure and also be relieved of this task this evening. (91)

With this gesture the Duchess effectively prevents all women from speaking for the duration of this particular evening.[17]

As Greene points out, Il Cortegiano is a Ciceronian or even, at times, a Socratic dialogue, not a medieval "debat"; however, women are not necessarily silent in a Ciceronian dialogue, so we may conclude that they have been silenced here for some purpose. In a topos in which myths of the origin of male authority are expected, Castiglione has created a new one representative of a particular notion of woman: women choose not to carry the burden of speech and authority even when given every opportunity to do so. Men are not shown to be repressors of women; women are seen to make the choice voluntarily, and men are exculpated from responsibility for their powerlessness. Far from being the "subjects" (in the modern sense of the people constructing the text) of the dialogue, the women defer the definition of the game, the society, and, ultimately, themselves to the men.[18] They will be what the men make them. The maternal court space, which is conducive to creativity in men, does not lead women to create.

When he introduces the controversy about womankind into Il Cortegiano in Book 2, Castiglione represents women as withdrawing from the opportunity to take control of what is said about them. The misogynist Ottaviano Fregoso

17. This scene underwent a good deal of revision from the first to the third versions of the text.
18. Floriani, Bembo (149–50) suggests that the female protagonists in Boccaccio and in Bembo's Asolani are objects: "finally, even the female characters in the Asolani, so clearly derived from Boccaccio, are still objects, not subjects of the debate that is undertaken in the work."

makes a series of digs at women, asserting that they are imperfect beings good for nothing but sex, and the ladies respond by physically assaulting him "come le Baccanti d'Orpheo" (328). When he suggests that they have made a physical attack because they are incapable of a reasoned one, Emilia does not respond with logic; she asks the Magnifico Giuliano de' Medici to be the "cavalier" who will defend women in the battle with the antifeminists. As in Strozzi's *Defensio mulierum* and Capella's *Della Eccellenza*, the metaphorical reference to the defender of ladies as a knight seems gay and amusing, but here it suggests the weakness of womankind even more than it did in the other works. In them a man chose himself to represent women in a written text; here women are portrayed as having chosen a man to represent them on an occasion when there are women present who might take up the "sword" of the spoken word in their own behalf.

Yet, given the society in which they live, the ladies' refusal to seriously engage in their own defense makes sense. At issue is not what woman really is but rather what men perceive her to be, and on this topic, men must speak to men. By polarizing the sexes and making women unworthy of love and incapable of being present at court, antifeminism cuts at the foundation of the entire system that we have seen so delightfully at work in the course of Books 1 and 2. It puts in jeopardy the most valuable constructs of civilization, Orpheus's inspired music and the elegant order of the Urbino court. The image of the bacchants dramatically represents the dreadful results of antifeminism without in any way making aggressive women look good, positive, or effective. Their destructive, angry (and comical) response needs to be contained by a definition of woman that will engage female allegiance to social stability. The creation of this definition is the goal of the profeminists, as the Magnifico Giuliano states it at the close of Book 2. He will prove women's worth as companions and objects of love and will validate their presence at court.[19]

It is important to note that the topic of the palace lady enters the text as a topic of debate. No one questioned the right of the courtier to exist when the topic was proposed for discussion on the first day. The debate was about the

19. "Ma, se la cosa avesse da esser pari, bisognarebbe prima che un . . . formasse una donna di palazzo con tutte le perfezioni appartenenti a donna, così come essi hanno formato il cortegiano con le perfezioni appartenenti ad omo; ed allor se quel che diffendesse la lor causa fosse d'ingegno e d'eloquenzia mediocre, penso che, per esser aiutato dalla verità, dimostraria chiaramente che le donne son così virtuose come gli omini" (331). [If the contest were to be equal, it would first be necessary for someone . . . to design a palace lady with all the perfections belonging to woman, just as they have designed the courtier with the perfections belonging to man; and then, if he who defended their cause were a man of mediocre wit and eloquence, I think that, being helped by truth, he would clearly demonstrate that women are as virtuous as men].

components that were to make him up, not about the ability of men to resemble the ideal. Their capacity for the cardinal virtues was taken for granted and received minimal treatment in a brief paragraph, whereas behavior that relies on these virtues—arms, for example—was given extensive coverage. The lady is different; her capacity for virtue (both cardinal and conventional feminine) is in doubt and because of this her very presence at court is challenged. The Magnifico Giuliano has to define her and defend her. The first Renaissance definition of a new role for woman occurs in the context of reevaluation and defense.

The outstanding characteristics of this new role are that it is neither an extension of woman's traditional private role of wife and mother nor in any way a version of woman's oldest profession. The very name of this role, "donna di palazzo," signifies its morality. It stands in opposition to the term that would have seemed the logical choice, cortegiana, and through its very awkwardness constantly proclaims what this lady is not: a sexual companion for the courtier. It also, however, signifies a difference between the lady and the gentleman. "Palace" designates a place, and "court" designates a social system, as "house" and "home" indicate the letter and the spirit of domestic organization. The court space that allows men to expand and develop aspects of themselves that are stifled by public political culture allows women a far more limited expansion. They can develop aspects of themselves that are stifled by private domestic culture, but they cannot move outward from the physical limits of the palazzo; it functions as the literal location of the lady's activity; away from it she is no longer a "donna di palazzo," whereas the "cortegiano" is a court man even when he practices his principal profession, arms, far away from the source of his identity.[20]

The practical discussion of the way the "donna di palazzo" ought to conduct herself while she converses with a courtier, the process called "intertenere," in Book 3 stands in the place of the long technical and philosophical discussion about the courtier's language in Book 1. She is a success if she stimulates him intellectually without engaging herself sexually. She does not even need to talk very much; Emilia Pia is an expert at "intertenere," and she talks very little. The activity of the "donna di palazzo" is creative, but it leaves no written documents by her hand, and so, although given an official public role as never before, women are left in the position of adjuncts who do not shape the image

20. The secondary nature of the role designed for the palace lady has been noted by modern feminist and Marxist critics. See Kelly (33) and Guidi (36). Lisa Jardine has made the salutary suggestion that the courtier is not a great deal better off than his female companion as far as real access to power goes; both play auxiliary roles (Still 55).

of the times that will remain for posterity. Their contribution is transitory—
the fleeting spoken word rather than the enduring written one.[21]

In Goggio's, Strozzi's, and Capella's texts we saw that the revelation that
nature suited women for an active, public role, but that custom has prevented
her from playing it led directly to the questioning of modern restraints on
women's conduct. By contrast, the Magnifico admits the possibility that woman
can ride, hunt, play ball, and handle arms as well as any man; she can play the
drums and the trumpet; she can rule nations; she can, but she ought not to.[22]
When challenged with evidence that women are capable of engaging in
strenuous physical activities, the Magnifico rules them out because they do not
fit his notion of the feminine:

> . . . non solamente non voglio ch'ella usi questi esercizi virili così
> robusti ed asperi, ma voglio che quegli ancora che son convenienti a
> donna faccia con riguardo, e con quella molle delicatura che avemo
> detto convenirsele. (347)

> . . . not only do I not wish her to engage in these virile exercises,
> which are so robust and harsh, but I wish that she would practice even
> those that are appropriate to a woman with care and with that soft
> delicacy that we have said suits her.

As a feminist does, the Magnifico separates gender characteristics from sex—
he admits that women are capable of being tough and "virili"—yet he
repeatedly restricts women to activities that he conceives of as feminine and
appropriate to woman's role as it already exists. This society needs the
"feminine," and he expects that women will give up "masculine" activities.

Similarly, the Magnifico makes the potentially radical argument that women
ought to aim at practicing the cardinal virtues just as men ought to, but the
contexts in which he sets the virtues deprive the argument of its equalizing
force. A comparison between the treatment of the cardinal virtues in Book 1
and Book 3 reveals the great difference between the courtier and the "donna
di palazzo." The parallel structure and reversal of emphasis in the two books is

21. It may seem that the courtier also produces nothing substantial, but this is not so. Cesare
Gonzaga's paean to woman's influence speaks specifically of the many authors who have written as a
result of "intertenere" (411).

22. He argues that, although women are capable of playing trumpets, they ought not to do so
because "la loro asprezza nasconde e leva quella soave mansuetudine" (348) [their harshness hides and
removes that gentile mildness] that ought to characterize female behavior.

striking. Count Ludovico da Canossa takes the importance of the cardinal virtues in a courtier for granted and discusses them in a single paragraph (156–57). Letters, which are "other than goodness . . . the true and principal ornament of the mind," need defending, and many chapters are devoted to explaining their importance. The dispute goes on for so long that Emilia Pia interrupts and ends it. In contrast, when discussing the court lady, the Magnifico's assertion that women are capable of practicing the cardinal virtues is disputed by Gaspare, who questions the utility of the virtues to women and asserts that many philosophers have said that women are "animali imperfetti" and are incapable of such virtues. The Magnifico's answer first addresses the issue of utility and then enters the larger territory of capacity; he goes on at such length and complexity in a philosophical defense that Emilia Pia interrupts him and unsuccessfully attempts to redirect the conversation.

The discussion of utility is brief; nothing analogous to letters is proposed for the lady.

> Although it may seem that continence, magnanimity, temperance, strength of spirit, prudence, and the other virtues have nothing to do with "intertenere," I want her to be adorned with all of them, not so much for the sake of "intertenere" itself, although they may be useful in it, but for the sake of being virtuous and so that these virtues make her such that she is worthy of being honored and so that her every deed is made up of them. (349)

Virtue is only of incidental value for a woman's performance of her assigned role; its primary value is to make her worthy of honor and make all her deeds virtuous. The distinction between virtue that leads to actions and virtue that infuses actions is very important. The first is public, the second private. The names of the virtues are not chastity, silence, and obedience, but the sphere of action is the same. Although woman can share in the cardinal virtues and, thus, is equal in theory, she remains different and powerless because those virtues do not serve as a foundation for action in the world.

This passivity is a quality peculiar to the court lady and not true of all women, however; it is a characteristic of the role, not the sex. This becomes clear when Gaspare Pallavicino points out that the logical consequence of attributing letters and the virtues to women is that "(they) govern cities, make laws, lead armies, and the men cook or spin" (349). The social chaos of which Gaspare speaks is an antifeminist's nightmare, which the Magnifico seems not to share. He cites Plato and hypothesizes that women might rule without positing as a corollary that men will lose all their authority and become effeminate. Just as the independent woman of the Strozzi manuscript can be glimpsed behind the prohibition of riding, jousting, and ball-playing, so she is clearly visible here. But the Magnifico does not develop this argument in support of rule by women because, as he says, "I am making a palace lady, not a queen" (350). With this stroke he cuts off the discussion of the "donna di palazzo" from the larger implications of the discussion about women.

It might seem that the references to queens and jousting and other physical activities represent a true challenge to the Magnifico's ideally cooperative "donna di palazzo," who willingly accepts a role that does not take advantage of her capacities. Castiglione may be wrenching control of the definition from his spokesman or at least be offering a strong alternative viewpoint that the reader may equally well accept. Although we as readers may choose to accept the alternate "truth" offered by the glimpse of the independent woman— indeed, the modern reader is very likely to accept that "truth"—it is important to note the damage that such a choice does to the court that Castiglione has gone to such efforts to create. The independent woman is inimical to the court because she does not contribute "una certa affabilità," and without this affability the lady cannot perform the role she has been assigned at court, and the entire protected structure collapses. If we choose the independent woman, we are refusing to play the game.

The Magnifico's formal defense of woman's capacity for virtue, which takes the place of the discussion of letters for the courtier, favors the interdependence of the sexes, not their sameness, and, thus, also represses the independent woman. He predicates his proof for women's excellence on sexual difference (as does Goggio), and his essential argument is analogous to Goggio's, though his use of paradox is less showy. He praises each sex for its special adaptation to its social role; that is, men gather and women safeguard the family's goods. He accepts that female bodies are colder than male, yet argues that this is an advantage. Women are temperate; their timidity can be true courage and magnanimity (361); and the quality that antifeminists perceive as stubbornness is constancy. In sum, like Goggio he presents a positive interpretation of the conventional characteristics of womankind in opposition to the negative interpretation of those same characteristics on the part of the antifeminists; he does not present a new definition as the Florentine manuscript of Strozzi's work does. Because this view of woman is positive, it can be described as profeminist, but as the Magnifico denies that a change in women's activities must be a result of perceiving her as good, it is not politically feminist.

In the course of this defense the Magnifico throws out some radical ideas and then withdraws from supporting them. These ideas join the suggestions that women can box and joust and govern in creating a subversive notion of sexual equality, a notion that threatens the peaceful relations between the sexes that are made possible by the character designed for the "donna di palazzo." An outstanding example, new to the debate, as far as I know, is the Magnifico's answer to Gaspare's statement that all women want to be men because of an instinctive desire to be perfect:

> Le meschine non desiderano l'esser omo per farsi più perfette, ma per aver libertà e fuggir quel dominio che gli omini si hanno vendicato sopra esse per sua propria autorità. (357)

> [The poor things do not wish to be men in order to be more perfect, but to be free and to flee the dominion under which men, through their authority, have vengefully placed them.]

Although it does assume that authority is proper to men, this statement has the earmarks of genuine political feminism, because it suggests that women are right to desire autonomy and that men have no natural right to tyrannical rule over them. "Meschine," "dominio," and "vendicato" speak of male cruelty and female suffering and foment resentment and revolt.

This definition of relations between the sexes is not inconsistent with the Magnifico's entire argument; women are still secondary in "autorità," but if discussed it would lead to the politically charged issue of social liberty for women, an issue that he has been avoiding. The Magnifico does not follow through on the political argument, but instead attacks the notion of female imperfection by arguing the necessity of both sexes for generation and by invoking the paradox that woman's coldness is superior to man's heat. Unlike the politically charged notion that women desire liberty from male oppression, the praise of coldness and even the argument for equal necessity perpetuate the status quo. They gain respect for woman's traditional role and attempt to change the reader's appraisal of it from inferior to different or even superior, but they do not question the appropriateness of the role to the sex.

Once again, the independent woman surfaces in the debate only to be repressed. The reference to female liberty suggests that the results of persistence in tyrannical antifeminism might be outright revolt like that of the bacchants. The solution is not to give women their liberty but to change male perceptions, so that their rule is not a tyranny based on scorn, but an authoritative rule based on respect. If men can be led to see women as companions who are equal in their difference, all will be well. As before, the suggestion of women's capacity and desire to be "masculine" serves as a warning extrinsic to the argument rather than as a genuine profeminist point intrinsic to the larger proof of woman's worth. It is not to be acted on positively, as part of a political program to increase opportunity for women, but rather negatively—something must be done to prevent this feared political act from taking place.

In this political context, one of the most interesting aspects of the philosophical defense of women is Emilia Pia's attempt to bring it to closure; her failure dramatically demonstrates the limits of female authority in this court and the formative importance of the male written word, as did the choice of a male champion and the substitution of "intertenere" for "lettere." A "donna di palazzo" engaged in "intertenere," Emilia tries to use the authority given her by the Duchess to direct the conversation away from its abstruse course onto one accessible to the entire group and, therefore, she thinks, more effectively defensive of women.

> For God's sake, she said, drop all the business of "matter" and "form" and "male" and "female" and speak in a way that may be understood; because we have heard and understood the bad things that signor Ottaviano and signor Gaspare have said about us, but now we do not understand how you are defending us; thus this seems to me to be off the subject and to leave in everyone's mind the bad impression of us created by our enemy. (358)

The effect of Emilia's interruption on the notion of woman being shaped by the narrative is very similar to the consequences of the ladies' bacchic frenzy. Gaspare began the philosophical debate with a caution that women would not understand what he was saying and would declare what he said to be untrue (356); so by stating that she cannot follow the argument, Emilia confirms the antifeminist's view of women's intelligence, just as the women's ineffective violence suggests their weakness and their failure to take on their own defense suggests their lack of reason.

The Magnifico's response to Emilia opposes the knowledgeable (male) reader with the ignorant, though not unintelligent, female listener and reveals the way that the limited kind of knowledge expected of the "donna di palazzo" restricts her sphere of action and her authority even within the court when its relations with the outer world are involved. He asserts that these abstract proofs are necessary because, if anyone should decide to write this debate down, readers familiar with these terms would expect to hear Gaspare's criticisms answered in kind, and, we the readers of the text, wise as we are in the ways of controversy, must agree with him and consider Emilia foolish for voicing her commonsense objections. Yet, Strozzi shows us that the Magnifico's method of defense is not the only possible one. By presenting a false dichotomy (either Gaspare's assertions will not be discussed or they must be attacked with exactly the arguments he has chosen), the Magnifico makes us overlook the possibility of asserting equality rather than difference. Emilia is right. If he does not leave a "mala impressione" of women, he at least leaves the impression that, superior as they may be in virtue, they are correctly placed in their traditional inferior role. By accepting her silencing, Emilia sets a good example of the tractability of a correct "donna di palazzo" and endorses male control of discourse.

Other actions would seem to contradict my discovery of repression of female independence even in their performance of "intertenere." Emilia successfully interrupts the discussion of *lettere* in Book 1 and the slander of friars in Book 3. In both cases she correctly labels the topic a digression, and her intervention succeeds because it serves the court's interests—*lettere* has been adequately covered and the friars sufficiently slandered—whereas her attempt to end the philosophical defense goes contrary to the purposes of the court, both as a dramatic action and as a truncation of a topic that builds the necessary framework for the positioning of the lady within the court's power structure. Similarly, the catalogue of famous women that brings the defense to a close is extended twice at the request of Margherita Gonzaga and Emilia Pia, but these examples promote the cause of the court by teaching women how to practice their virtues to the benefit of society; thus, the ladies are furthering the court's interests by requesting more information.[23] Every example that is developed beyond a name tells of wives who are constant to their husbands, wives who love their husbands more than their husbands love them, and women who have acted in the interests of social stability (Roma and the Sabine women). Once again men are represented as in control of the text, and the women's request for information confirms rather than denies their authority.

When the Magnifico decides to include independent women in a third and final extension of the list, it is in response to Gaspare's sneers about women of the present day, not in response to a request by the ladies, and he again subverts the radical profeminist potential of his case. He states that "if you will take the trouble to measure the valor of women against that of men, you will

23. In the second redaction of the *Cortegiano* the list is more radical than in the third. Castiglione omitted the names of many female poets and queens when he revised.

find that they never have been nor now are at all inferior to men" (383–84). The word "valor" in this statement makes the grounds of comparison a traditionally masculine virtue and would seem to establish equality between the sexes; however, the two-part list that follows does not support the scope of the generalization.[24]

In the first part we learn of politically valorous women who are isolated from the mass of womankind by social class and are extraordinary rather than exemplary of universal capacity. Anne of France, Isabella of Spain, Isabella d'Este, and other living noblewomen are eulogized as directly comparable with men, but the Magnifico declines to talk about "an infinite number of other ladies, and also lower-class women" and, again, "I could tell you of some who were highly accomplished in letters, in music, in painting, in sculpture; but I do not wish to dwell on these examples so well known to all of you" (389).[25] Earlier, the Magnifico took care to provide adequate information for a future reading public; now, he is satisfied to rely on the unwritten knowledge of his listening audience. The omission of the names of common women and accomplished women assigns them to historical oblivion.

The composition of this list makes it very different from those in the earlier defensive texts in which learning is extremely important, class is not an all-determining factor, and an effort is made to discover obscure women whose reputations need refurbishing. Sabadino features erudition as the outstanding characteristic of many of his ladies and even includes his own wife on the basis of her learning. Strozzi, of course, makes a plea for the education of women, as does Capella, and Goggio includes a wide variety of actions and social classes in his extensive biographical books. Even Castiglione developed both the categories of commoners and learned women, though not extensively, in the second redaction of the *Cortegiano*.[26] The author would seem to have been fully aware of how such lists conventionally were constructed and to have deliberately directed his text away from inclusiveness in its final version.

24. Vespasiano made a very similar claim but spoke of "virtù," not "valor," and did not make the claim of equivalence. "In ogni istato sono istate le donne ripiene di tante virtù" (292) [In every state there have been women full of many virtues].

25. The Magnifico does mention one group of commoners: the women of Pisa who actually took arms against the Florentines to defend their city in 1499, but this astonishing example of military valor among an unnamed mass of contemporary women cannot compete with the many names of noblewomen, and it also is an example of an isolated action outside the normal conduct of these women's lives. It confirms the validity of action for women within the context of defense of the home. Guidi notes the importance of the anonymity of the Pisans (58).

26. See Castiglione, *La Seconda Redazione* (258). Guidi points out that the final list also does not include many of the minor Italian nobility who were included in the second version and that the entire list reinforces a tendency toward exclusivity in the third version (68).

The restriction of the list to noblewomen of the highest order is consistent with the argument for nobility made in Book 1. It also was politically practical for Castiglione to flatter these particular families; indeed, the possibility that biographical descriptions of these ladies may be misinterpreted as flattery is raised more than once. In the context of the controversy about women in which this list is set, however, the limitation of the list recalls the extraordinary-woman thesis of Boccaccio. Here, it is birth rather than masculine spirit that enables these women to cross the threshold between masculine and feminine, but the practical result is the same. Emulation will not enable an ordinary woman to equal their achievements, and even a noblewoman can do so only when she assumes a position of power through marriage or inheritance. In this way, the catalogue of famous independent women, a trope essential to the proof of the equality of women, becomes another restraint on the ambition of the "donna di palazzo" and reinforces the secondary nature of her profession.

The isolation of women who perform political actions is increased by their contrast with the group that follows them: women famous for exemplary sexual continence. Paradoxically superior to men, this latter group of women happily remains excluded from political power. These examples are drawn from all classes of society, though even they are divided into two kinds: those whose actions are large-scale and public and those whose deeds occur in the privacy of their homes and hearts. The actions of these heroines can be imitated by all women. This is a valor open to all, commoner and noble, learned and ignorant.

It is also represented as a heroism that is particularly female. The few examples of male continence that Gaspare manages to introduce are attacked as being motivated by political rather than moral considerations. Indeed, Castiglione's analysis of the causes for Scipio Africanus's public display of his abstinence from sexual relations with the captive wife of one of the noblemen of a captured Spanish city is worthy of Machiavelli (400),[27] whereas his examples of female continence reveal the women to be motivated by shame; their goal is to keep even chaste actions out of the public view and to preserve privacy.

These examples are calculated to lead the reader to scorn men for their inability to be chaste and to admire women for their capacity for restraint. If they succeed, they will win for women the right to control their own bodies, but this does not lead to sexual liberty and social chaos because what women want to do with their bodies is exactly what society wants them to do with them: preserve them for use within marriage.

27. He is in enemy country, a new captain, in need of making his reputation, etc.

It is enough if you allow me the point that women abstain from the unchaste life more than men do; and it is certain that they are not held back by any brake other than one they apply themselves; and it is true that most women who are guarded too strictly or beaten by their husbands or fathers are less chaste than those who have some liberties. But love of true virtue and the desire for honor are usually a great restraint on women—I myself have known many who value these virtues more than life itself. (395)

Within the context of a society in which fathers and husbands exercise cruel restraints on the women of their households, the attribution of moral sense to women is liberating, yet the control that women win has no visible results: their public role does not change. Female autonomy and the interests of society are identical.

Even the way the examples of sexual continence are presented reinforces the importance of privacy. Almost none of these women are spoken of by name, and the examples are drawn from the speaker's private experience rather than from publicly accessible historical records. When an attempt is made to speak of the Duchess herself as exemplary of this virtue, she makes one of her rare entrances into the conversation in order to prevent her private life from receiving public exposure. This is women's history as it has always existed: marginalized, oral, ephemeral, and dependent on memory; it is at the mercy of time as conventional history is not, and Castiglione has represented it as women's choice by means of the Duchess's demurral. As a result, female independence in the realm of sexuality poses no threat to society's structures or written representation of itself. Men remain in control in all spheres.

Having established the commitment of women to chastity and to the social order, a necessary prerequisite to the presence of women in the public space of the court, the discussion returns to the topic with which it opened: the role of the "donna di palazzo," especially the refinements of her practice of "intertenere" when the topic is love. The potential conflict between her public profession and her private virtue, which caused difficulties in assigning her a name, is entirely resolved, as far as all but the most avid antifeminists are concerned, and the last pages of the third day record rules that a lady can observe in order to protect herself from advances she does not desire. Paradoxically, these rules provide her with liberty; without their external reinforcement of her inner desires the "donna di palazzo" would not exist at all because she would have no authority to reject the courtier's advances. As Greene demonstrates so elegantly, only because of the rules is there space for the game.

Liberty and restraint are inseparable companions; "la medesima libertà era grandissimo freno" (86) [this same liberty was a very great restraint].

This part of the dialogue resembles a *questione d'amore* rather than a Ciceronian or a Socratic dialogue, because conduct is being measured against an explicit standard to which all agree. The socially sanctioned secret love of medieval courtly literature is replaced with socially sanctioned public flirtation. Sexuality is replaced with speech. Roberto da Bari's wild suggestion that unmarried women ought to be allowed some license serves as a confirmation of this unanimity. Like the earlier suggestion that women carry arms, this casually tossed-out idea introduces the danger of social chaos, but the threat here does not come from women or even a potential within them. We know women to be chaste, and the suggestion serves as a reminder of the social chaos created by male sexual desire, against which the rules defend women. It is silenced by Emilia, who operates decisively here as would the queen in a medieval literary court of love. In this limited moral and generic space, women can rule actively. The shift in power can be seen in the response to Gaspare's final lengthy antifeminist tirade. Ottaviano, his former "companion at arms," greets it with laughter, as does Emilia. Neither a feminine bacchantlike attack or a masculine verbal defense is necessary. The battle for the "donna di palazzo" is won because female autonomy has been shown to be in the public interest and the threat of the independent woman has been contained.

If we return now to the context of the defense of women and measure Castiglione's presentation of the profeminist case against those we have already examined, the cautious conservative nature of *Il Cortegiano* emerges clearly. Topics that are commonplaces of defense because they are essential to the advocacy of a public role for women are neglected or given scant attention. That males have sovereignty is seen as a limit on women's freedom and even is lamented, but the male right to this sovereignty is never questioned. That women have the capacity to excel in the same virtues as men is repeatedly asserted, but in the lives of exemplary women, passive rather than active types of the virtues continue to operate, and magnanimity, courage, and wisdom lead down the same virtuous path as the more traditional chastity, silence, and obedience. That men control written records is an unquestioned assumption, and no examples of female control of written language are developed. Yet, the defenses by Strozzi, Capella, and even Goggio show that this separate but equal system of sexual difference, necessary for the generation of Castiglione's beloved court culture, was a mythical construct even at the time of its creation.

4

THE DEBATE ABOUT WOMAN
IN THE *ORLANDO FURIOSO*

Like Castiglione, Capella, Strozzi, Goggio, and Sabadino, Ariosto was a member of the Northern court circle, and, like them, he produced a defense and encomium of womankind: the *Orlando furioso*. From the very first lines, "Le donne, i cavallier, l'arme, gli amori, / le cortesie, l'audaci imprese io canto" [The ladies, the knights, the arms, the loves, / the courteous deeds, the daring undertakings I sing], the poem breaks with literary and social convention.[1] Epic would exclude ladies; romance and the custom of society would pair them only with knights and loves. Ariosto's paratactic syntax frees them to combine with arms, courtesies, and daring deeds as well, traditionally masculine territory in epic, romance, and society.[2] They are liberated to play the new roles constructed in theory and illustrated by historical example in the defenses and encomia produced by Ariosto's contemporaries.

In the poem as a whole, Ariosto attempts to replace the romance conception of love and sexual relations with a model founded on the notions of woman developed by the defenders of womankind. The genre of this attack is epic, and its heroine is Bradamante; her independent character and the story of her

---

1. All quotations from the *Furioso* are from the edition edited by Caretti; all translations are my own.

2. Ariosto conflates the opening line of the *Aeneid*, which defines the essential style and content of epic (arms, man, sonorous singing) with lines from *Purgatorio* that define the subject matter and tone of romance (men and women, exploits and pastimes, love and courtesy, nostalgia). Dante's lines read, "Non ti maravigliar s'io piango, Tosco, / quando rimembro . . . / le donne e' cavalier, li affanni e li agi / che ne 'nvogliava amore e cortesia" (14.103–10, passim). Shemeck also argues that the first line "refrains from assigning characters to spheres of action on the basis of gender" (70) and presents a detailed analysis of the ways that "Ariosto's ordered sequence raises questions regarding the ties between literary/discursive conventions and conventions of a social order" (71). See Blasucci for an excellent contrast of Ariosto's syntax with Dante's (143).

quest for Ruggiero and of his ultimate commitment to her offer an answer to Orlando's madness because their marriage offers a model of male and female relations based on love and knowledge on both sides.[3] The epic plot offers Bradamante opportunities for autonomy not available to women in the romance plot of Orlando, yet the representation of her as finally choosing to accept Ruggiero's dominion over her resolves the threat that her independence poses to the social and literary structure. Ariosto projects a new social, sexual, and generic order that can contain and, thus, benefit from the potential of women suggested in the opening lines.

Ariosto supports the overarching contrast of the kinds of love present in his two major plots with three structural and narrative devices that work to reconstruct the audience's perception of woman. First, he integrates into the poem an interconnected series of three fairly formal debates about the nature of womankind. Second, he creates a Narrator who is himself alternately a type of the volatile, irrational, idealizing, and antifeminist romance lover and a rational profeminist historian. Third, he fills the territory of his text with an astonishing variety of independent women, both good and bad, who illustrate the humanist argument that moral and intellectual potential is as varied in women as in men. As a result of the debates, the Narrator's comments, and the representation of other independent women, Bradamante's actions do not exist in isolation as manifestations of an extraordinary ability; she can be seen to be an exemplar of the new woman of humanist thought, eminently more lovable than the fleeting Angelicas of past ages, an autonomously chaste woman who willingly accepts her husband's dominion over her, yet who is active and capable in her own right—a woman on whose virtues a dynasty can be founded.

The participation of the *Orlando furioso* in the defense tradition was recognized by Ariosto's contemporaries. Several authors of texts in praise and defense of women refer to the poem's profeminism to increase the persuasive power of their own arguments in favor of women's capacity for virtue and against the male tendency to blame their own errors on women. Vicentio Maggio in *Un breve trattato dell'Eccellentia delle Donne* praises the poet's wisdom in representing Orlando's antifeminism as madness (23v).[4] Castiglione, in an early version of

3. Fichter speaks of the "inverse relationship" of the Bradamante and Ruggiero epic plot and the Orlando romance plot (71).

4. "Veggendo adunque noi le donne di ogni sorte virtu ornate, meritamente il Poeta Ferrarese introduce nel suo divino poema, un'homo Furioso & grandimenti turbato, per che ne dicesse male & alla buona lor fama detrahesse molte cose dicendo quali poi con niuna ragione prova & con niuno argomento fortifica, di sorte che evidentissimamente appare, ch'egli non si mova per guiditio ma per ira

the *Cortegiano*, refers to Ariosto as a praiser of women's virtues (Ghinassi ed. 277). In his *Della dignità e nobilità delle donne* (Florence, 1625) Cristoforo Bronzino (d. 1540) cites Ariosto as an example of a writer who wisely revised his original work to remove misogynist opinions (Bertana 183 n. 1).[5]

Twentieth-century critics also tend to read the *Furioso* as profeminist, but they see Ariosto to be borrowing elements of the defense tradition for his own purposes rather than to be working in that tradition himself. Many have explored the praise and blame of women as an example of Ariosto's famous unstable tone and as an example of the changes that he made in the 1532 edition (Petrini, Carrara, Bertana, Durling, Jvanoff, Dalla Palma, among others); some have brought the content of the texts about women that we have examined to bear on particular speeches or scenes in order to explain them (Santoro, Bertana, Valesio), and, perhaps, discover what Ariosto personally thought about women and marriage (Bertana and, to some extent, Brand), but no one has undertaken to examine the strategies of praise and defense that govern the entire text.[6] I suggest that, like the texts already studied, the *Orlando furioso* attempts to reform the reader's misogynist notion of woman or confirm his philogyny by demonstrating the excellence of womankind by means of historical examples and logic. The poem is an active participant in the controversy.

The Debate about Womankind

Orlando's madness stands at the center of the poem as an exemplum of the tragic consequences of adherence to the old system of relations between the sexes. It is caused in large part by his profoundly selfish misapprehension not

& sdegno contra di una donna conceputo dal qual odio commosso, tutte poi indifferentemente morde & trafige." [Therefore, as we see women decked with every kind of virtue, the Ferrarese poet introduces into his divine poem a man who is crazy and deeply disturbed because he spoke badly of them (women) and detracted from their good name by saying many things that then he did not demonstrate with any reason or fortify with any argument, with the result that it appears extremely evident that he is not moved by judgment but by anger and disdain against a particular woman and then upset by that hatred he bites and stabs all without discriminating.]

5. An exception is Michelangelo Biondo (1497–c. 1565), who celebrated Ariosto as a misogynist in his *Angoscia, doglia, e pena le tre furie del mondo*, a polemical tract against women (83). He does not, however, refer specifically to the *Furioso*.

6. Shemek offers a survey of the various positions; she argues that "because no resolution of *querelle* questions is available on the basis of the most explicit treatment of them in the *Furioso*, Ariosto's reader is obliged to proceed to the much more complicated task of examining the *querelle* arguments in relation to the other depictions of women in the poem" (97).

only of Angelica, but of all women. His expectation that she will be bound to him if he performs courteous and valiant deeds for her and that she will not desire to actively choose a husband, his vision of her as a helpless lamb in his dream, and his ignorance of what she really is like, all make him vulnerable to the complete disintegration of his system of values once he discovers she is not what he conceived her to be. His brutal antifeminism and insanity are a direct result. His experience of love—his translation of Angelica's ordinary clay into "angeliche sembianze" and his consequent disappointment at her performance—follows the pattern mocked by defenders of women because, for all its apparent gallantry, it is selfish and calculated entirely to bring pleasure to man.

That Orlando is a textbook case of the lover who turns misogynist is obvious to anyone who has read Goggio or Capella, but the poem does not explicitly offer this intertextual reading of him in any of the scenes in which he acts. Rather, the three series of debates about womankind, which are prompted by three other heroes' experiences of female infidelity, provide the philosophical context for understanding Orlando. Like him, Ariodante, Rodomante, and Rinaldo are all forced to confront evidence of their beloved's commitment to another man, and each of their stories is set in the context of a discussion of woman's capacity for fidelity and the right of society to demand it of her.[7] The misadventure of the chaste Ginevra (Cantos 4 and 5) prompts a discussion of whether society ought to expect women to be chaste and whether women are naturally capable of chastity or society needs to force them to conform to its expectations. The rejection of Rodomonte by Doralice (Cantos 27–29) leads to questioning of the notion that woman is morally inferior to man and of the reasonableness of society's founding laws on this premise. The release of Rinaldo from his enchanted love of Angelica (Cantos 42 and 43) leads to stories that reveal the male sex's greater potential for depravity. The three moments are linked by the similarity of the heroes' experiences, the voice of the Narrator who calls attention to the debate, the debate form itself, and the common source of their arguments in the contemporary controversy about women. In them Ariosto puts the romance experience of love on trial and finds it guilty of causing social chaos and bringing suffering to both sexes.

---

7. Elissa B. Weaver argues that the episodes in which Orlando, Rodomonte, and Bradamante are told stories about their beloveds and go mad form a chain and that they demonstrate that Ariosto worked by means of repeated modules that permit "reciprocal connections" and "interpenetration of contexts" at the same time that "the poem proceeds in a linear manner" (401). The sequence that I am examining confirms her argument and illustrates the complexity of Ariosto's "intreccio," as it offers another series of episodes centering on Orlando's experience of love.

The First Debate

The story of the "aspra legge di Scozia" represents misogyny and women's virtue dramatically in terms easily recognizable from the defenses of women we have been examining. At the center of the story is the ethical and emotional issue of woman's faith.[8] Ginevra, a Scots princess, refused cruel Polinesso's attempt to seduce her and remained faithful to Ariodante, her fiancé. The resentful villain made it appear that she had accepted him as a lover, and she was charged with fornication according to a law that requires that, unless a woman finds a champion who proves her innocent,

> . . . ogni donna, e di ciascuna sorte,
> ch'ad uom si giunga, e non gli sia mogliera,
> s'accusata ne viene, abbia la morte.
>
> (4.59.2–4)

[. . . every woman of every rank who joins herself with a man to whom she is not married must be executed, if she is accused.]

The justice of this law and its social utility are called into question by the various actors in the story, each of whom tells what he knows of the event and states his attitude to Ginevra's supposed action and to the "aspra legge." By the end of the episode the harsh law has been shown to be inadequate as a deterrent because women's virtue has its source within their hearts and cannot be legislated.

A conversation between a group of monks and Rinaldo, a knight-errant from Charlemagne's court, begins the episode. The monks tell him of Ginevra's need for a champion and encourage Rinaldo to take on her defense because chivalry obligates him

> a vendicar di tanto tradimento
> costei, che per commune opinione,
> di vera pudicizia è un paragone.
>
> (4.62.6–8)

[to vindicate from such a great betrayal she, who, according to general opinion, is a paragon of true chastity.]

---

8. Both the earliest commentaries and the most recent critics have demonstrated that this story illustrates the value of faith and its necessity for the maintenance of order in society. See Wiggins *Figures* (19–30, passim).

Their use of "vendicar" and "tradimento" and their assurance that "commune opinione" recognizes her as truly chaste indicate that a firm belief in Ginevra's innocence is the cause of their concern. They are not arguing that the law ought to be changed. If they thought that Ginevra was guilty, they would not seek a champion for her and would not perceive the law as "aspra." They accept the conventional expectation that a woman should be chaste. In answer to the monks, Rinaldo argues against the very premise on which the law is established: he asserts that sexual promiscuity is a woman's right. He sees Ginevra's only mistake to be her inability to keep her actions secret, and he vows to defend her from the consequences of this mistake.

This dialogue recalls a discussion in the *Cortegiano* about the proper response that a courtier should make to jokes at women's expense. Profeminist Giuliano de' Medici argues that because the ruin of her reputation means death or infamy for a woman, as it does not for a man, men must defend the honor of a falsely accused woman. Antifeminist Gaspare Pallavicino attempts to modify the Magnifico Giuliano's call to combat; he argues that unchaste women are in even more need of defense and claims that his argument makes him more a defender of women than the Magnifico (391–92). The monks' position resembles the Magnifico Giuliano's, and Rinaldo's resembles Pallavicino's.

The audience in the *Cortegiano* finds Pallavicino's suggestion amusing but invalid as a defense of women because chastity is at the center of their notion of the "donna di palazzo." By contrast, important modern critics of the *Furioso* episode have accepted Rinaldo's answer to the monks as a valid, strongly profeminist defense of women. Santoro defines Rinaldo as an accepted spokesman for Renaissance profeminism in his article "Rinaldo ebbe il consenso universale," and C. P. Brand suggests that Rinaldo's liberating words "seem to reflect Ariosto's own feelings" (118). I, on the contrary, suggest that, in Renaissance terms, Rinaldo is an antifeminist because he is motivated by male sexual interests, while the monks are Renaissance profeminists because they assume that a woman's chastity is maintained through inner strength, not external enforcement. The action of the story reinforces the value of chastity as an inner virtue beyond legislation and demonstrates the danger of Rinaldo's philosophy.

Rinaldo's greatest claim to the name of a profeminist is his assertion that he will argue publicly for a change in the law because it enforces a double standard of sexual behavior.

> perché si de' punir donna o biasmare,
> che con uno o più d'uno abbia commesso
> quel che l'uom fa con quante n'ha appetito
> e lodato ne va, non che impunito?

Son fatti in questa legge disuguale
veramente alle donne espressi torti;
(4.66.5–8; 67.1–2)

[Why must a woman be punished or cursed because she has done with
one man—or more than one—what man does with as many as he wants
and is praised for it, not punished. Many outright wrongs are done to
women in this inequitable law.]

Pleasing as it may sound to a modern ear, this endorsement of female
promiscuity goes against all the tenets of the sixteenth-century apologists for
women. Profeminists who state that women feel the same sexual desires as men
argue either that external restraints ought to be applied to male conduct as
well or that women are superior precisely because they are capable of restraint
as men are not; we saw Capella make this latter argument.

Rinaldo's antifeminism is made clear by his failure to make a substantial
argument against the double standard. He attacks the law because it denies
sexual pleasure to the male lover, not because it withholds equal rights from
women.[9] He thinks of women as objects that can satisfy men's sexual desires;
he sees the real criminals as the women who deny their would-be lovers sexual
pleasure by not allowing them "to vent their love in their loving arms." He
would reverse the terms of the law and punish women who do not grant sexual
release to their suitors (4.63.7–8)![10] He speaks the subliminal text of the law.
Be secret, be safe.

Again, the situation parallels the *Cortegiano*. There, when the group is
discussing the mode in which a "donna di palazzo" ought to conduct a courtship
or a flirtation, the Magnifico refuses Roberto da Bari's plea that she be allowed
to offer hope of sexual favors because his basic rule for a lady in matters of love
is that "she should show her lover all the signs of love except those which
might induce in his heart the hope of obtaining something dishonorable from
her" (420). Rinaldo, like Roberto da Bari, favors the older tradition of secret
love that the Magnifico, who represents the sixteenth-century profeminist

9. Wiggins makes a similar objection to Rinaldo's argument, but without referring to Renaissance
thought. "Rinaldo's opinions . . . reveal themselves to be an expression of a laissez-faire cynicism of
which Scotland's law is little more than the opposite extreme" (*Figures* 25). See also Shemek: "By
putting fair criticisms of the social gender system in Rinaldo's mouth, while at the same time making
their conclusions unacceptably extreme, Ariosto commences his own rejection of the *querelle*" (74).

10. When Rinaldo learns that Ginevra is innocent of the charges, he does not retract his previous
position; he simply expresses relief from his anxiety about losing a combat judged by God (5.75).

tradition, explicitly rejects; the monks, even though they are not so explicit in their rejection, favor the profeminist notion of a self-controlled chaste woman.

Santoro takes the monks' response to Rinaldo's ideas to be an enthusiastic endorsement, as his title, "Rinaldo ebbe il consenso universale," shows, but it is difficult to tell exactly what Rinaldo says that gains their agreement.

> Rinaldo ebbe il consenso universale,
> che fur gli antiqui ingiusti e mali accorti,
> che consentiro a cosi iniqua legge,
> e mal fa il re che può né la corregge.
> (4.67.5–8)

[The universal consensus was that the ancients were unjust and not very alert when they agreed to such an iniquitous law and that a king who has the capacity to correct it and does not does badly.]

That the "consenso universale" is on Rinaldo's side sounds impressive, but it is not clear that the monks (to whom this universal must refer, as they have formed his audience) have heard anything Rinaldo said. They agree that the law is "iniqua" and its institutors unwise, but they expressed this opinion before he spoke. Their response is merely a restatement of their original position that the law should be abolished because it exposes innocent women to punishment.

The harsh law, with its promise of safety in secrecy and its location of authority outside the woman, does not encourage the development of women's inner strength and puts society at risk from the very deed it appears to discourage. The maid Dalinda dressed in her mistress's clothes, received her lover Polinesso at the window, and gave the impression that Ginevra was unchaste, all because she was seduced by the promise of secrecy. Dalinda is weak, Polinesso is strong, and the law does not keep her from falling (5.8.3–4). Its failure illustrates the profeminist argument that chastity cannot be legislated because the desire to be chaste must come from within. In the Cortegiano, the Magnifico Giuliano defines a woman's best defense against falsity to be integrity. She needs to think of her reputation before her desires; inner strength and commitment to honor are her only defense against evil. Dalinda lacks this inner strength and has no defense against the wickedness of men.

Yet, finally, Dalinda provokes sympathy for the plight of women exposed to a double standard. Equity is the issue, but not the equity of license of which

Rinaldo speaks. In acting on her sexual desires and in allowing herself to go along with Polinesso's plan, she was unwise, but her foolishness and lack of malice combined with Polinesso's cruel and well-planned evil also point up the injustice of a law that would have punished her, had her crime been known, and left Polinesso alive and with no diminution in status. As the law is an extreme version of the double standard that existed in Ariosto's time, her case also points up the injustice of a social standard that punishes the victims and not the seducers.

Ginevra's situation as a woman in need of defense from slander is the situation of womankind as a whole in the defenses we have examined, and Ariosto, like the profeminists, makes his text speak in praise and in defense of her capacity for virtue and against the legitimacy of antifeminist authorities. Like the examples of chaste women in the defenses, her virtue refutes the absolutism of the traditional antifeminism expressed by Ariodante's brother Lurcanio, who finds in her supposed behavior confirmation of his belief in the complete immorality of womankind (5.63). In Polinesso's bitter response to Ginevra's virtuous rejection of him, we see acted out the malicious false-speaking about women that we have heard of over and over in the defenses. Antifeminists would kill women's reputation out of resentment at rejection; Polinesso, a subscriber to Rinaldo's tenet that "a cruel woman is worthy of death," would literally kill her.[11] The narration of his actions and the near-disaster that results from them represents the dangers that misogyny poses to women and to society as clearly as the rhetoric of profeminist writers does.

By naming this princess Ginevra (Guinevere), Ariosto makes his attack on romance love explicit. The name brings Arthur's queen to mind and makes a comparison between the two characters inevitable.[12] Guinevere's secret unchastity is essential to the Arthurian experience; as the primary kind of love in the Arthurian story, it not only offers opportunities for great heroism and suffering on the part of Lancelot, but also creates the conflict between love and society that brings about the collapse of the Arthurian world. Ariosto's transformation of Guinevere into Ginevra, a chaste woman who wants nothing more than to get married to her equally honest suitor, challenges the moral and literary values of Arthurian romance. The secrecy and the exciting tension it generates are replaced by an abhorrence of secrecy and the tension generated by the desire that truth about chastity be revealed in time. With Ginevra, Ariosto

11. In addition to the conversation from the *Cortegiano*, Goggio's citation of Boccaccio's *Corbaccio* at the beginning of the *De Laudibus* is relevant.

12. See Rajna on the topic of the "aspra legge" in romance before Ariosto (154ff.).

offers a new literary ideal for womanhood; she is chaste, and she is straightforward in her declarations of love.

Ariodante's true gallantry holds an answer to the problem of sexual inequality posed by the harsh law and by the antifeminism of Ariosto's own society, but it is an answer that few men are prepared to make. He is unique among the lovers in the *Furioso* who are confronted by evidence of their ladies' infidelity because he does not become an antifeminist, even though Ariosto represents him as completely believing the evidence set before his eyes.[13] His two attempts at suicide demonstrate how completely he is taken in by Polinesso, and his recovery from despair shows the intensity of his commitment to the chivalric code of conduct. He explains that he must defend Ginevra because

> Ella è pur la mia donna e la mia dea,
> questa è la luce pur degli occhi miei:
> convien ch'a dritto e a torto, per suo scampo
> pigli l'impresa, e resti morto in campo.
>
> (6.10.5–8)

> [Even so she is my lady and my goddess, she is very light of my eyes: it is appropriate that right or wrong for the sake of her safety I take up the exploit and die on the field.]

When Ariodante makes this speech, he is in exactly the same state of ignorance that Rinaldo was in when he pledged himself to defend Ginevra, but his attitude about her is as unselfish as Rinaldo's was self-interested. In Ariodante, Ariosto has created an exemplar of the perfect adherence to the idealizing values of the romance code. He truly gives his lady liberty out of respect for her, not because she is a weak woman and cannot be judged ill for actions she cannot control. He will fight for her out of love for her, not to disguise her guilt—as we just saw that Gaspare in the *Cortegiano* says men ought to do— and not to advocate a woman's right to sexual freedom, as Rinaldo would.

Finally, the story of Dalinda, rather than Ginevra, presents the real challenge to the antifeminism of the harsh law. She is seriously flawed; she is the kind of person with whom laws are intended to deal. Ariosto's representation of her case supports neither the harsh treatment of women who really are unchaste nor the reform of law to permit unchastity. She acts out of love, and the conclusion of the episode emphasizes the need for mercy in dealing with

13. Orlando, the king and Giocondo, Rodomonte, and Rinaldo himself become antifeminists.

human fallibility in sexual matters. When he pleads her case in front of the court, Rinaldo abandons his promise to attack the inequity of the law and begs for mercy for her, not for her right to loose morality (6.16.1–6). We are left with a sense of the need for greater morality among men. This mode of revising the double standard upward is typical of Renaissance profeminist writing; thus, Rinaldo's speech, which appears profeminist but is actually misogynist, is answered by an episode that is truly profeminist.[14]

The Second Debate

The second debate about womankind is generated by the pagan knight Rodomonte's disillusionment with Doralice, the lady he loves. When he offers her the choice between himself and another man and she chooses the other over him, Rodomonte flies into a fury and condemns all women as unfaithful. Hastening away from the scene of his discomfiture, he soon comes to an inn run by a cynical Frenchman who has managed to play both sides in the war and maintain his prosperity. This innkeeper unsuccessfully tries to comfort Rodomonte by attacking womankind and telling him a story that demonstrates that the best response to female infidelity is to shrug and accept it; an old man who is present at the inn defends women against the imprecations of Rodomonte and the innkeeper, but Rodomonte silences him. Traveling farther, the knight encounters the maiden Isabella, who is accompanying the corpse of her betrothed; he abducts her, but she saves her chastity by tricking him into murdering her. Her death converts him to love. The effect of this complex concatenation of episodes is analogous to that of a defense like Strozzi's or Castiglione's; the opposition is given full opportunity to voice its objections and cite its examples, but finally the selfishness of its motives is revealed and a rational profeminist position dominates: some women are flawed, but most will try to be good, if given models for behavior.

No matter which way you look at him, Rodomonte is an unpleasant character; pagan, irascible, and violent, he is given to cursing God, king, and women when things do not go his way. The cause for his antifeminism lies in

14. The episode of Ebuda forms a reprise of the issues examined in the Ariodante and Ginevra story. The law that condemns beautiful women to death as an offering to the orc was instituted because the king of the island was so angry at his daughter for becoming pregnant after being raped by Proteus that he killed her. In this case, as in Scotland, an extreme male response to female sexuality is the issue, but there is no question of the law's being legitimate, and Ariosto emphasizes the innocent female suffering rather than the issues of liberty.

the proprietary nature of the chivalric love relationship. Unlike Ariodante, who gives his love and demands nothing in return, Rodomonte expects his lady to prefer him because he has performed many deeds as tributes to her; he has honored her in jousts, tournaments, and war (27.105–6.2). When she chooses the other man, he feels he has been cheated of something that is rightfully his. He looks upon her as a property to be purchased with deeds, and this attitude causes him to deny her the freedom of choice that he appears to give to her and to blame her entirely rather than looking at the quality of his own love.

A typical antifeminist of the type Capella and other profeminists criticized, Rodomonte veers from conceiving of his lady as perfect to seeing her and all women as a burden and a plague. His tirade against Doralice (27.117–21) is a magnificent piece of misogynist rhetoric. The only reason he can find for his disappointment is "that you are a woman" ("che femina sei") (27.118.8). He exalts men and debases women. He associates women with beasts and their fertility with the proliferation of stinging insects and the growth of weeds, whereas he associates men with fruit trees and the tidy labor that promotes their asexual reproduction. He attacks nature because of its gender and withdraws praise even for women's part in generation; these are typical antifeminist ploys, as is the piling up of negative adjectives in the last lines—a form of condemnation without evidence.

The first response we hear to Rodomonte's ranting is spoken by the Narrator in his persona of disappointed lover (27.122–23). He offers a mock-defense of women. Acknowledging that his experience of women has been identical to Rodomonte's—all the women whom he has loved have proven unfaithful—he blames this situation on bad luck and refuses to blame women. He asserts that one must believe that for every bad woman there are one hundred good ones; he simply has had the misfortune to choose the bad ones (27.122.7–8). Although he claims to disagree strongly with Rodomonte's opinions of women, he sounds like a brave and idealistic man putting a good face on his persistence against terrible odds: for the sake of his sanity he *must* believe something that goes contrary to reason ("creder si *dee*").

The third stanza of the Narrator's speech presents a very different attitude toward the problem from the first two. It was added in 1532 and is generally taken to be a veiled reference to Ariosto's beloved wife, Alessandra Benucci. In it, the misogynist preoccupation with the division of women into groups of good and bad is replaced by the effusive offer of encomiastic writing. The stanza is permeated by the expectation that the poet's hope that the lady will be kind will be fulfilled; thus, unlike the mock-defense of womankind in the first two stanzas, the tone of this stanza really does contradict the blanket condemnation in Rodomonte's uncharitable speech.

As a whole, the Narrator's stanzas have the unsettling effect his pronouncements on love usually have.[15] His opinions are quicksilver; he is an excellent example of the irrationality of both profeminism and antifeminism when inspired by love or its disappointments. By establishing a parallel between Rodomonte's ideas and the Narrator's experience, the speech calls attention to the subjective nature of Rodomonte's response but prevents it from being seen as peculiar to him. It does not provide a substantial attack on his prejudice.

The French innkeeper introduces another kind of antifeminism into the episode. He accepts women's infidelity as inevitable and, thus, does not see it as a personal affront to the man who suffers from it. His antifeminism, like that of the gallant Gaspare Pallavicino in the *Cortegiano*, can masquerade as generosity because it does not damn women for immoral conduct; he finds a way for men to live in peace with women. Unlike Rodomonte's position, which is open to attack because it is so obviously vindictive, the innkeeper's is difficult to attack because he represents it as founded impartially on a "scientific" survey that proves that no woman is faithful and that any who appears to be so is "just better at hiding" ["più accorta era a celarse" (27.138)]. Rodomonte's arguments bear some twisted relationship to theology and philosophy; the Frenchman's are without any philosophical framework; they assert the validity of experience over idealizing expectations.

The innkeeper tells the circumstances of his survey in the tale of Giocondo, a story guaranteed to convert trust in women into cynicism. In this story, the handsome young husband, Giocondo, undergoes the same disillusionment about his wife that Orlando, Ariodante, and Rodomonte do about their ladies. Returning home unexpectedly, he discovers his wife sleeping in the arms of a servant only hours after she swore her husband's absence would kill her. He refrains from harming his lady or the servant, but he loses his famous beauty and would have died of grief, if he had not one day spied the King's wife at the same game with a dwarf. This teaches him that his wife's action "was not her fault, given that her sex never is satisfied with one man" ["Non era colpa sua più che del sesso, / che d'un solo uomo mai non contentosse" (28.36)]. The rest of the story consists of an apparently foolproof demonstration of the universal truth of Giocondo's discovery about women's naturally limited moral capacity. He and the King, a pair of Don Juan pollsters, attempt to seduce as many women as possible. They are never turned down and have a delightful

15. See Durling (150–76) for the most comprehensive discussion of the Poet-lover's voice.

time, but finally, when a young woman, whom they have placed between them in bed for safekeeping, makes love with a third man while they lie beside her, they give up and go home to their wives because they will give them satisfaction just as well as any other woman.

In this story, Giocondo progresses from naive belief in his wife, to disillusionment about her fidelity, to disillusionment about all women's fidelity, and, thus, to reconcilement to his wife's behavior. The love that he initially has for his wife disappears in the process, and he comes to think of her as an object to be enjoyed (*godere*). The inference is that only the cynical misogynist who has very limited expectations of women can have a successful relationship with them because he has no illusions to be shattered. Enjoyment, not love, is what one ought to look for. This is the lesson that the innkeeper would teach Rodomonte; Doralice's infidelity has liberated him to truly enjoy life.

Rodomonte does not accept the story's central premise—that woman is freed from responsibility for what she does because her promiscuity is the result of an inborn moral limitation. A misogynist but not a cynic, he responds with extreme bitterness and suggests that no amount of antifeminist writing could be adequate to the truth of women's depravity (28.75). Although Giocondo's appearance returns to its freshness once he learns that he is not uniquely cursed, Rodomonte continues to believe that he and other men could only be "giocondo" if women had never been created (27.119.4).

An old man who is present at the inn engages in a formal refutation of the innkeeper's antifeminist definition of womankind in an attempt to persuade Rodomonte that he and all men are culpable. A skillful apologist for women, he uses a three-pronged strategy frequent in the literature of defense. He argues against the authority of the innkeeper's source and his evidence, he attacks the moral soundness of the male sex, and he begins to cite examples of chaste women to counteract the Giocondo story, but Rodomonte silences him. The first stage of his argument is brief. He asserts that the person who told the story to the innkeeper was motivated by anger despite his disclaimers, and, thus, cannot be relied on as objective. A truly objective survey would show that chaste women outnumber unchaste by one hundred to one. Because both of these arguments are so timeworn, they cannot overturn the innkeeper's and Rodomonte's cases.

The old man's attack on the double standard is persuasive and truly profeminist, not merely a pretense as was Rinaldo's, because he attacks the superiority of the male sex and compares the general depravity of men with the specific problem of incontinence among women. He calls on the members of his audience to examine their own sexual behavior and asserts his confidence that not one of them has been faithful to his wife or would resist a woman if she gave him any encouragement; this is an argument that Strozzi made at length in the *Defensio mulierum* (46–51).[16] The old man is so confident in his evaluation of men, that he proposes a new law that unmistakably echoes the harsh law of Scotland.

> Saria la legge ch'ogni donna colta
> in adulterio fosse messa a morte,
> se provar non potesse ch'una volta
> avesse adulterato il suo consorte:
> se provar lo potesse, andrebbe asciolta,
> né temeria il marito né la corte.
> Cristo ha lasciato nei precetti suoi:
> "non far altrui quel che patir non vuoi."
>
> (28.82)

[The law would be that every woman caught in adultery would be put to death, if she could not prove that her consort had committed adultery one time: If she could prove this, she would go free and would not fear her husband or the court. Christ left among his precepts: "do not do to others that which you do not want to suffer."]

The use of "do not do" rather than "do" in this misanthropic version of the Golden Rule makes it seem that the most one can hope for is the avoidance of evil rather than the active doing of good. As he has already stated that he assumes no man in his audience to be free of guilt, the assumption is that no woman will be punished. Unlike Rinaldo, who gave sexual freedom to women providing they were good at keeping affairs secret, the old man is not making a plea for female promiscuity. He is advocating equality before the law. The difference is very important. For Rinaldo, extramarital sexual activity was good per se, whereas, for the old man, it is an occurrence that has to be dealt with equitably, but it is not good and should not be encouraged. He is willing to allow a woman whose husband has been chaste to be put to death, although it is unlikely that this would ever happen.

The old man's rhetorical method resembles Rodomonte's in his antifeminist tirade because he claims against the entire male sex the faults of some—a technique that he criticized when it was used against women; he differs from

16. See also the *Cortegiano* 395.

Rodomonte, however, because he admits that women are at times unfaithful. Women may be incontinent, he says, but one rarely encounters a female thief, murderer, or usurer (28.83). By admitting the single sin that has been imputed to women by the innkeeper, the old man makes his argument seem credible, as Rodomonte did not. Rodomonte would have had to gain our assent to the premise that men are perfect and would have no problems if women were not around; the old man only needs our assent that some women are continent and that women are very rarely thieves, usurers, murderers, practicers of large-scale fraud, or blasphemers—activities (except for the last) that their social role in the Renaissance generally precluded from being major temptations.

Because Rodomonte cuts him off before he can give his examples of good women, the old man's defense of women is limited: given the precondition of a fallen world in which no human actions are pure, women are not so bad as men. This is very moderate profeminism because it does not push the notion of woman to a positive extreme. It does not substitute excessive idealism for scorn; it removes women's sexuality from the context of its emotional impact on men and considers it in an ethical context in which a woman is judged, not by the pain she causes, but by how well she lives up to standards that apply universally to both sexes. The change in point of view from involved lover to disinterested observer permits the old man to see that all women are not the same.

Profeminism is not the necessary result of rational consideration of women in an ethical framework, of course, and arguments constituting a rational rebuttal to this speech's downplaying of the social importance of chastity in comparison with male social evils were available in contemporary antifeminist literature. For example, in the *Cortegiano* Pallavicino cites the effects of women's inchastity—illegitimate children and uncertain inheritance of family property—as reasons for enforcing a stricter standard for women than for men (391). Such a rational attack does not appear at this point in the *Furioso*; Ariosto does not represent any of the old man's auditors as offering any spoken opposition to what he has presented. Rodomonte violently silences him. As a result, the old man's argument that women are less sinful than men stands unchallenged in the debate thus far.

The Narrator quietly but authoritatively supports the old man's views. He does not represent himself as a lover here, but as a seeker after truth. From the moment he introduces the old man, the Narrator praises his wisdom. He is "un uom d'età, ch'avea più retta opinion degli altri, e ingegno e ardire" (28.76.1–2) [a mature man who had a more upright opinion than the others, and more wit and courage]. He is "sincero e giusto" [sincere and just] and, in silencing him, the Saracin fled the truth ["fuggia udire il vero"] (28.84). Therefore, the misogyny of the scheming innkeeper and impassioned Rodomonte is made to seem untrue and irrational in the face of the old man's sincere and just truth.[17]

Because he only has the chance to speak of ordinary women and is prevented from giving his examples of great chaste women, the old man's "truth" seems very sober; however, Rodomonte's encounter with Isabella provides the missing heroic example for him and for the defense of women in progress in the text. Isabella exemplifies the virtues that he denied women could exhibit. Through admiration of her heroism and shame at his own action, Rodomonte comes to believe in the existence of good women and to value chastity itself, a virtue that he had previously thought of only as one that would serve his sexual desires by keeping his lady true to him. Experience corrects his opinion of women and leads him to appreciate the truth of the old man's concept.

Ariosto does not leave the reader on his own to note the relationship between Rodomonte's adventure with Isabella and his previous beliefs; the Narrator becomes intrusive at this point in the narrative and speaks antimasculine invective of the type that appears in defenses of women. He breaks off his description of Rodomonte's murder of the priest who attempts to prevent his abduction of Isabella by ending the canto and beginning the next with an extended critique of Rodomonte's mutability and incapacity to distinguish among women, and he ends the entire sequence with an elaborate and hyperbolic eulogy of Isabella. The critique begins with an echo of Rodomonte's tirade against womankind: "Oh feminile ingegno . . . come ti volgi e muti facilmente" [Oh female wit . . . how easily you turn and change] (26.117) becomes "O degli uomini inferma e instabil mente! / come siàn presti a variar disegno!" [Oh uncertain and unstable mind of men! How ready they are to change their plans!] (29.1.1–2). This echo underscores the fact that Rodomonte proves about men the claim he made about women. He can hardly criticize women for infidelity and inconstancy if he is so quick to change. Rodomonte's inability to distinguish among women is criticized with equal harshness (29.3.3–8), and this criticism makes it clear that the judgment of men who are motivated by passion simply cannot be trusted. In neither anger nor love is he able to distinguish among women.[18]

---

17. Brand suggests that "we are inclined also to see Ariosto in the elderly man who is not prepared to accept the Fiametta story as valid evidence against the female sex" (118).

18. Turchi attributes Rodomonte's response to Isabella to the story of Giocondo (296). This inability seems to me to be native to Rodomonte; he expresses his belief in the uniformity of womankind before he hears the story of Giocondo; the story confirms his belief.

The Narrator makes no pretense of being impartial on the subject of women in this poem. He portrays himself as an offended defender of women who will use the rest of the story both as proof that Rodomonte's words against women were foolish and ignorant and as punishment for the blasphemous words so that others will be inhibited from speaking ill of women. Suddenly, a story that seemed a natural part of the narrative has been identified by the Narrator as a lesson aimed at the protagonist and any members of the audience who resemble him in their attitudes about women. We are reading a defense of women and, for both Rodomonte and for us, the story of Isabella functions as the example that illustrates the old man's argument as the Giocondo story illustrated the innkeeper's. Reinforced by the Narrator's eulogy of Isabella, it might persuade the male reader to admire women and the female reader to persevere in her virtue.

Ariosto's choice of this particular story to refute Rodomonte further confirms the presence of the contemporary controversy about women in this entire section of the *Furioso*. The tale of a young woman who engineers her own death to avoid rape had already been used by the humanist Francesco Barbaro in his marriage tract *De re uxoria* to illustrate the great value that some women place on their virginity. Thus, the Narrator's intervention replaces the story in its original context, the discussion about women.

In keeping with the source-story and with the tradition of the defense of women, Isabella exemplifies a particular kind of female virtue. Her most impressive characteristic is not chastity, which she shares with many women in the poem, but the independent self-reliance with which she maintains it. This quality she shares with only Bradamante and Marfisa. Most women in the *Furioso* who are threatened with rape or violence are helpless and passive; they rely on a passing knight to rescue them, and the rescue frees them from the threat of violence and the loss of virtue at the same time. Even Angelica, who is the most self-reliant of the other nonmilitary ladies, plays one knight off against the other to defend herself from unwanted advances and uses magic, not heroism, to get herself out of tight situations. Isabella is active and heroic; she relies entirely on herself and is only interested in preserving her chastity, not in escaping violence. She is a true martyr because she chooses physical suffering as a means of escaping physical and spiritual violation.

The Narrator's extremely enthusiastic eulogy of Isabella at the end of the episode provides a transition between the material of the controversy about women, with its serious ethical and social concerns, and encomia of the Estes. In this speech the lesson of Isabella, which in the context of the previous cantos applies to all women, is made to apply particularly to Isabella d'Este.

Thus, when speaking of the heroine Isabella as setting an example for women of his own day, the Narrator criticizes his own times, saying that few chaste women exist. Although this may appear to undercut the profeminism exhibited by the development of the episode up to this point, it does not. The change in mode, from defense of women to encomium of a single woman, dictates the handling of the material. In the genre of the defense of women, the example of a single woman sheds glory on all, but in the genre of encomium of patrons, the example of a single woman is linked as exclusively as possible with the patron.

Within this encomiastic context, the qualities for which Isabella is praised remain consistent. In comparison with Isabella, even Lucrece is passive, and God (who intervenes to establish a great destiny for the name "Isabella") identifies great intelligence and wisdom as primary among the qualities all holders of the name will exhibit (29.29). This is the ideal woman of the fifteenth- and sixteenth-century humanists and of the *Furioso*. Yet, the Narrator's extravagant celebration of Isabella and her heroic choice of martyrdom make it seem that she may be an extraordinary woman of the kind that Boccaccio describes. A reader is likely to wonder whether indeed such a woman could exist or, at least, whether such women, phoenixlike, exist only one at a time, as the innkeeper suggested. The action of Isabella is finally too perfect to disprove definitively the misogynic assertions of Rodomonte and the innkeeper. By isolating Isabella from other women, the Narrator leaves us with the question raised by the old man: What are we to make of the ordinary woman? Does the greater depravity of man excuse her sins? This is the topic of the third debate.

The Third Debate

The final debate about women (Cantos 42–43) occurs just after Rinaldo has been magically cured of his passion for Angelica. He arrives at the country estate of a melancholy knight, who begins their after-dinner conversation with the same question the innkeeper asked Rodomonte: "Do you have a wife?" When Rinaldo admits to being married (much to the reader's surprise), his host offers to let him drink from a cup that will reveal the truth about his wife's chastity; when Rinaldo refuses, saying, "ogni donna è molle" (43.6.5) [every woman is pliant], the host envies Rinaldo his wisdom and tells his life-story. He was happily married to a perfect woman who had received an upbringing along the most up-to-date humanist lines when he yielded to the temptation to magically disguise himself as a handsome former suitor of hers and offer her jewels in exchange for sexual intimacy. When she failed to withstand his appeal to her avarice, he revealed his true identity and she, shamed and indignant at such a violation of trust, left him and went to live happily with the very man whom he had impersonated. After a few words of wisdom, Rinaldo leaves and is told by his host's boatman a comic story in which avarice leads both the wife and husband to sexual corruption. In each story the husband's betrayal of his wife or his values is represented as greater than the wife's, and the essential antifeminist argument for restraining women more than men is overturned: women's morals are vulnerable, but they are equal or slightly superior to men's.

Before presenting the knight's tale, Ariosto creates a profeminist context. Rinaldo and his host have dinner under a fountain constructed in the shape of a pavilion supported by statues of ladies who will live in the future; the ladies are standing on the shoulders of men, the poets who will celebrate them. A plaque under each lady gives her name, briefly describes her, and names her poets. All these ladies are familiar figures from other encomiastic sections of the *Furioso* and from the catalogues of famous contemporary women that appear in Sabbadino and Castiglione. They are Lucrezia Borgia, Isabella d'Este, Elisabetta and Eleanora Gonzaga, Lucrezia Bentivoglia, Diana d'Este, Beatrice d'Este, and, finally, an unnamed widow of great beauty and honor who is held on the shoulders of only one poet, Ariosto's own Alessandra Benucci, of course. Each of these ladies is celebrated as chaste, beautiful, and the pride of her family or city; no details of their accomplishments or characters are given. The poets are the greatest scholars and court poets of the day; Castiglione, Bembo, Sadoleto are among them. An intrusion of Ariosto's present into the historical time of the poem, the figures not only flatter his patrons but represent the fame available to women who embody the ideals of Renaissance court society as we saw it in *Il Cortegiano*. [19]

In this environment dedicated to the celebration of virtuous women, the knight's offer to Rinaldo of the opportunity to drink from a magic goblet that will reveal to him whether his wife is faithful is surprising because it entirely changes the point of view from which women are seen. [20] Removed from the

19. The linking of art with female virtue resembles the paean to literature inspired by women that appears in the *Cortegiano* (412–13), though Castiglione mentioned only the poets and not the women who inspired them.

20. We have seen often in the *Furioso* how inaccessible certainty of both infidelity and fidelity is to lovers: Ariodante and Lurcanio are mistaken about Ginevra, Dalinda about Polinesso, Orlando about Angelica, Bradamante about Ruggiero. It would seem that in each of the cases, certainty one way or

pedestal where their integrity inspires art (both the fountain, a literal pedestal, and poetry) and provides an ideal of social conduct for all time, they become the objects of male sexual anxiety and jealous possessiveness. The knight speaks of the need to "spiare" (spy out) the truth about one's wife, of a wife turning a man into a beast when she cuckolds him, and of the shame of public knowledge of cuckoldry when the man himself is ignorant of it; in short, he speaks of the innocent man suffering disgrace through his wife, and he offers stolen knowledge as a safeguard against public disgrace and the private mistake of honoring someone unworthy of honor. The conflict of the beauty of the ideal suggested by his surroundings with the squalor of what the knight represents as real is shocking, but, by this point in the *Furioso*, so is the suggestion that an unfaithful wife is ipso facto worthy of desertion. Under the name of justice lurks the antifeminism of those, like Rodomonte, who demand absolute purity in women but not in themselves and who think of women as their property. The rest of this episode is devoted to the revilement of the misogynist attitude implicit in this speech.

The attack is begun by the Narrator; he interrupts his account of events before Rinaldo's response to the host's offer and begins the next canto (43) with a declamation against avarice. This speech attacks men as well as women; it, thus, undermines the notion that males are morally superior, just as antimasculine satire does in defenses of women, and assists the profeminism of the setting. Avarice, the Narrator says, diminishes the achievements and wastes the potential of the greatest male scientists, generals, and scholars by lowering their sights from abstract knowledge and glory to the most earthly concerns and rewards, and it destroys the virtue of women, who resist the entreaties of eligible suitors and then give in to old, ugly, or monstrous rich men.[21] Although this passage may seem inappropriate to its immediate context because Rinaldo and the host have not displayed avarice of material wealth, because its definition of male endeavors and female virtue is entirely conventional whereas the wife in the story we are about to hear was famed for her learning, and because the seducer the wife confronts is young and handsome, the Narrator insists that the speech is relevant to what he has just related as well as what is

---

the other would solve the problem, but, over and over, Ariosto employs the topos of the discrepancy of appearance and reality to show that the proof of the hero is in the trial, how he acts under the suspicion of or the apprehension or misapprehension of infidelity in his beloved.

21. Cesare Gonzaga makes a similar profeminist argument in the *Cortegiano*. He contrasts the resistance of women to the pressures suitors put on them with the all-corrupting power of avarice in men (403). Later, he describes the pressures suitors put on women and expresses sympathy with women's defeat (408–10).

to come. It is up to us to discover how it applies to Rinaldo, the host, and the wife.[22]

When he refuses the offer of the magic goblet, Rinaldo expresses an insidious kind of antifeminism that masquerades as profeminism because it allows a woman the freedom to be unfaithful: because a man is likely to find that his wife is unfaithful and to become miserable as a result, he would be foolish to seek to know the truth about her. As before, Rinaldo's laissez-faire approach to women's conduct is based entirely in a materialistic concern with male pleasure. The wife is free to act as she wishes, if she can keep her infidelities secret from her husband so that he suffers no disappointment or shame; the husband must do his part by not inquiring too closely into her conduct. Rinaldo has not changed; he is as pleasure-seeking, amoral, and antifeminist as he was in the fourth canto. Although there he spoke as a lover and here he speaks as a husband, his values are consistent: women are put on earth for the pleasure of men; take the pleasure and avoid the pain.

Yet, Rinaldo unwittingly provides an element of the profeminist foundation of the episode. He suggests that knowing for sure whether one's wife is faithful is as forbidden to man as was the forbidden fruit (43.7). This sounds like an exaggeration used to create a clever wisecrack at the expense of woman. It suggests the antifeminist commonplace that women have a great capacity for secrecy in sexual affairs. However, Rinaldo develops the analogy to draw a parallel between the consequences of knowledge in Adam's case and in the case of the inquiring husband and reveals the misogynist audacity of his analogy and the particular limits of his own philosophy. He suggests that, in both the case of the apple and of the wife, God forbade knowledge to man because it would bring man unhappiness (8).

This analogy is both comic and troubling because Rinaldo has confused the consequence of rebelling against the prohibition of the fruit with the cause of the prohibition; as always he is interested in the letter of the law and not the spirit. God did not forbid the fruit out of concern for man's future happiness, but as a test of obedience and as a symbol of faith and of the greater rank and power of God. It is true that, in the little world of human society, the disaster that follows in the wake of the discovery of infidelity is like that which followed

22. Mario Santoro also sees this proem as leveling distinctions between the sexes, but he perceives it as broadening the focus of the episode from the particular topic of female infidelity to the larger one of human frailty. He does not recognize the argument as part of the well-defined tradition of the defense of women. "Per questa ambiguità il proemio prefigura da una parte il tema, più evidente ed epidemico, della infedeltà femminile, dall'altra la cognizione della fragilità della condizione umana e della relatività della virtù, cognizione che costituisce la premessa del discorso di Rinaldo e, più largamente della *deep structure* della seguenza" (142). Like Durling, he constantly pushes the poem to less specific meanings, to general comments on the nature of life, while I find in it specific reference to topics of particular interest during the Renaissance.

the Fall: banishment from the paradise of the home and an eternal break in the continuum that existed between man and woman who are one flesh, but Rinaldo is concerned with the loss of "allegrezze" (cheerfulness), not with social and spiritual disaster.[23]

This irony against Rinaldo suggests the true reason why the knight's use of the goblet is perfidious: he is assuming power inappropriate to a husband, and he is betraying a lack of faith. Just as eating of the fruit of the tree was an act of pride (because it put man in a God-like relationship to all of creation) and of avarice (because he desired to possess forbidden power), so the attainment of certain knowledge of his wife's good or evil is an act of pride and avarice: it places the husband in a God-like relationship to his wife and satisfies his desire for unnatural power over her.

In suggesting by this analogy that such marital relations are wrong, Ariosto invokes a notion of marriage typical of the humanist defenders of women, whose essential premise that the sexes have equal moral and spiritual capacities resulted in a challenge of the traditional notion that woman's weakness created a need for superior male power in marriage. For example, Strozzi in his *Defensio* includes his discussion of marriage as a piece of evidence to disprove the antifeminist calumny that women are imperfect creatures. He argues that woman's soul came from God, though her body was drawn from Adam's. As a consequence she is man's spiritual equal, but submits to man because of a natural reverence as a child submits to its parent, not as an inferior as does man to God or a servant to his master. Strozzi reinforces this reading of the Old Testament with Pauline texts about the distribution of power within marriage. The apostle says, woman does not have power over her own body, man has; and man does not have power over his body, woman does, because she was not made from his feet to be "subdued in servitude" but from his side "so that he should know that she was given to him as a consort and as a sweet companion of humanity, and for the duty of mutual benevolence" (30–31).[24] As Strozzi reads Paul reading Genesis, Scripture teaches that the sexes reach perfection in union with each other; each sex is inferior on its own.

The knight's tale is a profeminist rewriting of the Fall in modern dress, although the knight himself, actor in the tale and retrospective teller, is not

23. Wiggins describes "Ariosto's irony in Rinaldo's allusion to Genesis" as "vitriolic. Rinaldo would have us avoid the forbidden fruit, not out of faith and obedience, but out of fear of disabusing ourselves of comfortable illusions" (*Figures* 35). Wiggins reads this speech as designed to undermine Rinaldo the man rather than as part of an ongoing attack on a particular attitude toward women.

24. "[A]ccio sapesse, che gli era data per consorzio e dolce compagna di umanità, et ad officio di mutua benivolenzia."

fully aware of its implications. Reading it in its context in the *Furioso*, we are led to feel and understand that the husband's lack of trust is a betrayal of *fede* as serious as an infidelity and that, as Paul said, the completion of the perfection of each member of a married couple lies in the other. The tale also challenges the misogynist assertions that Eve was solely responsible for the Fall and that, as a consequence, human suffering in this land outside the garden can be blamed on Eve's daughters.

The story of the Fall is immediately brought to mind by the knight's description of his wife and of the palace where he lives. She is the illegitimate daughter of a magician, who brought her up according to the humanist dogma that environment and education can produce a woman with excellent morals and an independent ability to maintain them. The palace is the home her father had demons build to preserve her from following the example of her mother, whose favors he had purchased with gifts. Another Eden in a fallen world, the estate derives its purity from its distance from the "commercio popular" (43.14.5), from the absence of any companions but chaste old women, and from its decorations celebrating chastity and its heroic preservation, such as the fountain that was described earlier and paintings of every woman who ever resisted lust ("ogni pudica donna che mai tenne / contra illicito amor chiuse le sbarre") (43.15).[25]

A humanist curriculum made the young lady the perfect feminine product of the new learning.[26]

> Ella era bella e costumata tanto,
> che più desiderar non si potea.
> Di bei trapunti e di riccami, quanto
> mai ne sapesse Pallade, sapea.
> Vedila andare, odine il suono e 'l canto:
> celeste e non mortal cosa parea.
> E in modo all'arti liberali attese,
> che quanto il padre, o poco men n'intese.
>
> (43.18)

25. The absence of any companions but old ladies is the most conservative part of her upbringing. Vespasiano da Bisticci advised that young women be kept separate from men and boys after the age of seven, but most humanists educated girls in company with boys and relied on the education alone to produce the desired moral sensibility.

26. Ariosto's characterization of the wife as extremely well brought up and as an example of feminine virtue is a major change from Ovid's version. There, the wife is an ordinary woman.

[She was so beautiful and well mannered that one could not desire anything more. She knew as much about trapunto and embroidery as Pallas ever knew. To see her walk, to hear her play and sing was to believe her a celestial and not a mortal being. And she applied herself to the liberal arts so well that she knew as much or a little less than her father.]

Just as profeminists suggested it would, her upbringing fostered her natural intelligence, beauty, and sweetness so that she was accomplished, moral, and modest, and, once married, found her greatest pleasure in being near her husband, as he testifies.

On the other hand, her husband, although well educated, was not raised in the garden and was not cut off from "commercio popular" during the time of his marriage, although he lived at the country estate. Sin enters the garden through him.

The reasoning process that leads him to test his wife appears to be profeminist. Melissa, a magician who is in love with him, suggests that he must give his wife the opportunity to be unfaithful; his constant presence at her side, she says, and the consequent lack of opportunity to sin may be the cause of the wife's morality. This argument is in line with a profeminist interpretation of a husband's role in marriage: too jealous a guardianship of a wife is wrong. The educated wife ought to have the ability to regulate herself and avoid sin, even when offered the occasion. Despite the seeming honesty of the reasoning, the test is corrupt for two reasons. First, it attributes motives to the husband that are not his. He has not been guarding his wife from the occasion of sin, as a traditional husband might do; he has been perpetually with her because he loves her and cannot bear to be parted from her. Second, the wife has already withstood exactly the test Melissa proposes; the husband tells Rinaldo that she had steadily refused the advances of a rich, handsome neighboring knight, and, thus, has proven herself to be the faithful and trustworthy wife she appears to be. The jealousy that Melissa's suggestion provokes is entirely irrational. He has eaten of the fruit and has lost his faith.

Having done so, he acts to corrupt his wife. In the most intimate circumstances—her private room when she is alone and at ease (43.36)—and in the magically assumed shape of her persistent lover, he appeals to her avarice. Given the overpowering circumstances, her struggle against temptation is almost as admirable as her fall is terrible:

> Turbossi nel principio ella non poco,
> divenne rossa, et ascoltar non volle;

> ma il veder fiammeggiar poi come fuoco
> le belle gemme, il duro cor fe' molle:
> e con parlar rispose breve e fioco,
> quel che la vita a rimembrar mi tolle;
> che mi compiaceria, quando credesse
> ch'altra persona mai nol risapesse.
>
> (43.38)

[At first she became very upset, she blushed and did not want to listen; but seeing the firelike flaming of the beautiful gems made her hard heart soft: and with brief and faint speech she answered that which it takes my life to remember: that she would satisfy me, when she believed that no other person ever would know.]

The worst of this moment is not the husband's knowledge of the wife's sin—after all, he has voluntarily created the situation—but the fact that a woman of such perfection has been lowered to desire secrecy to disguise her acts. Through his illegitimate temptation, the husband has made her equal to the most ordinary woman, Giocondo's wife, for example, yet she has already proven herself not to be ordinary. She would never have given in, if the husband had not betrayed her by taking advantage of their intimacy to create these extraordinary circumstances, and, thus, her action does not support the assertion "ogni donna è molle."[27]

The end of the tale stresses the husband's lack of faith. When his disguise is lifted, he confronts his wife with her betrayal. No other husband or lover in the *Furioso* does this. Giocondo leaves rather than shame his wife, the King keeps his promise not to harm his wife, and Ariodante refuses to charge Ginevra with adultery. All these men can be reconciled with their wives, but for this husband there is no comic resolution of his troubles. His cruel self-righteousness and lack of faith drive his wife away from him forever, and no reader is likely to think that he has gotten anything other than what he deserves. Through making us feel the loss of her innocence so strongly, the story demonstrates the truth of the Pauline and humanist axiom that when the best woman is part of a couple, her well-being is as much in her husband's

27. The wife in Ovid's story of Cephalus and Procris is put in a much less challenging position and falls. Her husband returns disguised as a stranger and does not speak of long unrequited love; he merely offers her jewels, and she accepts immediately. The story in that form, up to that point, is antifeminist, proving that avarice is stronger than virtue in women. Rajna (572) saw Ariosto's changes as attenuating the wife's guilt.

keeping as his is in hers. The wife's perfection alone is not enough; her husband must support it, not by restrictions as an old-fashioned husband would, but with *fede* as a new humanist husband should.[28]

The relative guilt that Ariosto assigns the two sexes in his story of the Fall is the opposite of that traditionally assigned in popular antifeminist literature, in which Adam's fall is nearly an act of charity done out of a sense of responsibility and commitment to Eve, and Eve's wickedness is the card that trumps any profeminist proof that women are as good as men. In the *Cortegiano*, for example, Frigio suggests that the praiseworthiness of women's great deeds is undercut by the fact that "those effects began when the first woman erring made another error against God and as a legacy left the human race . . . all the miseries and calamities that are experienced in the world today" (362). The Magnifico cites Mary to refute Eve and does not answer Frigio's argument directly. Other profeminists saw that it was essential to refute the placing of the responsibility for the Fall on Eve because it was based on the assumption that Satan chose the woman because she was morally weaker by nature and made an easy target.[29] The Scholastic arguments extolling Eve's place of creation and the materials with which she was made and Goggio's paradoxical defense of her as having benefited mankind by her error are both attempts to deal with this attack.

By means of this episode Ariosto removes the Fall as an a priori refutation of the defense of woman offered in the *Furioso*. The story attacks both antifeminist premises: the wife is morally superior, and the husband falls through lack of charity and absence of a sense of responsibility and commitment. Womankind is raised by this counterversion of the story that is usually used to pull her down; we are left with the impression that the man has behaved worse than the woman. In this profeminist garden, the man precipitates the Fall.[30]

In his response to the tale, Rinaldo reproves the knight for devising a test that his wife would be so unlikely to be able to resist because avarice is an all-but-irresistible force within all humans, men as well as women. "How many men have you heard of," he asks, "who have betrayed their superiors and friends for gold?" (43.48). His words echo the Narrator's introductory stanzas

28. This story is the opposite of the story of Ariodante and Ginevra. There, he conquered jealousy and maintained his faith despite his belief that she had betrayed him and was rewarded by the discovery that all the disappointment had been an illusion. Here, the husband is consumed by jealousy with no reason and loses his faith; he is rewarded by the fulfillment of his expectations and eternal regret.

29. Profeminists were not the only ones to refute this argument. Saint Thomas Aquinas saw it as pernicious as well because it made God's punishment of Adam unjust.

30. Melissa is a magician and might be a stand-in for Satan rather than an ordinary member of her sex. The appearance of the female snake-fairy in the next story suggests this may be true.

on avarice and make explicit their implicit suggestion that men and women are equally avaricious, but once again Rinaldo is reductive.[31] Unlike the Narrator, who laments that vice pulls people down and prevents great achievements, Rinaldo finds in human limitations a justification for low expectations, and he cannot understand the real tragedy of the knight's story or its profeminist lesson.[32] He can neither appreciate how great a woman fell nor understand the real essence of the knight's fault in regard to his wife. Because he does not value ideals, he is neither profeminist nor antifeminist. Unlike the profeminist "sincero and giusto vecchio," who invoked male sin as a standard with which to demonstrate the relative insignificance of female sin and who paired his disparagement of mankind with a vision of ideal conduct, Rinaldo invokes male sin only as an equalizer.

The defense of woman requires a positive representation of the sex, the example the old man would have given, not merely a statement that man equals her in vice. The knight's story offers this positive representation in the person of the wife, whom the knight himself so carefully describes as the best possible woman. But it is important that she does fall. Ariosto does not argue that women are perfect, but, rather, like the most serious profeminists, he shows that they have the potential to be very good and admirable, when supported by their society and trusted to be so. He represents his own society, and particularly the Este court, as appreciative of such women and as providing them support, literal and figurative, in the form of the poets upon whom they stand, whereas the husband's lack of appreciation of his wife and lack of support of her is set in relief by the setting in which he tells his story, and the analogy with that greater Fall makes us appreciate the seriousness of what has happened and how much has been destroyed. The story does not lead to despair because the situation could have been avoided. A good education, a good marriage, and a good society can safeguard a woman against such a fall.[33]

31. Rinaldo's suggestion in the last two lines that the knight might have behaved as badly as his wife, if put in the same situation, carries weight not only because the story has led us to see that he is not superior to his wife, but because they are the very words that Cephalus uses to beg forgiveness of his wife in the story of Cephalus and Procris. That Ariosto assigns the words to Rinaldo instead of the knight makes it possible for him to make the break between husband and wife absolute and makes the analogy with the Fall possible. Paradise is defined as their marriage which is lost forever.

32. Mario Santoro extolls Rinaldo's prudence here as elsewhere. For him, this episode stands for Rinaldo's reentry into reason and is a triumph of tolerance and moderation (*Anello*, passim, especially 152). While I would agree that Rinaldo is prudent, I would argue that the unheroic inadequacy of Rinaldo's response demonstrates the limits of prudence.

33. In my insistence on the specific relevance of the episode to the topic of marriage, I again differ from Santoro, who reads the story as unfolding on a "sempre più vasto orizzonte umano e morale" (*Anello* 144). He also seems to see the episode as undercutting the value of humanist education. He

The positive humanist profeminist values of this tale are oddly reinforced by the fabliau version of the story of Cephalos and Procris that the knight's boatman tells Rinaldo immediately afterwards. A fairy who must spend one day a year in the body of a snake is saved from death by a young man, and she rewards him with a magical jewel-producing dog. He approaches a young wife whose old and jealous husband is away on a trip and, with his looks and his dog, he seduces her. Her husband returns, alerted to his misfortune by a fortune-teller, and hires someone to take his wife into the woods and execute her, but the wife disappears. When the husband goes to look for her, he finds a magnificent palace. This palace is guarded by "a monstrous and hideous Ethiopian," who offers the husband great riches if he will bend his body to the Ethiopian's sexual desires. As he does so, the wife appears, draws a contrast between herself and him, and suggests they resume their marriage and never refer to the incidents again. The husband agrees. In this story the conventional hierarchy of the sexes is again reversed because the sacrifice that is made to attain the riches is unequal; the wife loses her virtue to a man more appropriate as her mate than her aged husband, whereas he loses his in degrading relations with a hideous being. Thus, we see evidence for the profeminist truth that women are less corrupt than men!

Everything is downgraded in this story. Although there is a real snake, the parallel with the Fall of man is not developed, and all the substantial themes contributed by that analogy are missing. This is not a story of betrayed faith, but of the power of avarice in a world where faith and idealism have no place. It is the previous story as heard by Rinaldo—only its materialistic elements are present. This is not a marriage of superior people. The wife is beautiful, too beautiful for her aged spouse, but she is not described as being educated or virtuous. The husband is a foolish scholar and murderously vengeful. The wife acquires power over her husband by arguing that at least she achieved her goal by doing it with someone handsome. Her argument is reminiscent of Giocondo's about his own wife after he saw the Queen sporting with a dwarf; however, his statement provided antifeminist consolation because his pride was eased by the recognition that there were degrees of corruption amidst the universal sexual immorality of women, whereas her statement provides profeminist consolation because it points out that, although all human beings are sexually corrupt, men are worse than women.

---

speaks of "la sottile ironia del contrasto tra tanta dottrina e i risultati pratici." The wife's father's education of her and construction of ideal surroundings went for nought; "eppure nulla impedirà che anche lei finisca per cedere alla seduzione della ricchezza" (*Anello* 150). Such blame of the wife is only possible if one does not blame the husband for betraying his proper relationship to his wife. The husband is indeed "nulla" when he ought to have formed another part of the protective shield around his wife.

Yet, finally the profeminism of this tale is not so crude as it appears. Although the wife achieves authority from having witnessed her husband's physical debasement rather than from doing anything positive herself, she relinquishes her authority in the best tradition of famous women. She offers a positive alternative to the "aspra legge di Scozia," a law that resolves all the problems that the others created.

> S'io ti parvi esser degna d'una morte,
> conosci che ne sei degno di cento: . . .
> pure io non vo' pigliar di peggior sorte
> altra vendetta del tuo fallimento.
> Di par l'avere e 'l dar, marito, poni;
> fa, com'io a te, che tu a me ancor perdoni.
>
> (43.142)

> [If I seemed worthy of death to you, know that you are worthy of one hundred . . . yet, I do not want to take any worse revenge than your failure. Make the having and the giving equal, husband; do as I do to you, you pardon me too.]

This law not only echoes the Golden Rule, as the old man's law did, but with its reference to pardon, it also brings to mind the paternoster's doctrine of reciprocal forgiveness. In this materialistic and ethically debased version of society, where we would least have expected it, a law has been written that resolves the sexual discrimination and bitterness that remained in all the other laws we have seen invented. It assumes the worst; it admits that we live in a fallen world and are ourselves likely to fall; it takes into account the fallibility of both sexes, and it encourages reconciliation. It works because, unlike all the other versions of the Scots law, it does not legislate sexual conduct for either sex.

This is the final version of the "aspre legge di Scozia" that appears in the *Furioso*. All the others have been attacked from various perspectives in each of the three debates and have been shown to be based on misapprehensions about the relative merits of the two sexes. We have seen the limitations of the Scots law, which grants absolute authority to the male sex over the female and condemns only women's public sexual license among women; of Rinaldo's law, which encourages secret license and punishes chastity; of Giocondo's law, which forgives female infidelity because nothing better can be expected of women; of the new law of the "sincero e giusto vecchio," which maintains an adversarial relationship between the sexes, although it permits women a defense against male accusations; of the knight's law, which deprives women even of the defense of secrecy and condemns them utterly for a single error; and, now, we have the wife's law. It too must be judged by what it achieves: for a society in which faith, chastity, and moral law have been utterly disregarded, it provides a new beginning, a new opportunity to act in good faith.

Over and over within these stories of sexual infidelity and abuse, examples of inwardly generated chastity and fidelity stand out to encourage the reader to look within himself or herself for the capacity to withstand temptation. Even this story, which has no example of fidelity, encourages the reader by provoking a reconsideration of its twin tale. The contrast of this story of base characters who come to a happy end with the previous story of high characters who come to a sad end retroactively makes the knight's error in not appreciating his wife appear worse. Because he adhered to a rigid code of unforgiving justice and refused to extend the grace of forgiveness, he ruined a happy and intellectually satisfying marriage with a wife of proven fidelity. The high quality of his marriage and his wife stand out in relief against the ordinariness and willing infidelity of the wife who formulates the new law; thus, by creating nostalgia for the high world of the previous tale, the second story confirms the idealistic humanist notion that education is of value in forming a wife.

The Debate as a Whole

In the several episodes of debate Ariosto demonstrates that man's problem with woman arises from his own limitations, from considering her an earthly good and object of desire whose steadfastness can be maintained by material restraints rather than by considering her as an independent being to be wooed and loved and won through steadfast faith and unselfish love. Because she is a principal object of male desire, it does not necessarily follow that woman is the "principal embodiment" of "the instability of earthly goods," as Durling argues in his discussion of the Poet's comments on women (175). The world is in flux; the constancy must be within.[34] The experience of woman that Durling defines

34. Marinelli also objects to "attempts to see the poem as centrally and essentially committed to a presentation of reality as inexorable flux and impermanence" and cites "Bradamante's love [as] the one immutable and constant thing in the poem. . . . Throughout she functions as the very human agent of providence's equally unrelenting pursuit of Ruggiero" (106).

is not the only experience of woman described by the book; it is the rejected experience, the one Ariosto discredits by showing the chaos and loss that occur when one considers woman in that way. Only when knights learn to distinguish between women and horses, can they can begin to be happy.

The defense of women plays an important part in this recommendation because through it Ariosto persuades his readers that women have the spiritual and moral capacity to make heroic efforts of chastity possible for themselves and worthwhile for their lovers. Women are worthy objects of love and desire when men are worthy in their love and desire. Voluntary obedience by both sexes to the virtue of chastity and to marital vows is the necessary prerequisite for happiness in marriage, not obedience forced by external law or even husbandly admonition.

This principle worked out through the adventures of characters who are extraneous to the main plot creates a framework by which to judge and understand the major characters. Because he has established this moderate profeminist context in the debate sections, Ariosto can present Orlando's romance adventures, which are directly analogous to those of Ariodante, Rinaldo, and the characters in the interpolated *novelle*, without appearing to teach or preach; alternatively, he can go over the misogynic deep end in the persona of the Narrator speaking on Angelica and not be taken entirely seriously. We can recognize in his speech the profeminist truth that disappointment in love produces antifeminism. In this series of debates, Ariosto has tested out misogynist platitudes and found them to be in error: women cannot be controlled by suspicion and rules, but they do have the capacity for true virtue equal to that of men.

5

PRAISE AND LIMITATION OF THE INDEPENDENT WOMAN IN THE *ORLANDO FURIOSO*

For all its positive appraisal of women, the debate sequence discussed in Chapter 4 represents female independence only as spiritual and moral autonomy: women control their own desires. Although this is an important basic step in Renaissance profeminism, we have seen that the defense of women was also based in praise of women's intellectual and physical strength. This part of the debate is associated with the epic plot of the *Furioso*. The lady knight Bradamante's sense of the kind of woman she is and her active role in the founding of the Este dynasty, her future sister-in-law Marfisa's active role as combatant, and the Narrator's praise of their deeds all directly speak for women's capacity to perform in what had previously been seen as the male arena. Despite the positive representation of women's capacities, their independence appears as a threat to society; autonomy can result in rebellion against marriage, reversed sexual hierarchies, and social chaos. As in the sequence of episodes discussed in the last chapter, the solution lies in womankind's voluntary self-restraint, not in male oppression. The ideal accomplished woman submits to marriage, its hierarchy, and its limited field of activity.

Both the original 1516 edition of the poem and the 1532 revision and expansion of it are concerned with the issues of the defense of womankind, but the latter frequently directly invokes the terms of the contemporary defense while the former renders the issues in narrative form and does not necessarily associate the poem with the tradition of defense. This suggests a growth in Ariosto's thought on the topic in the intervening years. Many of the great additions to the poem made in 1532 address the problem of gender definition and the social role of the independent woman; the episode at the Rocca di Tristano, the overthrow of the tyrant Marganorre, the story of Olimpia, and the marriage complications that occupy the last cantos—all are linked with the topics of defense. The clear deepening of thought about women in these passages led Enrico Carrara to suggest that a desire to "'rinfamare' il gentil sesso" [renew the reputation of the gentle sex] was one of Ariosto's major motives for adding these episodes to the poem (6).

Bradamante and Marfisa

The military women in defenses of womankind are of two kinds. There are Amazons and modern knights like Joan of Arc and Maria Pozzuoli, soldiers who are not interested in marriage;[1] and there are women who are or will be wives and who undertake military action only as a means of furthering the interests of their husbands and families. Marfisa fits neatly into the first category. She is exclusively dedicated to arms and considers her part in the war to be important both when she is on the Saracen side and when she converts and pledges herself to Charlemagne. Her role is essentially masculine, as is her sense of herself. Bradamante does not fit neatly into either category. Like Marfisa, she is a professional woman-at-arms; she does not take up arms merely to follow a man and not all her military endeavors are in the cause of love. Yet, her self-image is essentially feminine; she consistently chooses love over her duty to Charlemagne, thus making it possible for herself to do her duty to posterity by bearing the ancestor of the Este line.[2]

Because of her commitment to an independent life and her conception of herself as politically important, Marfisa might seem to offer the most potential for commentary about the role of women in society, but Ariosto does not develop this possibility. He uses Marfisa's ignorance of sexuality and love as a means of exploring the physical paradox of the masculine woman, and he uses Bradamante as the focus of the poem's discussion of the social role of the accomplished woman. Her adventures prompt other characters to discuss this topic, whereas none of Marfisa's do, and the Narrator's two eulogies of accomplished women focus attention on the interdependence of the sexes

---

1. On Pozzuoli, see Petrarch, *Familiarium* 5.4.

2. Ascoli suggests that Bradamante "comes closest to a resolution of the problem" of "conflicted faiths" that is "a repeated motif of the poem." He cites 45.101 in which "she promises to be both faithful and unfaithful"; that is, she will keep faith with Ruggiero no matter what other inconstancy it leads her into (329–31). This is, of course, a private solution available to a woman and not to a man because her superficial infidelity is part of a greater fidelity to the destiny that lies in her body. Ruggiero cannot retreat into the private.

rather than on independence, even though Bradamante is not a participant in one of the adventures that lead him to speak. As a result of Ariosto's connection of Bradamante to contemporary thought about women and his representation of her as feminine and because of his exclusion of Marfisa from this same controversy and his representation of her as masculine, Marfisa remains part of the past and Bradamante provides a precedent for the women of Ariosto's own day.

The lady knight was a standard feature of chivalric narrative before Ariosto wrote the *Furioso*, and he created neither Bradamante nor Marfisa, but no lady knight had ever before been represented in a manner that led the reader to make generalizations about the role of women. Even when the narrative includes an event that might have led to reflection on woman's role, the romances do not reflect. For example, Galiziella in the *Aspramonte*, a valiant professional soldier from the "regno feminoro" (realm of women), agrees to her brother's request that she marry only the man who can beat her in battle because she recognizes that her husband should be able to chastise her. Although the stipulation that her husband must be stronger than she suggests some anxiety about the effect of female prowess on social order, the problem is not discussed. In practice, the rule gives Galiziella the freedom to marry as she wishes; her beloved has already beaten her, and his rival is afraid to fight her. That the rule also deprives her of freedom by making her an inferior who is subject to physical punishment is not presented as paradoxical. Immediately after marriage she gets pregnant and seems to give up fighting.[3]

This same motif of requiring suitors to defeat the lady knight in armed combat was part of the traditional story of Bradamante. In *Bradiamonte, sorella di Rinaldo* a popular romance, the dedicated and proficient heroine wishes to avoid marriage completely, so, on her own initiative, she stipulates that she will not marry a man who cannot beat her in a contest at arms (162). When she is challenged by a prospective suitor, Amansor, the king of Barbary, she wins easily and her victory in single combat results in a victory over his retinue by the Carolingian army. In this case the condition that the lady sets for marriage effectively ensures her physical, emotional, and political autonomy, but the romance is interested in the autonomy only as an extraordinary feature of this woman's life that sets her off from other women and makes her a worthy topic for literary entertainment.

Even in the *Orlando innamorato*, from which Ariosto most directly inherited Marfisa and Bradamante, the heroines do not provoke discussion and are not

---

3. According to Ariosto, this Galiziella is the mother of Ruggiero and Marfisa.

seen as posing a serious challenge to conventional social organization; no connection is made between their behavior and the conduct of women of the poet's own time. The actions of neither woman in the *Innamorato* deeply resemble her conduct or adventures in the *Furioso*. Boiardo's Marfisa is a buffoon who spends much of the first book armed and on foot in pursuit of Pinabello, who has stolen her horse and who teases her by keeping the horse just out of her reach. Boiardo's Bradamante is a steadfast soldier of Charlemagne and is assigned important strategic duties. She does not fall in love with Ruggiero until near the end of the portion of the story that Boiardo completed. Although she gets lost immediately after falling in love and becomes the object of love by another woman who mistakes her for a man, her wandering does not have a clear symbolic significance and the case of mistaken identity does not reveal anything about the heroine's attitude toward the paradox of her profession and her sex.[4]

Ariosto's major innovation in the treatment of the lady knight was to explicitly analyze the social and personal implications of her independence. Two issues are dominant: Does a woman's anatomy determine how she is to be treated by society or do her abilities? Does a woman's capacity to defend herself necessarily invalidate a marital hierarchy that places woman inferior to man? In the first edition of the poem (1516) the first issue is present but primarily by inference rather than by direct statement, and the treatment of it is primarily comic; in the additions made in 1532 the second issue is extremely important and the first is handled openly and seriously. Through his representation of Bradamante and Marfisa in both editions of the poem, but especially in 1532, Ariosto leads his readers to think about the notion of sexual difference and sexually determined roles in a way that none of his predecessors do.

Anatomy versus Abilities

Ariosto poses the paradox of women capable of "male" conduct by calling attention to both Marfisa's and Bradamante's bodies. Each woman at least once surprises onlookers by removing her helmet and revealing her sex and then is forced to defend herself against claims that her feminine appearance and not

4. See Marinelli's detailed discussion of the meeting of Bradamante and Ruggiero in the *Innamorato* and of the ways in which Ariosto developed the relationship and themes Boiardo introduced (58–76). Marinelli's focus is on Ruggiero rather than on Bradamante throughout.

her masculine prowess should be the determining factor in how she is treated. In the episode concerning Marfisa, which was in the edition of 1516, the issue remains practical—Marfisa asserts her own liberty from convention but makes no reasoned statement explaining her position, whereas in the episode concerning Bradamante, added in 1532, the issue becomes theoretical—Bradamante argues for the primacy of what one does over what one's anatomy leads people to expect one to do. The 1532 edition is directly and explicitly involved in the political and social defense of womankind.

In canto 26 when Marfisa removes her helmet the description of the revelation of her sex is matter-of-fact. All see that she is a young woman because she has golden curls and a delicate and beautiful face (26.18–19); their response is not erotic. They cannot look at her enough because she is the author of such great deeds in battle, not because they are moved by her beauty. The fact of her sex is a surprise, but it does not lead them to consider Marfisa as a sexual object; her deeds are in their memories, and they determine how she is treated. Later, when Marfisa puts on a dress at the request of her companions, the Narrator explains where the clothing came from and that Marfisa rarely lets herself be seen without armor, thus making it clear that Marfisa does not travel with feminine clothing in her saddlebags and that this is a moment of particular intimacy, but he shows neither Marfisa behaving in a feminine manner nor her male companions taking advantage of this intimacy.[5] She does not become an object of desire to them; she remains one of a group of equals; the usual significance of feminine clothing is irrelevant for those who know her abilities.

Having established this image of Marfisa, Ariosto introduces a threat to her sexual neutrality that at once makes us admire her self-reliance and feel the distance that lies between her and most women. Mandricardo bursts in and challenges the men to a duel as soon as he sees Marfisa; he wants to win her to use her as an object to trade to Rodomonte in exchange for Doralice (26.70). He assumes that women are possessions to be controlled by the men who own them and that they have no will or identity of their own. Marfisa is in the same situation Isabella is in when she leads Rodomonte to kill her. This episode is comic as the other is not because we can predict a happy outcome to Mandricardo's attempt to possess Marfisa as we cannot for Rodomonte's attack on Isabella. Marfisa's martial conduct and her virile beauty have convinced the

---

5. Another example of Marfisa's comic ignorance about sexuality occurs when she dresses the horrible hag Gabrina in the finery of a young woman and cannot understand that this does not make her as attractive as a young woman. She has no objections to fighting over her.

reader of the complete inappropriateness and impossibility of treating Marfisa as a sexual object.

Mandricardo does not challenge Marfisa's right to act like a man; he is unaware of her ability. In her response to his claim that he has won the right to control her by defeating Viviano and Malagigi, whom he has taken to be her champions, Marfisa accepts that right and does not dispute the law of chivalry that mandates that women be treated as possessions.[6]

> Io ti concedo che diresti il vero,
> ch'io sarei tua per la ragion di guerra,
> quando mio signor fosse o cavalliero
> alcun di questi c'hai gittato in terra.
> Io sua non son, né d'altri son che mia:
> dunque me tolga a me chi mi desia.
>
> (26.79)

[I concede that you would be right and I would be yours by right of war if either of these men whom you have overthrown were my lord or knight. I am not his nor do I belong to anyone but myself: therefore whoever wants me, take me from myself.]

The position Marfisa assumes here is essentially that of Bradiamonte in *Bradiamonte, sorella di Rinaldo*. She grants the authority of the misogynist notion that is central to the chivalric code: a woman is property that belongs to men by right if they can win it, but she asserts that, as a military woman, she is not included under the terms of the code. She has control of her life. Although this assertion challenges traditional views, Marfisa does not develop the theory behind her assertion as I have here; she relies on physical power, not reasoned argument to persuade her opponent. Because the Narrator does not step in and defend her assertion either, the episode remains unconnected to the tradition of the defense of womankind.

At the "rocca di Tristano" (castle of Tristan), Bradamante's removal of her helmet leads her host to want to consider her as a woman rather than as a man, just as Marfisa's wearing of a dress leads Mandricardo to try to treat her as a woman, but this episode, inserted into the poem in 1532, is explicitly

---

6. Wiggins takes a contrary view. He sees Marfisa as being engaged in a "crusade to prevent women from being reduced to sexual objects" (*Figures* 188).

connected to the defense tradition because Bradamante makes a carefully reasoned defense of her rights as a military woman. At the "rocca di Tristano" it is the custom

> che 'l cavallier ch'abbia maggior possanza,
> e la donna beltà, sempre ci alloggi;
> e chi vinto riman, vòti la stanza,
> dorma sul prato, o altrove scenda e poggi.
> (32.94)

[that the most powerful knight and the most beautiful woman lodge there; the one who is vanquished leaves the room, sleeps in the meadow or wherever he or she ends up.]

This custom is borrowed from Arthurian tradition with one all-important change: no Arthurian romance includes the beauty contest between women (Rajna 502). This added element brings the episode into the controversy about women because it makes it possible for Bradamante to refuse to be a competitor in the beauty contest, to demand to be judged on her military skill, and to challenge the traditional categorization of people by gender rather than by deeds.

When Bradamante, who entered the castle because of her skill as a knight, is revealed to be a woman, a debate is held on the question "whether Bradamante should be considered a legitimate guest because she conquered in arms or in beauty" (Carrara 9). Her host is for strict divisions between the sexes. He wishes to treat her as a woman and to expel Ullania, the woman who arrived before her. Bradamante claims that she did not enter the castle as a woman and that she does not wish to be treated as one. She asserts that no one can really know what she is without undressing her and that she must be a man since her every gesture is masculine, but she admits, for the sake of argument only, the thesis that she is a woman and is less beautiful than Ullania. She argues,

> . . . non però credo
> che mi vorreste la mercé levare
> di mia virtù, se ben di viso io cedo.
> Perder per men beltà giusto non parmi
> quel c'ho acquistato per virtù con l'armi.
> (32.104)

[I do not, however, believe that you would want to take away the prize of my skill, even though I concede by my face. To lose for less beauty what I won by skill at arms does not seem just to me.]

Brand calls her entire speech "a fine legalistic argument, much of it, a *reductio ad absurdum* of the futile distinctions made between the sexes" (120), and, indeed, it is. Although Bradamante does not extend her argument from the single example of herself to a generalization on the rights of women, as the writer of a defense of the sex would, she does enunciate a doctrine that could provide the basis for a case for other women, as Marfisa does not when she defies Mandricardo: women who are capable of equaling or surpassing men should be compared with men. As Carrara says in his analysis of this passage, "a parità di prove parità di diritti" (9) [equal achievements deserve equal rights].

Clever as Bradamante's argument is, she concludes her speech with a physical threat, not a logical feint; she offers to fight anyone who contradicts her. Talk as he may about Bradamante's womanhood, the host would have very little hope of enforcing his law against her. What really destroys the rule of gender in this passage is not what Bradamante says, but what she is capable of doing: in her body the traditional definition of woman breaks down. The Narrator praises the cleverness of Bradamante's arguments, but emphasizes the importance of her physical strength in carrying her point (32.107). Her ability to force agreement is the final proof of her thesis that what she is is defined by what she has done, not by society's expectations.

Bradamante's attitude toward her gender in this episode invites comparison with Marfisa's in the land of the "donne omicide" (homicidal women), already present in the 1516 edition. To set herself and her friends at liberty, Marfisa must conquer ten men in the lists and ten women in bed. She does not recognize her inadequacy in the second contest but rather states that the sword at her side is able to "cut all knots" (19.74.7). We laugh at her because she does not acknowledge even to herself that her sword is not a male "sword." Bradamante nowhere gives this sense that her self-image depends on ignoring her sexual difference from men. Her speech at the "rocca" recognizes the female body even as it denies its relevance to the question at hand. By saying "who will say [that I am or am not a woman], if I don't undress completely" (32.102.5–6), she shows her awareness of what Marfisa seeks to forget.

Similarly, the narration stresses Bradamante's erotic beauty without undercutting the episode's explicit challenge to the traditional definition of gender roles, whereas Marfisa simply is presented as female but not desirable. Bradamante's sexual attractiveness is evoked, for example, when her hair tumbles out of its snood and reveals that she is a woman:

> La donna, cominciando a disarmarsi,
> s'avea lo scudo e dipoi l'elmo tratto;
> quando una cuffia d'oro, in che celarsi
> soleano i capei lunghi e star di piatto,
> uscì con l'elmo; onde caderon sparsi
> giù per le spalle, e la scopriro a un tratto
> e la feron conoscer per donzella,
> non men che fiera in arme, in viso bella.
>
> (32.79)

[The lady, beginning to disarm, had taken off her shield and then her helmet; when a net of gold, in which she compressed and hid her long hair, came off with the helmet; from which her hair fell down spread on her shoulders, and suddenly revealed her to be a maiden, not less beautiful of face than savage in arms.]

Although we are already in on the secret and know that this knight is a woman, Ariosto succeeds in using our knowledge to create anticipation; we hear of the "cuffia d'oro" in line 3 and anxiously await the inevitable cascade of hair, which Ariosto delays until lines 7 and 8. By presenting the revelation of Bradamante's womanhood in stages, Ariosto makes us rediscover what we know; he associates us with the physical point of view of the knight of the "rocca" and makes us participate in the startling discovery of her gender and sexual attractiveness.

In this episode Ariosto suggests an alternative to the old ideal of helpless beauty, represented in this case by Ullania. He does not replace it, however, with its exact opposite, the virago, a woman like Marfisa whose bearing and sense of herself divide her from her sex. He instead portrays a complex woman who combines physical strength with femininity. The episode demonstrates that women should be judged according to what they can do rather than what society has always said they are, but without denying all differences between the sexes. It makes it clear that Bradamante is equal to and yet different from men.

Women and the State

Although it has profeminist implications, the episode at the "rocca di Tristano" says nothing practical about the position of the independent woman in sixteenth-century society. This topic is introduced by the Narrator in two encomia: the proem preceding Marfisa's and Astolfo's disestablishment of the society of the "donne omicide" (canto 20) and that preceding Marfisa's, Bradamante's, and Ruggiero's overthrow of the misogynous tyrant Marganorre and their establishment of a matriarchy (canto 37).[7] The first proem and episode were present in the 1516 edition of the *Furioso*; they are not seriously engaged with political aspects of the topic of sexual equality. The second proem and episode were added in 1532, and they are.

The three stanzas that introduce canto 20 stood as the only profeminist speech by the Narrator on a topic other than love and fidelity in the 1516 edition of the poem. They use three conventional profeminist points to praise women and form a bond between the heroism of Marfisa and the women of Ariosto's own day. They enthusiastically celebrate the abilities of women to perform in traditionally male fields (stanzas 1 and 2), suggest that male historians have neglected woman's history (stanza 2), and praise modern women for the emergence of sufficient "virtù" among them to give work to numerous encomiasts and to silence antifeminists (stanza 3). They are specific about ancient women—Arpalice and Camilla, Sappho and Corinna represent military and literary success among women of the past—but give no examples of modern women; the Narrator merely asserts that they exist in great numbers. This is not unlike his assurance elsewhere that he will write about a hundred or a thousand good women to make up for one bad one. Without names and details, the assertion that positive examples exist has scant power to impress and no power to persuade.

In the second stanza, the Narrator attempts to throw a profeminist bridge over the silent gulf between named classical women and their vaguely suggested modern counterparts, but he offers too many possible reasons for the absence of records of female deeds from the postclassical period. Either no great women existed in the intervening years or they existed but male authors did not report their deeds. Either the male authors did not report their deeds because they did not know about them or because they were envious of them and wanted to deprive women of their deserved fame. The profeminism of the statement is

---

7. The strong distinction that I make between the voice of the Narrator in these two encomia, and especially in 37, and his voice in his many intrusions discussed in the previous chapter is similar to that made by Fichter at the beginning of his third chapter. Durling links these two passages but does not discuss the implications of their difference in tone and content from others spoken by the Narrator (150–52). Although Ascoli does not discuss these two voices, his complex discussion of the poet provides a context for considering the place of these personae in the overall system of tensions in the poem.

weakened by the concession that great women may not have existed for such a long time and by the suggestion that men may not have intended to neglect women but may simply not have known about their deeds. Deeds that cannot acquire fame even when no prejudice acts to repress them are hardly very spectacular.

Given the ambiguity of the causes for lack of fame in the second stanza, the assertion in stanza 3 that times have changed is not persuasive. Everything is too hypothetical. It *seems* to him that "virtù" among women is on the increase and that it will inspire writers. This statement requires corroboration from the audience to be convincing. A profeminist would find it in his or her own experience, an antifeminist would not. This is praise without defense, and its power is very limited. The Narrator's goodwill toward accomplished women does not seem to be in doubt, but the actual existence of such women does.

The story of the "donne omicide" makes the praise offered in the proem even more equivocal. These women founded their Amazonian society in response to the extreme cruelty and irresponsibility of men and instituted firm laws that forced women to rely on themselves, but these proved to be ineffective because they went against natural necessity: new citizens were needed and women felt sexual desire for and even fell in love with the men provided to create the citizens. By the time Marfisa and her companions reach the land, the provision of men to answer sexual needs has resulted in the reestablishment of male power, if not authority, within the society. Decorative bands of Amazons decked out in bows and arrows and buskins roam the city, but the captive men do their fighting for them and the women have restored themselves to the position of sexual combatants, as the test for any knight who wanders into their territory shows: the stranger must beat ten male knights on the battlefield and satisfy ten women in bed.

By showing the Amazon nation to be on the verge of disintegration from within, Ariosto obliquely attacks the profeminist notion that male rule is a man-made system imposed on women by male craft and physical force. Female rule seems to be an unsustainable aberration that arises in response to male misgovernment; the real issue is the need for men to treat women well so that women are not driven to such unnatural lengths to protect themselves against those who ought to be protecting them.[8] Rather than supporting the ability and right of women to govern, the episode diffuses male anxiety about Amazons

8. See Roche ("Ariosto's Marfisa"). After discussing the allegory of the horn and the legal history of the realm of the "donne omicide," he comes to the conclusion that "what Ariosto has done is to show the insufficiency of the Law of the 'femine omicide,' the insanity of setting man against woman, the impossibility of society without cooperation between man and woman, women and men" (132).

by showing that they really do not hate men and are not really a threat to men, but are a male creation: if men honor their obligations to women, these monsters will not rise up.

Because these ladies are "antiqui," like the women praised in the proem to the canto, and yet their achievements, now being recorded by a male historian, are not worthy of praise, the episode undermines the optimism of the proem. The contrast between Marfisa, whose actions provide the impetus for the praise of women, and the "donne omicide" does not work in the favor of independent women; she is the exception, the not-so-Amazonian Amazons are the rule. She is a true warrior, she has no sexual feelings, and she is a companion and ally of men, but her positive actions prove nothing about women in general. She functions outside the normal institutions of society, and the contrast of her ability to do so and the failure of the Amazons to create a society in which all women act like Marfisa shows that she is extraordinary and an outsider. Judged by the example of the "donne omicide," most women both want and need the traditional domestic structure of society. The conclusion of the episode with the blast of Astolfo's magic horn and the dispersal of the women and the evaporation of their community as though it had never existed is a narrative representation of the insubstantiality of the threat of female government.

The episode of Marganorre and the encomium of women that precedes it, both added in 1532, stand in marked contrast to the vague praise of women in canto 20 and the story of the "donne omicide." The new encomium is convincingly profeminist because it fills in the details missing from the earlier one; the episode, however, pushes the restructuring of society to a matriarchal extreme that is destabilizing and unnatural when considered in the context of the eulogy and the rest of the poem.

The twenty-four stanza encomium of women that stands as the proem to canto 37 is a masterpiece and an innovation in Renaissance profeminism. In it the Narrator does not merely defend women against attack and celebrate their accomplishments in an attempt to persuade a male audience to revise its opinion of the sex; he attributes to women a desire for fame, and he advises them to break the dependent relationship that exists between themselves and male writers. He tells them that they should take charge of their own fame by writing great works that will be read in the future and also by recording their deeds themselves instead of depending on men to do it for them.

The encomium has four movements, each of which focuses on some aspect of the relationship between women's fame and written works. Six introductory stanzas establish the greatness of women and the neglect of their deeds by male historians. Seven stanzas celebrate modern women and the modern writers, Castiglione and Capella among others, who accurately record their deeds and praise them; special praise is given to Isabella Colonna, who persisted in marrying the man who loved her despite papal opposition, and to her husband, who wrote poetry in praise of her. Nine stanzas encourage women to write and free themselves of the need for male historians and encomiasts and feature Vittoria Colonna as an inspiring example of woman's capacity to assure fame to herself and others. The final two stanzas summarize and apply the lack of historical records to the particular case of Bradamante and Marfisa and to the Narrator as celebrator of them. Although he himself is writing women's history in this very passage, and although he includes in the passage the conventional assertion that male historians are now very eager to write the positive truth about women, the Narrator urges women to overcome their dependence even on well-disposed writers and to take control of the means of representation by addressing future generations themselves to create the image that they wish to have seen by posterity. Power lies in the written word.

The assertion that male writers have distorted the history of women through envy and malice is a commonplace of profeminism as it is a commonplace of humanism that writers have the power to hand down to posterity their vision of events as *truth* (as Ariosto explains in the conversation between Astolfo and Saint John), but the encouragement of women to speak out for themselves is not.[9] The usual strategy used by the profeminist writer is to offer himself as the exception to the rule or as the evidence of the goodwill of modern men and to offer his work in defense of woman to rehabilitate her reputation and to establish her good fame for posterity. We saw Strozzi (93), Goggio (when speaking of the founding of Rome), and Capella do this, and even Boccaccio offered himself as a redressor of the wrong done to women by historians—although, of course, the fame he offered was not necessarily good. Some writers of defense do suggest that male history would be very different had women been historians because they would have recorded only the nefarious deeds of men as men have done of women, but they offer this point as evidence to make their readers believe that men have distorted history; they do not urge women to write history as Ariosto's Narrator does.

Most profeminists reveal over and over that they cannot really imagine an equality between men and women; we saw this in their myths about the origin of the social hierarchy and in their presentation of themselves as gallant defenders of women.[10] They convert their choice to write a defense of women

9. Ascoli briefly sets this passage in the context of other passages in which poetry is "figured as a kind of tomb and as that which may transcend the tomb" (371).

10. See, for example, my discussion of Strozzi's chivalry and of his account of women's decline from power and of Capella's chivalry at the beginning and end of his work.

into a need for such a defense on the part of women; implicit in the very genre of defense is the weakness of the defendant, woman; she is incapable of defending herself, so the male writer comes to the rescue. This strategy establishes modern woman's dependence on man as her champion and reinforces notions of her passivity that contradict the examples of energy and fortitude that make up the history the male defenders tell; the modern woman's appropriate response to a book written in her defense is gratitude, the sexual-courtly relationship of exchange is maintained. Ariosto breaks this relationship in this encomium, as he did not in the proem to canto 20. That passage was compatible with the characterization of the Narrator as a cynical lover writing in the profeminist mode to further his own purposes; this one is not because it encourages women not to depend on the Narrator; it encourages independence.

Yet, at the same time that the Narrator asserts that his efforts are not necessary and even makes a convincing case against himself, Ariosto is constructing the image of the ideal woman of his time for posterity. The two contemporary women he uses as examples of behavior to emulate were both self-reliant women and good wives. Isabella Colonna displays the strength of mind and commitment to withstand forces that would determine her course of action for her. Because she acts in the name of love and is faithful, her behavior might be taken for conventional female conduct, but she is not obedient to conventional authority. She is praised for

> l'amor, la fede, il saldo e non mai vinto
> per minacciar di strazii e di ruina,
> animo. . . .
>
> (37.9)

[the love, the faith, the whole spirit which was never conquered by the menace of torments and ruin. . . .]

Because she disdained Fortune's every blow with her "virtù" (sprezzando di Fortuna ogni percossa), she achieved her desired end and married as she wished.[11] Hers is a marriage of equals "di lei degna egli, e degna ella di lui" [he worthy of her, and she worthy of him], and her independence works for the

---

11. She is an example of Ariosto's exaltation of humanist "virtù" against "fortuna" of which De Blasi speaks. "Fortuna" is the political situation that would have forbidden her marriage and "virtù" her courage and enterprise in achieving her goal.

conventional social structure, though against certain authorities within it. She gets her reward—fame and an accurate historical representation of her deeds— through her husband's and Ariosto's poetry.

Because of her profession as poet, Vittoria Colonna would seem to represent a very different kind of independence from Isabella's self-reliance. She is one of the new modern women who make male celebrators of women obsolete:

> . . . molte, lasciando l'ago e 'l panno,
> son con le Muse a spegnersi la sete
> al fonte d'Aganippe andate, e vanno;
> e ne ritornan tai, che l'opra vostra
> è più bisogno a noi ch'a voi la nostra.
> (37.14.4–8)

[. . . many, leaving the needle and fabric, have gone and go to quench their thirst at Hippocrene's spring; and they return such that your work is more necessary to us than ours to you.]

Skill at writing gives these modern women freedom and power, two qualities necessary to break away from woman's conventional social role. That men need their praise suggests that women now have the power to determine how future ages will perceive the men of their own time. This could be threatening to male peace of mind, given the treatment women have received at the hands of men, but the way the example of Vittoria Colonna is developed puts this anxiety to rest.

> Quest'una ha non pur sé fatta immortale
> col dolce stil di che il meglior non odo;
> ma può qualunque di cui parli o scriva
> trar del sepolcro, e far ch'eterno viva.
> (37.16)

[This one has not only made herself immortal by means of her sweet style than which I hear no better; but she can raise anyone of whom she speaks or writes from the grave and make him live eternally.]

The main person whom she has raised from the grave is her husband, of course, and so Vittoria fuses the perennial tradition of fidelity with the humanist ideal of accomplishment perfectly in her work and in her life. Her ability as a poet complements her role as wife and poses no threat to domestic or social peace. The anxiety of male writers that causes them to write women out of history is without foundation.

The stress on fidelity in the descriptions of Isabella and of Vittoria connects the values of this proem with those that governed the Narrator's comments on women and love, but the statistics seem contradictory. The romance passages repeatedly stress the rarity of fidelity among modern women; this proem and that to canto 20 laud the ever-increasing numbers of accomplished women, yet clearly require fidelity as a necessary part of an accomplished woman's charac- ter. The two claims seem to be irreconcilable. Fidelity cannot be rare among modern women and yet many of them be worthy of fame. This discrepancy can be explained generically. In romance the Narrator is speaking of all women and the faithful are a small group compared with all womankind; the eulogy of Isabella and the statues at the Cispadono host's palace make it clear that these few chaste ladies are the members of the Este circle. In epic the Narrator is comparing a select group of women from his own time with comparable women from the past, not with all womankind. Even the learning of the male humanists and the leadership of great male generals and statesmen would seem rare if compared with the education and abilities of all men. Thus, those few faithful women exempted from the general condemnation of womankind are the same ladies whom the Narrator praises for their accomplishments; both sets of comments praise one group of women.

The Narrator uses his return to the adventures of Bradamante and Marfisa as a means of reasserting his ability to serve women as historical reporter, and this brings a return to the courtly voice of the conventional profeminist hoping to profit in some way from his endeavors on woman's behalf. He writes for two reasons:

> sì perché ogni bell'opra si de', dove
> occulta sia, scoprir, sì perché bramo
> a voi, donne, aggradir, ch'onoro et amo.
> (37.24)

[because one must bring to light all good deeds when they are hidden and because I burn to please you ladies whom I honor and love.]

This declaration of honor and love suggests a partiality on his part, a lack of objectivity about women that has not been apparent before in the encomium, which has persuaded by the strength of its examples. It helps to make the voice of this proem consistent with the tone of the Narrator's other speeches on women, but it does not have the strength to detract from the powerful and original profeminism of this passage.

Marganorre

The contrast between the values expressed in the proem and those embodied in the tyrant Marganorre, whose story follows it, is shocking. In his society women are considered to consist only of their sexuality and are banished from the city to an adjacent slum; foreign women who have the misfortune to arrive in the city are deprived of all clothing below their umbilicals so that their genitals are exposed and then the women are sent on their way. The powerlessness of these women contrasts both with the authority of those described in the proem and with Bradamante and Marfisa, who arrive on the scene, depose the tyrant (with Ruggiero's help), put him in the hands of the exiled women for torture and execution, and establish a matriarchy. The context, the presence of the lady knights, and the events make the episode seem to be a simple exercise in profeminism in which the evil of misogyny is countered by the positive good of giving power to women, but the story is not such a simple lesson. Although Marganorre is clearly wicked and his misogyny unnatural, the women are not idealized and matriarchy is not presented as natural.

Marganorre's laws do not just oppress women, as the Scots harsh law did. The society that he has constructed is an external representation of the misogynist mind. Women are forced to become the filthy animals that misogynist literature defines them as while their husbands and sons live in the city, which has been cleansed of their presence. The humiliating treatment of foreign women similarly debases them. These two forms of degradation of women result from a kind of misogyny that Ariosto frequently represents in the *Furioso*, the treatment of women as nonautonomous sex objects whose function is to satisfy male desire.[12] We hear Rodomonte define his notion of woman after

12. Peter DeSa Wiggins sees the treatment of Ullania and her companions as "poetic justice." In his discussion of the "rocca di Tristano" episode he argues that Ullania is like Angelica; she permits herself to be defined as a sexual object and, thus, it is right that she suffer the humiliation of having her skirts removed by Marganorre. "Squatting on the ground to hide their private parts, they have become symbols of what it means to seek distinction in the fulfillment of a sexual stereotype. Struggling now to hide that which they allowed to define them before, they are in ludicrous subjection to their physical being" (202). Ullania's mission is find the best knight for her lady, who defines herself as the most

Doralice rejects him, and we hear the Narrator speak his sadistic wishes when Orlando knocks Angelica off her horse; here we see the suffering that women undergo when forced to live the lives Rodomonte says they prefer and to suffer the violence of actions worse than those the Narrator wished to perform. Ariosto makes what we see repellent and by this means attacks misogyny.

He also attacks it by showing its inappropriateness. Like the more prosaic defenders of women, he offers examples of heroic women to counter the misogynist notion of woman. The story of the origin of the law is as follows. Two foreign married women rejected the sexual advances of Marganorre's two sons. The first woman survived the young man's attempt to abduct and rape her because her husband killed him. The second woman, Drusilla, was forced to rely on her own resources because the second son murdered her husband before making his attempt on her. She tricked him into drinking a poisoned wedding cup and had the pleasure of knowing that she had taken her revenge for her husband's murder before she, too, died. Marganorre reacted to the deaths of his sons by restructuring his society to exclude and shame women; he did not recognize any fault in his sons' behavior.

The story of Drusilla is part of the tradition of the defense of women. As the story of Camma, the tale appears in the *Cortegiano* and in Francesco Barbaro's *De re uxoria*. The major change Ariosto makes is in the context of the story. In the other works, it is told to illustrate the great love of which women are capable and forms part of a defense intended to persuade the reader to have a positive opinion of women. Here, Ariosto does not reach directly out to the reader in an attempt to persuade him to admire women (as he did in the similar case of Isabella) but rather juxtaposes Drusilla's heroic action with Marganorre's monstrous reaction. To a reader familiar with the story, his behavior is likely to appear as a gross misreading of the text of Drusilla/Camma's action. Rather than being primarily a celebration of women, the story is made into a persuasive illustration of the cruelty and injustice of misogyny by the elaborate account of Marganorre's response.

This story, added in 1532, reveals another aspect of Ariosto's rethinking of

---

beautiful woman in the world. Thus, she by proxy represents a rigid definition of the sexes according to beauty and strength, the principle that is attacked at the "rocca di Tristano"; Marganorre's stripping of her clothes could be a revelation of the true nature of the beauty that she represents, but to consider this behavior just and find truth revealed by the tyrant's action is to side with misogyny and punish woman for the desire her beauty arouses. It also is to ignore the pain it causes, to treat Ullania not as a character but as a symbol of a certain approach to womanhood, and to go against Wiggins's central thesis: that the story "is not primarily about actions, but about character—about the inner, irrational life of man" (*Figures* 206). It also ignores the intense concern that everyone has to restore the ladies to clothing that is proper for them, not just clothing that covers their genitals. They are first given male clothing; this is not sufficient. If we were being taught the lesson Wiggins is suggesting, male clothing might even be desirable. For more on this topic, see the section on the "rocca di Tristano" above.

the issues of the defense of women. This change can be seen when the events and presentation of this story are compared with those of the tales of female faith in the 1516 edition, especially the story of Isabella and Rodomonte. Like Marganorre's sons, Rodomonte is unmoved by a woman's faith to her deceased beloved and considers her only as an object to be desired and used; Isabella, too, uses her wits to save herself from sexual union with a man whom she despises. But there the similarity ceases. Rodomonte is converted from misogyny by his murder of Isabella because her heroism teaches him the value of chastity and respect for women and their autonomy. Misogyny, it seems, can be corrected by contact with good women. A similar conclusion can be drawn from the overturn of the misogynist law in the story of Ariodante and Ginevra and from the knight's regret for his mistreatment of his wife. By contrast, the story of Marganorre represents misogyny as an emotion utterly unreachable by reason or example. Faced with one of the most popular and persuasive exemplars of female faith and valor that exists in classical and Renaissance literature about women, he feels no shame at what his son has attempted and sees no value in the young widow's defense of her body against violation.

In their discussions of this episode, both Renzo Negri and Marcello Turchi see its strength as lying in the dark atmosphere that Ariosto creates in his description of Marganorre's society and its history; they consider Marganorre to be potentially a tragic figure.[13] Negri sees the study of Marganorre as a tragic father as the only valuable part of the episode. He describes the misogynist law as a bizarre creation that takes away from the coherence of the episode and complains that Ariosto's introduction of the law transforms Marganorre into a kind of Bluebeard from a children's adventure book. It cheats Marganorre of his tragic end (121). Turchi identifies the episode as important because of its "funzione fantastica," which lies in the dark passions that govern people's conduct and lives within it: the misery of the three ladies whose skirts are "murkily cut short" and especially the dark passions of Marganorre and Drusilla create a mythic "romanzo nero." In this context Marganorre's suffering is his triumph and his antifeminism is a stylistic and sentimental letdown (328–30).

It is true that Ariosto represents Marganorre's savage attack on Drusilla's dead body (the passage Turchi quotes to substantiate his praise of the mimetic force of the passage) with extraordinary vividness. It is quite horrifying, degrading, and ironic—in his violence against her body he is comparable to a

13. C. P. Brand judges the episode unsatisfactory. "The total effect is certainly not harmonious: the poet seems more concerned to press home some bitter truths about his fellows than to preserve a smooth facade. There are some touches of fine psychological penetration, particularly in the portraits of Marganorre . . . and Tanacro" (179).

snake and a dog that futilely bite the stick and the stone used as weapons against them. This is not an image to rouse sympathy for a father cheated of revenge; he is behaving like an animal. To interpret him as a tormented father rouses sympathy for him and gives justice to his actions. He is not tragic and he is not heroic because at this moment he is not shocked into horror at the negative notion of women that motivated his sons and he does not respond with admiration for Drusilla.

His antifeminism is part and parcel of his character; it does degrade him from his ideal potential as a man, but not from any potential that he himself has shown. From the moment he introduces the character, Ariosto represents him as a wicked man held in check only by the greater morality of his sons (37.44–45). His attack on Drusilla's body and on the women of his society is the result of attitudes he held before the death of his sons; his true feelings are released, he is not suddenly driven to frenzy, and he experiences no conflict. He is indeed a kind of Bluebeard and the land he rules *is* the nightmare world of children's stories. It is made so by the unnaturalness of the misogyny that Negri would discard as a disruptive "bizzarria" and that Turchi sees as somehow extraneous to his true character. The account of his treatment of Drusilla's corpse, of the women in the church, and of women in general is calculated to make us recoil at the monstrosity of his misogyny and to make us long for his overthrow.

Ariosto's representation of the behavior of the male members of Marganorre's society suggests that female rule is a punishment of their complicity with misogyny rather than being a positive institution in itself.[14] Drusilla, a "mere" woman, found a way to defy him; they did not. They went along with Marganorre, even though they cried out in their hearts against what he did. Ariosto describes the situation in Marganorre's country as typical of the behavior of men under a tyrant.[15] They become suspicious of each other and they permit him to hurt whomever he pleases without protesting.

> Ma il cor che tace qui, su nel ciel grida,
> fin che Dio e santi alla vendetta invoglia;
> la qual, se ben tarda a venir, compensa
> l'indugio poi con punizione immensa.
>
> (37.105)

14. Ariosto seems to have anticipated Calvin's notion that woman rule was a punishment sent by God.

15. For a discussion of the topic of tyranny in this episode, see Griffin (59–60).

[But the heart that is silent here, cries out above in Heaven and inspires God and the saints to revenge; which, although slow in coming, makes up for the delay with extensive punishment.]

Although the main person in need of punishment is clearly Marganorre himself, his male citizens have let things get to such a state that Providence has had to intervene in the form of the three knights; the consequence of this intervention is female rule.[16] The ease with which these knights overthrow Marganorre also reflects badly on the male citizens. Marganorre's citizens only dare to attack him once he is deposed and it is safe. Then their behavior is no different from that of their female relatives, who attack Marganorre in a mob.

Most critics who discuss this episode see Marganorre's overthrow and the establishment of rule by women as a kind of balance to or even retraction of the antifeminism they see at work in the episode of the "donne omicide" (for example, Turchi 327).[17] They speak of "the institution of laws more favorable to the cause of women" (Griffin 59). The assumption is that we are to feel that Ariosto himself endorses female rule or at least expects that we will see it as a positive alternative to Marganorre's tyranny. This would be an extraordinary view for any sixteenth-century author to hold; even the most extreme profeminists support only equal opportunity to rule, not matriarchy. Ariosto is not presenting a radical new political ideal here; as he represents it in action, female power is as comic in its unnaturalness as Marganorre's power was horrible.

Rule by women first appears as a simile that offers evidence that women can be as lethally antimasculine as Marganorre is antifeminist if they are given political power. When the three knights first arrive in the female suburb, Ruggiero worries that they have arrived in an Amazonian land:

> Non più a Iason di maraviglia denno,
> né agli Argonauti che venian con lui,

---

16. Molinaro in his discussion of sin and punishment in the poem speaks of the episode as though it ended with the humiliation and suicide of Marganorre, whom he offers as "a good example of a man who suffers in equal measure the harm he inflicted on others" (42). Torture and suicide are clearly punishments of Marganorre, but to see woman rule as directed at him—a punishment in that it reverses his most deeply held beliefs—is to ignore the effect it will have on the entire society. Molinaro might well have extended his analysis to include the punishment of the male citizens.

17. Brand speaks of the establishment of female rule as an "echo" of the Amazonian episode (117), but goes on to speak of the Scots law episode as striking "a more explicitly profeminist note" (118); it is difficult to know how he takes female rule here as it was not treated positively in the earlier episode, but Brand suggests it is somehow profeminist here.

le donne che i mariti morir fenno
e i figli e i padri coi fratelli sui,
sì che per tutta l'isola di Lemno
di viril faccia non si vider dui;
che Ruggier quivi, e chi con Ruggier era
maraviglia ebbe all'alloggiar la sera.

(37.36)

[The women who made their husbands die and their sons and fathers with their brothers did not give more amazement to Jason and to the Argonauts who came with him, since on all the island of Lemnos one did not see two virile faces; than Ruggiero here, and those who were with Ruggiero felt amazement when they took lodging that evening.]

While this stanza purports merely to record the amazement Ruggiero and the others felt at seeing a community composed entirely of women, the evocation of the murder of husbands, sons, fathers, and brothers by the women of Lemnos and the singling out of Ruggiero as the primary person who feels amazed creates a sinister atmosphere. It is chilling, as the portrait of the land of the "donne omicide" was not, despite its name. The reference to the women of Lemnos introduces the memory that women can be ruthless in their treatment of men who have mistreated them.

Ruggiero has no need to fear in this case at this moment—the women welcome him along with the lady knights—but the image of a violent antimasculine society that runs through his mind becomes potentially appropriate at the end of the episode when women are in control of the town. His own beloved Bradamante and sister Marfisa interrupt the course of simple summary justice of a male lynch mob because "they had chosen to make him die of suffering, discomfort, and martyrdom." They bind Marganorre and put him in the hands of women so they can have their revenge, and then they establish a matriarchal government.

But these vengeful women are not the women of Lemnos, and the representation of their punishment of Marganorre makes the tyrant look foolish without making the women look very terrifying. By the end of the story we have moved from the grandiose and passionate world of Marganorre to a world of petty concerns and human limitations. Drusilla's old female servant drives the naked and handcuffed Marganorre with a cattle prod till he drips with blood, but she cannot continue hurting him because she is out of breath. The three ladies who were deprived of all clothing below the waist (now clothed in borrowed skirts) use feminine weapons; stones, nails, teeth, and needles can wound only superficially (stones thrown by their weak arms, that is), and their use against a man of gigantic stature like Marganorre is comic. They are signs of his great humiliation and reminders of the weakness of those whom Marganorre oppressed. This image is reinforced by the comparison of Marganorre's fall with the diminishment of the flow of a torrential river in summer when a child or even a woman can cross it; he, the great enemy of women, has been rendered as harmless as a summertime rivulet.

The image of the women flocking around Marganorre and attacking him is a comic allusion to the Bacchae, an example of violent antimasculine mob behavior. Castiglione uses the notion of the Bacchae as a delicate warning of the potential for extreme female reactions to misogyny when he represents Emilia Pia and the other ladies playfully attacking Gaspare Pallavicino in self-conscious imitation of their ancient sisters; instead of developing the comic action into a threat by supporting it with other aggressive actions or words on the part of the ladies, however, Castiglione replaces attack with defense. In the *Cortegiano*, the battle against misogyny is entirely in male hands, and men are safe from real attack from female weapons.

In the *Furioso*, the situation is different. The misogynist has not merely spoken against women like Gaspare, he has maimed, murdered, and exiled them. Mock-abuse and reason are not sufficient to bring him down. The real and effective violence of the two lady knights and their male companion is necessary to deprive him of political power, but the attack by the ladies is necessary precisely because it humbles him and reciprocates the pain he caused; it is a personal not a political action.[18] The violence is not very threatening, but the double echo of the attack by the Bacchae in myth and in the *Cortegiano* paired with the reference to the women of Lemnos at the beginning of the episode suggests that misogyny is dangerous to men because it stirs up hatred of men in women. This hatred can go out of control and become antimasculine frenzy if men do not accept the value of women.

In the land of Marganorre, the men do not reassert control, but Ariosto does through gentle mockery. As we have seen, the very stanzas that bring the Bacchae to mind are comic; so are those that describe the restoration of order in Marganorre's society and the institution of the law reversing the roles of the sexes. The comedy makes it hard to take the role reversal seriously. Although we do not actually see the women take control of the government we do

---

18. For the argument that the torment of Marganorre by the women is distasteful and a literary failure, see Negri (121–22).

descend to the level of "feminine" concerns.[19] Events that appeared tragic earlier in the episode, such as the loss of skirts and the exposure of the private parts of the ladies from Iceland, are now seen from a pragmatic point of view. After all, it could have been worse; they could have been killed:

> Gli è pur men che morir, mostrar le brutte
> e disoneste parti, duro e forte;
> e sempre questo e ogn'altro obbrobrio amorza
> il poter dir che le sia fatto a forza.
>
> (37.114)

[No matter how hard and painful it is to show one's ugly and shameless parts, it is less painful than dying; and being able to say that it was forced on oneself eradicates all opprobrium.]

Suddenly a situation that was intolerable has been reduced to manageable terms. Their very powerlessness is turned to their advantage, and they are free to worry about their reputations and the condition of their clothing. When Bradamante and Marfisa leave, these ladies stay behind to make themselves some new dresses; after all, they would not want to appear in court in the ordinary clothes they hastily put on for modesty's sake! To find the Narrator gently mocking his characters is a relief after the intensity of tone in the earlier part of the episode, but the mockery also suggests the weakness of the regime that Marfisa and Bradamante have instituted in place of Marganorre's.

The law itself that Marfisa and Bradamante devise is comic, especially in contrast to Marganorre's law, because it assumes that such an enormous change in social organization can be effected with a simple law and the threat that Marfisa will return and burn down the town if the townspeople should not obey. How the law will be enforced against wandering knights is not explained, and the description of the oath they must swear is ridiculous in comparison with the rigor and cruelty of Marganorre's treatment of foreigners.

Enrico Carrara, the author of the only extensive study of this episode, described the imposition of female rule as a joke.[20] Although Carrara does not explain how he knows that Ariosto has passed from pathetic to jest, nor why the martyrdom of the tyrant and the full victory of women are to be approved

---

19. The entire denouement brings to mind Pope's *Rape of the Lock*; the return to normal concerns has a flavor of mock-epic.

20. "E solo allora il poeta si permette di sorridere" (7) (only then does the poet allow himself to smile).

of but the matriarchy is not, nor why he is confident that Ariosto's audience would have smiled with the poet or even how broadly they would have smiled, his is an astute reading. To smile at something is not to take it seriously either as a possibility or a threat. Ariosto's representation of female rule is hard to take seriously because no woman within the society has shown any capacity or desire for rule. Through the use of comedy Ariosto has made female rule seem unrealistic and unthreatening. We have not witnessed the founding of another homicidal female kingdom.

This is not to say that Ariosto is writing as a misogynist, subverting the ostensible antimisogynist message of the episode, or even as a misanthropist, scorning both sexes equally; he is representing the dangers of the rule of passion and the dangers of giving exclusive power over one sex into the hands of the other. The episode shows him to be no more idealistically in favor of female government than he is blindly in favor of male government. To merely take the establishment of female rule at the end of this episode as a balance to the story of the destruction of female rule in the story of the "donne omicide" is not to take the episode seriously enough. Either Ariosto is advocating a complete reversal of the social order of his society—a revolutionary concept without support elsewhere in the *Furioso*—or he is expecting us to draw back from the new form of government that Marfisa and Bradamante establish as a radical destabilizing innovation that does not solve the initial problem faced by this society, which was unnatural relations between the sexes. He led us to laugh at female rule in the story of the "donne omicide" and to see it as unnatural; here he has led us to feel terror at Marganorre's "feminicide" and to smile at female rule. The balance is corrected in that male tyranny is shown to be worse than female, but the lesson of the episode of Marganorre is not simply that misogyny is cruel and irrational, but that all societies based on extreme relations between the sexes are unnatural.

That Bradamante as well as Marfisa establishes this law seems to give some validity to it.[21] After all, Marfisa is clearly never going to marry and has no conception of herself fulfilling any of the roles defined by even the most radical sixteenth-century theorists of womanhood; she might reasonably be thought of as favoring a reversal of the social order, although she showed no allegiance with her sex among the "donne omicide." Bradamante, on the other hand, has shown a clear understanding of the social implications of her military skill

21. Most critics speak of this law as Marfisa's law (Carrara 178), but Ariosto says the "guerriere" make the people swear (115) and set up the trophy and have the law written (119), although he seems to put Marfisa in charge of the operation (120), and he makes her the one who will actually enforce the law with an inspection visit (117).

and is a future wife. Her sponsorship of the law might mean it ought to be respected, but Ariosto does not develop Bradamante's commitment to the law or the terms of the law thoroughly enough to make her participation in its institution part of a feminist program on her part. When he wants to make Bradamante pronounce on topics from the defense tradition, he makes her voice loud and clear, as we saw at the "rocca di Tristano." Here she does not speak; I suggest that Ariosto, having provided no substantial profeminist arguments for the foundation of a matriarchy, is using the lady knights for comedy and not suggesting that the belief in female supremacy is deeply held by either woman.

Marriage and the Independent Woman: An Epic Role

Although Bradamante is not represented as politically radical, the characterization of her as an accomplished woman who is not extraordinary is essential to the triumph of epic over romance in the poem. The story of Marganorre belongs to the romance world, which is constantly disordered by love because sexual passion distracts men from duty and physical autonomy is used by women as a means of maintaining power over men; men become slaves to passion and women, and the social order maintained by the traditional sexual hierarchy is upset. But Bradamante's main role is in the epic world, which is successfully ordered by love because sexual passion is mutual and is directed toward the laudable social end of founding a dynasty.

The characterization of Ruggiero is important to the elevation of epic over romance, of course, but Bradamante holds the key because she demands a new kind of love and a new kind of marriage. She is neither the romance lady who is a goddess to the man who loves her, as are Ginevra and Angelica, nor a passive Lavinia, who is considered a piece of property to be fought over and not consulted.[22] She is an accomplished woman worthy of love and willing to give it, and she abjures power over her beloved and uses her abilities to seek a secondary role. Through her, Ariosto establishes the moral, physical, and intellectual equality of women as an essential premise of his poem; at the same

22. See Levi (passim) and Marinelli (107–9). Marinelli describes Bradamante and states that she is initiated into the world of a specific kind of love, the love that contemporary Neoplatonism denominated "amore umano, neither bestial nor angelic, but coasting between" (108).

time, however, he demonstrates the social and personal value of the traditional hierarchical relationship between the sexes and makes mutual love a major epic value as it never had been before.

Although the episodes added in 1532 reinforce the new role assigned to Bradamante, the essential features of the role were present in the 1516 edition. Ariosto makes Bradamante's crucial role clear early in the poem in the episode in Merlin's cave (canto 3) in which she is given a knowledge of her destiny and descendants that is like Aeneas's in Book 6 of the *Aeneid*. This scene shifts a large part of the epic burden onto Bradamante's shoulders, but she does not thereby become a masculine figure.[23] Her bearing throughout the adventure is appropriate to her sex as sixteenth-century writers defined it. She reacts to the news of her future importance with lowered lashes, humility, and girlish delight. At the end of her interview with Merlin and Melissa, Bradamante is instructed in a method to save Ruggiero, who is Atlante's prisoner. Although these instructions correspond to Anchises's description of Aeneas's own immediate future of waging war, Bradamante is not a leader. Her duty is to find Ruggiero and marry him; her responsibility to the future will be fulfilled by her bearing children.

Bradamante is moved and impressed by this display of her male offspring, but she is not entirely satisfied with her knowledge. She is curious about her female descendants, and in canto 13 she asks Melissa, the magician, to tell her whether any of her female descendants will be beautiful and virtuous ("metter si può tra belle e virtuose"). Melissa answers with a descriptive catalogue of Este daughters and wives, Isabella d'Este and her sister Beatrice, Ricciarda di Saluzzo, Eleanora d'Este, Lucrezia Borgia, and Renata of France, ladies whose virtue and accomplishments are praised frequently in the encomia of women written by Ariosto and his contemporaries.

In her eulogy Melissa establishes the importance of women in the history of the Este family but also distinguishes clearly between male and female roles. While men will excel at arms, women will be mothers . . . guardians and sturdy columns of illustrious houses ("madri . . . reparatrici e solide colonne di case illustri") and be noted for piety, generosity, prudence, and continence. The description of Isabella d'Este emphasizes that her appreciation of and encouragement of courtesy do not divert her from her primary duty: just because she lived chastely, Penelope was not less than Ulysses ("sol perché casta visse / Penelope, non fu minor d'Ulisse"). Lucrezia Borgia is handled in a

---

23. Fichter (89) speaks of the divided roles of Bradamante and Ruggiero at different phases of their careers. He is feminine at times and she masculine.

similar fashion. Her beauty, virtue, and honest fame make her outstanding, but her most special quality is her ability to instill in her children a sense of upright habits. As the moral instruction of their children is one of the major duties entrusted to women by Renaissance authors, this appreciation of Lucrezia, like the praise of Isabella, appeals specifically to a sixteenth-century sense of what a good woman ought to be. By means of the portraits of these Este ladies, Ariosto establishes as an accepted value within the poem the accomplished but domestic ideal developed by his contemporaries and firmly connects Bradamante with it.

The encomium of women that Ariosto added in 1532 is consonant with the values of this catalogue of Este women, but, as we have seen, it emphasizes the pairing of female accomplishments and fidelity rather than the natural biological ability to give birth. Bradamante fits both categories of women, but as she is developed in Ariosto's additions to the poem her accomplishments become more important. The "rocca di Tristano" and the story of Marganorre pose the problem of integrating the accomplished woman into society; the story of the combat for Bradamante's hand, introduced into the end of the poem in 1532, resolves the problem.

In the first edition of the poem Ruggiero and Bradamante wed without difficulty soon after he is baptized; in the third edition, they must overcome a series of obstacles. Toward the end of the poem Bradamante finds herself in a dilemma. She and Ruggiero have declared their love to each other; her brother Rinaldo has formally betrothed them; Bradamante has returned home expecting to marry Ruggiero immediately. She discovers, however, that her parents have planned a marriage between her and the son of the Greek emperor and expect her to be delighted at the prospect. This is an oddly concrete problem to find treated in a poem that thus far has dealt with the less everyday side of the lives of its heroes. The concern with money and social position seems to bring the episode closer to the values that govern the *novelle* told to Rinaldo than to those that rule in the body of the poem. Critics have been unanimous in identifying this section of the poem as *borghese* and have lamented its lack of poetic inspiration. Interested as he is in popular social forces at work in the poem, Piromalli can see little value in the "dramma economico borghese" and asserts that the "fire of imagination has not touched this section.[24] Momigliano calls canto 44 "one of the worst in the *Furioso*" (139). He believes that the

24. "Le prime crepe del Rinascimento cominciano ad apparire e anche artisticamente si avverte una stanchezza e una decadenza nel canto dell'amore contrastato dalla morale e dalle ambizioni dei genitori: il fuoco della fantasia non ha toccato le ultime vicende di Ruggero e Bradamante" (117).

parental opposition to Bradamante's marriage offered Ariosto an opportunity to avoid tired Petrarchism, which he sees as a flaw in almost the entire treatment of the love of Bradamante and Ruggiero, but that "the motif never comes to life" (140). In other words, Ariosto has not succeeded in turning his middle-class subject into poetry.

Certainly Piromalli's and Momigliano's sense that this last section of the poem is *borghese* is accurate, but their demand that Ariosto should have raised this material above its origins and infused it with high beauty or *fantasia* and a universal quality is inappropriate. The entire story of Bradamante and Ruggiero is *borghese*. The hero and heroine derive from romance and Boiardo to be sure, but the plot that Ariosto devised for them in his poem is derived from the *Aeneid* and serves the material purpose of celebrating the family of Ariosto's patron, a family recently enough risen to appreciate a dynastic epic.

Throughout the poem Bradamante has the aim of getting married and raising a family; to criticize her for this is to disregard her entire role in the poem. Momigliano complains that when Ariosto came to write the end of his story of Bradamante the candor, abandonment, and sympathy that inspired all his unfortunate heroines were exhausted.[25] It is true that in this scene and, indeed, until nearly the last stanzas of the poem Ariosto treats Bradamante with delicate humor and affection rather than with the "abbandono" that Momigliano desires, but it is also true that Bradamante is not one of the "eroine sfortunate." Her position in the poem is unique. All the other romantic heroines are helpless and only able to achieve their desires through clever manipulation of men (Angelica and Isabella) or dependence on men (Olimpia and Ginevra); as a result, the poet's protective sympathy at their distress (Angelica excepted, of course) is appropriate. Bradamante is a new kind of heroine; as we saw at the "rocca di Tristano," she manages to be feminine while being self-sufficient and the Narrator does not attempt to arouse pity for her even in a scene where she is threatened with separation from the man she loves.

Of all the love stories in the *Furioso* the story of Bradamante and Ruggiero is tied the most specifically to Renaissance concerns. We have already seen that Bradamante is repeatedly set in a sixteenth-century context; she is the legendary ancestor of ladies of Ariosto's own time, yet in herself has already achieved the ideal of womanhood that will be admired in Ariosto's society. The efficacy of this ideal is at stake in the final cantos of the poem. She is confronted with

25. "Si erano esauriti il candore, l'abbandono e la simpatia che sono la fonte ispiratrice di tutte le sue eroine sfortunate" (142).

the dilemma of how to behave obediently and still marry Ruggiero, the man of her love and her destiny.

Faced with a conflict between her own desires and her parents' will, Bradamante recognizes that she ought to be obedient ["so quanto, ahi lassa! debbo far, so quanto / di buona figlia al debito conviensi" (44.43.1–2)]. Bradamante's sense of the propriety of filial obedience has drawn criticism from those, like Rajna and Tomalin, who believe that her independent status as a knight should give her courage to defy her parents' wishes. To think of Bradamante as entirely independent is to misapprehend Ariosto's characterization of her: she is always portrayed as an accomplished woman with domestic goals. Unlike Marfisa, Bradamante is a woman first and then a knight, and, as we have seen, according to the most sophisticated sixteenth-century thinkers, she can only remain a good woman if she is obedient.

The way in which Ariosto resolves the dilemma he has created for his character is consistent with the ideal of womanhood he establishes in the catalogue of Este ladies. Bradamante cleverly discovers that she owes obedience not only to her parents but to her brother:

> S'io non sarò al mio padre ubbidiente,
> né alla mia madre, io sarò al mio fratello,
> che molto e molto è più di lor prudente,
> né gli ha la troppa età tolto il cervello.
>   (44.46.1–4)

[If I will not be obedient to my father nor to my mother, I will be so to my brother, who is much much more prudent than they are and also has not had his wits taken away by age.]

This speech is comic, certainly, but the comedy does not work against Rinaldo's authority; it makes the heroine look a bit silly and juvenile. Bradamante's trick of choosing to obey her brother is very revealing of her thoughts about herself. She does not consider going directly to Charlemagne. Instead, she finds a way to maintain the form of a traditional woman's behavior by appealing to the authority of a male member of her family. She, thus, conducts herself correctly according to the thought of Ariosto's time and the ideal the poet has created.

Only after her clever transfer of power over herself to her brother is Bradamante free to act to bring about the marriage. She does this by reminding Charlemagne that he is in her debt because of her military actions and then asking him a boon: that he not let her be given a husband who cannot beat her at arms. Bradamante's skill at arms is the quality that makes her unusual, accomplished. Here, she wants to use her accustomed independence to put herself under the authority of a husband. She knows that only Ruggiero can beat her; her cleverness is finally the quality that wins her what she wants; she has found a way to have her own desire and yet stay within the limits of obedience. The fact that Bradamante's plan does not work smoothly and nearly loses Ruggiero for her does not take away from the dignity and cleverness of her action, but it does reinforce Ruggiero's superiority to her; she would not have fought her best had she known Ruggiero was her opponent. Because she believes she is fighting Leone, Bradamante really does not want to be beaten; she fights as well as ever she has, and her loss to Ruggiero in disguise proves that his ability in arms really is superior to hers.

It is clear that Bradamante sees marriage as a transfer of authority over herself. When she is separated from Ruggiero and afraid that he thinks she will marry Leone, she assures him that he is the only one she loves in terms that emphasize her freely given obedience:

> A voi, Ruggier, tutto il dominio ho dato
> di me, che forse è più ch'altri non crede.
> So ben ch'a nuovo principe giurato
> non fu di questa mai la maggior fede.
> So che né al mondo il più sicuro stato
> di questo, re né imperator possiede.
> Non vi bisogna far fossa né torre,
> per dubbio ch'altri a voi lo venga a tòrre.
>
> (44.63)

[To you, Ruggiero, I have given all dominion over myself, which is perhaps more than others believe. I know well that no faith sworn to a new prince was ever greater than this. I know that in all the world neither king nor emperor possesses a more secure state than this. You do not need to dig a moat or build a tower, for fear that others will come to take it away.]

In the mouth of a woman of Bradamante's ability these are not empty metaphors. Without deprecating her own value, she speaks of her complete acceptance of Ruggiero's dominion over her.

The last scene of the poem shows Bradamante acting as wife for the first time. Before Ruggiero's final battle with Rodomonte, the Narrator surveys the crowd of spectators, noting briefly the anxiety of the ladies, the commoners, and the knights. His gaze settles on Bradamante, who also is worried despite her certainty that Ruggiero is stronger, braver, and more honorable than Rodomonte; she wishes that she could protect Ruggiero by taking his place:

> Oh quanto volentier sopra sé tolta
> l'impresa avria di quella pugna incerta,
> ancor che rimaner di vita sciolta
> per quella fosse stata più che certa!
> Avria eletto a morir più d'una volta,
> se può più d'una morte esser sofferta,
> più tosto che patir che 'l suo consorte
> se ponesse a pericol de la morte.
>
> Ma non sa ritrovar priego che vaglia,
> perché Ruggiero a lei l'impresa lassi.
> A riguardare adunque la battaglia
> con mesto viso e cor trepido stassi.
> (46.114–15.1–4)

[Oh how willingly she would have taken on herself the undertaking of that uncertain fight, even if remaining bereft of life would have been the certain result. She would have chosen to die more than once, if more than one death can be suffered, rather than suffer that her consort put himself at the risk of death.

But she does not know how to find a prayer that has the power to persuade Ruggiero to leave the undertaking to her. Thus, she stood watching the battle with a melancholy face and a trembling heart.]

These lines show Bradamante in the moment of transition from her old role of warrior and protector of the, at times, ineffectual Ruggiero to her new role of wife obedient to and in need of protection by her husband. At the same time that Bradamante wishes she could stand in for Ruggiero in the duel, she recognizes that her chances of success are nothing compared with his, and the military superiority he established in his duel with her is confirmed. She is thinking here like a noble lady about to watch her lover fight a duel; her offer to fight in Ruggiero's place is animated by a spirit of loving self-sacrifice rather than by a sense of her own martial abilities. Ruggiero's rejection of Bradamante's offer confirms his dominion over her. She approaches him from the position of an inferior begging a favor, "non sa ritrovar priego che vaglia"; he has the authority to reject her plea and to expect her obedience.

In our last glimpse of Bradamante in the poem, she has lost all traces of her military character and is animated solely by love.

> Non fu in terra sì tosto, che risorse,
> via più che d'ira, di vergogna pieno;
> però che a Bradamante gli occhi torse,
> e turbar vide il bel viso sereno.
> Ella al cader di lui rimase in forse,
> e fu la vita sua per venir meno.
> Ruggiero ad emendar presto quell'onta,
> stringe la spada, e col pagan s'affronta.
>   (46.125)

[He was no sooner on the ground than he rose, stimulated more by shame than by wrath; because he turned his eyes to Bradamante, and saw her beautiful, serene face troubled. At his fall she was in doubt and was about to faint. Ruggiero to amend that shame quickly, gripped his sword, and confronted the pagan.]

This could be a description of Fiordiligi or Isabella, so beautiful, so inspirational, so passive has Bradamante become.

It is tempting to feel disappointment in Bradamante's withdrawal from action, but to do so is to misapprehend the quality of her excellence and ambition. Bradamante's inaction in these final scenes is justified by Ariosto's presentation of her throughout the poem. As we have seen, he consistently considers her talent subordinate to her goal, and her attitude toward womanhood is reinforced by rhetorical praise of women whose primary virtues are chastity, piety, and dedication to family. Because her desire always was to marry Ruggiero and her military exploits were incidental to her domestic goal, Bradamante's submission to her husband is not a humiliation. Like the ideal lady of the controversy about women, she freely chooses not to be independent.

6

THE NEW IDEAL IN ENGLAND:
THOMAS MORE, JUAN LUIS VIVES,
AND RICHARD HYRDE

In England, as in Italy, interest in the defense of womankind was stimulated by humanist educational theory and the practical results of that theory. In the first quarter of the sixteenth century, Thomas More formulated his ideas about education and put them into practice in his household, which consisted mainly of girls. More had great respect for women's intelligence and encouraged his children's tutor not to differentiate between them on the basis of sex. The results of his efforts with his daughters and wards were so impressive that many of his contemporaries who followed his example and educated their daughters cited his success as justification for their enterprise, and the names of the young women who were educated under his auspices became a fixed part of lists of famous women not only in England, but abroad.

That the accomplishments of these women could be so universally celebrated in an age in which the education of women caused deep anxieties was due to two factors. First, More believed that the goal of education for both sexes was spiritual rather than political; this meant that his learned daughters and wards appeared to conform to woman's traditional private role. Second, More himself did not publish his theories, and *The Instruction of a Christen Woman* by Juan Luis Vives, whose publications on women's education have been assumed to speak for More, restricted the curriculum for girls and emphasized repressive external social codes rather than More's internal spiritual codes. Unfortunately for More's modern reputation, the distinction between More and Vives that I am arguing here is not generally accepted; More usually is credited with the creation of a repressive model of female education.[1] It is my purpose to attempt

---

1. For the grouping of More and Vives together or the implied responsibility of More for a restrictive theory of education, see Wayne (19), A. R. Jones (299), and Hannay (9). Gloria Kaufman is an

to restore More's image. He was a profeminist educator who gave his female students spiritual and ethical autonomy, which the hierarchy of marriage did not require them to sacrifice or compromise. More was an anomaly among Renaissance educators because he did not place woman in a dilemma.

Although he did not publish theoretical writings on education, More's thought about the education of women is available in his Latin epigram on choosing a wife (published 1516) and in his private correspondence with William Gonell, one of the tutors he employed for his children (1518?), and with his children and the other young people living in his household (1517–23). In all of these works More pits the private world of the learned woman against society rather than praising her for conformity to society's values. He praises education for providing her with spiritual and moral autonomy, that is, the ability to know what is right, rather than with the reinforcement of the outward form of chastity; indeed, he never speaks of chastity. Through More's system of education a woman achieves a capacity for moral judgment and is freed from the bondage to male authority that characterizes woman's role in conventional marriage.

The letters and epigram are complementary to each other, the letters providing the personal and philosophical background for the public and formally polished epigram. Both genres idealize domestic life in opposition to public life, but they offer different points of view on the benefits of domestic life adapted in part to the sexes to which they speak. The epigram is designed to persuade a public male audience of the comforts of domestic life with an educated woman. It is written entirely from a male point of view and does not consider what marriage means to women. The letters are designed to persuade a private female audience and its tutor that women can live a satisfying intellectual life within the bounds of Christian humility. They directly address the educated woman's desire for fame and influence, and they acknowledge and attempt to resolve the dilemma of the intellectually independent woman who must restrict her activities to the home. Both the epigram and the letters reveal More's conviction that the primary purpose of the education of women is to improve their spiritual lives; that is, education is of great benefit to women themselves because it gives them an invaluable tool for achieving greater closeness to God. The epigram, however, focuses on the assistance that this closeness enables a woman to give her husband, while the letters focus on the

---

exception. She asserts, "if we compare Vives with his humanist colleagues—Erasmus, More, or Clements—he seems at best a middle-of-the-roader and at worst an antifeminist" (896). Unfortunately, she does not develop the comparison with More, Erasmus, or Clements beyond referring to Clements's respect for his wife's knowledge of Greek.

direct personal benefit of this closeness to the woman involved; her education provides her with spiritual autonomy within a society that provides her with no social autonomy.

The Latin epigram was the only description of More's female ideal available to the public in his lifetime in published form. In it he gives extraordinary prominence to the role of education in making good wives and to the value of female eloquence. As is typical of texts advising men on choosing a wife, More lists for his reader the qualities to be desired in her. After citing such conventional elements as a mother of excellent character, a modest but not severe countenance, a restrained demeanor, and virtue ("virtutis inclytae"), More completes the list with two items that make this future wife a product of the humanist imagination.[2] She must be neither too talkative nor too silent ("Proculque stulta sit / Paruis labellulis / Semper loquacitas, / Proculque rusticum / Semper silentium"), and she must be "either educated or capable of being educated" ("Instructa literis / Vel talis ut modo / Sit apta literis").[3] Much of the poem is devoted to an evocation of the pleasures of life with a learned woman and to praise of exemplary eloquent women.

With his assertion that there is a kind of female speech that lies between pointless garrulousness and boorish silence More challenges the reader to radically revise his notion of a wife. Traditional thought relegates woman to silence in marriage on the grounds that her speech is naturally bad. It indicates her foolishness and her rebellion against her husband's rightful authority whereas her silence indicates her sensible acquiescence to her husband's superior judgment. More undermines this theory by describing the silence as "rusticum silentium," a silence of ill-grace and ignorance, not obedience, that may even indicate that rebellion is fomenting under the silence and that woman as traditionally defined does not respect her husband's authority whether she openly violates it or secretly fumes. Rather than blame this problem on the nature of womankind, More suggests a remedy: education. The

2. "Virtue" is a pivotal term between the traditional virtues and the humanist ones. See Khanna, who argues that "the standard translation of 'chastity' is misleading here . . . because it does not include the intellectual, moral, and rhetorical strengths of the woman so important to More's description" (83). Bradner and Lynch seem to have taken her point because they translate *virtutis* as "virtue" in the Yale edition rather than as "chastity" as they did in the 1953 Chicago edition. Citations of the translation of More's epigram are to Bradner and Lynch's Yale edition unless noted otherwise.

3. I use Khanna's translation here rather than Bradner and Lynch's "Let her be either just finishing her education or ready to begin it immediately." By speaking of "finishing her education," this latter translation suggests that there is a limit to how educated a woman should be and that a woman's education might reasonably be expected to stop with marriage. We will see that More thought of Margaret's education as continuing long after her marriage.

wife described by More is freed to speak her understanding based on her education; indeed, she is chosen on the promise that she shows of being able to do so.

Learning and the ability to speak give the wife intellectual autonomy and authority within her marriage. Because of her education, the wife's company provides for the husband not only a retreat from the cares of the world, as the company of any wife might, but a solution to those cares through the husband's submission to her wise perspective on them.

> Quibus coherceat
> Si quando te leuet
> Inane gaudium,
> Quibus leuauerit,
> Siquando deprimat
> Te moeor anxius,
> Certabit in quibus
> Summa eloquentia
> Iam cum omnium gravi
> Rerum scientia.
> (lines 138–55)

[By her comments she would restrain you if ever vain success should exalt you and would comfort you if grievous sorrow should cast you down. When she speaks, it will be difficult to choose between her perfect power of expression and her thoughtful understanding of all kinds of affairs. (189)]

The key element in this description of life with a learned wife is the power of her wise speech. Female eloquence, which was potentially so dangerous a skill that many humanists argued for the need to prevent its acquisition, here is presented entirely positively. The wife's intellectual autonomy, which she gains through her education, and her willingness to use her wisdom to relieve her husband's cares are the essential elements of this idealized domestic life.

The wife's eloquence is not restricted to solace of her husband. More gives four examples of ancient eloquent women; two of them, Tulia (the daughter of Cicero) and Ovid's daughter, demonstrated literary eloquence; one, Cornelia, the mother of the two Gracchi, used her persuasive speech to educate her sons; and one, the wife of Orpheus, must have been eloquent because such a poet would not have married her had she not been so.[4] Although these women are still closely tied to their families, as their designation by relationship to a male relative indicates, the eloquence of at least two of them is said to have been appreciated by the public. This suggests that the educated woman's literary activity is not a threat to domestic harmony; rather, it is an occasion for pride on the part of her husband or father. The educated woman can be seen as a part of normal society, and she is not a threat to domestic and social order.

Feminist scholars have repeatedly noted the importance of eloquence in the humanist curriculum and the significant omission of the subject or even the explicit exclusion of it from girls' curricula, even when other items demand great sophistication.[5] Without public speech, learning remains personal and private; with it, the educated person has access to power. More seems to be advocating an intermediate kind of speech by means of these women. They are all sheltered from the view of the world by the names of their husbands or fathers, and they do not achieve prominence and power in the world by means of their speech, yet they do not all only use their speech for the benefit of their families.

More's fifth example of an eloquent woman goes beyond the domestic realm. More introduces the trope of encomium of the women of his own days, familiar from Italian humanist defenses of women and collections of biographies, but unlike the Italians, who praise their own age for producing so many accomplished women, More stresses that his age has managed to produce only a single woman worthy to be matched with his ancient examples. In this woman the poet offers his male reader a vision of a nation and world transformed by female eloquence.

> Utcunque ruticum,
> unam tamen tenet
> Nostrumque uirginem,
> Tenet, sed unicam,
> At sic ut unicam
> Plerisque praeferat,
> Cuique conferat
> Ex hijs, fuisse, quae

4. In his epigram on the coronation of Henry VIII (no. 19) More compares Queen Catherine with Cornelia, saying, "Eloquio facunda cui Cornelia cedat" ("the well-spoken Cornelia would yield to her in eloquence") (line 170).

5. See the discussion of Bruni in Chapter 2.

> Narrantur omnibus
> Tot retro seculis,
> Quae nunc et ultimam
> Monet Britanniam
> Perlata pennulis
> Famae uolucribus,
> Laus atque gloria
> Orbis puellula
> Totius unica,
> Ac modo suae
> Cassandra patriae.
>   (lines 182–200)

[After all our age, however rude it may be, does have one maiden, though it has only one, whom it may set above almost all others and compare with any of those women whose stories come down to us from ages past. Borne high upon the soaring wings of fame, she now gives warning even to remotest Britain, the one and only boast and glory of the whole world, not merely the Cassandra of her own country. (191)]

More creates a prophetic tone in this passage by contrasting the humbleness of his age with the glory of the woman and by portraying her as warning or teaching not just her own nation but the world. The identity of this woman is a mystery and, thus, the interpretation of the passage is problematic; by celebrating the geographical extent of her fame, More makes her seem the equal of the ancient women whose fame has triumphed over time, and, by speaking of her as a Cassandra admonishing the world, he makes her move in grander circles than the domestic ones to which the references to fathers, husbands, and children limited the ancient women.[6]

Whatever the historical reference, the prophetic vision makes explicit a monitory theme that has been running tacitly through the epigram: the learned

6. More's emphasis on the uniqueness of the woman (he refers to it three times) makes it seem that he is making a veiled encomiastic reference to a particular woman. Critics have generally assumed that the lady is of high birth (374, note to lines 183–200) and have suggested Princess Margaret and Princess Mary, sisters of Henry VIII, and Catherine of Aragon. For a discussion of the claims of these candidates, see the above-cited note. Warning or teaching of a nation does not necessarily come from a queen, however, and I suggest that More's own daughter Margaret may be intended by these lines. Although at the date the poem was published (1515 or 1516) she was only ten or eleven and did not yet have an international reputation and was not yet a teacher of "right principles," praise of his daughter in such terms would be in keeping in the context of this list of famous women in which Ovid and Cicero are cited as proud and loving fathers.

woman can be of benefit to society only if men recognize the value of her eloquence and employ her. The most significant fact about Cassandra is not that she prophesied doom, but that she attempted to teach and no one listened. In a poem about the need to change one's opinion of women and give them voice, Cassandra is a perfect example of silenced female eloquence: she was wise; she spoke the truth, and no one listened. Contrary to the usual feminist reading of him as a conspirator in the effort to silence women, in this epigram More consistently praises the efficacy of female speech in the home, in literary works, and even, in an extraordinary case, in the political realm.

More's letters on education deal with the practical problems of enabling women to speak wisely and discovering appropriate occasions for their speech. Two major themes run through all of them: the ability of education to create in the student an understanding of virtue that enables the student to judge right and wrong independently of society and the necessity for the learned person to hold himself or herself aloof from the opinion of society in order to be free to act in accord with conscience. More is, thus, not in the tradition of humanist educators like Bruni and Vergerius, who conceive of education as a provider of wise men trained in history, philosophy, rhetoric, and oratory who can apply their knowledge to the affairs of state, but rather in the more abstract moral tradition of Pico della Mirandola in his "Oration on the Dignity of Man."[7] Like Pico, More asserts mankind's need for education to exploit its full potential and raise it from the level of beasts; he focuses attention on the importance of the individual soul and of the individual's relationship with God, and he teaches disdain of the world's opinion. More applies this teaching specifically to girls as no Englishman had done before him; in doing so he makes Englishwomen part of the Renaissance.

In the letter to Gonell (63), his most extended statement of his educational philosophy, More defends the practice of educating women. He states his belief "that the harvest is [not] much affected whether it is a man or a woman who does the sowing. They both have the name of human being whose nature reason differentiates from that of beasts; both, I say, are equally suited for the knowledge of learning by which reason is cultivated" (105). In order to show its irrelevance to his line of argument, More admits as a hypothesis the misogynist thesis that "the soil of a woman be naturally bad" [Quod si muliebre solum suapte sit natura malignum et filicum quam frugum feracius (quo dicto

---

7. See, for example, Vergerius's *De Ingenuis Moribus* in Gundersheimer (1965); he praises the virtues of oratory and eloquence and says that fame is an appropriate goal for the student. More translated Giovanni Pico della Mirandola's life of his uncle and a few of Pico's letters.

multi faeminas deterrent a literis) (122)] and reasons that if it were true (though it is not), it would justify the education of women because if women are inferior to men, then they need education more than men do to make up for their natural defect.[8] With this statement, he frees his argument for the education of women from the necessity of proving that women are men's equals: education has a role in the formation of character no matter how weak the material with which the teacher must work. As More's aim in this letter is not to defend women but to defend the education of women and to direct that education to virtuous ends, this is a masterful strategy, but it has led some readers, who have not noted the use of the subjunctive, to the mistaken conclusion that he had a low opinion of women's intelligence.[9]

More presents the humanist defense of learning for women within the context of a discussion of his daughters' relation to society. He sees their sex as posing a special problem because people are unused to learned women and will watch for their mistakes in conduct as an excuse for attacking the concept of educating women. He suggests that they deal with this problem by turning their attention away from society to the true goal of education, a goal that applies to both sexes.

> Though I prefer learning joined with virtue to all the treasures of kings, yet renown for learning, if you take away moral probity, brings nothing else but notorious and noteworthy infamy, especially in a woman. Since erudition in women is a new thing and a reproach to the sloth of men, many will gladly assail it, and impute to learning what is really the fault of nature, thinking from the vices of the learned to get their own ignorance esteemed as virtue. On the other hand, if a woman (and this I desire and hope with you as their teacher for all my daughters) to eminent virtue of mind should add even moderate skill in learning, I

8. This argument resembles that made by Plato in the *Laws*. "He argues that because the woman's 'natural' potential for virtue is inferior to a man's she's a greater danger to social harmony than he. . . . She must not be left to her own devices or the state may lose control." To deal with this problem, he "would educate women 'in precisely the same way' as men for otherwise they will lack that common purpose without which the state is doomed to be but half a state." Elshtain (36), quoting the *Laws* (262–63). Although More dissociates himself from the antifeminism of this position and from Plato's obliteration of the distinction between ethics, economics, and politics, he gathers in Platonists with this strategy.

9. See, for example, Beilin, who quotes the passage and then argues, "With the consciousness that her education must begin by correcting her inherent defects, a woman like Margaret Roper had a kind of double original sin to redeem. Not only was she the daughter of Eve, but her mind was 'naturally bad' " (22). Similarly, in paraphrasing the letter, Richard Marius says, "even if a woman's brain is inferior to man's—as More clearly supposes" (223).

think she will gain more real good than if she obtain the riches of Croesus and the beauty of Helen. Not because that learning will be a glory to her, . . . but because the reward of wisdom . . . depends on the inner knowledge of what is right, not on the talk of men, than which nothing is more foolish or mischievous. (103–4)

This passage has three essential premises: that fame is not important, that the purpose of learning is to develop "the inner knowledge of what is right," and that women have the capacity to achieve this wisdom and make independent ethical decisions.

The ability to judge right from wrong is the key to all Renaissance defenses of women, as we saw consistently in Bruni, Goggio, Strozzi, and Capella, because it frees women to be responsible for their own morals rather than committing them to following male strictures on their conduct. This freedom may not result in any change in behavior—the moral code has not been changed, just woman's ability to rationally understand it—but the location of the code has been moved from outside to inside, and women have been made morally responsible members of society. Although the result of this judgment is virtue, More does not subject this virtue to public scrutiny or value it for its usefulness to society (as, for example, a guarantee of the legitimacy of heirs); he emphasizes its value to the person who practices it. Society is represented entirely negatively here: it assigns infamy; it envies; it is foolish and mischievous. Freedom from exposure to its opinion is a blessing to be desired.

Although this advice may seem to be the clever means of reconciling learned women to their domestic isolation and consequent powerlessness, it is not.[10] In the letter to Gonell, More goes on to generalize from the particularly sensitive situation of learned women to the case of learned men and asserts that they, too, do well to stay out of the public eye. Though they have less to fear in the way of infamy, they also stand to lose if they seek fame because the goal of education is identical for both sexes. More counsels Gonell to lead his students (including More's son, John)

> to put virtue in the first place among goods, learning in the second; and in their studies to esteem most whatever may teach them piety towards God, charity to all, and modesty and Christian humility in themselves. By such means they will receive from God the reward of an innocent life, and in the assured expectation of it will view death

10. For the contrary opinion, see Wayne, A. R. Jones, and Hannay.

without dread, and meanwhile possessing solid joy will neither be puffed up by the empty praise of men, nor dejected by evil tongues. These I consider the real and genuine fruits of learning, and though I admit that all literary men do not possess them, I would maintain that those who give themselves to study with such intent will easily attain their end and become perfect. (105)

More's definition of the benefits of education in this passage is the same twofold one we saw above: humanistic studies encourage spiritual growth and independent self-respect. Conspicuously absent from this definition is the Italian humanist notion of education as the shaper of civic leaders through its instilling of classical virtues (justice, fortitude, etc.); More's learned person is not a citizen in the secular state, but in the kingdom of God. There is a suggestion of retirement from the world in the virtues that are learned (piety, charity, modesty, humility) and in the ability the scholar acquires to scorn the opinion of the world.[11] Women would seem to be specially privileged in this scheme because their lives are customarily domestic and therefore solitary, whereas men have to decide to avoid public life and seek solitude. Qualities of women's life that usually demand apology and justification from their defenders who wish to maintain the traditional structure of society need no apology from More; they are assets, not liabilities. Women are in an enviable position.

The contempt for the world that is evident in both these passages is symptomatic of an attitude that runs through many of More's works, an attitude that More's biographers see as crucial to an understanding of the man, yet the motivation of which is disputed. Stephen Greenblatt in *Renaissance Self-Fashioning* identified in More "a lifelong current of contempt for a world reduced in his mind to madness, a rejection not only of all the pride, cruelty, and ambition of men, but of much that he himself seemed to cherish, a desire to escape into the fastness of a cell" (16). This psychologically formulated interpretation of More's withdrawal from the world represents More as in unhealthy retreat from his own passionate engagement in the world to an empty place where such engagement is impossible. The cell protects More from the side of himself that is attracted to the world. Although Greenblatt is

---

11. The stress on the spiritual benefits of education is typical of More's pronouncements on education; it is not peculiar to contexts in which the main topic is female education. He defends the study of Greek and all the liberal arts in his letter to the University of Oxford (no. 60) on the grounds that they are essential to the study of theology and that they "train the soul in virtue" (98).

discussing a statement More made in the tower in which he transformed his prison cell into a monastic cell, and in which the word "cell," therefore, suggests religious retreat, Greenblatt's use of it suggests nothing positive.[12] He sees the cell as the bleak setting for communion with self rather than as a place filled with the life of communion with God. In Greenblatt's terms, More's willing sacrifice of aspects of life that he cherished is folly because there is nothing genuinely desirable or positive about the alternative. Retreat is a negative and selfish gesture.

The letter to Gonell, written early in More's political life, suggests a very different interpretation of the cell. It represents the retreat for which More already longed as a place of liberty. It shows More's intense idealization of the life removed from political concerns; rather than the bleak and empty fastness of a prison cell, secure only because of the absence of temptations. The retreat in this letter is filled by the joy of the scholar's relationship with God. For More, as for a religious, retreat is a positive gesture that has nothing to do with selfish self-fulfillment.[13] More does not speak of a place of exclusion of the entire world, but rather of a way of life that permits its practitioner to live untrammeled by society's opinion and undistracted by its demands.

More's association of women with private life has left him open to inclusion in the general feminist critique of humanist educators begun by Joan Kelly, who argued that "the bourgeois writings on education, domestic life, and society constitute the extreme in this denial of women's independence. Suffice it to say that they sharply distinguish an inferior domestic realm of women from the superior public realm of men" (21). Valerie Wayne, for example, asserts that More's and other humanists' "emphasis upon ethical conduct for women could, however, easily become yet another means of restricting their behavior and intellectual growth. As humanists defended women, they also prescribed specific roles for them, especially domestic roles, and they identified a limited function for their learning" (19). In this view, virtues do not exist in any Platonic or Christian sense, but are created merely for the cynical purposes of those who hold the power in society, in this case, those interested in patrilineal descent and male social dominance. According to such a reading, ethics is merely a cover for politics and the fact that women seek a private

12. See More, *Selected Letters* (239), for the full context of the passage Greenblatt quotes on page 16.

13. It is, of course, possible to take a psychological approach and assert that all desire for religious retreat arises from personal anxieties, if one denies the existence of God and the reality of attraction to him.

audience and choose to write spiritual works is regrettable because such a choice leaves them without power in the world.[14]

By contrast, I suggest that More's acceptance of the conventional exclusion of women from public roles and positions of power is not a sign of oppression. Unlike the Italian humanists, who had to find a way to justify the exclusion of educated women from power after having argued that they had the moral capacity to benefit from a system of education whose goal was the right exercise of authority, More could uphold the conventional order of society with no taint of hypocrisy. Whatever modern attitudes may be about the value of public life and whatever his own importance in the public life of his time, More clearly thought that the spiritual life was superior. Given this attitude, to give women access to public roles would be to condemn them to morally ambiguous lives, to exile them from the demiparadise of the cell.

More's acceptance of a private role for woman frees her from the dilemma in which Italian humanists placed her. Unlike the educated Italian woman, who is put into the position of abdicating authority, which is intensely desirable, in the interests of social peace, More's woman is at liberty to pursue moral and spiritual perfection. Because of More's emphasis on spirituality for both sexes, the male student is put in a position similar to that occupied by woman in Italian works on women. He must give up a mode of life that he would prefer if he were free of social obligations. The Italian woman must give up a public role because her family commitments require it; the man who followed More's teaching would have to give up a private role because his family commitments required it. Inasmuch as the feminine role offers the freedom to be excluded from public responsibility, it seems possible to go so far as to say that More's letters to his family betray an envy of the female role. The woman who follows More's teaching is free to practice what More preaches.

More's letters to the members of his school, especially to Margaret, test the persuasive power of the notion that retreat from the world offers opportunities for the cultivation of virtue which make the retired life superior to the public life. He has educated his daughter and knows that she has the intellectual capacity to compete in the male world, yet he does not encourage her to look to the public for approval or to challenge the conventional public social order in any way. Judith P. Jones and Sherianne Sellers Seibel, in "Thomas More's Feminism: To Reform or Re-Form," describe More's approach in these letters as "traditional in emphasizing the importance of female obedience and virtue"

14. The notion of More's educational theory as restrictive of women's intellectual growth is widespread, and he frequently is blamed by implication in discussions of his daughter Margaret's works. See Hannay (9). Elaine Beilin is an exception. She suggests that More was not the only influence on his daughter Margaret's sense of herself as a writer (4).

and modern in their assertion of "the rational nature of humanity as a source of human salvation and perfection" (69). Although the letter to Gonell reveals that obedience and virtue are not restricted to females and that they are not opposed to the rational nature of man, it is true that More entirely accepts the traditional restriction of a woman's life to her home, although the quality of life that he prescribes for the home is untraditional in the extreme.

More repeatedly recognizes that Margaret may wish for fame but be deprived of it by society's prejudices against women, and he offers her two kinds of consolation: testimony that she does, in fact, have a good reputation for scholarship and praise of the unlimited opportunities for spiritual perfection that her restricted life offers.[15] We have Margaret's work and, thus, can see that she seriously aimed for spiritual perfection. We do not have Margaret's letters and, thus, can only rely on More's praise of Margaret's attitude as evidence that he succeeded in consoling her for her lack of a public connection with the scholarly world. More's advice to Margaret speaks of disappointment in the rewards that this world gives for hard work and directs her to look inside herself for satisfaction. The fastness of the cell seems to be one's own well-developed conscience, which is given the opportunity to operate freely in the fastness of the home (128).

> Something I said to you in joke came back to my mind, and I realized how true it was. It was to the effect that you were to be pitied, because the incredulity of men would rob you of the praise you so richly deserved for your laborious vigils, as they would never believe, when they read what you had written, that you had not often availed yourself of another's help: whereas of all the writers you least deserved to be thus suspected. Even when a tiny child you could never endure to be decked out in another's finery. But, my sweetest Margaret, you are all the more deserving of praise on this account. Although you cannot hope for an adequate reward for your labor, yet nevertheless you continue to unite to your singular love of virtue the pursuit of literature and art. Content with the profit and pleasure of your conscience, in your modesty you do

15. He twice sends her news that prestigious aquaintances have expressed incredulity upon being told that certain elegantly written letters are her compositions (no. 108, no. 128), and he once (no. 106) teases her by saying that the honor of her sex would have led him to excuse any inelegance of style but that she did not need to have such excuses made for her because her letters "have so little cause for you to dread the indulgent judgment of a parent, that you might have despised the censorship of an angry Momus" (148). His friends' astonishment and his own praise of her as superior in skill to most of her sex is flattering to her personally because her work has been mistaken for a man's and thus reaches the highest standards, but it is also discouraging because it reveals the low opinion in which women were held even by learned men.

not seek for the praise of the public, nor value it overmuch even if you receive it, but because of the great love you bear us, you regard us— your husband and myself—as a sufficiently large circle of readers for all that you write. (155)

The reference to Margaret's dislike of borrowed finery gives a strong impression of her as an independent girl determined to define herself and desirous of recognition in her own right. That More offers Margaret consolation for not receiving praise for her work confirms that she desired such praise; that More offers consolation rather than reproach for her desire suggests that More could sympathize with such a desire.[16] Yet, despite his sympathy, More does not suggest that reform of the world's opinion of women is possible or even desirable; he teaches his daughter contempt for the world's opinion and redirects her attention to her conscience, the seat of moral virtue where learning will benefit her directly. Isolation from the world brings freedom.

More imagines Margaret living her intellectual life in harmony with her domestic life. In a letter to her after her marriage (no. 106), More advises Margaret to

devote the rest of your life to medical science and sacred literature, so that you may be well furnished for the whole scope of human life . . . yet I am of the opinion that you may with great advantage give some years of your yet flourishing youth to humane letters and so-called liberal studies. . . . I need not say that by such studies a good judgment is formed or perfected. (149)

That More expects his daughter to continue her education after marriage and to practice a profession shows that he did not just consider education of girls as a preparation for marriage, a more sophisticated version of the moral education any girl ought to be given. Margaret exists for him as an independent person, not merely as a woman defined by her social relationships.

Later in the letter, More makes it clear that he conceives of her mind as free from her obligation to obey her husband. "I am ever wont to persuade you to

16. Margaret Hannay reads Margaret More's family audience and production of religious works as a restriction imposed by the men of her family (it would seem). She speaks of women being "forced out of original discourse and into translation" and states that "when their work was published, it was often anonymous; if it was known to be by a woman, it was usually restricted to manuscripts in the family circle, as was most of the work of Margaret Roper More" (9). I suggest that More's correspondence with Margaret offers a corrective to this view.

yield in everything to your husband; now, on the contrary, I give you full leave to strive to surpass him in the knowledge of the celestial system" (149). Although this passage is written lightly, the meaning for Margaret's intellectual development is quite serious. Just as men and women are rational creatures "equally suited for the knowledge of learning by which reason is cultivated" (no. 63), yet not equally suited for public life, so a wife is her husband's intellectual equal but his social inferior.

More's strong attachment to his family and his frequent expressions of regret at his absence from them (no. 106, for example) suggest that he would like to center the male role in domestic life too, although he sometimes reveals that withdrawal from public life into his domestic life would cause him great distress. Early in his correspondence with his children, he admonishes Margaret to report to him about the progress all the children are making in their studies because "rather than allow my children to be idle and slothful, I would make a sacrifice of wealth, and bid adieu to other cares and business to attend to my children and my family" (no. 69). Just as in his famous crisis More was torn between duty to his sovereign and to his God and His church, More here is torn between the duties and rewards of the office he has accepted and his domestic responsibilities.[17] Just as he advises Margaret to submit to her husband, he must submit to his sovereign. In each case the individual must submit to authority but is authorized to retain an inner freedom; Margaret is free "to surpass [her husband] in knowledge of the celestial system," and More retains his silence, a feminine virtue.

More's emphasis is not on the social value of virtues such as chastity, but on their value to the individual who gains spiritual autonomy through education, no matter what his or her position in society may be. While he does not deny the (masculine) power of the state, he is not writing in the service of oppression. Rather, he sees woman's life as offering an avenue of escape from the oppression of the state, and he perceives himself as liberating women by restricting their scope to their family and their subject matter to spirituality. He sees private female discourse as superior to male public discourse and envies women their opportunity to withdraw from the world.

17. It seems that when More was free to be home with his family he felt held down by his duty to go over the accounts and chat with his children and his wife. Activities that looked like pleasures to him from a distance seem to have become drudgery and impediments to study when he had the opportunity to do them. "When I have returned home, I must talk with my wife, chat with my children and confer with my servants. All this activity I count as business when it must be done—and it must be unless you want to be a stranger in your own home." Letter to Peter Giles in *Utopia* (4).

Positive and liberating as the place of woman is in More's own system, his acceptance of the traditional exclusion of women from public life and political action allowed those who came after him, especially Vives, to devise a very conservative program of female education while appearing to base it on the rock of More's example.[18] *The Instruction of a Christen Woman* (Latin, 1523; first English translation, 1529) is a book of rules for conduct in which education is conceived of entirely as the teaching of moral precepts that will lead to conduct beneficial to society. Vives was what I hope I have shown that More was not: a restrictor and a repressor whose insistence on the primacy of the single virtue of chastity created a very narrow field of activity for women.

A startling example of Vives's rewriting of More can be seen in Vives's statement of what he finds praiseworthy about More's choice to educate his daughters; he was "not content only to haue them good and very chast, wold also they shuld be well lerned, supposynge that by that meane they shuld be more truly and surely chast" (8r).[19] For More, learning opens up the spiritual world to women; for Vives, learning is a means of more securely ("surely") achieving the socially useful end of preserving a woman's chastity. In *The Instruction*, education of women serves the purposes of the male political authority that it subverts when imagined by More.

Yet, the notion of an independent woman exists in Vives's book, despite Vives. The *Instruction* appears decided on a narrow and negative definition of woman, but the method of presentation does not successfully repress the more positive notion of woman that is present in many of the examples used and that is implied by the simple act of including elements of a liberal education in a book that is essentially a conduct book.[20] Vives's subject was more powerful than he. The presence of the independent woman in the text may account for

18. The mere fact that he advocated education for women established Vives as a profeminist among historians for many years. Utley called it "a landmark in the history of woman's liberal education" (69). Robert P. Adams, *The Better Part of Valor*, chapter 13, passim (especially 226), assumes that Vives can be classed with More as a profeminist simply because he favored the education of women and rejected the erotic representation of women in romance. Recently a number of excellent reappraisals of Vives's thought have appeared. See Kaufman and Wayne.

19. Citations to Vives's *Instruction* are to the 1541 edition. The preface has no page numbers and is cited by signature.

20. In her excellent analysis of Vives's thought, Gloria Kaufman anticipated me in my feeling that Vives's work pulls in two directions. After such observations as "the notion that a woman's chastity is constantly endangered is the single idea that occupies most of Vives's attention and delimits his view of the formal education girls should receive" and after finding extensive evidence within the book of "profound suspicions regarding women" (895), she concludes by asserting that "the point to be made, however, is not that Vives is antifeminist but, rather, that he is ambivalent" (896). She seeks the cause of his ambivalence in his Spanish origin, his knowledge of the Aristotelian definition of woman as imperfect, his scant contact with More's household, etc.

the enthusiasm with which the book was received by Renaissance readers, who saw it as liberating; the attempt to repress her certainly accounts for modern dislike.

Vives's defense of learning for women is based entirely on the argument that it will lead them to virtuous conduct and arm them against the temptation of vice. He speaks neither of the simple pleasure of learning nor, more surprisingly, of increased closeness to God. Learning for modern women is neither speculative nor spiritual; it is entirely ethical.[21] A woman is "sufficiently appoynted" when she has learned enough to see to her honesty and chastity. Vives does not advocate putting this learning to any other use. Learned wives are to be as silent with their husbands as their less learned sisters, and learned women are not advised to write or translate. Learning opens no windows on a larger world. Even the chastity that learning is intended to reinforce is portrayed as a social duty, rather than as a physical manifestation of a spiritual purity that goes beyond the simple chastity of the body.

Vives's commitment to the traditional social roles of the two sexes is revealed by his differentiation of the curricula for girls and boys on the basis of these roles.

> Though the preceptes for men be innumerable: women yet may be enformed with fewe wordes. For men muste be occupied bothe at home and forthe a brode, both in theyr owne matters and for the common weale. Therfore it cannat be declared in few bokes, but in many and longe, how they shall handle them selfe in so many and divers thynges. As for a woman hathe no charge to se to, but her honestye and chastity. Wherefore whan she is infourmed of that, she is sufficiently appoynted. (A3r)

Distressing as this statement is as a theory of female education, it is equally distressing simply as a philosophy of education. Vives believes that all occasions can be met with rules. Because they lead more complex lives, men need more rules. Armed with these rules they will know how to handle themselves. Clearly, Vives does not consider the ability to reason and the ability to make independent moral judgments to be the quality to be cultivated in students. The men and women produced by his teaching would look outside themselves for authority. It is a system that produces conformity and intellectual dependence in both sexes. Vives is quick to admit this and to cite it as a virtue of his

---

21. As her thoughts are unstable, "she should be encouraged to read, not think" (Kaufman 895).

system; it is better not to give people a choice when it comes to virtue and vice because the good would choose virtue anyway and, thus, will not feel limited, whereas those inclined to vice need rules.[22]

There is no arguing with Vives. He defines those "unto whom my preceptes shale seme rigorous and sharpe" as immoral people, "that is yonge men, that be ignorant, wanton and unthrifty:which can nat ones beare the syghte of a good woman" (A3v). If one tries to object to his narrow view of women and the conduct appropriate to them, one reveals oneself to be immoral and loses all authority. He conceives of himself as dictating precepts whose truth will be unquestioned. Although in the body of the book, as opposed to the introduction, Vives uses examples and cites authorities in an attempt to persuade his reader of the wisdom and truth of the system he has devised; he has no confidence in the intellectual ability of his reader. He provides no material for analysis, considers no possible problems the reader may encounter; rather, he provides rules for the educator as he provides rules for those to be educated. He is the authority; that is reason enough that he should be accepted.

Yet, despite his efforts to retain authorial authority and male control, his plan to educate women cannot succeed unless he admits woman's capacity for self-control. His primary defense of education for women presents it as a means of strengthening their commitment to morality.

> She that hath lerned in bokes to caste this and such other thinges, and hath furnyshed and fensed her mynde with holy counsayles, shal never fynd to do any vylany. For if she can fynd in her harte to do naughtyly, hauying so many preceptes of vertue to kepe her, what shulde we suppose she shuld do, hauying no knowleg of goodnes at al:And truly if we wold call theolde world to remembrance, and reherse their tyme, we shall fynde no lerned woman that euer was yll, where I coude brynge forth an hundred good. (6r)

This passage represents the female reader of a book of "holy counsailes" as capable of retaining these precepts in her mind and of applying them to challenges that she herself faces. This representation of the results of education implies that woman has the capacity to be under her own jurisdiction rather

---

22. He imagines that some readers "wyll thynke my preceptes oversore and sharpe. How be it the nature of all thynges is suche, that the way of vertue is easye and large unto good men, and the way of vice contrarye, strayte, and roughe. But unto yll men neyther the way that they go in, is pleasant, nor the way of vertue large and easy inough: and seyng it is so, it is better to assent unto good men than yll: and rather to reken the bad folkes opinion false, than the good mens" (A3rv).

than that of a male authority; thus, it threatens to disrupt the politics of Vives's system.

Vives does not face this challenge directly. He avoids it by never following out the political implications of his assertion of woman's moral capacity; even more significantly, he frequently shows doubt that an educated woman can be trusted to stay within the "fense," thereby undermining his own thesis. On the topic of stepmothers, for example, he says, "therefore women muste be warned ofte, to rule theyr owne brayeds and fantasyes of mynde. . . . And if thou suffre thy braydes to rule the, they wyll brynge upon the a great numbre of troubles" (120v). Although the woman is spoken of as needing "to rule" her mind, the choice to rule it is not hers, and the author seems to have little confidence that she will remember the lesson for long; she has to be reminded "ofte." Despite the use of "thou" and "the" in the second sentence, the passage is aimed at the male authority who has the stepmother in charge. The second sentence would seem to be a model of a speech that might be made to the stepmother by the male reader, rather than direct speech by Vives to the female reader. He will do the warning to which she must respond.[23] Once again the social system as it stands is not challenged by education. In the very language with which the plan for their education is formulated, women are not represented as authorities over themselves. The educator is represented as having to keep close watch on his student and repeatedly interfere to remind her of the precepts she has been taught. The learned lady may respond well to prompting, but she cannot be relied on to recognize dangerous situations on her own.

Given his reluctance to trust women to apply what they have been taught, and given the moral basis on which he justifies the education of women, some of the examples that Vives selects from the "hundred good" women as proof of woman's capacity to govern herself and choose good are surprising. They go far beyond the limits of the role that Vives envisages for women and form the prime example of the uncontrollable eruption of the independent woman into his text. The list begins with

> Cornelia the mother of Gracchus, whiche was an example of all goodnes and chastite, and taught her children her owne selfe. And

23. The book of *Instruction of a Christen Woman* is addressed throughout not to the woman who is the object of its plan but to those who have her in keeping, even though it deals with the education of mature women, wives, and widows, as well as young girls. Vives directly addresses the male reader, but he stands aside from women and describes their behavior, speaking of them as "she" or "a woman." Even the rare times when he appears to address a female reader seem to be a form of indirect discourse to male readers.

> Portia the wyfe of Brutus, that toke of her father's wysedome. And Cleobula, daughter of Cleobulus, one of the. vii. wyse men, which Cleobula was so gyuen unto lernynge and philosophie, that she clerely dispised al pleasure of the body, and liued perpetually a mayde, at whome the doughter of Pithagoras the philosopher toke example, which after her fathers dethe was the ruler of his schoole, and was made the maystres of the college of virgins. (6rv)

In all these cases and the others that I have not quoted, Vives's praise of the exemplary women's virginity or chastity, while deserved, misses the primary point that the examples seem to illustrate and that most early Renaissance readers found in them. The entire list praises women who either put their virginity to some nontraditional use or who stand out for some other accomplishment that is not in conflict with virginity, but is not necessarily due to it. We saw that in More's epigram the role of the Gracchi as social reformers was stimulated by their mother's speech. Vives mentions teaching, but how and what are not specified. In the next chapter we will see that Sir Thomas Elyot praises Portia's political allegiance to her husband; here the nature of her wisdom is unspecified, and its paternal source is stressed. That the daughter of Pythagoras ran his school after his death is syntactically subordinate to her virginity here in Vives's account, but the action of running the school is what brings her to prominence and distinguishes her claim to fame from that of the other virgins included in the list.

The outstanding example of Vives's overlooking of the radical undercurrent in his examples is the following:

> Sulpitia wyfe unto Caleno, lefte behynde her holy preceptes of matrimony, that she had used in her lyuinge herself, of whome the poet Martiall writeth on this wyse.
>> Redeth Sulpitia all yonge women,
>> That cast youre mynde to please one man.
>> Redeth Sulpitia also all men,
>> That do entende to please one woman.
>> Of honest and vertuous loue, doth she tell,
>> Chast pastymes, playes, and pleasure,
>> Whose bokes who so considereth well,
>> Shall say ther is none holyer.
> And it is playnely knowen, that no man in that tyme was more happy of his wyfe than was Caleno of Sulpitia. (6v–7r)

The result of Sulpitia's actions was moral, and, thus, supports Vives's precept that the only end of learning is moral action. Martial's epigram, however, stresses her writing as the means by which she achieved moral action. Martial advises his female and male readers to turn to Sulpitia's written works for instruction in virtue; Vives does not make clear what he wants his reader to do beyond admire her holy living and Caleno's happiness. He does not exploit the fact of her writing to its full potential, but, by including it, he stimulates thoughts of imitation. Sulpitia wrote books and advised men as well as women; therefore, it would seem, this is an activity that Vives favors.

When we come to the program of study for the contemporary young woman a few pages later, however, it becomes clear that Vives does not intend that the modern lady should imitate the actions of her ancient sisters, but rather their attitudes. The examples are in implicit and sometimes direct conflict with modern standards of conduct. Although the topic of instructing others through writing as Sulpitia did does not come up, this is not benign neglect. Despite his praise of her, Vives does not seem to have thought of women using their learning to create anything new.[24] Writing would seem to be an extension of speech and teaching, and, therefore, forbidden. For example, although he notes that the daughter of Pythagoras was famous for having run her father's school after his death, Vives explicitly bars women from running schools for men. "Let her lerne for her selfe alone and her yonge children, or her systers in our lorde. For it neyther becometh a woman to rule a schole, nor to lyue amonge men, or speke abrod" (9r).

Once, Vives has to explicitly steer his reader away from too liberal an application of one of his examples to modern times. He praises Hortentia because she made an

> oration unto the iuges of the cyte for the women, which oration the
> successours of that tyme dyd rede, not only as a laud and prayse of
> womens eloquence, but also to lerne counnynge of hit, as well as of
> Cicero or Demosthenes orations." (7r)

He then finds himself needing to discard the awkward feature of Hortentia's eloquence when he comes to say what a modern woman ought to study.

---

24. Valerie Wayne notes that "although *The Instruction* treats most aspects of a woman's life, Vives does not address the subject of women's writing or translating at all; he seems not to have seen such work as a possibility for them" (21). She goes on to discuss Vives's description of a woman's tuition in handwriting as a means of imprinting morality in her mind. "The purpose of her activity is not to communicate but to learn better her duty, and Vives does not suggest a larger purpose for handwriting elsewhere in his book" (22).

> As for eloquence I have no great care, nor a woman nedeth it not, but she nedeth goodnes and wysedome. Nor is it no shame for a woman to holde her peace, but it is shame for her and abomynable to lack discretion, and to lyue yl. Nor I wyl not here condempne eloquence, which both Quintilian, and Saint Hieronime folowyng hym, say, was preysed in Cornelia the mother of Gracchus, and in Hortentia. (8v)

Although Vives says he will not condemn eloquence, he bounds it with such cautions about the danger that attends its practice—it may lead to indiscretion and thus to shame—that he effectively bars it from the curriculum. Vives must excise the example after bringing it up because he wishes to praise women's silence, yet the only reason for including the example in the first place was to persuade the reader that women could speak and should be listened to. Paradoxically, if Vives could succeed in stilling the voice of the independent woman, which he invoked in his examples, his entire proof of the compatibility of learning and virtue would fall and his defense would fail.

Vives does not account for this difference between modern women and ancient ones except to say that the modern "nedeth it nat," but his emphasis on goodness and wisdom suggests that his overwhelming concern with chastity leads him to limit women to the home, despite the evidence that he himself has given for their capacity for virtuous action outside the home. The historical and living examples of morality and wisdom that Italian humanists used to force a redefinition of what woman is serve for him only as examples of what women can do if they are properly fenced in by precepts. He does not really have confidence in women despite his use of the famous-woman tradition. Unlike More, who uses the example of Cornelia in his epigram to establish women's praiseworthy capacity for speech, Vives must excise the example after bringing it up because he wishes to praise women's silence.

Vives justifies his low opinion of women's intelligence and the limitations he puts on her conduct in consequence by reference to the Fall.

> For Adam was the fyrst made, and after Eue, and Adame was not betrayed, the woman was betrayed in to the breche of the commande-ment. Therfore bycause a woman is a frayle thinge, and of weake discretion, and that may lightly be disceyued. whiche thinge our fyrste mother Eue sheweth, whome the dyuell caught with a lyght argument. (9rv)

This statement, which is a fundamental part of the traditional misogynist case against women, sits very uneasily with the examples of famous learned and eloquent women that appear just a page before it. For Vives, this archetypal example of female foolishness is more powerful than all the many, many examples of the wise, learned women he himself has already adduced, but it will not necessarily persuade a reader who has been impressed by the accomplishments of women that fill four and a half pages. The examples themselves provide an alternate system of female conduct on which women could model themselves that goes directly contrary to the conduct Vives wishes to recommend. He has borrowed a method of argument from humanists more liberal than he and by so doing he reveals possibilities for women only to withdraw them. This is a serious rhetorical error; Vives has weakened his own authority by allowing the ancient world to speak contrary to him. Whether a woman, or the man providing education to her, restricts herself to Vives's mode now depends on her confidence in his judgment. The independent woman exists as an alternative within the text.

The first English translator of the *Instruction*, Richard Hyrde, confirms the openness of Vives's text to a more positive reading of woman's capacities. Hyrde was a student and, perhaps, a tutor in the More household, and in his preface to the work, he speaks of More's response to it as well as his own reasons for translating it. [25] Both men value Vives's work, but Hyrde's comments and those he attributes to More subvert Vives's prescriptive and proscriptive method by speaking of women themselves as the audience for the work and as actively engaged in procuring education for women. It seems that Hyrde dedicated the translation to Queen Catherine at the suggestion of More who

> nat onely for the matter it selfe was very gladde therof, but also for that (as he than shewed me) he perceyved that hit shulde be to your noble maiestie for the gracious zele that ye beare to the vertuous education of the woman kynde of this realme. (A.iii r)

Hyrde here represents More as seeing Catherine as an active patron of the education of young women. The book is not represented as initiating the move toward the education of women, but rather as forming part of a movement whose head is the queen. Valuable as his work is, Vives is not in control; the queen is.

This is certainly a gallantry on the part of a writer looking for royal approval,

25. This preface was included in the 1529 edition of the translation and omitted from 1541 on. Citations of the preface refer to the 1529 edition. On Hyrde's relationship to More, see Bayne (5–6) and Stapleton (92).

but other elements in the introduction suggest that the appreciation for independence of mind in women is genuine. The very act of translation itself addresses the work to women, who Hyrde says were excluded from the audience of the original work because their education had not included Latin as it ought to have done. Such a work ought to be available in the vernacular so that women can make use of it. Hyrde imagines his female reader as actively and critically engaged with the text; he speaks of it as having to persuade her of its truth and utility.

> And surely for the plantynge and nurysshynge of good vertuous in everye knynde of women/virgins/wyues/and wydowes / I verily beleve there was never any treatis made / either furnisshed with more goodly counsayles / or sette out with more effectuall reasons / or garnisshed with more substanciall authoritiees / or stored more plentuously of convenient examples / nor all these thynges to gether more goodly treated and handeled / than master Vives hath done in his boke. (A.ii v)

In this passage Hyrde perceives the book as expecting its reader to use her judgment and be influenced by its reasons, authorities, and examples; he does not anticipate that his work will be transmitted to women by way of male authorities, and he does not expect that women will accept without thought what Vives, himself a male authority, has written.

The vocabulary Hyrde uses here in this original passage anticipates the one that he will use for Vives's Latin words, but the context makes a significant difference in their connotations. Within Vives's text "counsayles" furnish and *fence* the woman's mind, for example, whereas Hyrde suggests that the book itself is furnished with "counsayles" and represents the woman as receiving the advice as a plant that will grow inside her, rather than as a fence that pens her in. Hyrde's conception of the relationship between the book's morality and the reader's is organic, whereas Vives's is mechanical. Hyrde's "counsayles" nourish growth, Vives's "counsayles" limit it; they are restrictive precepts under another name.

Hyrde reproaches men for their past abuse of their authority over the education of women. Men complain about women's moral frailty, he says,

> yet havyng the education and order of them in their own hands, not only do litell diligence to teach them and bring them up better, but also purposely withdraw them from learnyng. (A.ii v)

Vives's book offers a remedy to this situation only by means of Hyrde's translation, which will put learning within reach of women themselves. Although it does not question the right of men to have authority over women, Hyrde's complaint against their abuse of their power sheds an Italianate profeminist light on women's past. If women have been less than moral in the past, it is because men have cut them off from the knowledge that would have led them to be virtuous. By this means, Hyrde identifies as circular the reasoning that would use examples of female immorality to restrict women's access to education, and he argues for the moral capacity of women. This profeminist confidence in woman's intellect and ethical capacity is absent from Vives's text even in Hyrde's translation.[26]

In sum, careful analysis of More, Vives, and Hyrde shows that thought about women's intellectual and moral capacity and about their education at the beginning of the sixteenth century was diverse and in the process of developing. Vives is not the exclusive representative of his times, and comparison of his precepts with the theories of More and Hyrde reveals that the generations of women who were educated in England during the century may not all have been oppressed by a sense of limitation and inferiority in themselves and in the genres open to them. When Margaret More put herself into her translating, as Rita Verbrugge argues in "Margaret More's Personal Expression" (39–42), and continued her studies and production after she was married, she was living according to expectations established by More that conflict with those advocated by Vives. When Mary Sidney translated the Psalms with great poetic skill and put the mass of *The Arcadia* into publishable shape, she too was the beneficiary of a liberal tradition in English Renaissance thought that fostered intellectual inquiry in women and did not restrict them to learning that would increase their private virtue. More and Hyrde did not question the political division of the sexes as the Italians did, but they did challenge the intellectual division, and they encouraged women to develop the autonomy that would enable them to act on that challenge.

---

26. Vives did not attempt to exclude women from learning altogether, of course, but rather to limit what they did with their learning. In his other published work, the preface to Margaret More Roper's translation of Erasmus's commentary on the Paternoster, Hyrde went far beyond Vives's limits. He encouraged women to actively engage in scholarship and even publication.

7

VIRTUE AND POLITICS IN
SIR THOMAS ELYOT'S
THE DEFENCE OF GOOD WOMEN

Sir Thomas Elyot's *Defence of Good Women* is the first native English work that fully and self-consciously participates in the Renaissance controversy about women in genre as well as in subject matter. More's letters and Vives's *Instruction* promoted the new humanist notion of woman to some extent, but they did not attempt to break down their audiences' preconceptions by means of ambiguous and complex rhetorical strategies, whereas Elyot's work, both a dialogue and a defense, is a neglected literary and philosophical masterpiece of the humanist controversy. In it Elyot sustains radical Platonic theses that had never been proposed in England before. He reasons that one system of virtues exists for both sexes, that women participate in virtue equally with men, and that, as a consequence, educated women are as capable of governing nations and living moral lives as educated men.[1] To illustrate the truth of his assertions, he creates one of the most philosophically consistent independent women in the controversy, Queen Zenobia of Palmyra, who has successfully governed herself and her nation.

As the presence of Zenobia suggests, the dialogue is set in classical Rome at the time of the Emperor Aurelian. It has two scenes. In the first, a conversation between two male speakers, the profeminist Candidus uses Platonic dialogics, Aristotelian paradox, and Plutarchan biographies of famous women to lead his antifeminist opponent Caninius to admit that the sexes have equal ethical capacities and that, as a consequence, women are as able to govern as men. In the second part, Caninius brings on Queen Zenobia, recently taken prisoner by the Emperor after having ruled as regent for some years and expanded the

---

1. See Jordan, "Feminism and the Humanists," for a discussion of her understanding that Elyot shares with other humanists a reluctance to accept "Plato's notion of women as endowed with the same virtue as men" (251–52).

boundaries of her nation. She discourses on the importance of a humanist education in her successes as wife, queen, and political prisoner.

The character of Zenobia is conventionally read as a figure of Catherine of Aragon in "exile" in Richmond, and Constance Jordan in "Feminism and the Humanists" recently has interpreted the dialogue as a political allegory that had the practical political goals of persuading Catherine to be prepared to act as regent in the case of a successful uprising against Henry VIII or of assuaging the antifeminist fears of potential supporters of the conspiracy. By 1540, however, when the dialogue was first published, Catherine was dead; thus Elyot, who dedicated the published work to Anne of Cleves, must have considered the work to have some truth beyond the immediate political one. When read in its philosophical and humanist context, the dialogue can be seen to be a justification of the education of women on the grounds that it will improve their performance in all roles they may be called on to play. In this case, its readers would not be potential political conspirators, but rather Elyot's fellow humanists, who would be capable of appreciating his clever use of Plato and Aristotle, and a more general audience, who might be moved to accept the notion that educating girls would not produce moral and political chaos.

The discussion between Candidus and Caninius, the first scene of the dialogue, is Platonic in structure and content. In firm control, the Platonist Candidus, through a process of question and answer, draws the profeminist truth out of his friend Caninius by revealing the inadequacy, inconsistency, and inaccuracy of his conventional Aristotelian antifeminism. The formal debate redefines woman by means of two questions: Can women be faithful? and, Is Aristotle's assertion that woman is an imperfect animal correct? Each question is answered by an attack on antifeminist authorities and by a demonstration of the greater veracity of profeminist authorities, with the result that woman's capacity for virtue is shown to be equal to man's. Elyot even incorporates, as two set pieces within the overall Platonic structure, a paradoxical proof of the superiority of women and a catalogue of famous women, two major Aristotelian rhetorical structures that profeminists conventionally use to break down antifeminist assumptions. By the end of the conversation, Candidus has demonstrated that the political woman has always existed, but that man's limited understanding has prevented him from recognizing her, and the reader who has assented to each logical step must necessarily agree to this conclusion.

Candidus's entire proof of the ability of women to rule turns on two notions developed in Book 5 of the *Republic*. First, whatever biological distinctions can be made between the sexes, woman does not "differ from man with respect to what we are talking about [i.e., being a Guardian]" (*Republic*, Book 5.453d–55c). Second, economics and politics are not two separate spheres but rather exist on a continuum.[2] In this passage Socrates argues that there are not two sets of virtues, one for men and one for women, but rather a single set of virtues that indicates the ability of the two sexes to perform the same tasks, and, thus, women must be included in the ruling class.[3] There must be philosopher-queens as well as philosopher-kings. He asserts that the sexes differ only in their generative functions and that neither sex is exclusively suited for any particular art or pursuit. He argues that the duties and laws of the republic should extend equally to both sexes.

Radical as he is in his attack on the definition of woman as essentially different from man, however, Socrates preserves the traditional hierarchy by asserting that women possess virtues to a lesser extent and by denigrating traditional female domestic accomplishments. Socrates asks,

> Can you mention any pursuit of mankind in which the male sex has not all these gifts and qualities in a higher degree than the female? Need I waste time in speaking of the art of weaving, and the management of pancakes and preserves, in which womankind does really appear to be great, and in which for her to be beaten by a man is of all things the most absurd?
>
> You are quite right, he replied, in maintaining the general inferiority of the female sex: although many women are in many things superior to many men, yet on the whole what you say is true.
>
> And if so, my friend, I said, there is no special faculty of administration in a state which a woman has because she is a woman, or which a man has by virtue of his sex, but the gifts of nature are alike diffused in both; all the pursuits of men are the pursuits of women also, but in all of them a woman is inferior to a man.
>
> .   .   .   .
>
> You will admit that the same education which makes a man a good

2. *Republic*, Book 5, argues the abstract case for the inclusion of women on a par with men. See also Elshtain, chapter 1, and Maclean (*Renaissance Notion* 48).

3. See Bluestone (3–4) on the neglect of this passage by commentators. She discusses the Renaissance in a single paragraph in which she mentions Ficino's Latin translation of the *Republic* but concentrates on Bruni's deliberate decision not to translate it "because he knew its suggestion of the 'community of wives,' as he put it, would be offensive to his Florentine audience" (4). She seems unaware that Plato's attribution of equal political power to women was a cornerstone of Renaissance humanist defenses of women.

guardian will make a woman a good guardian; for their original nature
is the same?
Yes. (716–18)

This reasoning has both profeminist and antifeminist implications. Socrates
makes it impossible to exclude women from power by asserting that few of
them have accomplished anything in comparison with men or by asserting that
many bad women exist, a traditional antifeminist tactic. It is not important
that all women are not capable of being good at gymnastics or philosophy
(after all, all men are not good at such things), as long as one accepts that
some of them inevitably will be. Yet, the rejection of the positive value of
woman's domestic role implied by Socrates's scorn of the making of "pancakes
and preserves" makes it impossible to praise women for "womanly" qualities
and, thus, may result in a lowering of esteem for women as long as Plato's ideal
state is not in operation.

Elyot's *Defence of Good Women* is a proof that women are capable of the
political virtue of justice because they display the virtues that compose it. He
takes over Plato's notion that the sexes do the same things and must be
considered in the same category; rather than talking in general terms about
"gifts of nature" as Plato does, however, he narrows the grounds of argument
and demonstrates that both sexes manifest the same virtues. Most important
of all for the dignity of woman, he discovers these virtues at work even in the
domestic realm that Plato denigrated. By proving that women have a capacity
for these virtues and that their practice of the virtues is of the same kind as the
male, he frees women to rule and to equal ethical status with men.

In true Platonic fashion, the groundwork for the proof of women's capacity
for justice is laid in an apparently irrelevant discussion about the private virtue
of "faith." In an attempt at ad hominem argument, overheard by Candidus,
who is late for their appointment, Caninius unwittingly provides a definition
of "faith" that Candidus can use to pivot the argument from the topic of
private love to public politics.[4]

CANINIUS. Candidus will not be long; his noble nature will not let him
break promise; for lack of faith defaceth all virtues. [*enter Candidus*]
CANDIDUS. Ye spake never a more true sentence, nor a more honest,
for undoubtedly faith, which some do call trust is of justice so great a
portion, that without it, neither God may be pleased, nor any weal

4. All citations of Elyot's *Defence* are from the edition edited by Watson.

Public may be surely [e]stablished. And they which do lack it themselves, with a little touch broken, be not a little offended.

CANINIUS. It is truly spoken, and now to talk of the matter, for the
which you willed me to meet with you. (214)

Caninius's casual definition of faith as the virtue necessary to make all other
virtues function ("lack of faith defaceth all virtues") is a personal ethical
statement of the social principal that Candidus states here ("faith . . . is of
justice"). Faith is not merely the confidence that authorities will take care of
those in their charge, the meaning that moderns seem to give to the term
(faith in God, the Constitution, or institutions): between equals it signifies
being true to one's word and the keeping of bargains; between unequals it
signifies a reciprocal hierarchical relationship that imposes responsibilities on
the inferior to obey and respect as well as on the superior to give worthy orders
and protect. Not only does lack of faith deface all personal virtues, but it
makes a proper relationship with God impossible, and it prevents the establishment of any "weal Public" because it prevents the establishment and maintenance of the hierarchies between the individual and God, between individuals,
and between the individual and the state.

The notion that justice is the central virtue necessary in the ruler, the state,
and the citizen is Platonic and essential to the *Republic*.[5] Elyot considers this
topic at great length in *The Governor*; he explains that justice (faith) is
composed of temperance, fortitude, and prudence.

only (saith Tully) men be called good men, as who saith that without
justice all other qualities and virtues cannot make a man good.

The ancient civilians do say justice is a will perpetual and constant,
which giveth to every man his right. In that it is named constant, it
importeth fortitude; in discerning what is right or wrong prudence is
required; and to proportion the sentence or judgment in an equality, it
belongeth to temperance. All these together conglutinate and effectu-
ally executed maketh a perfect definition of justice. (159)

5. John Major in *Sir Thomas Elyot and Renaissance Humanism* examined the relationship between
Elyot's thought and Plato's in detail and determined that the political ideas in *The Governor* are deeply
indebted to Plato, not just to the Platonic tradition. "In *The Republic* Plato describes the well-ordered
state in terms of an analogy with human virtues; the good society, like the good man, will possess the
virtues of justice, wisdom, and temperance (courage is the peculiar virtue of warriors and rulers). . . .
In *The Governor*, however, Elyot put this Platonic notion to practical use and attempted to prove that a
humanist education in these virtues would improve an already existing political system by preparing the
ruler and his magistrates to rule well, whereas, as its Platonic form suggests, the *Defence* is an idealistic
work, more like the *Republic*" (186).

That Caninius substitutes the private ethical sense of faith in this Ciceronian definition of what makes a good man shows the narrowness of Caninius's thought. He thinks in personal terms, and Candidus must correct his perspective by leading him to recognize the political implications of the private ethical judgments that he makes.[6] Despite his having been moved to make the statement by political considerations—that is, Candidus has an obligation to him to fulfill—he reduces faith to the most personal level as the central virtue of a code of noble ethics. Caninius does not recognize the political implications of his own statement, but Candidus does. Candidus's identification of faith as the fundamental component of justice is analogous to Caninius's identification of it as the fundamental component of noble private virtue, but Candidus's is a definition that links the particular instance of faith to the general concept from which it derives.

Although Caninius may seem right when he objects that Candidus's serious philosophical response to his platitudinous comment on his friend's possible tardiness has no connection with their debate about women, he is not. Sexual faith is at the center of the controversy about women; it is the root of the male denial of female autonomy and of the restriction of woman to the private sphere. Because neither woman nor sexual faith seems to be at issue here, Candidus easily gains Caninius's assent to the integration of the concept of faith with justice, the overarching virtue of which it forms a part; Caninius's acknowledgment of the truth of Candidus's assertion makes it impossible for him later to deny that the capacity for private sexual fidelity indicates a capacity for public justice. If Candidus can lead his adversary to admit that women are capable of faith, the most difficult part of his job will be done.

To prove women's capacity for fidelity, Candidus uses the standard profeminist strategies of discrediting seeming authorities by demonstrating that they are not impartial witnesses but disappointed lovers, asserting that particular examples have been wrongly used to build a case against all women. He cites numerous examples from philosophers and historians to prove that fidelity does

6. In saying that faith is the essential element of justice, Candidus is asserting a principle that Elyot formulated in his own voice in the *Governor*. "That thing that I spoke of is faith, which I by the authority of Tully do name the foundation of justice. For thereat not only dependeth all contracts, conventions, commutations, intercourses, mutual intelligence, amity, and benevolence, which be contained in the word which of Tully is called the society or fellowship of mankind; but also by due observing of faith malefactors be espied, injuries be tried out and discussed, the property of things is adjudged. Wherefore to a governor of a public weal nothing more appertaineth than he himself to have faith in reverence, and most scrupulously to observe it. And where he findeth it to be condemned or neglected, . . . rigorously and above all other offences punish it . . . remembering this sentence, 'Of faith cometh loyalty, and where that lacketh there is no surety' " (182).

exist in women, but he pushes toward a specifically political and Platonic conclusion. For example, he cites four historical women for their exemplary fidelity. All were married to men who died for their political ideals, and his accounts of the women suggest that they were motivated not just by personal ethics but by their sense that they formed a domestic and even a political unit with their husbands; their sexual fidelity was part of a more complex relationship that included fidelity to their husband's ideas. Indeed, the concern for sexual purity, which is usually the motive for the suicides of faithful wives, is entirely missing in this list.

Panthea is the most traditional example of chaste fidelity (she committed suicide rather than marry her husband's vanquisher), but Candidus suggests that she was committed to her nation as well as her husband by mentioning the detail that she embalmed her dead spouse "after the fashion of her own country." This makes it seem that her motive for dying was as much a concern not to subjugate herself to a foreigner as it was a desire "to be with her husband" (219). Portia's suicide is reported straightforwardly: hearing of the death of her husband, she hastily devoured hot burning coals. No indication is given of her motive, but as no threat to her chastity existed, she represents a fidelity that goes beyond sexuality. Paulina makes this theme explicit: she was "desirous to be continual companion with her old husband"; companionship, not a sense of her husband's exclusive right to her body, motivated her (220).

In the last and longest example, the wife of Ligavius explicitly identifies herself as a political unit with her husband.

> [He] being led to be beheaded, his loving wife continually followed, desiring the ministers to put her also to death with her husband, alleging that also to die she had well deserved, for as much as she had kept her husband at home, after that she knew that he was attainted. But seeing that no man did take regard to her hearty request, she returned home to her house, and shutting fast all the doors, and abstaining from all meats and drinks, finally with sorrow and famine she ended her life, and departed to her husband, whom she so much loved. (220)

That no man is willing to put her to death indicates that the men did not consider that a woman's action could be considered to be political even when the same action on the part of man clearly would be, yet Elyot represents the woman's argument as the cause of his praise of her and thus, to some extent, endorses the notion that a woman is responsible for her own actions even within the context of marriage when society might consider her to be obeying orders and not free. Behind the wife's argument is the notion that an inferior must only obey just orders; a wife is free to judge her husband's demands and reject those that are unjust. Her husband's seditious desire to be hidden from the state was unjust from the point of view of the state; thus, she would argue, she freely chose loyalty to the "economic" realm rather than the state and is culpable. Although her goal is the same fellowship with her husband that Panthea and Paulina sought, her attempt to be judged as a conspirator breaks down the barrier that imprisons woman within the domestic. Candidus's list of famous women has managed to imply a political role for women by suggesting that sexual fidelity is a private form of the virtue faith, and that a woman who demonstrates sexual fidelity is capable of political faith.

Having proved woman's ethical capacity to rule, Candidus goes on to prove her rational capacity and to mock the Aristotelian notion of her as "a work of nature unperfect," lacking in hardiness, wisdom, and constancy, or, by their formal ethical names, fortitude, prudence, and temperance. To prove that not only women display inconstancy, Candidus undermines Aristotle's reputation. It seems that the great man himself had a malicious nature and rebuked all other philosophers including Plato, from whom he learned so much; he also worshiped Hermia even though he disparaged women as imperfect.[7]

To prove women's prudence or reason, Candidus bases an astonishing paradoxical defense of the superiority of woman to man on the notion of the complementary roles of the sexes found in the pseudo-Aristotelian *Economics* and in Xenophon's *Oeconomicus*. According to these texts a wife's safeguarding of the provisions provided by her husband is as important an activity as the husband's provision of the items. Her timidity is a virtue in the context of the home, although it would be a liability in the larger world, just as his courage is a virtue in his business ventures but would lead to waste in the home. This sex-linked system of virtue is in complete contradiction to the Platonic argument. It freezes the sexes in their traditional roles, whereas Plato's understanding of virtue opened new roles.

Candidus's paradoxical proof makes flamboyant use of Platonic dialogical method to make an Aristotelian text prove a point of view entirely opposed to

7. John Major does not take this attack on Aristotle seriously because it is "leveled at the 'historical' person of Aristotle, not at anything he wrote (excepting the slander of women in *Historia animalium*). . . . It would be foolish, however, to take this isolated incident as representing Elyot's true opinion of either Aristotle or poetry" (148). Major's grounds for dismissing the attack on Aristotle, thus, are that the topic of the *Defence* is not important; he does not deny that Elyot leveled an attack at the slander of women.

that of Aristotle and of Plato. He leads Caninius to admit that safeguarding takes more reason than providing and thus to draw the conclusion that the activity that has always been perceived as having been assigned to woman because she is physically weak offers proof that she is mentally strong. It follows that if reason makes her successful in the home, it can make her successful outside the home as well.

In a logical chain that leads Caninius to accuse him of dallying with him (sophism), Candidus gets Caninius to agree to a series of statements that inevitably yield the following conclusion:

> Behold, Caninius, where ye be now. Ye have so much extolled reason, that in the respect thereof, bodily strength remaineth as nothing, forasmuch as the corporal powers, with powers of the soul can make no comparison. And ye have not denied, but that this word, Man, unto whom reason pertaineth, doth imply in it both man and woman. And agreeing unto Aristotle's saying, ye have confirmed, that prudence, which in effect is nothing but reason, is more aptly applied to the woman, whereby she is more circumspect in keeping, as strength is to the man, that he may be more valiant in getting. And likewise ye have preferred the prudence in keeping for the utility thereof, before the valiantness in getting. And semblably them which be prudent in keeping, before them that be only strong and hardy in getting. And so ye have concluded that women, which are prudent in keeping, be more excellent than men in reason, which be onely strong and valiant in getting. And where excellency is, there is most perfection. Wherefore a woman is not a creature unperfect, but as it seemeth is more perfect than man. (229–30)

This conclusion goes against both Aristotle and Plato. Plato dismissed the making of pancakes and preserves as beneath contempt, thereby depriving the female sex of any grounds for maintaining its superiority to the male, without in exchange asserting that women were as capable as men in the political world that had previously been closed to them. The *Economics* closes the kitchen door on women in its apparently generous attribution to them of dominance in a separate sphere. Elyot uses women's household skill as a lever to pry open the door and give women political opportunity. Although he ends by stating that woman is "more perfect than man," Candidus's point here is not that one activity, and, therefore, one sex, is really better than the other. Like most paradoxical defenses, *The Defence of Good Women* pushes to an extreme and then pulls back to what in contrast appears to be a conservative position. That logic can prove the superiority of women's reason as well as of men's suggests that the entire opposition is false and that the sexes are equal as regards reason.[8]

Of course, Elyot was not the only humanist to cite the *Economics* as evidence that women have a positive contribution to make to society, but he was unique in his use of the *Economics* as a base from which to argue the superiority of woman's reason. For example, in the *Cortegiano*, the Magnifico laughingly refers to the philosophical axiom that soft flesh means a strong mind and concludes that women are more adapted to speculation than men, but then in his development of the argument that the male skill at gathering and the female skill at safeguarding are based in the sexes' respective strength and weakness, he does not develop the topic of intelligence but rather concentrates on perfection in difference. He then goes on to assert the sexes' equal virtue (Castiglione, *Cortegiano* 354). The connection of the superior-reason assertion with the perfection in difference and with the equality of virtue is not logical and clear; the former two topics reinforce the notion that the two sexes are different. Women are soft and, if we are willing to accept the paradox, intelligent; men are tough, and again, admitting the force of the paradox, not so smart.[9]

Candidus does not make a virtue of weakness. His exposition of the *Economics* reveals that reason is natural to women as to men, and it neither praises nor denigrates women's physical capacity. Far from being irrelevant to politics, as Plato would have it, or being a sign of inferiority, as Aristotle would have it, domestic science is an activity that demands the exercise of intelligence like other activities. Unlike the Magnifico, Candidus shows us that the qualities of "Discretion, Election and Prudence which do make that wisdom, which pertaineth to governance" (231) reside in the actions that we all have seen women perform, actions that we perhaps previously dismissed as thoughtless and contemptible, as Plato did.

Because of his novel reading of the *Economics*, Candidus is able to present his examples of virtuous women, especially Zenobia, as exemplary of what women can do if given the proper preparation rather than as extraordinary and essentially different from other women. He first cites numerous wise women

8. See my discussion of paradox in the introduction.

9. Jordan compares these two passages and comes to an opposite conclusion from mine. "The two versions of the argument are different only in tone . . . both Candidus and the Magnifico commit themselves to the proposition that physical weakness entails a compensatory intellectual strength" ("Feminism and the Humanists" 250).

conventional in the humanist controversy, Nicostrata, Minerva, Diotima and Aspasia, and others, and some more unusual figures such as Leoncium, who "excelled all men of her time in wisdom and eloquence, in so much as she wrote against Theophrastus, the most eloquent disciple of Aristotle, in women's defence, which book, if it now had remained, should have been sufficient to put you to silence" (231). He then turns to his culminating example, Queen Zenobia, who presents not just women's capacity for learning, but also their "strength and valiant courage" or fortitude. His exposition of her virtues leads Caninius to "confess that in women is both courage, constancy, and reason" (233), the qualities necessary for rule. She is the final argument that breaks down the Aristotelian notion of female difference and opens politics to women.

Because Candidus's Platonic logical strategy dissolved Aristotle's consideration of women as a separate class, different from men and imperfect, one might expect Elyot to conclude that they must be freed from a hierarchical relationship to man. Not necessarily positioned below (or above) him, women ought to function as he does in the political and domestic orders. This is an extremely radical position, one that attacks the fundamental structures of society because it invalidates all conventional rules for relations between the sexes—and, of course, Plato bravely followed through on the consequences and abolished private domestic life and all private hierarchies. Elyot does not. By means of Zenobia, he maintains that the intellectual, ethical, and physical equality of educated women with men is consistent with conventional English sexually based social hierarchies because the virtue of faith, whose linking of the private and public spheres was so carefully developed in the first part of the dialogue, is a conservative virtue. Faith dictates a commitment to existing systems. Elyot does not question the preexisting hierarchical order of society or the distribution of authority on bases other than merit; he argues that at certain times, given a disruption in the normal system of authority that puts the nation (or a family) at risk, a woman may take up the position of authority.[10] Thus, rule by woman remains extraordinary even though the woman who rules does so by virtue of capacities she shares with all women. She is not an extraordinary woman.

Elyot's representation of Zenobia's life and conduct establishes her as outstanding but not extraordinary; her humanist education provides a rational explanation for everything that she accomplishes. We learn about her from a

10. Elyot does not question the hierarchical order or the distribution of authority on other bases than those of merit in *The Governor* either. He merely argues for the education of those likely to assume such authority.

brief biography that Candidus recites before her entrance and from her own description of the role that her education in moral philosophy played in her life. Candidus tells us that

> there dwelleth here by me a lady, late a great queen and wife to Odenatus King of Palmyra, which is a city and country in Surry. Her name is Zenobia. She hath had of our host victory twice, and now late was taken prisoner by Aurelian the Emperor, albeit for her nobility, virtue and courage, she was pardoned of her life, and a fair home is appointed to her in this village. She is well learned in Greek, and doth competently understand Latin, but excellently the Egyptian language. She herself teacheth her children good letters, and being now vacant from other business, writeth, as they say, of Alexandria and the other eloquent stories. (232–33)

To this information Zenobia adds that she "spent the years between sixteen and twenty" in the study of moral philosophy, that she married at the age of "twenty years and above," and that

> during the life of my noble husband of famous memory, I was never, or seen, say or do any thing, which might not content him, or omit anything which should delight him, such circumspection good learning ministered unto me, that in hunting and other pastimes, I retained alway such gravity, that of any dissolute appetite, none could conceive of me any suspicion, and yet my learning was had of none honest men in any derision. (236)

According to Zenobia it was only after the death of her husband that she became active in politics. The terms in which she describes herself make her seem the ideal humanist prince, wise in choice of councillors, capable of avoiding war, and devoted to justice. Her learning enabled her to retain her infant children's control of the nation by making the necessary orations persuading the people to "retain their fidelity" and by rebuilding the kingdom's defenses. She describes herself as particularly successful in law-giving and explains that "renown of just and politic governance" enabled her to add territory to her empire without employing force of arms (238). Once she is a prisoner, magnanimity, which Zenobia learned from her study of "noble philosophy," enables her to "keep in as strait subjection all affections and passions, as the Romans do now me and my children" (238).[11]

The humanist terms of this biography stand out on comparison with the traditional biography of Zenobia told by Boccaccio and Christine de Pizan. According to both these sources, Zenobia was an extraordinary woman. She led a childhood typical of Amazonian figures, scorning womanly exercises and men and devoting herself to hunting. She chose to marry of her own accord, but only engaged in sexual relations with her husband in order to become pregnant. She joined her husband on the battlefield as an officer and a soldier. At his death she took over the nation and was a strong ruler; de Pizan stresses the chivalry of her rule, and both agree that enemy nations feared her physical power. She also was learned in Egyptian, Greek, and Latin and may have made summaries of histories written in those languages; de Pizan adds that she made sure her children were educated. De Pizan stops here, but Boccaccio goes on to describe Aurelian's triumph over her and mentions that she ended her life as a private Roman matron with her children on an estate near Tivoli.

This Zenobia is not an example of a humanist prince, nor is she a model contemporary women could hope to emulate. Her Diana-like youth serves as an explanation of her strict devotion to chastity and of her later military excellence rather than her humanist education. There is no mention of laws, orations, wise assessments of action to be taken in crises, let alone the pacific expansion of the realm. A distaste for sexuality rather than magnanimity governs her sexual behavior. Even the single use to which she is said to put her learning, the writing of summaries of histories written by others, is less impressive than the active writing of history that Candidus attributes to Zenobia in the dialogue. As Boccaccio frequently reminds his reader, his Zenobia is extraordinary and unlike most women in her chastity and courage.[12]

In contrast, Elyot's Queen Zenobia is a great example of the ethical and political efficacy of humanist education. Both the practical skills, such as the oratory she employed to retain the loyalty of the kingdom's subjects, and the understanding of "faith" that was behind her strategy were results of her education, and her skills as wife, mother, and political prisoner were too. It enables her to function perfectly in whatever position she finds herself within

11. Although Elyot does not specify what Zenobia studied before she studied moral philosophy, the placement of this subject last in the curriculum suggests that Zenobia had been following the course of study that Elyot laid out for boys in *The Governor*, Book 1, chapter 11. There, the study of moral philosophy begins at seventeen after the study of logic, rhetoric, oratory, cosmography, and history. Moral philosophy is studied "to the intent his courage be bridled with reason" (39).

12. I have grouped de Pizan with Boccaccio here because the events they retell are essentially the same, but de Pizan's approach to Zenobia lies somewhere between Boccaccio's and Elyot's. She does not compare her unfavorably with other women, but she does depict her as an Amazonian type and does not connect Zenobia's learning and her administrative and military skills with her chastity.

the hierarchy. As his unconventional handling of the *Economics* shows, Elyot did not consider the abolition of the private sphere to be necessary to achieve sexual equality, whereas both Boccaccio and de Pizan represent Zenobia as an alien to the normal life of women.

Zenobia is the Platonic ideal of woman brought to dramatic life in order to persuade the reader out of whatever doubts may linger after the verbal definitions of Candidus's philosophical disquisition; she is also a historical person and as such proves the existence of the ideal in real time and space.[13] That she may also represent Catherine of Aragon, a real person in Elyot's own time, projects the ideal into the actual. Zenobia is a "speaking picture" of feminine virtue both public and private; by means of her, Elyot uses the "poetic fusion of moral abstractions with actual characters" (F. Robinson, *The Shape of Things Known* 100) to lead not to an understanding of the moral abstractions, as Sidney later would have it (we already achieved that through Candidus's philosophical speech), but to the belief that such abstractions can exist in real people.[14]

Elyot's use of a female voice is an innovation in Platonic dialogue; he makes woman actually public instead of potentially so. Zenobia's role in the *Defence* is in keeping with her ideal status. She is in the dialogue, but not of the debate. The question of the equal capacity of women is resolved before she enters, and Candidus relinquishes to her his role as leader of the dialogue. He no longer leads the ignorant Caninius toward the truth but instead interviews the woman who embodies the truth and teaches it to the men by means of logic.[15] Zenobia's authority derives from her experience as an educated woman, an experience neither Plato nor Aristotle chose to examine. Elyot's dramatic representation of female experience and his attribution of authority to a woman's voice go against both Platonic dialogic convention and the Aristotelian notion of woman. Aristotle deprived her of a public voice because she did not possess reason and goodness.[16] But even Plato, who urged a public role for

13. Elshtain argues that "*The Republic* exemplifies a purely abstract vision of a future condition which bears no relation to humans-in-history, with no coherent connection to some recognizable past and the beings who lived in it" (39).

14. Although the speaking picture is a Sidneyan term and postdates Elyot, Forrest G. Robinson in *The Shape of Things Known* demonstrates the source of the concept in Platonic and Neoplatonic visual epistemology. He also defines the relationship between Platonic visual epistemology and Aristotelian. Aristotle "brought Plato's Forms down to earth, stripped them of their transcendence, and joined them with matter as the actualizing constituents of all Being" (22).

15. See Jordan's argument that the physical presence of Zenobia is the key to the power of the example. "By representing Zenobia as a character in a dialogue, a living voice, he endows her with a kind of 'vital authority' " ("Feminism and the Humanists" 248).

16. See Elshtain (47).

women, never gave them a voice in his dialogue, and he disparaged their private speech.[17]

The central premise of Zenobia's apology for the education of women is that the study of moral philosophy promotes virtue in women in all the roles society calls on them to play. She explains that the classical virtues of justice, temperance, fortitude, and prudence operate in women's lives and keep them from "error and folly," which would make them "unmeet for that company whereunto they were ordained, I mean to be assistance and comfort to man" (235). Although phrased entirely in domestic terms, this is the same argument for the unity of virtue that Candidus made. Zenobia argues that a woman's good conduct can be understood in the same terms as a man's and that rational understanding of the nature of the virtues assists her to be good, just as it helps a man. For example, she explains the usefulness of an understanding of justice.

> Justice teacheth us women to honour our husbands next after God, which honour resteth in due obedience, whereby mutual love betwixt them is in a more fervency, for undoubtedly no woman him loveth, whose hate or displeasure, she nothing feareth. Also Justice restraineth us to do any thing which is not seemly. (235)

This justice is the same one of which Candidus spoke at the very beginning of the dialogue, but Zenobia speaks of the role of justice in the economic sphere, the one realm of experience that Candidus did not name in his initial definition of justice.

In this passage Zenobia presents willing subjection in the domestic sphere as an act of justice (faith). This subjection does not seem to be a humiliation and a waste that is admirable only as a generous sacrifice of personal ambition for the sake of domestic order, because Elyot represents no conflict between the educated woman and her role. Faith and obedience to her husband are for a woman what political faith and obedience to a sovereign are for a man; they indicate no qualitative inferiority.[18] Without them no marriage may be surely established: "faith . . . is of justice so great a portion, that without it, neither God may be pleased, nor any weal Public may be surely [e]stablished" (214). Although the behavior being advised for women is absolutely conventional,

---

17. See Elshtain (24).

18. Jordan sees this notion as politicizing marriage because it gives the wife the right to judge and disobey orders. "No humanist . . . gives a wife as much autonomy as Elyot does by casting her in an essentially political role" (256).

the notion of woman behind the advice is anything but conventional. A woman's faith to her husband is not caused by her first sexual experience, as some would have it, nor by keeping her isolated from all men, nor by making her perceive lack of chastity as sin; it is caused by teaching her that faith is a part of justice. In this context faith is a social rather than a personal virtue, and it is based in reason.

The representation of woman as motivated by a rational understanding of the same four virtues that govern male political behavior places women on the same continuum as men and makes a transition from private woman into public woman possible as the consideration of the same good behavior without the framework of the classical virtues does not. Elyot is arguing that women are not fitted by nature to a single role but rather by circumstance; just as a virtuous male who does not hold authority and is elevated to it is capable of performing his new role well, so a virtuous female in the same situation performs well. [19] He is countering the Aristotelian argument that "the courage of a man is shown in commanding, of a woman in obeying" (*Politics*, Book 1, chap. 13 [1260a 20]) with the argument that courage is not sex-linked but rather role-linked; a man at times shows courage in obeying and a woman in commanding.

When Zenobia turns to the topic of the success of her reign over Palmyra, she asserts the fundamental importance of the cardinal virtues, especially justice (faith), to good government just as Candidus did in the first scene of the dialogue. Zenobia explains that upon the death of her husband she "considered the state of things which then happened together" (236) and "determined to prepare remedies quickly" (237). The remedies that she determined applied the same virtues to the political situation that she had previously applied to the domestic situation; indeed, as she was head of her household as well of the realm, the continuity between private and public was more complete than it might have been under a male ruler, who would not have been directly in charge of the household. For example, Zenobia explains that "I caused good laws to be published, observing them first in mine own household, and caused them in all other places to be well executed" (238).

19. In his discussion of 'practical philosophy' Maclean explains that "in the context of practical philosophy, man is a complex being with a multiplicity of roles and functions, sometimes private, sometimes public, sometimes master, sometimes subject. Historical moment, social conditions and conventions, sex, age, climate, diet all affect one's moral and political being. The variations in individuals and in the conduct most suited to them derive from such factors as these; sex is but one of them" (*Renaissance Notion* 49). While antifeminists give sex precedence over all other qualities as a disqualifier, Elyot reduces it to a minor factor and permits woman the capacity for multiplicity, if not frequent opportunity to exercise it.

This suggests that there is no difference between governing the household and the nation. This notion of law-giving confirms the appropriateness of female experience to government just as Candidus's exposition of the *Economics* did.[20] The royal household sets an example for the entire nation.

In addition to creating a system of justice for her household and nation, Zenobia put herself under this virtue's rule. "I made Justice chief ruler of mine affection, and in all consultations would I be present, where I heard all other people speak first, that I would not be ignorant, and then shewed mine advice wherein I seemed not to be negligent" (238). Zenobia is not saying that she needed to follow this procedure because she was a weak female in need of advice and in danger of being carried away by passion; she is saying that she acted as a good humanist prince and did not form her "advice" until she had heard the evidence; then her feelings, or goodwill, and reason would work together. Zenobia so successfully placed herself and her realm under the rule of justice that even those who were her declared enemies "chose rather to leave their hostility, and to remain in our subjection, than to return to their own country" (238). All in all, Zenobia's career proves without a doubt that women can govern because they can understand justice, can practice it, and can command and inspire it in others. Zenobia attributes her great success in "wisdom and policy" to "the study of noble philosophy" (238); thus, her example proves that if women are given the same humanist education in ethics as men they can achieve the same results. She was an ideal prince and other women could be as good as she, if given the preparation.

The continuity of virtues from private life into public life, which forms the basis for Zenobia's ability to rule successfully, does not mean that there is no difference between masculine and feminine social roles. Zenobia consistently assumes that women for the most part will play subservient roles to men and will be active only in the private sphere. She distinguishes carefully between her private and public selves and the behavior that goes with each. When she speaks of how she went about taking control of her husband's country, she explains that

> to the intent that the name of a woman should not among the people be had in contempt, I used so my proceedings that none of them might

---

20. The slight ambiguity of the word "observed," meaning either that Zenobia observed the value of laws that had arisen naturally within the household or that she caused such laws to be observed in the household, strengthens the impression that Zenobia governed well. It suggests that she placed all units under her control in harmony with the natural order imposed by God.

> be said to be done womanly. Wherefore I sat alway abroad among my nobles and councillors and said mine opinion, so that it seemed to them all that it stood with good reason. (237)

In this speech Zenobia breaks the connection between masculine and feminine manners and the sex of the person who displays them. To act masculine is appropriate for a woman if she is in a position of authority as it is not if she is in her conventional subservient position. To not have acted masculine would have cost Zenobia her political success; in Zenobia's view there is no way to act feminine and rule. Virtue is not indicated by conduct alone, as traditional feminine etiquette would have, but by conduct appropriate to the situation.

Ideal as she was, however, and skillful at expanding her territory without war, Zenobia lived in a less than ideal world, was conquered by Aurelian, and taken to Rome as a prisoner. This is the stage of her life that she is in when she enters Elyot's dialogue, of course, and it is important to note that Elyot need not necessarily have chosen this moment. He might have set his dialogue in the period of her triumphant rule; he might have omitted all mention of her defeat, as Christine de Pizan did. He might have written about some other heroic queen who ruled until her death. That he chose to represent Zenobia, and in this period of her life, suggests that the captivity forms an important part of Elyot's analysis and defense of woman. Elaine Beilin sees him as turning a blind eye to the probable real consequences of educating women.[21] Constance Jordan takes it as an indication that "Elyot . . . wrote the *Defence* half-heartedly and perhaps to fulfill an obligation" ("Feminism and the Humanists" 256). I long read the choice as a strategy of containment: Elyot created an independent woman but he was made uneasy by her and chose to represent her in a period when she was no longer a threat, much as Ariosto concluded the *Furioso* with the domestication of Bradamante.

All of these interpretations assume that there is something demeaning about Zenobia's captivity and something particularly "feminine" in the situation in which she finds herself, but Elyot does not present it in this light. When Candidus describes her career he does not attribute her defeat to any specifically female failure; any general fighting the Romans might have suffered it. She did not lack courage or judgment but rather "hath had of our host victory twice,

---

21. "To Elyot, there seems to be no problem inherent in educating a woman while assuming that she will continue content to be private and domestic. The writers against women's education may have more nearly analyzed the reality when they claimed . . . that once a woman began to learn, men would no longer be able to choose her reading lists or prevent her from preferring the pen to the needle" (11).

and now late was taken prisoner by Aurelian the Emperor, albeit for her nobility, virtue and courage, she was pardoned of her life" (232). Fortune, not a flaw in her character, led to her fall; her character protected her from disaster after the fall. Once again, Elyot overturns conventional assumptions about women's weakness; Zenobia's captivity is not a sign of weakness but of strength. [22]

The same knowledge of virtue that enabled her to be a good wife and to rule makes Zenobia capable of living the role of prisoner with dignity. She particularly demonstrates the virtue of magnanimity, an aspect of fortitude. Through her study of "noble philosophy" she "acquired such magnanimity that now I keep in . . . straight subjection all affections and passions" (238). In *The Governor*, Elyot defined "magnanimity" as "good courage," that is, "the practice of those things not only which be great and most profitable, but also them that be very difficult, and full of labour and peril" (194–95). It is the virtue that rulers call on when faced with great challenges, and Elyot's use of it here indicates that Zenobia is not to be conceived of as passively and patiently enduring suffering, as a Christian or an uneducated woman might, but rather as meeting it head-on and conquering it as she would a physical challenge. [23] Even in captivity, she remains in control. If magnanimity is "the garment of virtue, wherewith she is set out . . . to the uttermost" (*Governor* 195), then the representation of Zenobia exhibiting magnanimity is an appropriate completion to Elyot's portrait of her independence.

Zenobia reveals her magnanimity by remaining entirely in control of both her public and private selves during her captivity. She takes care to behave appropriately to her lost regal status and to her private virtue and avoids leaving her home to attend dinner parties because this might lead people to suspect her of immoral conduct, a suspicion injurious to her reputation in both her capacities: "For the remembrance of my princely estate may not sustain words of dishonesty. And because I am now as a private person, I fear the common

---

22. That Zenobia was a queen but is no longer one at the time of the dialogue may be tied to the specific occasion of the work for which Jordan argues in her article. Her position is similar to that of a regent who must be trusted to relinquish her power when her children come of age; this is the situation that Catherine would have been in had she gone along with Chapuy's conspiracy. If read in this way, Zenobia's conduct answers the anxiety of an English reader who would not want Spain to seize control of his country by means of the foreign-born regent. The same virtues that enable women to be good wives and good rulers enable them to be good prisoners, and, perhaps, regents willing to cede their position when the time is right.

23. Usually, it would seem from Elyot's examples, these are challenges that can be overcome with physical courage, but not necessarily, as Plato exhibited verbal magnanimity when he insulted Dionysius, King of Sicily (*Governor* 194–97).

success of familiarity. . . . For I dread infamy . . . more than ever I did the loss of my liberty" (233–34). Once again Zenobia is demonstrating that virtues cannot be distinguished according to sex. Princely honesty and feminine honesty are two versions of the same virtue. Her "feminine" concern with her reputation as a chaste woman is analogous to her previously demonstrated "masculine" concern for her reputation as a strong ruler. Her concern to be perceived as chaste does not mean she is weak and passive and accepting of a male-imposed restriction—even a male prince must worry about his reputation—rather, it indicates her liberty and her ability to control her life even within the larger context of political defeat. That her control over herself is expressed in anxiety to have the reputation of being sexually chaste may be distasteful to modern readers, but any other attitude would have been inconsistent with the moral philosophy that governs all her actions because it would show a lack of self-control. Zenobia's concern for her reputation arises from the same commitment to faith that produced her political success.

The division between Zenobia's private and public selves resembles the Renaissance doctrine of the king's two bodies; indeed, her sex makes the doctrine even more necessary because her female body serves to remind people at all times that her private self exists, but in her there is no gap between the behavior of the public and the private self. The same virtues govern the conduct of each and so, although as a queen she operates under the rules designed for the public self—the ruler of whatever sex—she does not cease to obey the private code because the virtues motivating public and private conduct are identical. Chastity and public action are not opposed to one another. A woman can act unwomanly without foregoing sexual restraint because public and private faith are founded in the same virtue.

By means of the notion of the unity of the virtues and by representing Zenobia as living a retired life, Elyot defeats the major argument made against women in his time: that whatever their intellectual and physical strength, their entry into public life would cause private moral chaos and public disorder. She is not an extraordinary woman who rises above the rules that apply to others; she is a representative of the potential of womankind, if given the proper education. Her wise rule arises out of an understanding of faith that would be available to all women were they educated in moral philosophy. The same virtue that enables her to perform successfully as an inferior in one relationship makes her capable of being a superior in another. At no stage in her life does Zenobia face a dilemma about how she should behave as wife, ruler, or prisoner because no contradiction exists between what she is and the roles that circumstances and convention lead her to play. Both obedience and rule are natural because both are founded in "faith."

Finally, however, despite the heroism of Zenobia and the radical assertion that women and men participate in the same system of virtues, the *Defence*, like *The Governor*, remains politically moderate; it argues the capacity of women to rule, but not their right.[24] It defeats Aristotle, but stops short of the most radical Platonic consequences of its logic. Rather than questioning the conventional structure of society and suggesting that educated women (and men) must be given equal power, as Plato does, Elyot demonstrates that women can safely be called on to perform male roles if they are needed. He is not impatient with established hierarchies that make the educated person of either sex inferior, but rather he objects to the treatment of women as a class that must be excluded from authority under all circumstances. For an Englishman of his time, this itself was a radical argument.

Although it may have been intended to inspire real subjects with real faith in the abilities of a woman ruler, Elyot's *Defence* remained a theoretical argument because the planned revolt against Henry did not take place. When female monarchs finally did accede to the thrones of England and Scotland, Elyot's radical arguments in favor of the naturalness of rule by women did not form the basis of the many defenses of their right to rule written by Catholic and Protestant supporters. Elyot's great vision of the possible results of a humanist education for women did not serve the propagandistic purposes of queens who needed to fend off the claims of competing female claimants to the throne. Philosophically, politically, and generically daring, Elyot's *Defence of Good Women* had almost no influence on the controversy about women in succeeding years.

24. Jordan argues that Elyot does not accept "Plato's notion of women as endowed with the same virtue as men" and that he does not "accept the politics that Plato then constructs on this premise" and does "not pursue the notion of women as 'guardians,' rulers and governors of the state—an investigation that might have concluded in justifying in principle the right of women to govern men." ("Feminism and the Humanists" 251) As we have seen, Elyot very clearly accepts Plato's notion of a single system of virtue, but it is true that he does not go on to prove the "right" of women to rule men. Jordan seems to find an antifeminist bias on Elyot's part and sees his failure on these two points as finally invalidating his entire defense.

8

THE POPULAR CONTROVERSY
IN ENGLAND

In England in the years between the
publication of Elyot's *Defence* (1540) and the death of Elizabeth (1603),
humanist thought about womankind is clearly evident in the serious analysis of
the relations between the sexes in marriage manuals, in the numerous long and
densely argued tracts that were written in defense of Elizabeth's rule, and in
translations of Continental works such as Capella's *Della Eccellenza* and Agrippa's *De nobilitate*.[1] It is almost entirely absent from the debate about women as
it appears in original works by English writers for the popular press.[2] With the
partial exception of one work, the *Dyalogue Defensyve for Women, Agaynst
Malycyous Detractours* by Robert Vaughan (or Burdet), these native English
works do not challenge the traditional valuation of women on the basis of their
sexual purity; nor do they employ the rhetorical methods of paradox; nor do
they engage in a serious analysis of woman's social role as defined by the
classical authorities Plato, Aristotle, the pseudo-Aristotelian *Economics*, and
Xenophon.[3] They are conservative works, and they reinforce traditional stereo-

1. The defense of woman rule, an important issue because of the accession of two queens, is
discussed in chapter 9 because the texts are a special case and not part of the mainstream discussion.
2. The translations are David Clapham, *A Treatice of the Nobilitie and excellencye of woman kynde*
(1542), a translation of Heinrich Cornelius Agrippa von Nettesheim's *De nobilitate et praecellentia
Foemenei sexus*; William Bercher or Barker, *A dyssputacion off the nobylytye off wymen*, which was
borrowed without acknowledgement from Lodovico Domenichi's *La Nobiltà delle donne* and from
Galeazzo Flavio Capella's *Della Eccellenza et dignità della donna*; John Allday, *The Praise and Dispraise of
Women*, translated from a French original (1579); and Anthony Gibson, *A Woman's Woorth, defended*,
a translation of Alexandre de Pontayméri's *Paradoxe apologique* (1599).
3. The native English works are *A Dyalogue Defensyve for Women* by Robert Burdet or Vaughan
(1542), *Mulierum Pean* by Edward Gosynhill (1542), *Defence of Women* by Edward More (1560), *The
Praise and Dispraise of Women* by C. Pyrrye (1569), *Her Protection for Women* by Jane Anger (1589), and

types of ideal conduct and roles for each sex by means of antimasculine satire and sentimental portraits of women.

Both the satire and the sentimentality suggest that the desire to reform morals back to standards that have been abandoned is the occasion for these works, rather than the humanist desire to rethink social structures and their components. Under cover of titles that suggest the new, they defend the old. They represent a resistance movement, a commitment to a notion of woman that was being threatened, and the enemy *against* whom the authors defend is the independent woman. They defend against her threat by denying that women either have the capacity for independent action or desire it; they celebrate a docile, chaste, conventional ideal.[4] They are not profeminist texts.

The Exception to the Rule:
A *Dyalogue Defensyve*

In light of the overwhelming choice of English defenders of women to stay with the conventional notion of woman, A *Dyalogue Defensyve for Women* by Robert Vaughan or Burdet stands out because it is a bird debate—that most medieval of genres—dedicated to proving up-to-date humanist ideas.[5] The

---

The Praise of Vertuous Ladies and Gentlewomen by Nicholas Breton (1597). Sections of numerous other texts take up the topic. I have not included such works because of lack of space, primarily, but also because I have tried to distinguish between works that were devoted exclusively to the controversy and those that include it as part of the entertainment. (The *Orlando furioso* and *The Faerie Queene* are obvious exceptions to this rule.) See, for example, A *petite Pallace of Pettie his pleasure*, which includes the story of Alexius, who wrote praise of women and gave it to his wife as long as he enjoyed marriage but who, having tired of marriage, wrote blame of women; *Euphues*, which includes "A Cooling card . . ." and a letter "To the Grave Matrons . . . ," a *remedia amoris* and an apology for love respectively; and George Whetstone's *Heptemeron of Civill Discourses*, which includes a very sophisticated and interesting debate about women that seems indebted to *Il Cortegiano*.

4. The approach to womanhood in numerous works in other genres connected with the controversy about women but not directly part of it supports this contention that the popular defenses are defending traditional ideals against the threat of the humanist notion of woman. Compendia of advice to women and marriage manuals such as Thomas Salter's *Mirrhor of Modestie*, itself a translation of a nonhumanist Italian work, stress division of labor and praise woman's domestic role. The latter works are explicitly Protestant, and the defenses of women, though not partisan in tone, cater to the same Protestant commitment to the primacy of domestic life.

5. Utley (272) gives a good summary of the discussion about the author of this work. A popular medieval forum for discussion of women and love, the bird debate was rarely used in the Renaissance. Utley lists only one other Renaissance bird debate on the topic of women, Feylde's *Contrauersye bytwene a louer and a Jaye*. (On bird debates see Malcolm Andrew.) Utley argues that the *Contrauersye* is the slanderous text to which Vaughan is responding (275–76); however, the *Contrauersye* and the *Dyalogue Defensyve* belong to two very different branches of the debate because the former focuses entirely on the topic of love and the latter on the humanistic topic of the perfection of woman in body, mind, and virtue. Utley also suggests Agrippa's *De Nobilitate* as a source (276).

thesis is "That to knowledge and vertue, women apt be / And yf of theyr lyves, comparyson thou make / More godly than men, they seme" (E1v). The story is simple: the pensive narrator, troubled by a book that has made him think about the vice of "detraction," wanders out to the woods one December morning and overhears a debate between a Pye, who is a detractor of women, and a Falcon, who is their defender. At the end of the dialogue, the Pye admits that he has slandered women and flies away pursued by the Falcon, and the author goes home and writes down what he has heard. Given the genre, one might expect the discussion of women to be comic and to turn on their sexuality, a subject about which birds are usually well informed, but woman's lust is only a small part of the Pye's complaint against women, and the Falcon's defense uses their chastity as only a secondary element. Instead, the humanist topics of equality of body, soul, reason, and will (moral capacity) structure the debate, although the dialogue stops short of raising doubts about woman's conventional social role.[6]

As its title states, the dialogue is "defensive . . . against malicious detractors"; that is, its purpose is to establish a positive notion of woman in the reader's mind to replace the negative notion that has formed as a result of reading antifeminist literature. Its simple structure is directed entirely toward the goal of defeating these detractors. The Pye states an antifeminist assumption about women, and the Falcon disproves it by means of catalogues of famous women and reference to Scripture and classical philosophy (often glossed in the margins); the Pye admits defeat on this point and raises another, and so on until the major tenets of antifeminism have been demolished and replaced by the profeminist "truth." The birds then briefly discuss what motivated the Pye to speak such falsehoods about women.

The debate falls into the three sections of most humanist defenses: the discussion of body, reason, and will. The Falcon rejects male physical strength and female beauty as indicators of value. Reason rather than physical strength divides man from beast, and beauty does not indicate nobility; thus, woman's physical weakness is not a sign of inferiority, nor is her more pleasing shape grounds for asserting her superiority. In the realm of reason, woman is man's equal, he asserts. She has made substantial contributions to culture in both natural knowledge and spiritual knowledge. The defense of woman's will

6. Very little critical work has been done on the *Dyalogue*. In addition to Utley, see Woodbridge (22–24). The *Dyalogue* was placed in the context of the *Scholehouse* controversy by Beatrice White and Louis B. Wright (468).

receives the most attention. The Falcon asserts Adam's responsibility for his own fall, proves woman steadfast, blames men for their lust and for the destruction their "hot" composition causes, praises women for their "cool" composition and their efforts to bring peace, cites the *Economics* as proof of women's thrift and usefulness to their husbands, reminds men of the value of women's nursing skills, blames men for seduction and praises female martyrs for chastity, defends women's clothing as usually appropriate to the society in which they live, and denies that one bad woman indicates that all women are bad. As this briefest of summaries indicates, this "truth" would be conventional, even conservative, in a Continental treatise, as in Elyot's *Defence*, because the topic of reason appears but briefly and the *Economics'* division of labor is unchallenged.

The greatest difference between the *Dyalogue Defensive* on the one hand and the *Defence*, Italian humanist texts, and their English translations on the other is that the *Dyalogue Defensive* has no interest in politics.[7] Having accomplished his defense, the Falcon turns to the literary question of the motivation for slanderous writing, "detraction." He does not examine the historical causes of women's inferior social status, nor does he argue in favor of leveling social distinctions between the sexes. He does not use his reconstruction of woman's character as a platform for change in anything but attitude toward women. He is trying to change what is said. For example, in answer to the Pye's complaint that women are inconstant, the Falcon counters with numerous examples of constant women, and among them is Judith, that cornerstone of humanist defenses of women's ability to rule. The Falcon, however, does not use Judith to introduce the topic of the identity of sexual and political constancy, as Elyot uses Zenobia, and he does not argue for the participation of women in government. He merely mentions her constancy along with that of Lucrece and other sexual exemplars to prove that constancy is part of woman's character and to defeat the slanderous assertion that it is not and has never been. He does not attempt to provoke women to become independent or society to define a new role for woman that suits his definition of her.

There is one area of discussion for which this statement does not hold true. At the end of his defense of women's "intellectyve power," in which he has cited some of the same classical examples as Elyot, the Falcon breaks new

---

7. The *Dyalogue* has long been considered indebted to the *Defence*. The case for Elyot's influence was made most thoroughly by Catherine Henze, but her description of the *Defence* is far from accurate and the similarities are so general as to be of little use.

ground and encourages female independence in the field of writing, a topic Elyot did not include in his general defense. Just as Italian humanists praised writing women of their own times, the Falcon praises the writing of contemporary English women, and he suggests that if education were reformed, women would have no need to have recourse to male authors.

> In our countrey natyve, women thou mayst se,
> In both tongues experte, the Latyne and the Greke
> In Rhethorycke and Poetrye, excellent they be
> And with pen to endyte they be nat to seke
> If women in youth, had suche educacyon
> In knowledge and lernynge, as men use to have
> Theyr workes of theyr wyttes, wolde make full probacyon
> And that of men counceyll, they nede nat to crave.
>
> (B2r)

In these lines the *Dyalogue Defensyve* is radically politically feminist because it suggests that women ought to use their skill at writing to benefit themselves as a group. The suggestion that women need to take control of the means of production would not be unusual in an Italian defense; indeed, it would be part of the larger argument that male writers have misrepresented women by omitting their actions from the historical record and would be followed by the assertion that women must use their literary skills not just to avoid dependence on male advice, but to write themselves back into history, a point Vaughan (Burdet) does not make. Yet, commonplace as it may have been in Italian texts, the suggestion is unique in English defenses. No other English defender of women during the first three-quarters of the sixteenth century made this extremely important feminist point. Nothing like it appears in More, Hyrde, Vives, Elyot, Gosynhill, Pyrrye, Edward More, or Anger. Vaughan (Burdet) is the first English participant in the controversy, indeed, the only one for at least two generations, to be interested in the problem that arises when writing remains entirely in male hands, and he is the only one to recognize the political significance of women's writing.

This interest in the political nature of writing reappears in the *Dyalogue*'s discussion of the causes of antifeminist detraction. Both the prologue and envoy (which are signed Robert Vaughan) and the bird debate itself assert that antifeminist literature is caused by male dominance of the patronage system. Rather than attributing antifeminism to a lover's bitterness at a woman's resistance to his courtship or to his resentment of her infidelity, the work attributes antifeminist writing to the materialistic calculations of male authors, who figure that male patrons enjoy hearing antifeminist slander more than they enjoy hearing praise of women's virtues.[8] The male patronage system encourages antifeminist texts. Those who write against women do so "throughe avaryce," Vaughan says in his prologue.

The Pye elaborates on this theme in his final speech in response to the Falcon's demand for an explanation of why he slanders women more than men.

> Womans power is small, in felde and in towne
> Therfore I them sclaunder, therfore I them skorne
> Men rule and gouerne, by see and by lande
> Promocyons and profytes, by them I may haue
> Therfore to catche somwhat, into my hande
> I laude them, I flatter them, whan I begyn to craue
> He that wysheth with welth, in this worlde leade his lyfe
> Placebo he must play, his kne both bowe and bende.
>
> (E2r)

This extraordinary passage anticipates twentieth-century New Historicist readings of Renaissance literature, and it makes explicit a notion that has been implicit throughout this study: the increase in women's capacity for and interest in patronage resulted in the increased production of defenses of women during the Renaissance. Almost all the texts examined thus far were addressed to female patrons, but they cite admiration and/or love as the cause of the dedication and the motive for writing. Vaughan (Burdet) is unique in his citation of economics and politics and not love and its attendant malaise as the causes of antifeminist and profeminist texts. He argues that woman is trapped; as long as she remains powerless, profeminist books will rarely be written. The solution to the problem of slander of the female sex would seem to be, not the vigilant practice of sexual virtue, but the cultivation of power.

Although the dialogue proper does not develop this radical political point, the prologue and envoy represent the very book we are reading as an example of the positive results that female patronage can have. In the prologue, Vaughan explains that Mistress Arthur Hardberde has received previous works of his kindly, and "Your bownteous benygnytie, imboldeth my rudenes / This treatyse folowynge, unto you to dedycate" (A1v). In other words, the generosity of a

---

8. Woodbridge states that "he hints obscurely that misogynistic tracts are written to gain great men's favor" (22). I do not find the treatment of the topic obscure or hinting.

female patron on previous occasions has resulted in the production of a profeminist work. The direct relationship between female patron and kind of text produced is made even more clear when Vaughan states that this work, which he claims was delivered into his hands by an unnamed friend, has special relevance to a situation in which Mistress Hardberde finds herself at this very moment.[9] Its defense against slander may do her a service, and the understanding it provides of the motives that lead men to disparage women may bring her comfort.

> Than in my mynde, I thought that you were
> Your cause consydered, and also your estate
> Moste worthy to whom, I myght sende or bere
> It to present, or els to dedycate
> And because it declareth, howe the Pyes do prate
> And what them causeth, suche pratynge to use
> I trust in God, it shall your mynde recreate
> Throughe to rede it, yf you wyll nat refuse.
>
> (A2r)

The close relationship between the sex of the patron and the subject of the book is asserted again at the end of the work in the envoy. Vaughan commits the book "to her womanly wysdom." He is sure she will bind the loose leaves together nicely with silk thread because she knows the text to be true.

> I have than no drede, to be in her protection
> As thou dost her, so wyll she the defende

. . . .

9. It may be that Vaughan is answering an individual instance of slander against a particular woman, whose name he seems to have disguised. Mistress Hardberde as the dedicatee for a bird debate seems suspect and, as many have noted, the name Madeline Vernon appears in an acrostic in the prologue. His method of defense is to associate the individual woman with womankind and to argue that what has happened to her happens to women in general. By this means he makes a generic defense of women serve as a defense of an individual woman and avoids giving a detailed defense of this particular woman, which would have forced him to identify her, something he clearly does not want to do. In this he resembles Elyot, who, it would seem, made a general defense of woman rule serve to promote rule by one particular woman. Each author speaks of the individual case behind the veil of a universal issue, but this suggests that the problem faced by each woman could not be solved by negotiation for the rights of that individual woman but required a change in the reader's notion of woman. This is obvious in the case of Elyot's *Defence*; to promote the assumption of power by a woman who is not in the direct line for the throne, Elyot must persuade his reader that such power has legitimacy. It is not so obvious in the case of the *Dyalogue Defensyve* because the occasion of the piece remains a mystery, but it would seem that, again, the individual woman can only be justified if what she has been accused of can be shown to be appropriate to women. The universal justifies the particular.

> Therfore, whan thou shalt come to her syght
> Whiche wyll be shortely, as far as I gesse
> Say thou arte sende, to pleade in her ryght
> As in the quarell, of thyne owne maystresse
> Than shall she se, what thou canst expresse
> For her defence, her ryght to recure
> And from detractours, that wolde the suppresse
> In her Cypresse cofer, she wyll kepe the sure.
>
> (E4r and v.)

This representation of the lady's relationship to the text is domestic; in keeping with the teachings of the *Economics*, which the Falcon quoted in woman's defense, she will care for the book as a household object, sewing it and keeping it in a chest. A product of male labor, it will be kept safe by female thrift. The text's need of defense is real, however, and the task of defending it is here assigned to the lady; the fact that she is the one doing the defending is important and should not be obscured by a too-literal reading of the domestic terms in which her defense of it is represented. Finally, the author is warning the patron that the book may be controversial and that he is counting on her to stand up for it. This approach would be conventional were the dedicatee a man, but addressed to a woman, it is a last attack on the repression of women. If the lady accepts the book and makes herself his protector, she is assuming the kind of power that he urged on women in the dialogue.[10] Even though she herself has not written the book, her protection of it will be a sign of her independence.

The Popular Defense in Mid-Century

The other three popular defenses written between 1542 and 1569 are ostentatiously controversial. All either were published in the same volume as an antifeminist piece, state that they were written in response to one, or both. *Defence of Women* by Edward More (1560) was printed and bound with the

10. It is too bad that the identity of "Mistress Arthur Hardberde" is unknown, so she cannot form an entry in the growing list of female patrons of Renaissance works. Utley suggests that the name "Margaret Vernon," which appears in an acrostic in the envoy, may be the maiden name of Mistress Arthur Hardberde (273). It might, of course, also be the real name of his patron.

Scholehouse of Women, an antifeminist satire that was probably written by Edward Gosynhill, the author of *Mulierum Pean* (1542), which itself calls attention to the *Scholehouse* as the text which it is refuting. C. Pyrrye presented two separate pieces printed together in *The Praise and Dispraise of Women* (1569). In each case, the result of the parallel presentation of the two sides of the debate is that neither has the last word; neither conclusively wins because neither concedes the victory.[11] This method of presentation emphasizes the controversial nature of the material being offered and suggests that the conflict is irresolvable.

Contrary to appearances, however, the conflict between these antifeminist and profeminist texts is not irresolvable; it is nonexistent.[12] They appear to offer alternative views of women, but, in fact, the same notion of woman and her proper social role lies behind all of them. They argue about how successfully woman is chaste, obedient, and silent, not about whether she ought to be. The defenses as well as the attacks are innocent of the humanist notion of woman. None of them is dedicated to a woman or concerned with women's patronage and political power.[13] None makes a serious philosophical argument for the equality of women's ethical capacity; lacking this, none argues for a change in woman's social role. All are concerned with Christian virtue and vice and speak of lust, gluttony, and anger instead of the classical virtues of prudence, temperance, and justice. In order to make woman's traditional role valued, the authors attempt to persuade the reader to appreciate the excellence with which women, more morally pure but less intellectually and physically tough than men, play that role.

11. Joan Kelly asserted that Gosynhill's "sentiments clearly lie with his castigation of the argumentative, loud mouthed, gossiping, lazy, greedy, inconstant, immoral, and disagreeable nature of women in *The Scholehouse of Women* (1541), which went through four editions by 1572, rather than with his own rebuttal, *The prayse of all women, called Mulierum Pean* (c. 1542), which enjoyed no such popularity" (75). It is not clear on what basis she makes this assertion, which is one of several she makes to prove the insincerity of male defenders of women. She seems to assess Gosynhill's own sentiments by counting the editions of his two works; clearly, however, publication had nothing to do with the author's commitment to his ideas, but more likely was tied to the profit the publisher expected to be able to make.

12. The participation of Gosynhill and Pyrrye on both sides of the question and Edward More's willingness to appear in company with the notorious *Scholehouse* have led most critics to skepticism about the sincerity of the profeminist views expressed by the three writers in their respective works. See Linda Woodbridge (37). This concern with sincerity has diverted attention from the issue that I find to be most important: the notion of woman developed within the texts.

13. Edward More's *Defence* is addressed to "Mayster Wyllyam Page, Secretary to Syr Phillip Hobdy"; Pyrrye's speaks "to the reader" and seems to expect that she will be female because he speaks of her as learning a moral lesson from the examples he gives; Gosynhill's title page proclaims the book to be "very fruytfull and delectable unto all the readers," but there is no dedicatory letter or formal address to the reader.

Gosynhill, More, and Pyrrye make no use of the rhetorical techniques that humanists used to persuade their readers. Rather, they show "real" scenes of women behaving virtuously to oppose the conventional antifeminist scenes of female immorality.[14] We are led to discover that women are chaste even though we thought they were not, but we do not discover that their chastity is a form of constancy and, thus, an indication of their capacity to rule. Antimasculine satire forms a major part of the content of most of these works; women are set up as a standard against which male conduct can be measured, but no connection is made between conduct and social role. Given the ready availability of humanist models in the earlier native works of Elyot and even Vives, in the translations of Continental works, and in the *Dyalogue Defensyve*, this conservative insularity in thought and method is striking; in England in the mid-1500s two very different ideals of womankind were current.

Gosynhill is the most sophisticated of the three authors in form and in the evidence he cites. He opens *The prayse of all women called Mulierum Pean* with a clear imitation of Chaucer's *Legend of Good Women*. The poet is visited in a dream by an assembly of women among whom is Venus, who reproaches him for having written against women and demands that he record her speech in favor of women. The rest of the work consists of this speech written somewhat inconsistently from a feminine point of view and an envoy written in Gosynhill's voice. The use of the dream-vision form and a feminine voice amplify the ambiguity about the truth of the narrative that already exists because the author has written on both sides of the question. Is the goddess of love speaking in favor of women more likely to tell the entire truth than a man speaking against the sex?

Venus's speech is pro-woman, but not profeminist, even when she includes evidence that humanists use to prove the political potential of women.[15] She focuses on the suffering that women's role imposes on them and on the resolution with which women perform their duties. She describes in exaggerated detail women's pain in childbirth and self-sacrifice in the care of their children. She represents women as helpless creatures on whose behalf external forces intervene. For example, the list of women famous for their chastity

---

14. Edward More, for example, denies that women speak to excess, but argues that if they were to "it is but a small fault, in authors syd we fynde, / True to be and credyble, wordes to be but winde. / Theyr tonges I think offended have on earth no lyving man" (lines 553–55). He diminishes the importance of speech rather than finding a virtue in it.

15. For a contrasting view, see Woodbridge, who argues that Gosynhill knew Agrippa because many of his examples and even the order in which the examples occur also appear in *De nobilitate et praecellentia Foemenei sexus* (44–45).

includes some chilling cases. We learn of Sarah, the daughter of Raguel and future wife of Tobias, whose seven lustful husbands were destroyed by a devil on their wedding nights because she was so virtuous and they so vicious, and of Dinah, the daughter of Jacob and Leah, whose brothers destroyed the city of the father of the man who raped her.

Venus portrays as helpless even the famous women whom the humanist tradition represented as independent. Judith, Deborah, Jael, and Esther are cited as proof that women make war and are wise only when moved by God. They are contrasted to Ishmael:

> So can be nat rede of any woman
> Namely in wryttynge autentycall
> To be so cruell as was this man
> At warre to be with one and all
> O that ye men can fyght and braule
> And kyll eche other comenly
> Whiche is nat sene in the femynyne.
>
> Howe be it there is founde in holy wryt
> That some women haue done lyke case
> Nat to them selfe but marked to it
> Of god onely, by specyall grace
> Suche dedes marcyall to brynge to passe
> That man myght nat Judyth to wytnes
> Whiche slewe alone myghty Holofernes.
>
> And in lyke case of Delbora
> Whom god electe his prophete to be
> The deth to declare of Sisara
> Where and whan to sygnyfye
> And gave her also more specyally
> Knowlege in many other cause
> And made her iudge over the lawse.
>   (C3v)

Rather than presenting the ability to make war and to judge as virtues that women share with men, these stanzas stress that these activities are not natural to women; they become involved in them only when God inspires them.

The emphasis on grace distinguishes Gosynhill's approach to female heroism from the humanist approach. The women do not act out of strengths natural to women, as Elyot's Zenobia does; rather, their perfection in passive virtues raises them to an extraordinary role. This approach is even more conservative than Boccaccio's in the *De mulieribus claris* because Gosynhill cites these women in an exclusively Judeo-Christian context that emphasizes the virtue that attracts God's grace to them rather than the deeds that they perform while under its influence. He contrasts them with immoral Old Testament men and compares them with New Testament women favored with special knowledge of Christ. They do not demonstrate women's capacity for independent action or for public action but rather women's ability to excel in conventional virtue.

Even Venus's celebration of the wives of the owners of great estates for the organizational and financial responsibility that they bear does not move *Mulierum Pean* onto humanist profeminist territory. Venus states:

> Estates comenly where I go
> Trust theyr wyues to overloke
> Baker, brewer, butler, and coke
> With other all, man medleth no whytte
> Bycause the woman hathe quycker wytte.
>
> My lady must receyue and paye
> And euery man in his offyce controll
> And to eche cause gyue ye and nay
> Bargayne and bye and set all sole
> By indenture other by court roll;
> My lady must ordre thus all thynge,
> Or small shal be the mannes wynnynge . . .
>
> (E3r)

What this lady does is impressive: she oversees the men who manage the businesses on the estate that have to do with supplying the household—baker, brewer, butler, cook. She draws up their contracts and pays them. A representation of the Renaissance manor lady's actual responsibilities observed by an eyewitness, this passage has substantial potential to support a profeminist argument for women's capacity for a larger social and political role, but Gosynhill makes no argument. The example stands at the very end of the text in a section devoted to miscellaneous bits of evidence in women's favor; Venus gives no clear reason for presenting it; it just shows women in a good light.

This passage is unusual in *Mulierum Pean* because it draws on experience rather than authority. Venus, or perhaps Gosynhill himself, is reporting what women actually do on estates "where I go."[16] But, of course, the behavior observed by the speaker is consistent with the division of labor described in the *Economics*, and the reference to women's practical intelligence ("Bycause the woman hathe quycker wytte") suggests the author's awareness of at least the relevant passage in the classical text, if not the whole text. Yet, the use of a classical rather than a biblical source does not in itself make an argument humanist. These two stanzas do not form part of a demonstration of either women's intelligence or their administrative ability, as similar paragraphs do in Elyot's *Defence*. Gosynhill does not apply the particular example to the general situation. He does not identify the virtues being employed, and he does not suggest that the kind of reason women demonstrate when they "overloke" bakers and butlers might be applied outside the home. Household management is a source of value in itself here; it is part of the traditional ideal.

Edward More's notion of woman in *The Defence of Women* is the same as Gosynhill's, and his evidence and his form are even less sophisticated. His strategy is to counter the entertaining antifeminist stories of the *Scholehouse* with entertaining antimasculine stories—to counter antifeminism with satire against men—but, despite his title, he has no serious, substantial profeminist case to make. His primary, almost only, argument is that women are often blamed for men's faults, and he proves this by analyzing numerous historical and modern situations in order to demonstrate the real fault of men.

More's method of argument does not advance the dignity of women and does not open for them the possibility of being compared with men on equal grounds. For example, he cites the condemnation of Eve as evidence of the male tendency to blame women for faults committed by men.[17] Because of her feebleness, he says, Eve ought not to be charged with responsibility for the fall.[18]

Her lacke of strentgh [*sic*], and nothyng els, was cause of her forlore:
Yf lacke of strength, bewty, wyt, in women be detecte,
It lyeth not in them these sayd thyng to correcte;
Nature fourmeth folks accordyng is to Gods wyll,

16. Henderson and McManus annotate this line, "at this point Gosynhill is clearly speaking in his own voice, although he had earlier in the poem maintained (albeit fitfully) the fiction that the work was dictated to him by Venus" (169).

17. He also cites women's financial dependence on their husbands as a defense. For example, women's gaudy apparel should not be blamed on them but on their husbands who pay for it; women may wear farthingales, but men invented them.

18. All quotes from More are from Utterson's edition.

In God it lyed and wan els then to make or spyll:
But Adam beyng ruler of see, and eke of lande,
That Eue to hym was subiect it may well now be skand,
And [Adam] hauying strenght [sic] sufficient, wanting nowght but grace,
So wolde offende our sauyour Christ to lese that ioyfull place,

.   .   .   .

And yet men wyll transpose the faute to seely Eue,
But no man, that the trouth doth rede, wyl them I thynk beleue;
Wherfore I trust I haue declared here at large,
That fawth commytted by the men are layde to womens charge.

                                                    (lines 58–72)

The very notion of women *against* which the humanists defended woman is here used to defend her.[19] More admits that woman lacks in "strength, bewty, wyt" and concludes that she has no responsibility for her own actions. She is Adam's natural subject because she is weak. She entirely lacks autonomy and independence. If a reader should accept More's assertion and cease blaming Eve, he would in the process be freed of any belief he might have had in her intelligence. This is not a humanist defense.

Weak as it is, the discussion of Eve is the longest logical exposition of a topic in the treatise. More's strategy throughout the rest of the work is to present a series of stories and vignettes loosely strung together to illustrate the theme that women are blamed for men's faults. The result is a satire that contrasts male selfishness and vanity with female generosity; its appeal lies in the skill (or lack of it) with which the examples of good women are presented, not in the strength of the argument. For example, a great deal of evidence is given to demonstrate that women who give in to lovers suffer, whereas the men "pretende to loue" and "with sundry dryftes" "bereue" girls of their virginity "which being lost and gonne, what greater losse can be, what better thing haue maydens now then theyre virginite?" (lines 281–88, passim). More briefly retells the story of Dido, whose experience with Aeneas taught her never to trust men, and then tells at great length (seven pages out of a total of thirty-nine) of the young Scots daughter of a prison warden. This woman learned never to trust Englishmen when she was moved by promises of love and marriage to set an Englishman free and then found herself abandoned.

19. This argument is not theologically sound. Aquinas, for example, attacked the defense of Eve as "seely" ("her ignorance did not excuse, but aggravated her sin, in so far as it was the cause of her being puffed up with still greater pride"), although he accepted the defense of her according to rank ("the circumstance of personal condition, on account of which the man's sin was more grievous than the woman's)" (Pt. 2.2, Q. 163, Art. 4).

In telling this pathetic story, More leaves its profeminist potential un-touched. He concentrates on telling a delightful narrative; he includes the false speeches made to persuade the young woman and feelingly portrays her passionate responses and her despair when she learns how she has been deceived. The very limited moral at the end—"thus may ye se exprest the nature here of men, / And yet they wyll affirme women worse then them" (lines 446–47)—does not build a positive profeminist case. More handles his next example in the same fashion. He tells a comic story of Virgil's attempt to lie with a woman and her successful exposure of him to all the town, but his lesson is merely "That women are ryght honest, and men are very lewede" (line 470). The same story might have been used to illustrate the woman's use of wit to defend her chastity, but More offers no praise for her wit nor does he suggest that women can be depended on to make correct moral decisions.

More's defense serves as a reproach to man. In the course of reading the work, the reader is led to reprove all men as he reproves Adam at the beginning. Example after example shows man, with his acknowledged greater capacity for reason and virtue, betraying, misleading, and mistreating the "weker vesselles" (line 559). The book ends with a description of the return of a drunken husband to his home and his definition of his wife's just reproach of him as "skolding." The representation of the wife as a moral authority is shocking and troubling because it reverses what ought to be true. The scene shows us a husband debased, not a wife raised to her proper level; she is a moral authority by default. The antimasculine satire works to encourage a male to resume his abdicated authority; it does not encourage a change in the status of women.

C. Pyrrye's 1569 volume has three distinct sections: "Disprayse of Women," "Prayse of Women," and "A Fruytful short dialogue uppon the sentence, knowe before thou knitte." In the prologue "To the Reader," the author clearly states the moral purpose that seems to underlie Gosynhill's and More's works and connects the popular tradition of praise and blame of women to the topic of marriage. He explains that he has written so that those women who feel moved to vice may read their dispraise here and be moved to virtue and so that good examples will lead them to do what they ought and, thus, gain a good reputation before man and God. This suggests that the antifeminism of the "Disprayse" is intended to appeal to the very group it satirizes and move it to reform, although it is also directly addressed to men, warning them to stay away from women if they wish to be happy. The praise of women stands as an ideal for women to follow and the dispraise as a warning against vicious conduct; a woman who follows Pyrrye's positive examples will lead a happier life than one who remains enmired in cruel vice.

While it is conventional for satire to suggest that its purpose is reform and for Renaissance literature in general to suggest that it has educational value, Pyrrye's volume does what it says it will do. The antifeminist satire is rough and holds up an entirely vicious image of womankind that should move any female reader to desire not to be identified with that group. The profeminist section is pleasant to read and concludes with a hymn to love; it holds up a positive image of womankind that is likely to move a female reader to feel a desire to be identified with this group.

The "Disprayse" is brief and uninventive in its antifeminism; in order to warn men away from matrimony, it emphasizes the duplicity of woman. Woman appears to be pretty and sweet but actually paints herself and is nasty. By reading history one can find example after example of women who delighted in bloody acts and vanquished men through their hatred. The reader should take heed before it is too late because woman is not what he would like her to be.

The "Prayse" is far more extensively developed than the "Disprayse." It is a blatant example of the playfulness of the popular genre of defense. Although the volume is entitled *The Prayse and Disprayse of Women* and states its author's name on the title page (an unusual procedure for attacks on women, standard for defenses), the praise section begins with the conventional assertion that its author has been motivated to write by the discovery of an anonymous book against women:

> I chaunced once to come in place,
> where I a booke did finde:
> Which booke did spitefullie disgrace,
> the gentle woman kinde.

> Then thus unto my selfe I thought,
> good Lord what man was he:
> That with such painfull studie sought,
> disprayse of femenie.

> How coulde he teache his penne to write,
> how coulde his hart devise:
> Such foolish fansies to endite,
> that all men may despise. . . .

> Thus musinge did I syt long time,
> at last my pen I toke:

And so beganne to writ in rime,
against that shamles booke.

(A5r and v)

The "Prayse" could, in fact, have been written before the "Disprayse" and could have been motivated by Pyrrye's reading of an antifeminist text by someone other than himself, yet the printing of Pyrrye's own "Disprayse" immediately before this text makes the "Prayse" a refutation of Pyrrye's own attack.[20] This opening makes it clear that the seemingly sincere and self-righteous attacks on antifeminist authors with which profeminist works ritually begin are often comic rhetorical devices that serve to polarize opinion and do not indicate anything about the author's real opinions or the real occasion of the work.

This brief passage has other qualities that undermine its sincerity and the depth of its commitment to women. The attack on the supposed author of "Disprayse" also suggests that the entire defense may be tongue-in-cheek, and, by extension, suggests that Edward More's sincere and valiant attempt to refute the *Scholehouse* after waiting for some older and more experienced man to take up the topic may be merely a pose designed to boost his popularity by connecting him with a popular topic. Pyrrye's reference to women as "poore wretches" and his suggestion that he is defending them because they are incapable of defending themselves indicates that Pyrrye's defense of women will appeal to our sympathy for their hard lot rather than being grounded in a humanist reevaluation of their capacity for reason and the classical virtues. When one turns to the text itself, however, its tone and its length in comparison with the "Disprayse" suggest that it may not be entirely facetious.

Pyrrye praises women for the same qualities that Gosynhill does, but he includes no antimasculine satire.[21] Woman suffers pain in childbirth, she goes to the trouble to raise her children and treats them kindly, and she cares for them in sickness. He states that the woman runs the house because her wit is quicker at getting the business done. Like Gosynhill, however, he does not develop this material into a defense of woman's intelligence and political ability; he leaves her in the home. He lists an extensive number of famous women, many of whom were heroic in battle, but he does not offer them as

20. Utley suggests that Pyrrye may not have written both works (206). He is inconsistent in his doubts, as in his discussion of the dialogue "Know before thou Knytte" he suggests that the "C" by which one of the interlocutors is identified may be the author himself, C. Pyrrye.

21. Utley sees Pyrrye as deeply indebted to *Mulierum Pean* (294).

models of what women can do but rather as models of virtue. This is his strategy with Judith, for example, "who in dead time of night: / Cut of the head of Holiferne, / and not by strength in fight" (D1r). "Sara Raguels daughter dere" appears, as she did in *Mulierum Pean*, as an example of God's preservation of women when they lead virtuous lives.[22] Pyrrye, like Gosynhill and More, defends women against allegations that they are unchaste and are the enemy of man; he is not interested in the role they play in society but in their virtue.

Although Pyrrye's authorship of both works and the clever placing in doubt of his sincerity in the introduction to the volume would seem to make the "Prayse" as suspect as the "Disprayse": the last speaker can dominate a debate, and Pyrrye at the end of "Prayse" allows the speaker of "Prayse" to assume an authoritative and sympathetic voice. The concluding section draws back from the extreme position held up to that point and suggests a moderate course. This is possible because there has been no antimasculine satire to replace hatred of women with hatred of men. Pyrrye makes the conventional admission that some women have been bad, but he reproaches their detractors for blaming all women, and he goes on to encourage his readers to rational love of women. His conclusion suggests that he is attempting to bring the sexes together: What creature other than man fights with his own kind? he asks, it is folly to slander those we should praise and love (D7r). He ends with nine specially set stanzas inviting the reader who has used his judgment while he read to join in his praise of woman. While it might seem that woman has been restored to her position as object of worship from which the antifeminists, including Pyrrye himself, knocked her down, Pyrrye's request that the reader "judge" suggests that he is invoking rational and disinterested appreciation and praise for woman's good qualities rather than the self-interested and indiscriminate praise offered by lovers. The reward for appreciating woman's good points seems to be satisfied love.

The final "Fruytful short dialogue uppon the sentence, knowe before thou knitte" instructs the reader to think carefully before taking an irrevocable step; marriage is implied, although not mentioned, as the specific act to which the two male speakers refer. For the male reader, the lesson of the entire volume would seem to be that one ought to inform oneself about womankind before committing oneself to marriage. This suggests that a good marriage is possible if entered into wisely, and this in turn suggests that the reader is being asked to synthesize the praise and disparise sections and arrive at a judgment of

---

22. This unusual interpretation of the case of Tobias and Sarah may show the closeness of the texts of *Mulierum Pean* and Pyrrye's, as Utley suggested.

woman that lies somewhere in the middle. This is possible because, as we have seen, the ideal that lies behind the two sections is the same. The woman who has learned her lesson from the reading will be loving, generous, chaste, devoted, a good mother; she will have no desire for mastery over her husband and, so far as we know, no intellectual curiosity. The woman being selected for the marriage that cannot be unknit will not be an independent woman.

Jane Anger Her Protection for Women and the Problem of Feminine Silence

Among the contributions to the popular literature in defense of women, one book stands out as different: *Jane Anger Her Protection for Women* (1589), written by Ja.A.Gent, as the title page says.[23] This work stands out because it is the only full-scale defense of women attributed to a female author in the sixteenth century, and the supposed sex of the author has gained a good deal of attention for the book in recent years.[24] *Protection for Women* has generally been accepted as putting forward "feminist" ideas, primarily because it is assumed to be written by a woman and because the authorial persona is angry at men; she speaks to women as a woman and advises them on the male temperament and character so that they may be "protected" from injury in the future.[25] Even those critics who doubt the female sex of the author or who suspect the sincerity of the piece accept it as making a profeminist argument.[26] Despite this near-consensus, analysis of its ideas and rhetoric will show that *Protection* is a conservative piece that undermines the foundations of Renaissance profeminism.

It is not possible to determine whether the author of *Protection* really was a woman. Most modern scholars agree that Jane Anger is a pseudonym but still argue that the author was a woman. For example, Hull asserts that "the 'Gent.'

---

23. All quotations from *Jane Anger Her Protection* are from the 1589 edition; for the reader's convenience I have also cited page numbers from Henderson's edition.

24. I stipulate "full scale" because in 1579 Margaret Tyler prefaced her translation of *The Mirrour of . . . Knyghthood* with a long defense of her right and ability to translate a secular romance. For discussions of *Protection*, see Woodbridge (63–66), Hull (120–21), and Kelly (101–2).

25. For example, see Ferguson, *First Feminists* (10). Louis B. Wright's description of the work as an "old fashioned recital of man's iniquity and woman's virtues" is unusual (476).

26. Woodbridge argues very persuasively against the assumption that Anger's defense is sincere, but she does not question whether the defense is in fact a defense, and she does not identify the notion of woman that is being defended.

appears to be a gentlewoman" because she identifies with her female readers" (120), and Woodbridge denies the work's sincerity but does not question the author's claim to be a woman.[27] Despite all this faith in the female sex of this pseudonymous author, it seems most likely to me that the pattern of authors writing on both sides of the question is being followed and that the most likely author of this work is the same unknown person who wrote the lost *Complaint of a late surfeiting lover*, which the *Protection* identifies as the impetus behind its invective.[28]

Whatever the gender of its author, the *Protection* shows no familiarity with the latest thought about women, and it has no feminist program. Although the female authorial persona "speaks" in the text, she does not encourage her female readers to do so and does not formulate a new notion of woman to refute the traditional, sexually based one. She does not address women with any hope to provoke them to aspire to anything but a very limited sexual autonomy. The work is a "protection for women" because it teaches women how to protect themselves from masculine wiles; it teaches self-defense not self-esteem or independent action. At once an art of love and a *remedia amoris*, it tells women that they need to know about men and men's perceptions of them in order to survive relationships with men with their reputations intact. Stylistically, it shares more with the genre of antifeminist satire than with humanist defense. It is an experiment in the manipulation of a created voice, a sort of dramatic monologue spoken in the persona of an angry woman, just as much of *Mulierum Pean* is spoken in the voice of Venus, and just as antifeminist pieces, such as the *Scholehouse*, are spoken in the persona of an angry man.

The unprecedented use of an angry female voice as author of the piece is the

27. Woodbridge suggests the name may be "allegorical" (63). Henderson and McManus offer a series of reasons for accepting all the defenses written under female pseudonyms as being by women (20–24). For example, they find that "the hypothesis that these treatises were actually written by men is not logical. Men write under female pseudonyms when there is some definite benefit to be gained . . . but in the Renaissance a female name on a defense treatise was an anomaly which would enhance neither the prestige nor the sales of the work" (21). Kelly discusses the text in a footnote to the statement "A number of well-identified English women published such rejoinders, as well as some pseudonymous authors who are clearly women" (76). In the note she recognizes that Anger may be a pseudonym, and that the work "may be questioned for male authorship" but notes that "there were a couple of Jane Angers living at the time." Kahin's entire argument that the work is sincere would make no sense if the author were not female; she admits that the name may be a pseudonym but she cites the research of Miss Ruth Hughey, who "discovered two Jane Angers living in England in 1589, either of whom might have written the pamphlet" (31 n. 3).

28. In this work, according to Anger, the author wrote on two kinds of matter: "the one in the dispraise of mans follie, and the other, inuective against our sex" (B1v; 175). There has been much speculation about this lost work. See Shepherd (*Women's*) and Kahin.

key to its attractiveness, its seeming radicalness, its ambiguity, and, finally, to
its support of the status quo.[29] Anger represents her act of speaking as a radical
departure from traditional female behavior; she asserts the persuasive profeminist topos familiar from *Dyalogue Defensyve* (and from most Italian tracts) that
power lies in male hands because they have control of speech and writing, yet
she does not represent her own speaking out as signaling the dawn of a new
age, a time in which control of the female image will be or should be wrested
from male hands. Indeed, analysis of what she actually says about writing shows
that she, unlike the Italian humanists whose voices she would seem to echo, is
not a believer in a new age of female verbal power.

Anger describes men as being quite cold-hearted in their use of their control
of the written word; they malign women even when they are moved to write
not by anger and disappointment but merely by lack of other matter to write
about. Men are free to do this because they know that women will not respond.

> But iudge what the cause should be, of this their so great malice towards
> simple women. Doubtles the weaknesse of our wits, and our honest
> bashfulnesse, by reason wherof they suppose that there is not one
> amongst us who can, or dare reprooue their slanders and false reproches:
> their slaunderous tongues are so short, and the time wherin they have
> lauished out their words freely, hath been so long, that they know we
> cannot catch hold of them to pull them out, and they think we wil not
> write to reprooue their lying lips. . . . (B1.r; 175)

Although the topos arguing that men are able to control society's notion of
woman because they control the pens and the presses usually concludes with
an appeal to women to right the wrongs of the past and record history
themselves so that their deeds will be correctly represented to future generations, Anger never suggests that women take control of the recording of
history; she nowhere praises any kind of writing by other women.

Anger makes it impossible for writing by women to take place in a morally
unambiguous context. That she herself, contrary to male expectations, is now

---

29. About this persona Shepherd says, "However Anger's pamphlet came to be printed, what is
striking—and I think new—about the text is the way in which it stresses the person of the author. The
particular feature of the women's pamphlets (whether the authors were really women or not) is their
'we women' manner: the authors used themselves as subjects, they drew examples from their experience
as women; this was the only way they, as 'voice' of women, could challenge authority and received
ideas. In men's writing, by contrast, the author tended to efface himself and to write as if objectively:
the male author could be 'objective' about the male world (*Women's* 30).

writing "to reprove their lying lips" is a breaking of the pattern of female silence and an assertion of independence on the part of at least this woman. Her act of writing defies the definition of woman as weak-witted and bashful; it would thus seem that her assignment of these traits to women in this paragraph is an ironic mocking of the male notion of woman. Yet, through associating women's bashfulness with honesty ("honest bashfulness"), Anger makes it impossible to maintain that women are not bashful without sacrificing the notion that they are honest. While she represents male lying as an external verbal act that can be indulged in at will and manipulated for power, she represents female honesty, expressed in "bashfulness"—a reluctance to speak— as an essential ethical virtue whose loss is sinful. Her bold act of writing puts her in jeopardy of being called dishonest.[30]

Rather than deny the traditional connection between silence and sexual virtue, Anger defends her appropriation of speech, printing, and audience on the grounds that she is angry and has been driven to speech by male action. In the dedicatory letter "to all women in generall, and gentle Reader whatsoeuer," she says,

> Shal Surfeiters raile on our kindnes, you stand stil & say nought, and shall not Anger stretch the vaines of her braines, the stringes of her fingers, and the lists of her modestie, to answere their Surfeitings? Yes truely. And herein I coniure all you to aide and assist me in defence of my willingnes, which shall make me rest at your commaunds.
> (A2v; 174)

Self-defense, as we have seen, is an implicit component of all defenses, but while male authors defend their right to speak on such a subject, Anger defends her right to speak at all. Her defense is not her wisdom or even her experience, but her anger, which drives her to do this act, which is at the limits of modesty. She does not represent her act of writing as natural but as in need of excusing, as she says in the letter "to the Gentlewomen of England," "for my presumption I crave pardon, because it was ANGER that did write it" (A2r; 173). Again in the verses with which she concludes the book, Anger says,

> If ought offend, which she doth send,
> impute it to her moode.

30. Anger's defense of her writing as the result of anger and, thus, of unreason, and her neglect of the topic of defense of female writing as a class suggests to me that the author of the *Protection* is not a woman, as women who speak usually defend their right and ability to do so. Margaret Tyler, for example, prefaced her *Mirrour* (1578) with an explanation and defense.

> For ANGER'S rage must that asswage,
> as wel is vnderstoode.
>
> (D2r; 188)

As these two symbolic uses of her name suggest, her identity is reduced to the single quality "anger," which has led her to write. This, of course, focuses attention on her passion, but it also redeems her morally because it portrays her writing as unpremeditated and her bashfulness as overcome by passion but still active in her—she must apologize and ask for understanding for what she has done. This moral justification is necessary because Anger has accepted the notion that silence is a sign of female purity and speech is a violation of that purity. That she is angry and is writing are themselves a reproach to men and a sign that their maligning of women produces antisocial results. Male slander has forced her to play an independent role that is not natural to women.

Anger builds a new understanding of woman to replace the one constructed by antifeminist male authors, but she does this primarily by discovering positive meanings in conventional negative phrases, rather than by inventing her own terms of praise (or taking over humanist ones). She wittily finds a profeminist truth in timeworn antifeminist platitudes such as the etymology of woman as meaning "woe to man" and the pseudo-Theophrastan definition, "mulier est hominis confusio."

> We are the griefe of man, in that wee take all the griefe from man: we languish when they laugh; we lie sighing when they sit singing, and sit sobbing when they lie slugging and sleeping. *Mulier est hominis confusio*, because her kinde heart cannot so sharply reprooue their franticke fits, as those madde frensies deserue. (B3r; 178)

Through her redefinition of such phrases, Anger takes away from antifeminist men the power to define what woman is, but she rejects only the negative vision of woman offered by tradition, not the positive ideal. Through Anger's writing, womankind is restored to purity, but she is not assigned any power or voice other than sighs and sobs. The result is a sense of women as long-suffering and patient moral superiors to men. The very qualities that she has identified as exposing women to mistreatment at the hands of men are the ones that are held up for praise.

Formal praise of women takes up only a brief section of the *Protection*, and the grounds for praise are entirely traditional. The purpose of this praise is not to persuade a male audience of the excellence of women, but to persuade women themselves of their own value. Anger begins her praise by excluding male readers, "let us secretlye our selues with ourselues, consider howe and in what, they that are our worst enemies, are both inferiour unto us, and most beholden unto our kindenes" (C1r; 180). As this phrasing suggests, what follows is praise with a vengeance; it proves that women are good at the same time that it continues the invective against men.

The defense of women is shallow and comic. It relies on old tropes such as the assertion that man was made out of "drosse and filthy clay" (C1r; 180) and "woman of mans fleshe, that she might bee purer than he, [which] doth euidently showe, how far we women are more excellent then men" (C1r; 181). Much is made of men's dependence on women in everyday life and in sickness, and men's virility is attributed to women's solicitude: "Without our care they lie in their beds as dogs in litter, & go like lowst Mackarell swimming in the heat of sommer" (C1v; 181). Argument is piled on argument with little or no development, and the evidence against men for women is far more witty than it is authoritative.

The defense of women's wisdom and wit, for example, is highly entertaining, but uses none of the readily available evidence of accomplished women to prove the point; indeed, it mocks the topic:

> And now (seeing I speake to none but to you which are of mine owne Sex,) giue me leave like a scoller to proue our wisdome more excellent then theirs, though I neuer knew what sophistry ment. Ther is no wisdome but it comes by grace, this is a principle, & *Contra principium non est disputandum*: but grace was first giuen to a woman, because to our lady: which premises conclude that women are wise. Now *Primum est optimum*, & therefore women are wiser then men. That we are more witty which comes by nature, it cannot better be proued then that by our answers, men are often droven to *Non plus*, & if their talk be of worldly affaires, with our resolutions they must either rest satisfied, or prove themselves fooles in the end. (C2r; 182)

This passage is a clever parody of the sophistic logic of antifeminist reasoning—as Anger's denial of knowledge of sophistry suggests it will be—and the end displays real wit by forcing men to accept women's rejections of their suits or look foolish. The passage proves that this particular woman is as clever as men; it says nothing about real wisdom. A send-up of the method of arguments made against women, it offers no substantial positive notion of woman's wisdom to follow up on its erosion of antifeminist slander.

Finally, as Anger said at the beginning, this text is a defense of women against men not an encomium of womankind. Anger sees male profeminism to be as suspect as antifeminism because it is a tool of seduction and deception. Not only are "their faire wordes allurements to destruction: and their large promises tokens of death, or of euils worse then death" (C3v; 183), but their published retractions of antifeminism, their defenses of womankind, are traps to catch women. In her conclusion, Anger advises women to be suspicious of those familiar figures in the debate, the profeminists who repent their former essays in slander:

> You must beare with the olde Louer his surfeit, because hee was diseased when he did write it, and peraduenture hereafter, when he shal be well amended, he wil repent himselfe of his slanderous speaches against our sex, and curse the dead man which was the cause of it, and make a publique recantation: For the faltering in his speach at the latter end of his book affirmeth, that already he half repenteth of his bargaine, & why? because his melodie is past: But beleeve him not, thogh he should out swear you, for although a jade may be still in a stable when his gall backe is healed, yet he will showe himselfe in his kind when he is traueiling: and mans flattery bites secretly, from which I pray God keepe you and me too. Amen. (D1r; 186)

Thus does Anger undermine and explode the pretensions of Gosynhill, More, and Pyrrye to heartfelt speech in defense of womankind—though, of course, none of them fully admitted to having written slander of the female sex before they wrote praise.

This closing speech is Anger's most radical profeminist move; she cautions her woman reader against accepting the positive notion of woman offered in the defenses as anything other than flattery designed to entrap her into a situation that will prove not so pleasant for the woman once she has accepted the man as her traveling companion. She urges her readers to become skeptical listeners and mistrusters of men, but she gives them no alternate role to play. Female power remains sexual power: the withholding of favor because of suspicion, the rare granting of favor to the rare honest man are the strategies Anger counsels. That and prayer.

Anger's cynical reading of the English popular defenses of women may well be accurate: as we have seen, none of the authors, except Vaughan (Burdet) removed the discussion of womankind from the context of love, not even Anger (her)self. None defined women in any way not previously conceived of by the most conservative male tradition and none used his voice to persuade women to take up their pens and speak. They do not urge education and freedom from domestic drudgery; they do not catalogue exemplars of women who excelled in the classical virtues. They consent to the validity of the traditional ideal, which demands purity of women and binds them in a nurturing role. In England, throughout the sixteenth century, the old ideal of woman dominated in defenses of womankind aimed at the popular market. Though some readers might have found more newfangled ideas in translations of Italian and French humanist texts, any reader whose taste did not run to serious literature might well have remained innocent of the notion that woman is man's intellectual, moral, and physical equal.

9

THE DEFENSE OF FEMALE REGIMENT: PRACTICAL POLITICS

To turn from the popular defense of women to the defense of rule by women during the reign of Elizabeth I is to turn from jest and play and a very traditional notion of woman to deepest seriousness in tone and in method of presentation and a confrontation with the independent woman of humanist thought. Gone are the obvious literary devices, the wit, the matching pro and contra cases, the references to Ovid and to the readers' own experience. The comic trope of the lover's self-defense and hope of advancement in love is replaced by extensive defense of the loyalty and patriotism of the author or his party and hope of advancement in the Queen's regard. These long and sober volumes present careful analysis of the case against rule by women and then give detailed answers to the objections on grounds natural, civil, and spiritual, buttressed with extensive references to canon and civil law and to the Bible.[1] No one would have read them for pleasure; indeed, no one interested in the defense of womankind would have been likely to identify them as being relevant and read them. They are, however, important to this study as a practical offshoot of the humanist analysis of woman's social and political role. In them the tropes and strategies of the defense are used to close off discussion, not to provoke it.

The need for such defenses arose at the accession of Elizabeth I, when John Knox challenged the Queen's right to the throne and her capacity for authority in his *First Blast of the Trumpet against the Monstruous regiment of women* (unwittingly, of course, as his object was to discredit Mary Tudor). The Queen's sex was perceived as a weakness in need of defense throughout most of her

---

1. Jordan points out that this method of argument is very different from that of the anti–woman rule party whose claims are "generally supported by an appeal to authority, chiefly scripture and Aristotle" ("Woman's Rule" 426).

reign and, even when no written attack on her right to rule was made or when the attack was aimed not at herself but at Mary Stuart, supporters from various parties produced defenses of her right.[2] Knox's *First Blast* was answered by the Marian exile John Aylmer in his *An Harborowe for faithfull and trewe Subjectes against the late blowne Blaste, concerninge the Government of Wemen* in 1559 and by John Calvin in a letter written to Burghley in the same year.[3] George Buchanan's attack on Mary Stuart in his *History of Scotland* was taken to be an attack on Elizabeth's right to rule as well and was answered by Roman Catholic Henry Howard, Earl of Northampton, in *A Dutiful defense of the lawful regiment of women*, a work commissioned by Lord Burghley himself.[4] The Norfolk conspiracy and the Northern uprising provoked Burghley to defend Elizabeth's rights and his own conduct in *Salutem in Christo*. The Pope's bull excommunicating Elizabeth and liberating her subjects from obedience received an authoritative answer from Bullinger. And the last machinations of the Guise party on behalf of Mary Stuart seem to have stimulated George Whetstone to write a retrospective response to Knox in *The English Myrror* (1586). John Bridges's *A defence of the Government* . . . (1587) also dates from this period.

These defenses can be divided into two distinct groups defined by the ambition of their authors and by their resolution of the dilemma posed by the independent woman. Protestants who hoped for or held ecclesiastical and secular political office espoused the extraordinary-woman theory. A professional writer, Whetstone, and a Catholic under suspicion of disloyalty, Howard, advocated female autonomy. The former group can be further subdivided into two approaches. Calvin represented female government as a disruption of the order of nature that God visited on man as a reprimand. He acknowledged no legal or natural authority in Elizabeth's government and gave her no grounds on which to base her claim to the throne other than a shadowy divine right revealed in her personal virtue. Alymer, Bullinger, Bridges, and other Protestants of Calvinistic orientation, attempted to reconcile Calvin's notion with the English situation. They defined the Queen's accession as a positive example of divine intervention in history. They showed that Elizabeth had the right

2. Even loyal members of the government resorted to blame of Elizabeth's sex when exasperated by her conduct. R. B. Wernham, in *Before the Armada*, cites state papers that show that her indecisive attitude toward Mary in 1568–69 drove "her loyal Puritan Councillor Sir Francis Knollys into exclaiming that it was time to end this feeble female government and for the Queen to let the men of her Council take over the management of affairs" (298).

3. For an excellent summary and discussion of Knox and many of the defenses and an interpretation of them in light of political doctrine, see Jordan, "Woman's Rule."

4. John Leslie defended Mary against the charges in his *Concerning the Defense of the Honor of* . . . *Marie Queene of Scotland*.

and the capacity to rule, but they did not treat her as a typical woman, representative of the capacities of all women if they are given a chance. Whetstone and Howard represented Elizabeth as exemplary of the powers of her sex; others could emulate her. Essentially, Calvin, Aylmer, and the other radical Protestants defined their works as defenses of the Queen, but they were, in reality, equally as much defenses against queens and female autonomy. The independent woman was the primary enemy against whom the society and the text needed to be protected. Whetstone and Howard defended the independent woman.

In her own speeches, Elizabeth I was very successful at taking neither side. In her famous speech at Tilbury before the attack of the Armada, she neatly enunciated the central paradox posed by her being at the head of the government:

> I know I have the body but of a weak and feeble woman, but I have the heart and stomach of a king. . . . [R]ather than any dishonor shall grow by me, I myself will take up arms, I myself will be your general, judge, and rewarder of every one of your virtues in the field. (542)

She is able to transcend the limitations of her ordinary woman's body and act with the spirit of a king, the highest of men.[5] Because of this male spirit within her she will not engender the typical female offspring—dishonor; she will function successfully as a man.[6]

But where does this male spirit come from? Elizabeth does not say. Why and how the male spirit that enables her to fight, judge, and reward has come to reside in her female body is a question that she does not raise. Boccaccio would have attributed the presence of "the stomach of a King" in her female body to the action of God; it would have been an example of a miraculous infusion of male spirit into a female body, and Elizabeth would have been an extraordinary woman. (See my Chapter 1.) By speaking of her own resolve to defend herself and her nation against dishonor, however, Elizabeth opens the possibilities that the male spirit has entered her body by natural means and that women are actually more powerful than their bodies may make them seem, and, thus, that

5. Elizabeth is referring to the political doctrine of the king's two bodies here. See Kantorowitz and Axton.

6. The speech gains force from its subtle suggestion that the men present are effeminate, just as in Boccaccio's *De mulieribus* the valor of women often showed up the effeminacy of men. If Elizabeth really has to fight, her taking up arms will have been in some way caused by the male soldiers' inadequacies. The speech provokes them to desire to fight so that she, so patently unable to do so, will not need to.

she is exemplary rather than extraordinary. Because, at the end of the speech, she turned her authority over to her lieutenant-general, her exercise of the male prerogative of combat was left in the symbolic realm of costume, and her government was distanced by a male intermediary. An expert at "exploiting her ambiguous position" (Crane 10), she makes it possible for men who hold a variety of views on the topic of women to be inspired by her speech and not to fear that her independence will crush their masculinity or their authority.[7]

This kind of rhetorical skill served the Queen well when she had to speak publicly on issues that needed an immediate response. As a long-term approach to the problem of her sex, however, such an ambiguous pose presented serious dangers: on the one hand, the weakness of women could be asserted as a reason why Elizabeth herself ought to be barred from rule; on the other, the possibility that woman's capacity to govern arose naturally could be used to defend the right of Elizabeth's competitors to the throne and to erode the image of Elizabeth as the divinely chosen leader of the elect nation. To adequately defend the Queen's position as legitimate ruler, her defenders had to resolve the dilemma, and she had to choose a side to favor.

In this competition for influence and power, Elizabeth's patronage went to Aylmer and those who followed his line of argument. As often as she flirted with the possibility that she was capable of self-defense and defense of the nation, as she did at Tilbury, when the legitimacy of her rule was attacked she favored defenses of her rule that distinguished between her legal and natural right to rule and the capacity of other women for office. Calvin's rigid defense of her as extraordinary and Howard's open defense of her as exemplary both fared badly. Both threatened the entire political system, the former by denying the Queen's hereditary right and the latter by opening the field to all competitors. Calvin got the cold shoulder, although, of course, the reasons for this did not lie only in his attitude toward rule by women. Howard was accused of sedition, according to his preface, and delayed circulation of his manuscript. (Whetstone was exceptional in that he integrated his defense into a larger work, and he does not seem to have been participating in the political contest.) As a result of the practical problems posed by rival claimants to the throne and of the Protestant notion that England was an elect nation, rule by a woman in England resulted in the theoretical restriction of fields of activity for women rather than their expansion as one idealistically minded might have expected.[8]

7. I wrenched this phrase from its context in Crane's discussion of a speech Elizabeth made in 1563 on the topic of marriage. In this speech, the Queen also plays with the trope of her female weakness. Although Crane does not discuss it, the speech at Tilbury might also be considered an example of counsel, as she is advising the troops to be valiant and to obey her lieutenant-general.

8. In "Woman's Rule," Constance Jordan describes the contrast between the potential and actual

The notion of the independent woman advanced by humanist thinkers was politically inopportune in Elizabethan England.[9]

Of all the texts written in defense of the Queen, John Aylmer's *An Harborowe for faithfull and trewe Subjectes* and Henry Howard's *A Dutiful defense of the lawful regiment of women*, when set against each other, best illuminate my thesis that the independent woman was an enemy in practical political thought in England—Aylmer's because it was the first English Protestant defense and set the tone and method for the rest, Howard's because it is the only freestanding extensive defense of the humanist position. That Howard's text was never printed and is extant in only three manuscripts and a few fragments whereas Aylmer's exists in numerous printed copies provides physical evidence of the dominance of the extraordinary-woman theory. Textual comparison will reveal defensiveness against female autonomy in *An Harborowe* and praise of it in *A Dutiful defense* and will provide evidence of the strategies used to contain or encourage the independent woman. Howard's text demonstrates that practical politics mitigated against the development of the profeminist thesis. It shows that an Englishman could conceive of a new role for women, but that it was not politic for him to do so.

Despite their different religious parties, both men had reason to fear for their political security when they wrote their defenses; Howard also feared for his liberty. Alymer was a Marian exile who hoped to return to England and become a power in the reestablished Protestant church, but he feared that his party would be out of power because of John Knox's ill-timed attack. His work is an attempt to prove his loyalty, to gain authority for his particular branch of Protestantism, and to gain power for himself within that group. It is addressed to the Lords Francis Earle of Bedford (Privy Council member) and Robert

---

results of this literature and the presence of a female monarch on the throne. "However convincing these arguments for gynecocracy were in the short run—when the stability of the English throne depended on the future of a single woman—they proved almost negligible in their real consequences over the long term, at least in any practical way. Neither the presence of a woman on the throne for the better part of the century nor the arguments for the legality of her rule seem to have encouraged an acceptance of the idea that women could assume magistracies or participate in political life in other capacities" (423–24). She finds this situation paradoxical. I suggest that the answer may lie in the careful limitation of the scope of the arguments themselves, as I explain below.

9. John King demonstrates that Elizabeth could be represented as part of a group of exceptional learned queens when the topic was piety and not government. In the woodcuts to Thomas Bentley's *The Monument of Matrones* (1582) she is shown with Marguerite de Navarre, Katherine Parr, and Esther. Bentley also includes Elizabeth's writings along with other women's devotional works. Both these aspects of his work suggest that when the topic was not the politically sensitive and precedent-setting topic of female government but rather piety and learning, Elizabeth could be seen as representative of the best of her sex.

Dudley. Howard was a member of the Roman Catholic Howard family. By his own testimony, he was favored by Elizabeth in the early years of her reign, when his family was in disgrace, but he was troubled by pursuivants in the years while he was compiling his defense. His work was commissioned by Burghley, perhaps as a demonstration of his loyalty, which he attempts to prove in the text. The work is addressed to the Queen herself, and he begs for her mercy at great length.[10] In both cases, self-defense rather than any intrinsic interest in the topic of rule by women led them to write in defense of the Queen. In this they both resemble the many defenders of womankind who express a hope that their work on behalf of the sex will win favor with some particular woman.

Aylmer's extensive dedicatory letter makes it difficult for anyone to call Elizabeth's right to rule into question: to do so makes one not only seditious but heretical; it divides one from "Christes church" and indicates that one is not a member of the elect. Aylmer speaks with the authoritative voice of a minister of God and seems privy to God's plans. He works by casting aspersions on his opponents and even on his friends, and he divides the loyal from the disloyal on the grounds of their religious beliefs rather than their political ones. He begins with a list of sects and heresies that poison the world: Anabaptists, freewillers, justiciaries, Adiaphoristes, Papists, all of whom are "god's enemies, by whom our aduersari Satan seketh to disturb the true vnitie of Christes church . . . and to dim that excellent lighte . . . [God] determined shuld shine to the unspeakeable comfort of his elect, in these our dais." Among the heretics are numbered those who "called into question among us such thinges, as good subiects before neuer doubted of, whether it wer lawful for women, inheritours of kingdoms, to gouern and guid the same, or no." This error may seem not to be related to salvation, but "the quiet of common weales is the nurse of religion" and the apostle damns rebellions, so it is not a trifle to stir up controversy about a subject never before mistrusted (A3r).

Aylmer's defense of himself in this letter is not directly stated, but it is implied. Having associated himself with the elect, Aylmer goes on to represent himself as heroic. He is the only one of his party conscientious enough to take on the necessary labor of refuting the *First Blast*. He has waited a year for some learned man to make an answer, but none was forthcoming.[11] He has written

10. Perhaps the assignment was given to him by Burghley as a sort of loyalty test: when he began to write the work, Mary Stuart was still alive, and the loyalty of all Catholics was suspect. He succeeded in writing the defense of Elizabeth without defending Mary, a neat trick as Buchanan's book, to which he was responding, was aimed at Mary.

11. Edward More offered the same defense of his entry into the *Scholehouse* controversy.

"so that neither our sworn enemies the papists shal . . . belie us . . . nor the highe powers themselves . . . fear us . . . We honor and esteme true obedience to the high ministres of God. . . . Thus me thinke I may saye in the name of al" (A3v).

In these pages Aylmer offers the alternatives of the babbling opinion of sects and the truth of the unified church, for which he has made himself the spokesman. His church is identical with the "excellent lighte" of God; loyalty to Elizabeth and loyalty to his church are one. He moves himself from the position of outcast to one of authority; he successfully defends himself from a charge of treason without ever suggesting that he could have been so charged. The extensive defense of rule by a woman, which follows this dedicatory letter, is the proof of his own obedience. He cannot be charged with treason, as he is the first to throw a stone at it.

Howard's dedicatory letter is far longer than Aylmer's; it runs from twenty-one to twenty-nine folio sheets in the various manuscripts.[12] It is an extraordinary example of the genre of defense in its own right. He begins from an extremely weak personal position and ends up as an authority warning the Queen against detractors. His defense of himself is inextricably entwined with his defense of his topic, which he presents as a controversial subject, one that it takes courage to broach.

His letter gives some sense of the political ambiguity of the defense of woman rule. It seems that, despite its clearly announced patriotism, Aylmer's book was not entirely well received (fol. 3) and that some who had been in print against the Queen and had never recanted became fat and wealthy (fol. 2v). Trust in the Queen's love gave Howard the courage to begin to write the work Burghley had requested of him, but he had no sooner started to write than the accusations began. It was said that he was writing the book only to flatter the Queen, and, worse, he was indicted at a Privy Council session and judged guilty, without having been asked any questions.

Howard represents the topic itself as the problem. Some Privy Councillors thought the topic should not be written on because it "should be used in present as a meane of working laudable effects then allowed as a president in matters of like weight to dispose of like authoritie." In other words, although defense of rule by women was judged to be politic at that moment of English history, it was seen to present a challenge to long-term political stability. For these Privy Councillors, defense of gynecocracy was an expedient means of achieving immediate political goals, and writing down the defense was a

---

12. All quotations will be from the manuscript in the Pepys library.

dangerous step to take because it could not be written in sand. To people who thought like this, Howard's book would have been more offensive than Aylmer's, and his representation of his effort as a continuation of his predecessor's is disingenuous and in itself a strategy of defense. Aylmer does not set precedents; Howard does.

As Howard represents his troubles here, the Queen herself does not seem to have taken part in the persecution of him and his topic; it seems that he is trying to sway her in favor of the work by dissociating her from its attackers. Her councillors, pursuivants, and unnamed slanderers have persecuted Howard and attacked Aylmer, whereas the Queen is represented as a loving protector whose best interests may not be supported by those who would suppress the writing of the defense. The very act of addressing the work to Elizabeth when it was commissioned by Burghley is strategic; Howard both begs her protection and warns her of her needs. He attempts to appear one of her party, one who has the privilege of addressing her directly and personally. He reminds her of her previous protection of him: when "He was but lately crept or swept out of the ruins of his house her majesty . . . regarded him with pity and warned him of traps."

Howard shows the Queen why such a work is in her best interest by presenting an extensive encomium of her in which he directly praises her policies, while making it clear that there are others who do not praise them; his praise of her is, thus, also a defense of her and delicately suggests that she is in need of defending. He especially praises her commitment to justice and her refusal to allow herself to swerve from it despite the claims by such philosophers as Machiavelli that rulers may do so with impunity. He compares the nation's response to her justice with past societies' responses to Deborah, Astrea, Velleda, and Margaret of Norway. Because he is asking for mercy, a form of justice, he is reminding her to be true to the quality that best serves him; if she is not, all this glorious praise will not rightfully be hers. Like Aylmer, Howard completely turns the balance of power by the end of his letter. He is an ally of the Queen, and those who would suppress such writings as his are her enemies.

The praise Howard offers the Queen inseparably links her with the general humanist defense of womankind. It is truly glorious. By the end of the encomium, she stands for all womankind, "all these accomplishments should be thorns in the eyes of declaimers against the virtue of the female sexe—when asked for proof of women's sufficiency to rule it should be enough to say your name" (fol. 17). Elizabeth is the convincing example in a proof of women's virtue. Whereas Aylmer in his letter condemned those who questioned "whether it wer lawful for *women, inheritours of kingdoms*, to gouern and guid the same, or no" (A3r, my emphasis), Howard condemns those who question "the virtue of the female sexe." The former does not speak of Elizabeth's ability but of her legal right; the latter makes ability the issue.

These two different approaches to the question in the introductory letters forecast the territory encompassed by each defense, but Howard attempts to blur the distinction. Toward the end of his letter, he returns to the theme with which he opened—writers who have preceded him in praise and defense of Elizabeth as a female ruler—but now he describes these writers as being numerous and having unquestioned authority. Howard hides himself among these wise, mostly Protestant, men. He is not flattering the Queen, he says, if he but traces their steps. Aylmer is mentioned again (his work is extant and very worthy to be read) along with at least twelve other defenders including the Archbishop of Canterbury, Jewell, the Bishop of Salisbury, the Bishop of Ross, D. Harding, D. Stapleton, Calvin, Peter Martyr, Bullinger, and Beza. He concludes, "the manifest authorities of learned men affected both waies in religion may serve to prove that howsoever they do vary upon pointes betweene themselves, yet still the beames of your approved vertues break out of the thickest cloudes and lighten both the one part and the other of our English hemisphere" (fol. 19v). As will become clear when we examine the body of these works, this statement is not entirely true. It is Elizabeth's approved (inherited) status that lightens the other writers' hemisphere.

Howard uses a strategy opposite to Aylmer's. Aylmer wins authority by making himself stand out from the group and by making his party seem to be the only one that believes in the Queen's right to rule *despite her sex*. Howard wins authority by blending himself in with the crowd. By refusing to acknowledge the true terms of Aylmer's defense, he makes himself appear to be part of an extensive tradition and, most important, an ecumenical one. For Aylmer, the community is defined by religion, and Elizabeth deserves defense as leader of the elect; for Howard, the community is defined by nationality. Elizabeth is a ruler who unites all sects, and defense of her is a topic that draws a Catholic such as himself into the circle of the faithful.

Having located himself within the establishment, Howard concludes with a warning against those who oppose woman rule; they are potential rebels. He enforces this point with a list of men who rose up against woman rule. Elizabeth must not trust the men in her court who speak against rule by women; no matter what authorities they cite, they are wrong and they are dangerous. The tables are entirely turned; the accused has found reason for suspicion in his accusers' temporizing. His book in defense of rule by women appears to be patriotic and necessary as a work to which Elizabeth can refer for proof of her rights. His cause and her cause are bound together.

Aylmer's and Howard's treatises appear very similar because they use the same methods of organization. Each writer outlines the main points of the specific work that spurred him to write and refutes them one by one. Each proves that female regiment is not against nature, civil or canon law, or Scripture (joined with canon law in Howard). Each cites numerous examples of great queens. Beyond these similarities, however, lie essential differences. Aylmer's defense is exemplary of the left-wing Protestant approach; it is extremely narrow in scope. It defends Elizabeth, but it does not defend womankind; it does not attempt a revision of the traditional notion of woman's social role, and it could not be used to justify government by any woman (Mary Stuart, for instance), only Elizabeth. Howard's is not typically Catholic, but rather humanist; it is broad in scope.[13] It defends Elizabeth and womankind. It redefines the notion of woman and her social role. Although it offers no refutation of Buchanan's specific charges against Mary, it is the kind of work that the Privy Council said it was: a book that offers a dangerous precedent for the future; it could be used to justify government by any educated woman. It is no wonder that Aylmer won his bishopric and that Howard's work remained in manuscript.

Aylmer's work is intensely partisan. He begins by establishing his position in relation to Knox's book and offering a defense of Knox the man whose "errour rose not of malice but of zele: and by loking more to the present crueltie, that then was used: then to the inconvenience that after might follow." Like Polymnestor and Hippolitus, who cursed all women for the fault of one who hurt them, so he "seyng the tormentes of Martyres, the murdyrynge of goodmen . . . the losse of Englandes honour, . . . and all out of ioynt: He could not but mislike that regiment from whence such frutes did spring" (B1v–2r). His mistake was to attack the general when he really wanted to attack an individual, Mary Tudor. Aylmer turns Knox into an overzealous religious patriot; by defending a misguided member of the sect even as he attacks his views, Aylmer continues the work he began in the dedicatory letter. He establishes himself as an important Protestant spokesman.

Aylmer considers that the right of women to rule can be legislated; it is not a right that is naturally women's because their nature fits them for it. He suggests that to question the right of women to rule is not in itself unreasonable,

---

13. The defense of female regiment in Catholic John Leslie's *Defense* is far closer to Aylmer's line of reasoning than to Howard's.

but that Knox was wrong to raise the issue when he did. To object to female rule when a woman was ruling was seditious; the same question might be raised under a male ruler and the laws "be redressed . . . without manifest and violent wrong of them that be in place" (B2r). For now it is "stablyshed by lawe, confirmed by custome, and ratefied by common consent of all the orders in the Realme [that woman may inherit]" and one cannot take away what nature gave by birth, and God called them to. "If he hable women: shal we unhable them?" (B2v). Thus, Elizabeth's legal right to the throne made her a candidate for God's choice.

Aylmer's argument is grounded in God's decision to give power to a woman, not in woman's demonstration of virtue. He readily admits women's lack of aptness, but "when God chuseth him selfe by sending a king, whose succession is ruled by enheritaunce and lyneall discent, no heiris male: It is a plain argument, that for some secret purpose he myndeth the female should reigne and governe" (B3r). Antifeminist as the description of woman may seem, her weakness is in good company. As his examples of other work that God did on his own out of unlikely materials, Aylmer mentions that he made the world and man, he caused the Red Sea to part, "he saved his people by the hande of a woman, poore Deborah," (B3v) he enabled David to kill Goliath, Christ to succeed against Satan, and Luther, "a poor friar," to restore God's word. His final example of God's secret purpose is Anne Boleyn, Elizabeth's mother.[14]

> Was not Quene Anne the mother of this blessed woman, the chief, first, and only cause of banyshing the beast of Rome . . . was there ever in Englande a greater feate wrought by any man: then this was by a woman? . . . If God had not gyuen Quene Anne fauour in the sight of the kynge . . . the Cardinall, Wynchester, More, Rochester and other wold sone have trised up Mardocheus. . . . Wherfore . . . the croppe and roote was the Quene, whiche God had endewed with wisdome that she coulde, and gyuen her the minde that she would do it. (B4v)

In all these examples Aylmer is trying to stress the power of God rather than the weakness of his agent, be it Deborah or David or Anne (or Elizabeth). Natural weakness is an asset that gives greater glory to God at the same time that God's choice to strengthen her enough to make her a good ruler gives greater glory to the elect nation, be it Israel or England. It is not clear how one knows that God is behind a monarch, but it would seem that the results of

---

14. Fox also saw God's favor acting in Anne. See Levin's discussion, "John Foxe" (123–24).

the monarch's actions reveal God's hand.[15] Goliath needed to be slain, and David did it; English Protestantism needed to be established, and Anne made the way for it.

Aylmer's Protestant notion of human weakness prevents his refutation of Knox's central argument—that it is against nature (monstrous) for woman to govern—from being a defense of womankind. He does not reinterpret woman-kind using humanist medical and philosophical constructions of the female body and character—the cornerstones of the humanist defense of a more responsible social role for women—rather, he redefines natural law so that it includes government by women as an unusual but normal event. Anything that has happened without interfering with "the preservation of the whol" (C3r) is natural.

> We see by many examples, that by the wholle consent of nacyons, by the ordinaunce of God, and order of lawe, wemen have reigned and those not a fewe, and as it was thoughte not againste nature: Therefore it canne not bee saide, that by a generall disposition of nature, it hathe bene, and is denyed them to rule.[16] (C3v)

And again, "the rule of women hath preserued common wealthes, ergo, it is not against nature" (D2r). Woman rule is like a woman having twins or an old person not having gray hair; it is unusual but not unnatural (D1v).

This approach to nature as accommodating of variations is extremely important because, as Jordan argues, it permits "the status of women [to be] considered in light of social expectations and cultural norms" ("Woman's Rule" 438):

> Aylmer redefines nature so that it no longer can be thought to provide laws but only to indicate the general patterns into which certain kinds of events tend to fall. Knox's notion of a "Rule" against gynecocracy, sanctioned by a law of nature, gives way to Aylmer's idea of magistracy that predominently favors men but does not exclude women. (439)

15. This argument is close to Calvin's. He maintained that as rule by a woman "was a deviation from the original and proper order of nature, it was to be ranked, no less than slavery, among the punishments consequent upon the fall of man; but that there were occasionally women so endowed, that the singular good qualities which shone forth in them, made it evident that they were raised up by divine authority; either that God designed by such examples to condemn the inactivity of men, or for the better setting forth his own glory" (34–35).

16. Compare Whetstone (*English Myrror* 136) discussed at the end of this chapter.

Aylmer has no sound philosophical basis for the inclusion of women in the pool of candidates appropriate for magistracy. He relies on assertion rather than proof, and his assertions often are inconsistent with what he says when he speaks of God's mysterious choice of weak vessels to work out his plan of history. For example, Aylmer says that God does not have to alter the ingrafted properties of a woman to make her capable of rule as he had to change the properties of water to make it a wall (C3v). Previously, Aylmer used the parting of the Red Sea to illustrate God's power to work great results out of unlikely material. There, the wall of water was analogous with rule by women, both were extraordinary events; here, the wall of water is miraculous and rule by women is not; it is merely unusual.

Aylmer's discussion of woman's capacity for virtue, the natural quality that fits her for rule, is short and confused. He relies on the simple assertion that "in a woman is witte, understanding" and cites Aristotle's authority; Aristotle states that women are capable of "the same vertues that be in a man, sauinge that they differ. Secundum maius et minus, that is moore in the man then in the woman" (C4r). This is not Aristotle, but Plato in the *Republic*, and Aylmer, by identifying the statement as Aristotle's and himself as an Aristotelian, undercuts his attempt to invoke famous classical philosophers in the cause of womankind and reveals his real allegiance to the view that the sexes display different virtues and that women are unsuited to rule. His confusion is clear in an analogy that he offers as positive proof: Just as a young man is not as suitable to rule as an older man so a woman is not as suitable as a man (C4v). Ian Maclean discusses a similar comparison of old men, young men, and women and their ability to govern:

> One commentator asks whether prudence is present in equal measure in all human beings, and concludes not, as both the humours . . . and experience make older men (being cold and dry) more prudent than younger men, and the male in general more prudent than the female. It seems that both Plato and Aristotle agree on this point. Now, prudence, according to Aristotle, belongs especially to the person who commands (imperans), and this authority (imperium) can derive either from convention, as with tyranny or monarchy, or from nature, as is the case with man's authority over woman; the male is *naturally* more robust, more rational, less subject to fluctuating emotions. (*Renaissance Notion* 49–50)

Aylmer recognizes that Aristotle, like Plato, discovers prudence in both sexes, but he does not understand that Aristotle discovers the prudence of old and young men to be constructed by their role in life, whereas woman's prudence is constructed by her physical nature. The analogy he draws just does not work as proof of woman's capacity to rule.

Aylmer is consistently Aristotelian and not profeminist in his neglect of the topic of woman's demonstrated abilities in fields that might contribute to proficiency in ruling (learning, for example), since Aristotle did not acknowledge their existence in quantities sufficient to make them worth mention. The only connection Aylmer makes between other activities of women and the duties of a queen is domestic. A woman rules men within her household; therefore, she can be said already to rule over men in her everyday life—although, of course, she is only a minister in this little kingdom as her husband rules her. Aylmer does not develop a proof that the virtues that the woman uses to govern the home are the same virtues a prince uses to govern a state, as Elyot does; he relies merely on the analogy between home and state to prove the point.

The single profeminist item that Aylmer develops in detail is the list of ancient and modern successful female rulers; his list is extensive, and he is concerned to prove that women can do a good job. "So that I wyn at his hand that these women reigned, and kept their countries in as good order or better than any men did: it is a great likelihod, that this sexe is not so unapt to rule, as he maketh them" (E2r). This is Aylmer's most profeminist statement by far and is in no way reconciled with his earlier statement that woman is weak in nature and soft in courage. Aylmer seems to recognize the truth of his examples, but it does not cause him to rethink his entire argument. As he explains, this list is necessary to demonstrate the naturalness of rule by women because, to be natural, it must have been successful. He is not interested in the greater implications for womankind. These independent women are not set into a philosophical or historical context that explains how they came to achieve what they did, and so their achievement does not set a precedent for other women's independence, merely for Elizabeth's. There is still need for the will of God to act to bring women to power.

Finally, Aylmer's difference from Knox is not substantial. He is politically aware, and he is willing to see the hand of God as imaginative in its choice of tools. Individual pieces of evidence that he cites offer great potential for a theory of government based on human capacities, but Aylmer never develops this potential. He consistently neglects topics that would be necessary to the case that women have the ability to rule—the kind of virtue they display, the role of education and culture in their behavior—and focuses on the narrow question of their right to rule if historical forces should bring them to power.

This he answers resoundingly in the affirmative, and in so doing fills precisely the need that he defined in his dedicatory letter: the need to refute the heretics who "called into question among us such thinges, as good subiectes before never doubted of, whether it wer lawful for women, inheritours of kingdoms, to gouern and guid the same, or no" (A3r). He has shown it is lawful for women to govern as long as they are inheritors of kingdoms, but he has not suggested that women *ought* to be inheritors. The line between Elizabeth and other women is quite firmly drawn by law, nature, and Providence.

The patriotic notion of England as the elect nation is absent from Howard's defense, as it was absent from the dedicatory letter. A partisan concept that could be used to exclude a Catholic female monarch from the right to rule, it was unavailable to Howard, whose only hope of successful self-defense consistent with his position as a Roman lay in the general defense of female rule. This is what he wrote. In addition to defending the consistency of woman rule with canon law and secular law, a strategy he shares with Aylmer, he offers a defense of the regiment of women based on a humanist defense of woman's character as endowed with the same virtues as man's.

The politically astute Aylmer attacked Knox for generalizing from the particular case of Mary Tudor; he might well have attacked Howard for generalizing from the particular case of Elizabeth Tudor. His argument could have been used to justify Mary Stuart as well as Elizabeth, although by the time he completed the work and circulated it, Mary Stuart was dead.[17] As Howard himself says in his dedicatory letter, the general nature of the strategy of defense seems to have bothered the Privy Council and may explain why the work remained unpublished. Perhaps the pursuivants who let the book fall through their hands when they destroyed his other papers should have read his work more carefully.[18]

Howard's work is divided into three books: "the first conteyneth reasons and examples grounded on the lawe of nature. The second reasons and examples grounded on the civile lawes. The third reasons and examples grounded on the sacred lawes of god with an answer to all false and fryvolous obiections which have been most unwisely countenaunced with deceitfull colours forced of theis

17. In chapter 5 in which he argues that all nations of all faiths have allowed the regiment of heirs general, Howard disproves Buchanan's denial of Mary's right to the throne, a right that was accepted by the Scots. He says Mary is deceased (fol. 35r). Perhaps the death of Mary Stuart made it seem to Howard that circulation of the manuscript would be safe.

18. *A Preservative against the Poison of supposed Prophesies* (London, 1583), another of Howard's works, "was suspected of seeming heresies and of treason . . . and in 1583 Howard was sent to the Fleet" (DNB 29).

lawes in disgrace of their approved and sufficient authoritye" (fol. 2r). Each book is divided into a series of chapters, which are followed by a series of objections and answers to them. The most important book for this study is the first; it treats material parallel to that treated by Aylmer in his refutation of Knox's assertion that woman rule was unnatural, but it gives more extensive and more sophisticated consideration to philosophy. Its chapter headings outline its approach: chapter 1: "What the lawe of nature is and howe yt ought to be lymited"; chapter 2: "That Eve was not subject to Adam at the first Creation"; chapter 3: "That the best philosophers have not reproved the regiment of women"; chapter 4: "That the guifts of the mynde and vertues appertaining to a prince the female sexe is not inferiour"; chapter 5: "That all nations as well heathen as christian have allowed of the Regiment of heyres generall." This is clearly an argument that is in sympathy with the notion of woman sustained in Elyot's *Defence of Good Women*.

Howard's definition of the law of nature is much more refined than Aylmer's. Rather than declaring that anything that occurs without upsetting the preservation of the whole is in accord with natural law, Howard distinguishes between the law of nature that applies to all created things and that which applies to man (the "ius gentius").[19] This law has its source in reason, does not distinguish between man and woman, and therefore does not favor male rule as the norm. His evidence is drawn from various fields: philosophers say that either sex may rule; if Eve had been created inferior, she would have been judged more leniently by God; and women in Christ's time were more faithful than men. The philosophers to whom Howard refers most frequently are Plato (*Republic*, Book 5), Aristotle (*Politics*, Book 5), and Plutarch, and the virtues are the classical virtues of temperance, fortitude, prudence, and justice. He consistently argues that women are endowed with virtues of exactly the same kinds as men and that these virtues qualify them for rule.

Howard does admit that men are superior to women, but he states this "truth" in a way that diminishes its consequences. Objection 4 states: "Since women have all gifts in less proportion than men it seems nature has barred them from all authority." The answer pays lip service to the notion that "some men are more excellent in comparison with women which no one will deny" but says that the important question to be answered is "whether this poor difference will give sufficient exception to the right of blood which is due by nature" (fol. 63r). By defining the difference between the sexes as a "poor difference" and by saying that only some men are more excellent than all

---

19. Leslie also makes this distinction. Also see Jordan ("Woman's Rule" 444).

women, Howard makes it seem that most members of the two sexes are comparable and that the difference does not matter; he goes on to assert that, if the succession is settled, men's greater aptness to rule cannot overcome woman's right to rule, because women have the capacity for the job. Even though he tries to restrict the application of this relative equality of the sexes to the specific case of a woman who has inherited a kingdom, the argument could be applied to a wide range of cases.

Many of the objections give Howard the opportunity to develop the thesis that women are intelligent and have a capacity for the cardinal virtues, which are necessary for a ruler. Objection 5, for example, states that temperance is a necessary virtue for a ruler; because women are not able to moderate fear, anger, and affection, they ought not to rule. Objection 6 states that a prince ought to be able to debate among the council and reject or accept advice, but women follow pleasure. Howard answers these objections with historical examples and with logic. He asserts that the intellect of men and women is about the same and lists examples of learned women, including Lady Jane Grey (fol. 71v), and examples of women who gained the trust of their husband or son who was a sovereign (Isabella of Castile and Blanche, mother of Lewis of France). As these women were not all monarchs themselves, they demonstrate the capacity of female monarchs to apply reason to problems of state, not by saying that women who become rulers have some special quality that distinguishes them from ordinary women, but by demonstrating that woman's nature includes reason and the ability to make sound judgments. They justify Elizabeth's rule by showing that she, as a woman, is naturally equipped for her duties.

Like Aylmer, Howard makes use of woman rulers of the past as evidence of the conformity of woman rule with nature. He states that he wishes to prove that Bodin and Buchanan were wrong to assert that all countries excluded women from rule. He cites the usual classical figures, Semiramis, Thomiris, Artemisia, among many others, but also "Cordrila, Martia, and Bunduica" of Britain. Again like Aylmer, he uses positive historical examples, including Isabella of Spain, to refute the argument that most queens have been unfortunate in government. Throughout, his goal is slightly more positive than Aylmer's; he tries to show that woman rule existed at some time in all societies, and, thus, is itself a law of nature, rather than showing that it has existed here and there, and, thus, is not monstrous. The context Howard has established supports his evidence better than Aylmer's; because he has shown that women are intelligent and capable of temperance, fortitude, justice, and prudence, the examples of queens who ruled well do not come as a surprise. Aylmer represents women as weak and foolish, and their successful rule does not fit their nature as he establishes it; it can only be explained by divine intervention.

Despite the greater liberality and truth to nature (as we know it) of Howard's arguments, he is not writing out of commitment to women or even in a humanist spirit of exploration and redefinition. The real ability of women is not the issue in his work. Unlike Elyot's *Defence of Good Women*, in which defense of women and self-interest were harmonious because the work's political purpose could only have succeeded if women were as capable as Elyot claimed (if Catherine had been made regent and proven incapable of ruling because she was a woman, Elyot would not have achieved his goal), Howard's defense would have succeeded no matter what the truth about women was, had its strategy been correct. His dedicatory letter established a clear purpose for his work: to produce a defense of women that would please Elizabeth without betraying his Catholic party. He was defending women not to make an action possible, but to affirm one that had already taken place.

For Howard and for Aylmer, the independent woman was outside the text in the person of the Queen, and the very writing of the text that demonstrated her right to exist was an indication of the male author's dependence on her power and munificence. In each case the author has done something to put himself in the wrong with regard to the Queen, and in each case the author writes a work that suggests that Elizabeth herself has been charged with doing something wrong. Each author creates a need for his services as advocate and then performs them in order to prove himself on the right side of the law after all. The issue of her sex has been raised by the male author to create the illusion that he is needed or to create a position of leadership and authority for himself among other men or to demonstrate his obedience to her authority; he does not have the authority to confer power, only to confirm it.[20]

Aylmer's and Howard's political engagement is revealed by comparison with Whetstone's *The English Myrror*, a defense with no immediate need for the Queen's protection. In this work, Whetstone answered Knox's attack of many

20. Burghley's *Salutem in Christo* is a concise example of the introduction of the issue of the Queen's right to the throne entirely for the purpose of self-defense. He states that the work was written to explain why the Duke of Norfolk had been committed to the tower, but this topic is dispensed with quickly: he planned to marry Mary Stuart without the knowledge of Queen Elizabeth. Most of the rest of the work is an attack on Mary, who refused to keep her promise to recognize Elizabeth's right to the throne. Burghley defends this right extensively, but the right is not in question; his right to have imprisoned Norfolk is. The defense of Elizabeth lends him authority; it is not material to the case.

years before by taking a position still more profeminist than Howard's, even though Mary Stuart was still alive and a potential threat. He argues that

> although the soueraigne place of rule, the chiefe credit of knowledge in Artes and Mecanicall craftes, together with all other giftes of grace, nature, and education be giuen unto man, yet there haue beene women, that in all maner of artes, qualities, and vertues, which have equalled the perfitest of men. (136)

Here, Whetstone takes women's native ability for granted, and attacks custom and the historical record for ignoring women's achievements. The crux of this sentence is the idea of the bestowal of credit. Men are credited with rule, knowledge, etc., but women should also be given credit because they have performed as well as the best men.

In this context Elizabeth shines as an exemplary member of her sex rather than as someone who goes beyond it: "But if the enuy of men would suppresse and murther the worthines of women, yet the divine virtues of our soueraigne Queene Elizabeth, doth and will alwaies keepe alive their divine memorie" (136). The theme of the envy of men that undoes the truth of history is familiar from Italian humanist defenses of women; Whetstone's statement acknowledges the contemporary English situation and presents modern men as possible enemies of women. Rather than celebrate male authors as having broken with the behavior of their predecessors and begun to give women due credit—as Ariosto does—however, Whetstone attributes the triumph of modern feminism to the Queen. He glorifies her by representing her as truly independent: in her the entire tradition of female accomplishment is secure. By means of her virtues, Elizabeth will triumph over male efforts to discredit women. Whetstone represents her as beyond the ebb and flow of male opinion of women, beyond the need for defenders such as himself.

Aylmer and Howard present themselves very differently from Whetstone. Their strategy depends on creating a real anxiety on the part of the Queen and the selection of themselves as her advocates. If she does not recognize that her sex is a delicate point that might cause her difficulties in maintaining authority, the chivalrous offer to defend will not bring the author his wished-for results. He must be capable of welding his cause with the Queen's; his self-defense only can succeed if he can persuade her that she is vulnerable and should accept his help.[21] Paradoxically, England's most independent woman becomes less independent if their texts are successful.

21. Aylmer indicated this delicate interrelationship of authority and dependence when he ended his dedicatory letter by appealing to Bedford and Dudley to defend "this pore treatise, which is the defence of them, by whome we be defended all" (A4v). He asked his immediate patrons (male) to use their authority to defend the work that he had used his authority to write in defense of the monarch (female), who had power and authority to defend all her people; that the Queen is referred to as "them" suggests how completely she does hold power, despite the author's assertion that she needs defending because of her sex. "Them" refers not just to queens (that would make no sense), but to all rulers, the generic group by whom all subjects are defended. Before the case for the defense has even been presented, the Queen has been represented as masculine and as holding the power to defend, yet, if the author can make his defense appealing, he will deprive her of some of her independence and create an interdependence of his fate and hers.

10

Praise and Defense of Woman
in *The Faerie Queene*

Successful as they may have been in their day, all the encomiastic defenses of Queen Elizabeth's rule have long faded into literary and political obscurity. They were occasional pieces and, their occasion gone, they are of interest only as cultural records of an age trying to accommodate itself to an uncomfortable fact. Edmund Spenser's *The Faerie Queene* is, of course, a very different case. It is surely the longest-lasting and most persuasive of all the defenses and encomia of Elizabeth's rule, and its representation of the Queen as "the most high, mightie and magnificent Empresse Renovvmed for Pietie, Vertue, and All Gratious Government" (22) remains one of the great attractions of the poem and is a major force in forming many people's impressions of what the Queen was like.[1] This success is due not only to the delight of the Spenserian text as contrasted with the tedium of the formal defenses, but also to the context the poet establishes for his praise of the Queen. Books III through V present the most extensive and eloquent defense and encomium of the feminine and of a female monarch to be written in the Renaissance.

Like the Italian writers of paradox (especially Goggio), Spenser defines the feminine and its role in positive terms. He establishes chastity as the basis of its power and woman's capacity for procreation as its most material manifestation, but chastity in Books III to V of *The Faerie Queene* is not a private virtue whose practice restricts the sphere of women's actions to the home, as it does in the rigidly divided complementary spheres of the Aristotelian *Economics,*

1. See the many New Historicist analyses of Elizabeth that are based on the Spenserian representation of the Queen; Montrose's "Elizabethan," for example. For an alternate version of Elizabeth that attempts to reclaim the characterization of the Queen from the hands of male eulogists and male critics, see Crane. All quotations of *The Faerie Queene* are from Hamilton's edition.

and procreation is not a passive activity. Rather, Spenser subscribes to the Platonic notion that ethical, economic, and political actions are all unfoldings of the same core virtues, although he differs from Plato in that he identifies different particular manifestations of the virtues in the two sexes. Chastity is the private manifestation of the public virtue of justice, as faith was in Elyot's *Defence*; it operates in the personal, economic, and political spheres and makes woman's participation in the natural, social, and historical process possible.[2] Spenser's Platonic understanding of virtue and the central importance he gives to chastity resolve the *discordia* of romance and epic. He feminizes the epic and is able to celebrate the feminine in his queen.

Others have argued for the centrality of the feminine to *The Faerie Queene* but have read the representation of the feminine as allegorical, that is, as bearing no relationship to social and political forces and to real women and the debate about them, or they have read the feminine as inferior, that is, as propping up the patriarchal order, masculine endeavor, or the male psyche.[3] Kathleen Williams pointed in the direction that I am headed when she drew an analogy between the action of justice and of love: "true justice is a tempering of cruel dooms as love is the establishing of concord over discord, and this is best expressed by feminine dominance" (175). Similarly, Humphrey Tonkin found Spenser's desire "to examine the process of generation in all its aspects—natural . . . , social . . . , and historical" to be the reason that he moved "femininity from the subsidiary position it normally occupies both in everyday thinking and in the psychomachia of the knightly quest to a position of dominance" (412). According to these interpretations, Spenser is not committed to feminine dominance or partnership; he merely brings to the foreground

2. Fichter makes a similar point about the importance of female virtues to justice, but he speaks in terms of evolution: "to represent empire as it can be under the dispensation of New Testament grace, justice must be wedded to the virtues associated with Britomart as she evolves in the course of books 3–5: love, equity, and mercy" (157). Similarly, Lillian Robinson states: "Spenser's concern, throughout, is not simply to demonstrate that some women do hold power legitimately, but also to show that legitimate female power means virtuous government" (297–98). She illustrates the point with examples.

3. Stevie Davies speaks of a depersonalized "feminine principle" and excludes social literature and the real condition of women from the disciplines of which she speaks. Goldberg and Quilligan suggest that Spenser regarded the feminine as less valuable than the masculine. Goldberg seems to argue that Spenser offers women encouragement to accept their traditional roles. "The feminine experience depicted in the [third] book centers on the acceptance of the maternal role" ("Mothers" 5). And again, "Britomart completes her initiation into maternity, thereby abandoning the matriarchal perspective" ("Mothers" 22). Quilligan argues against the importance of maternity but still defines woman's role as supportive of male order. "Woman's work is to be no longer physically productive for the new marketplace—or even preeminently reproductive—but psychologically and spiritually supportive of another's work" (177). Both suggest that because Spenser's heart lies with politics and the marketplace, he excludes women from the field.

something that is usually held back in order to get a better look at a process of which it is part.

Rather than being a mere abstraction, a prop to male order, or a useful tool for literary exposition, the feminine is an essential principle in the grand scheme of *The Faerie Queene*; it represents an alternate order. The feminine is essential in its own right both in the ideal golden world that Faerieland sometimes represents and in the real political world that it often shadows. In *The Faerie Queene*, the feminine is defended against male attempts to dominate and marginalize it, and the Queen is defended against those who would isolate her from her femininity by focusing only on her "stomach of a king" and against those who would devalue her femininity by focusing on her "body of a weak woman." Like Elizabeth herself, who spoke of this opposition in her speech at Tilbury, Spenser finds strength in the paradox. For him, danger lies in the devaluation of the feminine, which results in the loss of the benefits that it contributes to the cosmos, to society, and to individual relationships. The possibility of peace lies in the feminine, and the independent woman is an enemy in this text because she is masculine.

Spenser's method of praising and defending the feminine and his female monarch is extremely complex. He uses three interconnected techniques. First, he creates a feminine cosmology for his poem by means of female figures (primarily, but not only, Venus in Book III and Isis in Book V) who have the strength to control male destructive forces and turn them to positive natural, personal, social, and political use. Second, he creates a new model for active female virtue when he tells the story of Britomart, lover, fiancée, not-queen, and not-mirror-of-the-Queen, whose chastity gives her the strength and impetus to range freely through Faerieland. Third, he addresses himself directly to Elizabeth, defends her in the Proems in which he names her mirrors, Belphoebe and Glorianna, and presents an allegory of her government in Mercilla. These approaches together create a radical new notion of the feminine as a force waiting to be tapped should God elect to bless the nation by raising a queen to power, but essential to peace, justice, and order in any case.

Venus and Adonis

At the center of Book III lies the Garden of Adonis, a *locus amoenus* whose philosophical system has given explicating critics great trouble, but whose sensual poetry has given great pleasure. At the center of the garden is located a thicket where the goddess Venus engages in "everlasting" lovemaking with Adonis, the mortal whom she seduced and, according to all other versions of the story, lost to death when he was gored by a boar. This mysterious thicket is the philosophical and erotic center of Spenser's revaluation of the feminine. In describing the lovemaking of the goddess and the mortal, he contradicts the traditional philosophical explanation of the biological process of generation, according to which the passive female contributes matter and the active male contributes form, a scheme that places the female in an inferior position. Like the Italian defenders of womankind, Spenser denies the passivity of the female and makes it impossible to relegate woman to inferior status on the basis of her body or her sexual desire; he liberates women from the tyranny of biological inferiority. But the representation of Venus, the beauty of the verse, and the power of the allegory move this episode into territory untouched by the paradoxical logic of Italian defenses; the account of the activity of Venus in the thicket in the Garden of Adonis frees female sexuality from the stigma of male scorn and from the notion that purity lies only in passivity.

Spenser twice associates Venus and the female with form.[4] First, just before the description of the Garden of Adonis, he speaks of Venus's "heavenly hous, / The house of goodly formes and faire aspects, / Whence all the world derives the glorious / Features of beautie, and all shapes select" (III.vi.12.1–4). Then, he describes the union of Venus and Adonis in terms of form and matter.

> All be he [Adonis] subiect to mortalitie,
> Yet is eterne in mutabilitie,
> And by succession made perpetuall,
> Transformed oft, and chaunged diuerslie:
> For him the Father of all formes they call;
> Therefore needs mote he liue, that liuing giues to all.
>   (III.vi.47.4–9)

The passage is confusing, but its overall effect is profeminist. According to lines 4–7, Adonis is changeable matter being acted on by Venus, who is eternal form; he is transformed; he is changed; he is not the agent of form and change. Therefore, he plays the role traditionally assigned to the female and Venus the male role of impressing form on matter. In line 8, however, the term "Father

---

4. My reading of the philosophical scheme of the Garden is indebted to Tonkin's extensive discussion of the association of Venus with form and Adonis with matter. C. S. Lewis also suggests that Venus contributes form during the lovemaking (155).

of all formes" may restore the masculine role to him. Venus's impression of forms on him results in making him capable of generating other forms. Yet, it is possible that, in this feminizing context, his paternal role may be confined to providing the "living" matter to the unbodied forms, the role that the mother is traditionally thought of as playing; thus, lines 8 and 9 may be entirely consonant with lines 4–7. That he is father of forms does not necessarily identify paternity with the active provision of the form.

The role that Spenser's redefinition of woman's role in procreation plays in *The Faerie Queene* is like the role the same topic plays in Italian humanist defenses; it prevents woman's physiology from being used against her. If she is to be man's equal and equivalent, her body cannot be considered to be an opaque filter for her intellect or to make her incapable of strenuous physical activity; the assertion that her contribution to the child she carries is active and shaping prevents dismissal of her as naturally passive and even accidental and permits a positive valuation of female sexuality.[5] This is not a topic that was of interest to English popular controversialists, who were satisfied to arouse their readers' sympathy for women's hard lot by evocative images of their suffering in childbirth and their tender care of husbands and children, nor to Elyot and the defenders of the Queen, who were especially interested in woman's political role, but Spenser founds the natural cosmology of his poem on it.[6]

Spenser's rewriting of the relationship between Venus, Adonis, and the boar provides a mythological basis for his philosophical radicalism; in it he shows female eros directing male sexual energy to productive ends. In the traditional Ovidian version of the myth, Adonis and the boar are allied against Venus; that is, Adonis's masculine desire to hunt finds its match in the phallic boar; he dies because he chose masculine aggression over love; the boar is an external representation of a quality within himself. Venus does not try to restrain the boar; her goal is restraint of Adonis; because she fails, he dies. The force of death is defeated in this version of the story only by means of his metamorphosis into a single flower. In Spenser's Garden version of the story, Venus restrains Adonis and the boar. Adonis does not die but rather lives forever, eternally transformed in his embrace with Venus, and the boar is "emprisoned for ay . . . In a strong rocky Caue . . . / Hewen vnderneath that Mount, that none him losen may" (III.vi.48). The female dominates in the cosmic forces that control the natural world.

5. The two versions of Strozzi's defense discussed in Chapter 2 illustrate this point.
6. By natural cosmology I mean his explanation of the forces that govern creation seen in non-Christian terms.

The peculiar image of Venus restraining the boar with his lethal tusk beneath her "mount" represents female erotic power as positive because it is capable of restraining male aggression. Her control over the boar gives her the power to prevent death itself from touching Adonis (III.vi.48), and her power over Adonis permits the process of generation to continue unceasingly. As in the Ovidian myth, the boar only seems to be separate from Adonis. Given the conflation of topography and physiology in this entire passage, if the boar is imprisoned in a cave beneath her "mount," the tusk of the boar would seem to have become the phallus it symbolized and Venus would seem to have trans- formed masculine, death-dealing aggression into a life-force by her erotic power. In Spenser's rendition of the myth, feminine erotic creativity overpow- ers masculine aggressive destruction. In a way, Venus can be said to be in control of the tusk-phallus. It is said to be within her body (or cave) and seems almost to have become a part of her. Her erotic power directs its energy, and the episode illustrates the value of active female eroticism as well as the active female contribution to procreation.

The image of Venus in control of the boar's tusk is one of a series of images of female characters wielding phallic objects that runs through Books III, IV, and V; each represents the power of the female to transform male aggression into productive energy. Elizabeth's white rod restrains the disruptive force of Philip II in the genealogy revealed to Britomart (III.iii.49), and Isis's white rod subdues the crocodile (V.vii.15) in an image that unites sexuality and politics. The statue of Venus has a snake lying tamely at its feet at the Temple of Venus, and Mercilla keeps a rusty sword at her feet. Each image will be discussed in its context. Unlike most allegorical Venuses, who merely play with their lover's arms after having conquered him, three of these powerful females possess their own and put them to good use.

Britomart is the poem's most thoroughly developed exemplar of the erotic, psychological, and political power of the feminine, and she, too, has a weapon—her magic lance. The first lady knight in English literature (if one does not count those present in translations of Continental works), she is a new kind of woman warrior. As the representation of Venus suggests, feminine power is a force that subdues masculine violence and generates peace and unity in the home, among friends, and in the political world. In the contemporary political world, as represented by Spenser, this triumph of the feminine occurred because of the Queen. In the fictional world of the poem, it comes about because of Britomart.

Yet, Britomart does not enter the poem as this exemplary force; she, at first, uses her phallic magic lance in a masculine fashion and disrupts concord rather than bringing it. Britomart is not a static emblematic image like Venus or Isis; in her errors and successes Spenser represents the unfolding and maturing knowledge of virtue in time.[7] Her virtue is chastity, but the vices that tempt her on her path to the accomplishment of her quest are not sensuality and illicit sexuality, as one might expect from the term "chastity."[8] Rather, she is tempted to misunderstand chastity and identify it with the invulnerability and masculinity of virgin independence, to believe that her virtue's purpose is to divide and conquer and to defend herself from involvement, to think she has failed because she loves and would submit.[9] In short, she is tempted to the vice of the independent woman against which we have seen so many Renaissance texts defend themselves: the complete identification with the masculine, an identification that leads to social chaos. Spenser's representation of Britomart's conquest of this vicious tendency within herself and her discovery of the pleasure of her virtue defend his text and his society against the threat of the independent woman.

Britomart Overgoes Bradamante

Spenser defines Britomart as a woman and a warrior by creating a constant implied contrast with Ariosto's Bradamante. Although the ladies seem comparable, Britomart is not the same kind of woman as Bradamante; she is a refutation of her, of the case for women made in the Italian poem, and, thus, of the Italian humanist notion of the equality (sameness), of the sexes. As any reader of the *Orlando furioso* knows, the basic structure of the Britomart—

7. Rose also insists that "[it is not possible,] especially at this early moment in her story, absolutely to identify Britomart with chastity. Britomart is not chastity personified; rather, . . . she is . . . a chaste woman" (80). Williams sees her as emblematic right from the beginning (91ff.).

8. Many critics redefine the titular virtue of Book III; they treat it as the book of love and Britomart as the knight of love or of "love directed by the virtue of chastity" (Roche 52). As a result, critical attention has primarily focused on Britomart's heart and passions rather than on her understanding of virtue and has, at times, hunted hopelessly for sexual wrongdoing. I am trying to redress the balance without denying my indebtedness, especially to Roche's and Rose's studies of love in the poem.

9. By contrast, Thickstun's assumption that chastity's natural enemies are lust and male seductiveness, paired with her assumption that Spenser paid allegiance to the notion that good women do not feel attraction to or attract attention from men other than their husbands, leads her to the conclusion that Spenser was not free in his representation of Britomart. "Spenser cannot allow Britomart to experience similar [i.e., like Red Cross] sexual temptation because she is a representative female character, an unmarried woman, whose chastity can be assured only by her continuously focused desire for Artegall" (40).

Artegall plot is conspicuously similar to that of the Bradamante–Ruggiero plot;
Britomart finds herself in many of the same situations confronted by her Italian
predecessor, and her actions often lead the Narrator to comments on womankind that echo the lines of Ariosto's Narrator.[10] Yet, in each case the similarity
of material—actions, setting, character—provokes an awareness of difference.[11]
Britomart, placed in the same situations that led to Bradamante's most radical
feminist speeches, consistently demonstrates the difference of her sex and is
not an advocate of women's rights. Nowhere does Spenser's effort to "overgo"
Ariosto in substance and style show more clearly than in his handling of
Britomart.

The descent of the English lady knight from the Italian is a commonplace of
Spenser criticism, but few critics have gone beyond the simple assertion of
similarity to discuss exactly how the two compare and what the effect of the
presence of a character so clearly indebted to another work is.[12] Since
McMurphy's preliminary study *Spenser's Use of Ariosto for Allegory*, the pages in
the *Variorum Spenser*, and the catalogues of episodes by Dodge and by Gilbert,
only Bender, Alpers, Wiggins, Silberman, and Bowman have discussed Britomart's relationship to Bradamante in any detail; of them all, only Bowman is
interested in the woman question. Bowman looks to episodes in the *Furioso*
"for guidance in interpreting" *The Faerie Queene* and uses the Italian poem to
supplement the English poem when information about motivation is missing
(516). Silberman uses Spenser's reworking of Bradamante's adventures to
illustrate his modification of Ariosto's tone and the text's relationship to the
reader (27 and 32).

10. Britomart's appearance and story line resemble Bradamante's quite closely. Both women enter
the poem precipitously, carry a magic lance (at times), encounter Merlin and learn of their dynastic
role in the history of their respective nations, share the role of Aeneas with their beloved, enter castles
with sexually restrictive laws, are mistaken for a man and receive amorous advances as a consequence,
aid a knight whose lady is imprisoned by an enchanter, engage in chivalric combat with a rival for their
beloved's affections, and are bested in a duel with their intended husbands.

11. Spenser's method of imitating Ariosto's text resembles the "heuristic" strategy that Thomas
Greene discovers in certain humanist imitations of classical texts. "Heuristic imitations come to us
advertising their derivation from the subtexts they carry with them, but having done that, they proceed
to *distance themselves* from the subtexts and force us to recognize the poetic distance traversed" (*Light in
Troy* 40).

12. Woods, for example, states, "although the warrior/woman figure has antecedents in and is a
convention of epic and romance, and Britomart has much in common especially with Ariosto's
Bradamante, Britomart's character is unusual in its fullness and centrality" (151), but she does not
elaborate on this assertion by comparing the two characters. Similarly, Fichter says, Britomart is
"derived from Ariosto but from that part of the *Furioso* . . . that attempts to assimilate the *Aeneid*"
(158); he then focuses on *The Faerie Queene*'s direct relationship with the *Aeneid* and makes very few
connections with the *Orlando furioso*.

Wiggins suggests that Spenser was aware of Ariosto's concern with "the divisiveness of all recourse to gender for self-definition," but he uses Britomart's relationship to Bradamante only as one in a series of examples of Spenser's "ambivalency" toward immoral and brilliant Ariosto (85).[13] Bender limits his discussion of the contrasts between the descriptions of the two lady knights' removals of their helmets to the pictorial. Alpers uses Spenser's reworking of Bradamante's adventure at the Castle of Tristan as an "especially interesting" example in support of his assertion that "the major sign that the *Orlando furioso* was continually present in Spenser's mind is that episodes that are important to him characteristically appear in more than one episode of *The Faerie Queene*" (196); Alpers does not, however, explore why this particular episode (or any other) might have been important to Spenser. I will explore the uncharted territory of Spenser's reworking of his major narrative antecedent on the topic of womankind.

Spenser's method of working with the *Orlando furioso*'s heroine is extremely complex. He often interweaves several Ariostan episodes to produce one adventure for Britomart and, as Alpers points out, he often uses the same Ariostan story more than once. For example, the account of Radigund and Britomart's defeat of her is conspicuously indebted to the representation of Bradamante's battle with Marfisa, but Radigund herself owes something to the *donne omicide*, and the resolution of the conflict is indebted to the story of Marganorre. The story of Malecasta is a composite of the stories of Ruggiero and Alcina, Bradamante and Fiordispina, and Bradamante at the "rocca di Tristano," and the "rocca" contributes not only to the story of Malecasta but also to Malbecco and to the opening of Book IV.[14] Bradamante's unprovoked unhorsing of Sacripante yields the overthrow of Guyon and of Marinell. The text of the *Orlando furioso* is thus rewritten several times within *The Faerie Queene*, and this repeated rewriting provides a very clear framework for the definition of the English heroine against her Italian prototype.

To a reader familiar with the *Orlando furioso*, Britomart's sudden entry onto the scene and her unhorsing of Guyon with a single blow of her lance in canto 1 indicate immediately that she is a lady knight in the tradition of Bradamante: the Italian lady behaved in much the same way when she entered her poem;

13. Wiggins identifies his essay as preliminary and points to the need for a detailed comparison of the two lady knights. "Spenser's use of the 'rocca' di Tristano is the firmest of all of the links in *The Faerie Queene* between Britomart and Bradamante and deserves to be discussed in an essay devoted exclusively to comparison of the two heroines" ("Spenser's Anxiety" 84–85).

14. Alpers (196–97) discusses the latter two examples but does not identify the Malecasta story as also indebted to the "rocca."

however, with this identification the differentiation of the heroines and their poetic contexts begins. In the Italian poem, the episode establishes Bradamante as part of the masculine political world. She rides off as quickly as she came, but a messenger, who is in pursuit of her in order to gather her back into the Carolingian war effort, reveals her female identity to her miserable opponent, thereby increasing his misery; Angelica, whom he had been attempting to rape, comforts him with excuses. The messenger's revelation of Bradamante's identity and of what she ought to be doing establishes that the conflict between duty and love typical of the epic hero is also typical of the epic heroine; Sacripante's comic shame when the messenger informs him of who has beaten him demonstrates that the military ability of women is perceived as threatening to self-esteem by at least some of the male knights in the poem. Our introduction to Bradamante poses the social problem caused by the accom-plished woman at the same time that it illustrates the similar capacities of the sexes.

Instead of raising the social issue of equal competition between the sexes when his lady knight first enters the scene, Spenser evokes the mystery of feminine otherness and the threat it poses to male stability. The focus of the episode is on Britomart's mysterious lance and on the reconciliation of the combatants rather than on the fact that Guyon has been beaten by a woman. The Narrator, not a messenger from the political world of the poem, explains who the victorious knight is and what her purpose is in an apostrophe to Guyon.

> But weenedst thou what wight thee ouerthrew,
> Much greater griefe and shamefuller regret
> For thy hard fortune then thou wouldst renew,
> That of a single damzell thou wert met
> On equall plaine, and there so hard beset;
> Euen the famous *Britomart* it was,
> Whom straunge aduenture did from *Britaine* fet,
> To seeke her louer (loue farre sought alas,)
> Whose image she had seene in *Venus* looking glas.
>
> (III.i.8)

Unlike the messenger's speech, which provoked an antifeminist outburst by a character, the Narrator's speech predicts what a character's response *would* be. We never see this response, and Britomart's sex never becomes an issue for the characters involved in the episode. The reader may follow the Narrator's hint and wander down the paths of antifeminism if he or she wishes, but the path leads away from the heart of the episode.

In this episode, Spenser reconstructs the lady knight; he makes her into a person driven by love; for this reason, she does not threaten patriarchal order here or elsewhere in the poem. According to the Narrator's introduction of her in the passage quoted above, Britomart's reason for being out in the world is exclusively a private and feminine love stimulated by Venus, whereas Bradamante's public duty was made clear by Ariosto's Carolingian messenger. This distinction remains throughout *The Faerie Queene*; whatever adventures Britomart encounters, she meets them as interruptions in a private quest. She never is torn between love and duty; her love is her duty. She is never assigned or asks for a masculine political role, however successful she may be in the masculine realm of combat.[15]

In this scene, the cause of her success is her "enchaunted spear," that oddly phallic object that undoes so many knights and critics in the hands of the virgin warrior. The final lines of stanzas 7 and 9 assert the danger of the spear, and almost all of stanza 10 is devoted to an explanation of its "secret virtue." Although Bradamante also possesses such a lance, she acquires it later in her career; she unhorses Sacripante in the scene to which Spenser is referring entirely with her own power and, thus, establishes her military strength. By attributing the victory to the spear and devoting so much time to evoking its powers, Spenser displaces attention from the potentially shocking disclosure of Britomart's sex to the provoking mystery of the spear. It is not possible to figure out why she has it at this point, but speculation may run wild, and the reader is led to expect that psychological and allegorical avenues of interpretation will be more profitable than the sociopolitical ones suggested by the Ariostan episode.

The scene ends with the emblematic reconciliation of the combatants, who assume their abstract identities as the virtues of their respective books, "goodly temperance, and affection chaste" (III.i.12).[16] Goodness, temperance, affection, chastity, male, female—all are yoked together on one plane in this *discordia concors*. That Guyon's temperance leads to peace suggests that anxiety about female power will not be a property of the good male knight, just as the invocation of Britomart's affection suggests that her military manner does not

15. In her discussion of Britomart's first taking up of arms Suzanne Woods makes a nice distinction between her feminine ambitions and her masculine means of accomplishing them. "Her woman's love makes her a manlike warrior" (152).

16. For another examination of the indebtedness of this scene to the *Orlando furioso*, see Cheney (83–87).

represent hostility to men. We are a long way from the scene in the *Orlando furioso*. There, no allegory of concord between the sexes is represented but rather its opposite, the division caused by female encroachment on male prerogatives. By creating this emblem and by focusing on the mysterious lance with its potential to entirely undo the male rather than on the social shame that the male combatant feels, Spenser directs attention away from the issue that interests Ariosto most, the actual social threat posed by accomplished women and how to accommodate it, and toward his own particular interest: the power of chastity.

This power is the subject of Britomart's next adventure, her visit at Malecasta's Castle Joyous. To summarize briefly: Britomart unhorses six knights outside the castle, gains entry, and wins the lady of the castle, Malecasta; she refuses to remove her armor when invited to do so, is courted and then joined in her bed by Malecasta, who thinks she is a man; Britomart responds with outrage at the violation of her bed, is joined by Red Cross in a skirmish with the six knights, and is wounded lightly by Gardante before routing all of them and departing. In the course of this episode, our visual perception of Britomart changes and with it our understanding of her virtue. She begins as a woman who trusts in her armor to protect her from unwanted approaches, and she ends as a woman dressed merely in her smock with unbound hair who lays about with her sword and receives only a light wound.[17] This image of Britomart militant is an emblematic representation of the mystery of the power of the feminine. The rest of Book III explores the possible private meanings of the image, Book IV the public meanings, and V its political dimension.

This adventure is the first of three imitations of Bradamante's big profeminist scene at the "rocca di Tristano" (see my Chapter 5).[18] The others are Britomart's entry into Malbecco and Hellenore's castle and into the unnamed castle at the beginning of Book IV.[19] Reading these episodes against their Ariostan prototype reveals that they play a major part in the development of Britomart's particular personation of the paradoxical figure, the lady knight. None of the three carries the sociopolitical content of the *Furioso* episode, which urges that accomplished women be allowed to compete directly with

17. See Hamilton's linking of this wounding with other relevant passages in his edition (Spenser, *Faerie Queene* 416). See also Roche's reading of Britomart's ignorance of love and her initiatory wound (*Kindly* 69–71).

18. Wiggins calls the triple imitation "the firmest of all of the links . . . between Britomart and Bradamante" ("Spenser's Anxiety" 84–85).

19. Fowler points out that Malecasta's and Malbecco's castles "share the same set of sources in Ariosto, in such a way that the alternate borrowings dovetail together" (588). He does not develop the comparison with Ariosto.

men for fame and privileges, because Bradamante's speech in favor of woman-kind is not imitated.

To recapitulate briefly: at the "rocca di Tristano" Bradamante encounters a law that challenges her right to hospitality at the castle; it states that only the most beautiful woman and the strongest man may stay. The heroine defeats the knight who arrived before her and enters the castle. When she removes her helmet and her cascading hair reveals her to be a woman, the host attempts to reclassify her as the most beautiful lady and to force Ullania, who was already occupying that post, out into the rain. Bradamante refuses to remove the rest of her armor and definitively disclose her sex; in a major statement of profeminist humanist doctrine, she defends her right to be treated according to her accomplishments rather than her anatomy. Her great strength—her real capacity to fight extremely well—forces her host to acquiesce to her demand.

Like the "rocca di Tristano" episode, the one at Castle Joyous turns on the issue of the newly arrived knight's hidden female identity, but Britomart succeeds in maintaining the secret of her sex. She refuses to remove her helmet and, thus, her flowing hair does not give her away. That she does not take off her helmet when invited to disarm is a surprise to a reader of Ariosto who, expecting the episode to continue along the lines of the "rocca," anticipates that her hair will fall down and cause problems. Without the revelation of the knight's sex, the debate about social roles that was the central focus of the Ariostan scene cannot take place, so the absence of the topos of cascading hair brings with it the absence of the political topos. This episode is not about the role of independent women in society.

In considering the events at Castle Joyous, it is important not to think of Britomart's armor as the "whole armor of God;" she is not Red Cross Knight. In Book I his removal of his armor is always a sign that he is exposing himself to spiritual danger; Britomart's *refusal* to remove her armor exposes her to psychological danger because it is a male shell that hides her female body from others and signifies her own lack of understanding of her sexual desires and erotic appeal.[20] When Britomart raises her umbriere and does not disarm, Spenser calls her a "brave mayd," but the epithet underlines her present fear. Having successfully fought Malecasta's knights on the jousting field, she thinks that armor provides a secure way to confront them in a social situation; however, Castle Joyous's attack is internal, not external, and hiding behind a masculine identity, which is what Britomart does by keeping her armor on,

20. As Shepherd stresses in *Amazons*, "the aggression is not worn like a disguise, but is something inner" (8).

cannot protect her. It gives her a false sense of security and leaves her ignorant of the real danger that she faces: the possibility that her own newly rooted feminine love for Artegall will travel along the path indicated by Gardante, Parlante, Iocante, Basciante, Bacchante, and Noctante.[21]

Britomart's vulnerability to these six knights, despite her armor, is suggested when we are told that when disarmed they are "faire knights, and goodly well beseene, / But to faire Britomart they all but shadowes beene." This may mean that in comparison with good-looking Britomart these handsome knights seem insubstantial; it may thus prepare for Malecasta's strong response to her, but it also may mean that despite the fact that these knights are so handsome, Britomart barely notices them. Because, as we shall soon learn, Artegall first appeared to her as a shadow, her unwariness of these knights is not at all an indication of their lack of power to secretly attack her.[22] The next stanza reinforces the second meaning; it explains that they are shadows to her because

> . . . she was full of amiable grace,
> And manly terrour mixed therewithall,
> That as the one stird vp affections bace,
> So th'other did mens rash desires apall,
> And hold them backe, that would in errour fall;
> As he, that hath espide a vermeill Rose,
> To which sharpe thornes and breres the way forstall,
> Dare not for dread his hardy hand expose,
> But wishing it far off, his idle wish doth lose.
>
> (III.i.46)

The perfect balance of the masculine and the feminine in Britomart and the image of the thorny rose describe her perfect ability to hold off men's base affections and rash desires, yet they have no deterrent effect on Malecasta's *female* desires nor on Britomart's own desires. Glorious as this image is, it is irrelevant to the situation in which Britomart finds herself. When Malecasta courts her, deceived by Britomart's masculine exterior, Britomart is moved, not, of course, to accept Malecasta's advances, but to sympathy. Malecasta's

21. See Rose's excellent suggestion that "seeing is the first rung on more ladders than that of lechery." Another is the stairs to marriage, which is "the one Britomart actually will climb, but Spenser's presentation of Castle Joyous indicates that another and less virtuous life might also have been hers" (93).

22. I am indebted to Hamilton's notes for the irony of the reference to shadows (Spenser, *Faerie Queene* 312).

speech and actions bypass "brave" Britomart's "manly terrour" and awaken her "amiable grace."

Britomart's refusal to remove her helmet marks the end of this episode's imitation of the "rocca di Tristano" passage and provides a transition into another moment from the *Furioso*, the time when Bradamante's short cropped hair led the lady Fiordispina to mistake her for a man (25.26ff.).[23] Thus, the imitation of the *Orlando furioso* stops just before the social import of the events comes to the surface. Instead of hearing of the social and political consequences of the heroine's military conduct, we see the private sexual and psychological consequences of her refusal to admit her feminine gender. Malecasta burns with lust for the male body that she assumes accompanies this face, and Britomart fears female sexuality. By substituting the second episode from the *Orlando furioso* for the one that he initially was imitating, Spenser successfully changes the focus of the episode from political to personal while continuing to lead his reader to compare his heroine with her Italian counterpart.

In the *Orlando furioso*, the episode reinforces the notion that the only significant difference between the sexes is the presence or absence of male sexual organs. The solution to the sexual problem posed by Bradamante's male appearance and female gender is comically efficient. The heroine wisely recognizes that blandly ignoring the lady's advances will only cause pain, but her declaration that she is a woman does not dissipate Fiordispina's desire, so she substitutes her twin brother for herself. The trick relies on the complete public interchangeability of Bradamante and her brother.

In *The Faerie Queene* the episode is not about the sameness of the sexes; it is about their difference. Unlike Bradamante, who recognizes Fiordispina's love and immediately admits her sex, Britomart recognizes Malecasta's feelings as similar to her own pain, but does not reveal that she is a woman because "she her sexe vnder that straunge purport / Did vse to hide, and plaine apparaunce shonne" (III.i.52). Her fixed habit of disguise and her desire to be treated as a man lead her into danger literally because her feminine sympathy with Malecasta's pain appears to Malecasta to be encouragement from a man and figuratively because she is attempting to repress her feminine desire.

The reader who knows the Ariostan prototype expects a comic discovery of the real sex of this "male" and an account of Malecasta's disappointment. This is what occurs in Britomart's bedroom when she awakens and finds Malecasta

---

23. Wiggins states that the allusion to the Fiordispina episode "masks" imitation of the "rocca," but he does not explain why he perceives the one imitation to be hidden by the other ("Spenser's Anxiety" 84). I see both allusions as conspicuously present.

in her bed, but all the attention of the narrative is focused on the startling beauty of Britomart's feminine presence and not on the mechanics of finding a genuine male body to make Malecasta happy. The poem suddenly moves into something magnificent: the emblematic representation of female chastity. When Britomart leaps out of her bed in her "smocke, with locks vnbownd," we finally see the female body and hair that have been hidden by the armor and by the poet's delaying tactics; if anything, they are more powerful suddenly released into view after the moment when their revelation was expected has passed. Amiability is entirely absent and "terrour" is fully present.

> . . . they saw the warlike Mayd
> All in her snow-white smocke, with locks vnbownd,
> Threatning the point of her auenging blade,
> That with so troublous terrour they were all dismayde.
>   (III.i.63)

Terror is an attribute of both Britomart and the spectators; she is terrified and terrifying.

The spectators are terrified because Britomart is not what they expected and because her physical courage and skill at arms are not what they expect of women. The pun on the word "dismayde" makes the point. Britomart's fear that the intruder in her bed will deflower her causes her to unleash her "troublous terrour" on Malecasta's male servitors, yet her sword, phallic like her lance and the thorns of the rose to which she was compared, "rapes" her male opponents—"they were all dismayde." In their dismay at her anger the male knights are helpless; they have already fought this knight the day before and know her strength. Her violent response is a kind of rape because it puts the men entirely in her power and violates their masculinity.

The conclusion of the episode concentrates attention on the central importance of Britomart's sexuality rather than on the importance of her social role or female physiology to others. Britomart feels "troublous terrour" because she thinks Malecasta is a male "loathed leachour." Yet, illogically, she remains enraged after she discovers that Malecasta is a woman, and she is wounded by an arrow shot at her by Gardante. After having kept her female body hidden for so long, she has finally been seen ("Gardante" meaning "looking") for what she is. Painful as it is and administered in a place of low sexuality, the wound inflicted by Gardante offers hope because it indicates that the militant/chaste woman is accessible to male sexuality.[24] The description of the wound as a

24. My reading of this entire episode, especially of the wound and its relationship to Britomart's

metamorphosis from a lily to a purple flower suggests an emblematic change of state from virgin to woman (her *lilly* smock with stains of vermeil steepe" [III.i.65]). Britomart has acquired knowledge of who she is that she did not possess before she faced her own desires in the mirror of Malecasta. In both imagery and action Spenser's episode ends with an insistence on the feminine sexuality of the lady knight, which was absent from both the Ariostan episodes to which it refers.

This scene begins the process of feminizing the epic that results in the resolution of the *discordia* of romance and epic. Whether we read her as Chastity defeating the first onslaught of the forces of courtly love or as an emblem of the real capacity of women for military action, Britomart has muscled her way into the ranks of the heroes as feminine, whereas Bradamante makes her way by arguing that she is masculine. Inasmuch as Bradamante is "male" at the "rocca," she wins the right for herself and similar women (poets, for example) to compete freely with males and receive the same rewards. Her strength puts pressure on society to disregard physical gender in making its laws; it establishes equal opportunity and puts her in competition with men. As a consequence, when she finally meets her superior in Ruggiero, she retires and resumes an entirely traditional female role. Because the value of the feminine is never established in the *Furioso*, Bradamante's role as wife and mother cannot be perceived as anything but secondary, unheroic, and non-political. The Este dynastic plot remains purely epic and masculine. Inasmuch as Britomart is female at Malecasta's, however, she wins the right for chastity to be perceived as a heroic virtue and she establishes that her quest for her husband, for love, and for her own identity as a generative female is heroic in its own right. We will see that, because she has something different to contribute, Britomart does not retire after she fights Artegall. The victory of the English poet over the Italian at this point, thus, lies in his overcoming the need for his lady knight to speak a profeminist speech.

Yet, precisely because her encounter with Malecasta locates the source of the lady knight's heroic power in the virtue of chastity, it leads to a rejection of the notion that women should govern men. The detailed account of Malecasta's aggressive courtship of her demonstrates the personal, interpersonal, and moral disorder that results from female initiative and female

---

femininity, is entirely different from Kathleen Williams's. She argues for the importance of a perfect balance of masculine and feminine in Britomart. She states that "Britomart believes that she recognizes a genuine emotion like that she has felt herself, and through the consequent lack of care her feminine side takes momentary control so that she has to defend herself without her armour and suffers a skin wound from Gardante's arrow of sight. But this is her only mistake" (112).

government in love, a danger of which Britomart should be especially wary as she has taken the initiative in looking for Artegall. For Britomart, Malecasta's name, which symbolizes the allegorical experience of her castle, can translate, granting Spenser a rather atrocious pun, "chaste in a male manner," which is another way of saying "not chaste at all." The good female warrior's male exterior cannot lead her to imitate a male sexual role, because, in the Platonic terms of this text, her physical strength has its source in her virtue; she would lose her fight with Gardante and his companions if she became "malecasta."[25]

The magnificent emblematic vision of chastity in action at the end of canto 1 is followed by the most explicit reference to the controversy about women in all of Book III: the encomium linking Britomart to great women of the past and to Queen Elizabeth (III.ii.1–3). The terms of the connection will be discussed in Chapter 11, but here it is important to note that this sudden move from the personal to the political prevents an exclusively allegorical and psychological reading of the prowess displayed by the lady warrior confronted with Malecasta. The Proem insists on the necessity of reading Britomart's skill at arms as a literal representation of women's natural abilities (otherwise the praise of the Queen is pure nonsense), and it begins the flashback in which we learn that her future lies in being a lady knight devoted to family interests and not an autonomous Amazon like Radigund.

This encomium is an imitation of the Proem that begins canto 20 of the *Orlando furioso,* and the episode that prompts the encomium in the Italian poem shares a number of elements with the Malecasta episode; by means of the proem, thus, Spenser introduces yet another Ariostan context for understanding his heroine's encounter with Malecasta and her particular kind of knighthood. Just before the *Furioso* encomium, Marfisa contracts to fulfill two obligations, for only one of which she is physically equipped. Like Britomart, who gets into an awkward situation by becoming Malecasta's "man," Marfisa must beat ten knights on a battlefield and must satisfy ten Amazons in bed. Herself an Amazonian type, Marfisa attempts to quell her companions' fear that she cannot meet the second challenge by pointing to her sword as the tool that will give her victory. She seems to be unable to distinguish between phallic symbol and the phallus itself. The Narrator speaks the encomium after a temporary truce has been called in the battle and just after Marfisa has let down her hair and revealed that she is a woman. The letting down of her hair

25. My suggestion that Britomart struggles with the need to choose between two kinds of female warriors within her contrasts with Williams's entire discussion of "her completeness as woman and warrior, an armed figure like Minerva or Venus armata, in whom feminine and masculine qualities are balanced" (91).

prevents the continuation of the military combat and forestalls the sexual combat because it leads to the discovery that members of her party are friends with her opponent and to the formulation of plans for the destruction of the Amazon realm.

In *The Faerie Queene*, the joust in bed, the letting down of the heroine's hair, and a reprise of the military combat occur, all in rapid sequence. Britomart does not get off so easily as Marfisa, who never has to face up to her physiological difference from men and remains a virgin and sexually inactive for her entire life. Thus, the analogy between Marfisa's encounter with the Amazons and Britomart's with Malecasta stresses the difference between Britomart and lady knights of Marfisa's type. Her initial persistence in her male identity is like Marfisa's belief that what is underneath the armor makes no difference. The encounter in bed jolts her into awareness of female sexuality. By superimposing this analogy with Marfisa on the already established analogy with Bradamante Spenser confirms Britomart as a lady knight of a kind distinct from both Marfisa and Bradamante, her two literary predecessors.

This is not to say that Britomart's martial ability is just an allegory. Spenser's dramatic representation of her decision to take up arms after Merlin tells her about her role in the future of England demonstrates that the physical strength required for Britomart's deeds can arise naturally in the female sex. In this, he is like many of the Italian defenders of women and the most extreme of his contemporary compatriots, Whetstone and Howard, and unlike the majority of Elizabethan writers, who favor the sudden infusion of valor theory typical of Boccaccio's *De mulieribus*. However, he does not follow Whetstone and Howard to their conclusion that physical capacity for arms demonstrates that distinctions between the sexes are culturally caused.

In her attempt to persuade Britomart to take up arms, Glauce, her nurse, uses two sets of examples of military women: a good group of great British ancestresses of the heroine and the glamorous but threatening Saxon Queen Angela. Both kinds of women are represented as literally having used arms; they locate Britomart's martial actions in the real capacities of womankind for such actions, not in the allegorical tradition; they do not represent a feminine moral quality. Glauce suggests that Britomart join the line of militant British women.

> And sooth, it ought your courage much inflame,
> To heare so often, in that royall hous,
> From whence to none inferiour ye came,
> Bards tell of many women valorous

> Which haue full many feats aduenturous
> Performed, in paragone of proudest men:
> The bold *Bunduca,* whose victorious
> Exploits made *Rome* to quake, stout *Guendolen,*
> Renowmed *Martia,* and redoubted *Emmilen.*
>
> (III.iii.54)

It is important that the examples Glauce chooses to inspire her charge are English and not the traditional classical Camilla and Pentheselia, who were known for their lifelong commitment to arms and for their lack of dedication to woman's traditional role. These female members of Britomart's "hous" took up arms for a particular cause. According to the descriptions of Bunduca, Guendolen, and Martia in the history of monarchs that Arthur reads in Book II, canto x, Bunduca acted when men failed and Guendolen when her husband was unfaithful. Mertia was famed for her discovery of laws, which her husband instituted.[26] They all demonstrate that women by nature have the capacity to perform "in paragone of proudest men"; thus, they do not fit the pattern of the extraordinary woman established by Boccaccio because, in each case their actions arise from a natural capacity, not a divine infusion of male force. At the same time their actions do not challenge the traditional order of society as those of Amazons do. These are women whose female virtues lead them to find the strength to act in the interests of family and nation.[27] They are very similar to Elyot's Zenobia.

The armor that Glauce suggests that Britomart wear has Amazonian connotations. It belonged to the Saxon Queen Angela, and it has just been

26. "A woman worthy of immortall prayse, / Which for this Realme found many goodly layes, / And wholesome Statutes to her husband brought" (II.x.42.4–6). I take "found" to mean discovered, not "established" as Hamilton glosses it (Spenser, *Faerie Queene* 265). That Mertia did not create the laws out of whole cloth and her own wisdom is suggested by the pun on "goodly" that Hamilton identifies and by the suspicion that Mertia was a fay (line 7), a being with access to hidden knowledge, and is consonant with sixteenth-century notions of law as naturally existing. An Emmilen famous as a warrior is not known. Hamilton suggests that Spenser may be referring to the widowed "Queen of Cornwall and mother of Tristram," who sent her son out of the kingdom to protect him from his uncle during his minority; see VI.ii.29. She conforms to the pattern of women who act in a crisis for the good of their family.

27. In *Monstrous Regiment* Lillian Robinson makes the very important point that Spenser provides Britomart with historical ancestresses of her type, unlike Ariosto, who provided Bradamante only with literary antecedents (300–301). However, she speaks of Mertia and Bunduca as activists (301), and she also argues that "in none of the instances that the chronicle cites, is there anything about the way the women rulers exercise authority that is specific to their sex, any intrinsically 'feminine' contribution that they make to government" (298–99), whereas I suggest the opposite, that their contribution is feminine. I contrast them with Angela; Robinson does not distinguish them from Angela.

conquered; not only did warrior women exist in the past, they even now exist. According to the description of her, Angela was a leader of troops, a virgin, rashly vengeful, a killer of men, and an enemy of Britomart's family. She is the kind of woman warrior Britomart pretends to be when describing herself to Red Cross, one schooled in fighting since infancy. That Britomart feels "great desire / Of warlike armes . . . / And generous stout courage" (III.iv.57) after she puts on Angela's armor introduces an important ambiguity into her character. It may be that with the armor she has put on a spirit alien to her family tradition and deadly in its results, as her aggressive entry into the poem and her lie to Red Cross suggest, but her "generous . . . courage" toward Guyon after her initial roughness suggests that she will finally reject militancy in favor of her dynastic mission.

The rejection occurs gradually. We emerge from the flashback to see her attack Marinell and ride off unconcerned in a reprise imitation of the opening of the *Furioso*. The complete closing of this dichotomy in her character does not occur until her encounter with Radigund. Progress is evident, however, when Britomart arrives at miserly Malbecco's house after her long absence in the middle cantos of the book. To summarize briefly: Britomart arrives at a castle in a rainstorm, discovers that its lord will allow no one in because he is so jealous of his wife; fights with Paridell for the right to enter a hovel where he is sheltering with Satyrane; joins ranks with these knights and gets permission to enter the castle by threatening to burn it down; and, then, once inside, removes her helmet and admits her identity. This scene is the second imitation of the "rocca di Tristano" and the third of the opening of the *Furioso*, although the elements are quite jumbled in their distribution between the fight with Paridell outside the hovel and the subsequent scene inside the castle.[28] Here, however, the focus is on the open revelation of Britomart's gender from which attention was diverted in the other episodes. Still conspicuously absent is the issue of women's rights that predominates in the original Ariostan episode. No one perceives Britomart's skill as infringing on male prerogatives.

28. Her battle with Paridell recalls her encounter with Guyon in that Satyrane intervenes to reconcile the knights as Arthur and the Palmer did and in that the topic of defeat by a female knight comes up. That she fights to gain entry recalls the "rocca" and its law, however, because it is so quickly followed by the removal of the helmet, another element from the "rocca" incident. Alpers suggests that "the special rule that makes a knight gain his entrance into the Castle of Tristan is due to the jealousy and inhospitality of its original owner . . . and this may have suggested to Spenser Malbecco's jealousy" (197). Hamilton glosses III.ix.16.5 "In contrast to earlier encounters in which she triumphs by her enchanted spear; hence steel-hed spear (1)" (Spenser, *Faerie Queene* 387). Although it is true that this is an odd description of the spear, I do not see what is gained by the interpretation of it as a different spear. How has Britomart changed so that she does not use her magic spear against Paridell?

The primary quality that stands out in contrast with both the Malecasta episode and the *Orlando furioso* original is the ease with which Britomart disarms and assumes female dress. When she removes her helmet, her hair cascades to her heels, but this disclosure of her femininity does not dismay her. She continues to disarm quite unself-consciously, even letting down "her well plighted frock, which she did won / To tucke about her short, when she did ryde." Even when he draws away from this homely and realistic portrait of the female warrior after battle in order to create a magnificent simile, the Narrator stresses her feminine power. He compares her with Minerva, a female goddess of war, who, like Britomart, is military without being masculine, and whose Gorgonian shield suggested the power of chastity to Renaissance mythographers.[29] The conflict between male and female that dominates both Spenser's and Ariosto's previous representations, though in such different ways, is entirely gone.

The response to the revelation of her sex is also different from reactions to the same revelation earlier in Book III. It is not the anxiety felt by the Narrator and by Guyon (had he known) nor the terror felt by Malecasta and her household; it is universal wonder and adoration. The residents, delighted by having mistaken her for a man, "meruaild at her cheualree, and noble prowesse, which they had approued" (III.ix.24). Even Paridell becomes easy with the idea that he has been beaten by a woman.

> And *Paridell* though partly discontent
> With his late fall, and fowle indignity,
> Yet was soone wonne his malice to relent,
> Through gracious regard of her faire eye,
> And knightly worth, which he too late did try,
> Yet tried did adore.
>
> (III.ix.25)

This is the scene that the Narrator's address to Guyon in canto 1 suggested would be one of distress; instead, Britomart's sex poses no problem to the overthrown male adversary. This response is conclusive. The unfolding of the private virtue of chastity continues through the end of the book, but the armed representation of it poses no more problems because the source of the strength

---

29. Hamilton (Spenser, *Faerie Queene* 387) refers to Comes's *Mythologiae* (1616), IV.v., where "the shield is said to symbolize power over lustful eyes" and to Petrarch's "Triumph of Chastity" where Laura bears Medusa's shield.

has been demonstrated to be in generative feminine virtue, not in antimasculine Amazonian vice. Only an old fool like Malbecco still mistrusts it.

Britomart hides her female identity under a male disguise once more in a comic scene at the opening of Book IV that ends with another imitation of the "rocca di Tristano" episode. Here, the tensions of the previous book are quickly resolved in an emblem of friendship, the virtue of this new book in which the informal and transitory concords established in Book III become formal and lasting; Britomart reveals that she is a woman in order to help an unknown knight. The episode begins with a reprise: because of her prowess, Britomart is mistaken for a male knight by a beautiful woman, as she was at Malecasta's, but Britomart plays her male role with humorous zest rather than defensiveness. Riding along with Amoret after having rescued her from Busyrane, she flirts with the poor lady and makes the socially awkward situation worse by making it possible for anyone who sees them to conclude that Amoret's honor is at risk. There is no tension in the scene. Amoret's defensiveness is a comic parody of her conduct at Busyrane's, and Britomart's imitation of lust is overdone and inconsistent; she doesn't make a very convincing "malecasta."

Although Britomart's reason for playing the male with Amoret is that she wishes to "maske her wounded mind" (IV.i.7), her motive at Malecasta's, the denouement firmly establishes Britomart's ease with her femininity and at the same time completely subverts the political content of the "rocca" episode. She and Amoret arrive at a castle with a law that requires that a knight who arrives without a lady must win one or sleep outside (IV.i.9). A knight with no lady attempts to win Amoret from Britomart and fails. Britomart takes pity on him and devises a scheme whereby all three travelers can obtain a night's lodging. She gets the host to agree that she is Amoret's male escort; she then reveals that she is a woman and acts as the knight's companion. She, in turn, receives the rewards of friendship when, in a comic reversal of the end of the Malecasta episode, she voluntarily enters Amoret's bed and the two spend the night talking about their loves.[30]

This happy outcome is made possible by Britomart's witty manipulation of the misapprehension of her body as male. Her strategy recalls Bradamante's at the "rocca," but, in recalling it, undermines it. Bradamante denies the sight of her body to those around her in order to succeed in her argument that women who are capable of performing like men must be given the rights of men. This

---

30. A night with Amoret offers all the comforts of the sharing of passions that occurs in teenaged female friendship. Britomart's frank conversation about her love for Artegall distinguishes this episode from conversation about Artegall with Red Cross when she was deceitful. There, her sex was acknowledged, but not her love.

argument denigrates the traditional female role and achieves respect for women only inasmuch as they can perform like men. Britomart flaunts the feminine gender of her body. True, she first claims her rights as a "male" knight, but she does not do this out of any interest in the rights of women. She is not interested in the rule's gender restrictions at all; she is distressed by it as a violation of hospitality—as a lack of friendship—and she manipulates its terms in order to extend friendship to both a man and a woman. Her ability to bring concord out of conflict between three characters is emblematic of the action of the Legend of Friendship, as her reconciliation with Guyon set a model for the acceptance of her chastity as a heroic virtue in the Legend of Chastity. Thus, women's virtue produces the strength that provides the solution in social and personal dilemmas; the narrative illustrates the Platonic notion of the continuity of the private and social virtues.

One of the essential conditions for the success of Bradamante's ambition is the interruption of the Narrator's blazon of her body. We see her beautiful head, but the pleasure of seeing the rest of her is frustrated because it must remain possible for her to claim that she may be a male. By contrast, the Narrator reveals all of Britomart's body and, unlike his full-length portrait of her at Malbecco's, this description is erotic.[31] There, the representation is realistic (she wears a dress neatly folded under her armor) and modest; here, our attention is drawn along the curves of her figure by the lightning simile that describes the motion of her hair.[32] No one present, other than Amoret and the young knight, can find a natural explanation for her appearance. They mistake her for Bellona, an enchantment, and a character in a "maske of strange disguise." But we know better; at this moment she has broken free from the mask she wore with Amoret and has left behind all "masques" and enchantments in Book III. She has definitively chosen not to be a woman warrior of the type of the destruction-bringing Bellona.[33] She is a human woman who has fully realized her sex's potential for virtue and valor, and she is luminous with the energy and power this virtue produces.

All is not perfect at the end of this first episode in Book IV, however. The male worship and adolescent female intimacy that conclude it must both be discarded if Britomart is to move from the private to the economic and political spheres and achieve marriage (the ultimate friendship), join Artegall in bed,

31. See Hamilton (Spenser, *Faerie Queene* 429).
32. See Bender (60–61) for a discussion of the nonerotic aspects of the description.
33. Hamilton suggests that Spenser changed Bellona to Minerva when he described Britomart at Malbecco's because Bellona has more violent associations. See Spenser's references to Bellona at VII.vi.3.32.

fulfill her dynastic promise, help to establish justice in society, and, thus, demonstrate the active power of chastity in every realm of human activity. The fight between Britomart and Artegall (and Scudamour) and their reconciliation, courtship, and engagement in canto 6 bring the process near to completion. They emerge committed to a marriage in which Artegall will be the authority and Britomart the moral center, a role that she plays in Book V.

Once again Spenser presents this essential development by reworking and refuting the *Furioso* and the notion of woman represented by Bradamante. The reconciliation is initiated by the removal of Britomart's helmet and the consequent revelation of her sex and her beauty, and the duel between the lovers recalls the duel between Bradamante and Ruggiero that begins the denouement of the *Furioso*. The duel in *The Faerie Queene* is a more authentic test of the lady knight's skill, however: Ruggiero in the *Furioso* restrains his violence because he knows that he is fighting his beloved, whereas Artegall does not know who Britomart is; Artegall fights with all his strength and is winning when chance leads his sword to destroy her helmet but not her head. Her beauty overpowers him, as her military might could not. He thinks that she may be "some heavenly goddesse" deserving of his obedience because of her "beauties excellence," and horror at his temerity makes "his manly hart to quayle" (IV.vi.21–22). Meanwhile, when Artegall raises his visor, his face acts on Britomart's memory, and she begins to soften. Neither her arm nor her tongue obey her will to fight, and she behaves and speaks mildly. She does not, however, worship him upon seeing his face; she remains standing above him.

Although it may seem delightful to see Artegall so devoted to Britomart, this is a dangerous situation. As long as the heroine remains in a superior position, their relationship will fit the unproductive courtly pattern whose drawbacks are represented by the allegory of Malecasta's Castle Joyous and by the story of the failed union of Amoret and Scudamour. The latter's teasing suggestion that Artegall's servile posture means that he is going "to live a Ladies thrall" signals the danger to which the hero has exposed himself (and to which he will succumb with Radigund). Britomart's "modest countenance . . . so goodly grave, and full of princely awe" has the positive moral effect of causing him his "looser thoughts to lawfull bounds withdraw" (33); it holds him off, just as her rose-thorn–like manly expression held off male desire at Malecasta's. If their relationship is to be fruitful, however, he must get up off his knees.

Glauce's efforts to effect a truce among the three combatants exacerbate the problem because she does not recognize that Britomart's victory over Artegall is erotic, not military. She imagines that he needs to be consoled for having been conquered by a woman, just as the Narrator imagined that Guyon would have needed such consolation, had he known the nature of his opponent (III.i). Even though Artegall has shown no distress at the sex of his opponent, she counsels him not to

> . . . disdaine, that womans hand
> hath conquered you anew in second fight:
> For whylome they haue conquerd sea and land,
> And heauen it selfe, that nought may them withstand.
> Ne henceforth be rebellious vnto loue.
>
> (IV.vi.31)

This equation of military and erotic conquest is inappropriate to the immediate occasion of Britomart's conquest of Artegall and to Book IV because it perpetuates the sexual inversion of tyrannical Petrarchan love.[34]

Glauce's advice to the heroine is equally inappropriate because it encourages her to think of herself as playing the courtly role. She begs that Britomart,

> faire Ladie knight, my dearest Dame
> relent the rigour of your wrathfull will, . . .
> graunt him your grace, but so that he fulfill
> the penance, which ye shall to him empart.
>
> (IV.vi.32)

Glauce considers Britomart to hold the power in the relationship. The advice to give up her wrathful will and to indulge in grace offers alternatives appropriate to a sovereign, not a wife. Britomart is not to be a virgin queen, and the model of female political supremacy is not appropriate to marriage. If Britomart is not to be to Artegall what Belphoebe is to Timias, he must conquer her in yet a third fight: courtship.

The rest of the episode celebrates Artegall's successful assertion of his masculine sexual force and domestic mastery. The wooing scene takes place on territory that he has chosen and at a time that he determines. Although he offers "meeke seruice and much suit," the dominant metaphors that describe

---

34. Upton noted that this encomium of women's accomplishments is an undisguised compliment to the Queen (Hamilton, ed., *Faerie Queene* 470). Glauce's advice to Britomart in the following lines is similarly complimentary to the Queen. They echo the poet's praise of Belphoebe, and, thus, of his sovereign's gracious use of her authority, and pay a tacit compliment to Queen Elizabeth herself without being good advice for Britomart.

the courtship are of war and the hunt. He lays siege to her heart, he brings her "unto a bay," and she yields "her consent / To be his loue, and take him for her Lord, / Till they with mariage meet might finish that accord" (IV.vi.41). That Artegall becomes Britomart's "Lord" does not indicate that she becomes his "thrall," however; he has to win "her will to suffer him depart," and on parting from him, Britomart sadly leaves him to "his fortunes gouernment" (46), which suggests that some other form of government obtains when they are together. What form is developed when they meet again in Book V.

This hierarchical realignment of the hero and heroine does not go counter to the notion of womanhood that Spenser has been developing for Britomart throughout the poem; as a consequence, her subjection is not like Bradamante's in similar circumstances, because it does not entail a complete relinquishment of her previous role. At the end of the *Furioso*, the heroine feels a social necessity to submit to Ruggiero and arranges a battle with him so that she can lose to him. She later stands on the sidelines in a dress and watches as he fights his archenemy. Her prowess is not a product of the same virtue that will make her a good wife, and Ariosto plays up the drama of her self-sacrifice. In contrast, Britomart becomes Artegall's companion-at-arms, although she cannot accompany him on his present quest; she must keep her obligation to Scudamour and find Amoret. Because her excellence arises from sexual difference and because she is represented in the context of the Platonic notion of the continuity of the virtues, she is impelled to continue her martial activities after marriage; whereas, because Bradamante's excellence arises from her similarity to men, her martial and marital roles are in conflict, and she must give up the former when she assumes the latter. Once again, the English author demonstrates the superiority of his notion of woman to the Italian.

There is one troubling aspect of this scene, however, that leaves room for further development in the relationship between Britomart and Artegall: Britomart is very reluctant to part from her beloved. While this might be taken as touchingly accurate psychological verisimilitude—what young woman would willingly part with her newly discovered fiancé?—the terms in which the Narrator speaks of their parting evoke the possibility that Artegall or she will go wrong. In the stanza in which he represents Artegall as engaging "his faith with her," the Narrator defines the period of time he will be gone by reference to "the horned moon," hardly a reassuring formula in the context of fidelity. Britomart is far from satisfied with Artegall's assurances, and her anxious, clinging parting from him and her commitment of him to "his fortunes gouernment" give a sense that he is going off into danger that she is not sure he can meet successfully.[35] What goes wrong will become clear when we look at their relationship in its political context in the next chapter.

The Temple of Venus

Before turning to politics, however, a discussion of the Temple of Venus is necessary to complete my study of Spenser's defense and definition of the feminine; it is in this episode that Spenser defines the social behavior proper to ladies. As its name suggests, the Temple is sacred to Venus in her social aspect, as the Garden of Adonis is to her generative aspect. It is located within the bounds of this world—Scudamour visits it, and it is a less happy place than the Garden, which exists in some strange zone within creation and time but beyond the limits of direct human experience. The Garden asserts the importance and value of the feminine contribution to generation and cosmological order: at its center is the erotic thicket where Venus and her lover join form and matter; no restraints on eros apply. The Temple of Venus asserts the importance and value of the feminine contribution to social intercourse. At its center is a statue of the goddess surrounded by lamenting lovers, and "at the Idoles feet apart / a beuie of fayre damzels" sits (IV.x.48). These damsels represent the restraints on eros that are essential if the sexes are to encounter each other in social situations. Ignorance and abuse of these restraints provides the material for many of the unfortunate experiences of the characters in Books III and IV, and this very episode ends with Scudamour's abduction of Amoret.

These damsels are Womanhood, Curtesie, Cherefulnesse, Silence, Obedience, Modestie, and Shamefastnesse. All are said to be peers of Womanhood yet obedient to her. The last four of these virtues are conventional feminine virtues; if Spenser were demanding absolute adherence to them from his female readers, then his notion of the feminine would be far more limited than the Garden of Adonis and the story of Britomart have made it seem. The presence of Curtesie and Cherefulnesse in the group, the organization of the virtues in a circle, and the specific value attributed to Silence and Obedience all work to prevent Womanhood from being restricted to her traditional domestic location and role.

35. Compare this departure scene with that at the end of Book I when Red Cross leaves Una "to mourne." There, no anxiety is created. Similarly, as we will see, in Book V the parting of Britomart and Artegall is not fraught with worry.

Curtesie and Cherefulness, as Spenser describes them here, are social virtues with a larger scope than the home. They permit Womanhood to engage in delightful conversation with whomever she pleases. Like Castiglione's Court Lady, who was an expert at *intertenere*, Curtesie "unto every person knew her part." She clearly has contact with a variety of people, if she is praised for being able to play a variety of parts, and, of course, her name suggests her presence at court. Similarly, Cherefulnesse facilitates conversation by making it delightful. These are the feminine social skills recommended by humanist authors, not by Protestant advisers on domestic conduct.

On their own, however, Curtesie and Cherefulnesse can lead to trouble because they may invite conversation and sexual advances, and they cannot restrain them. In Spenser's elaborate circle each is counterbalanced by a restraining traditional feminine virtue—Silence, Obedience, Modestie, and Shamefastnesse.[36] The relationship of each virtue to her companion varies. Shamefastnesse is placed opposite Cherefulnesse. The former never lifts her eyes; the latter's eyes "darted forth delights." In their pure form, obviously, these two virtues cannot be practiced simultaneously; a woman must decide which is appropriate. Modestie and Curtesie face each other; they can be practiced at the same time, but in combination each is different from what she is on her own. Just as the Magnifico set limits on the flirtatiousness and suggestiveness of his Court Lady in the *Cortegiano*, so Modestie might temper Curtesie. In the weightiest pairing of all, Womanhood is opposite the paired Silence and Obedience. This is something of a paradox, as all the virtues are said to obey Womanhood. She has authority, yet she obeys. The description of Silence and Obedience resolves the apparent paradox: they are not exclusively domestic virtues any more than the rest; they are the virtues of religious martyrs. "Both gifts of God not gotten but from thence, / Both girlonds of his Saints against their foes offence" (IV.li.8–9). Spenser's Womanhood is a Protestant ideal, but not the narrow and unexciting one that the presence of Silence, Obedience, Modestie, and Shamefastnesse at first suggest.

The final element necessary to womanhood in this Venerian temple is the erotic, the quality whose social expression many, but not all, of the virtues are designed to permit and control. It is present in the midst of this group of virtues in the person of Amoret, who sits in the lap of Womanhood. All these social virtues, however, cannot safeguard her from abduction by "Cupid's man," who roughly proclaims the inappropriateness of her virginity to Venus's

---

36. I am indebted to Hamilton (Spenser, *Faerie Queene* 505) for my understanding of the physical organization of this circle.

service.[37] He is right, of course, yet his methods do not get him very far. Like Orpheus, to whom he compares himself, he loses the object of his affection because he is rash and breaks the rules. His rape of Amoret from this setting is the result of an unresolved conflict between Womanhood and Venus; unsocialized Venus winks at him; Womanhood rebukes him for being "ouer bold." If Scudamour had participated in the social processes defined by the circle of virtuous women sitting "apart" from the statue, he might have produced less (or even no) pain for himself and for Amoret. The story provides a retrospective explanation for much of the suffering in Book III at the same time that it makes a profeminist point by exonerating good women from guilt for the violent erotic response that their beauty sometimes provokes in men.

The story of the Temple of Venus concludes the exposition of the private and social aspects of chastity. In Books III and IV womankind and the feminine have been defended and praised as governors of the passions; we have seen them turn men and the masculine from undisciplined destructive courses to restrained and productive paths. The positive political power of chastity is also present in these books, and it is fully developed in Book V. It is to that topic that I now turn.

37. If one compares the Temple of Venus with the Garden of Adonis, the most outstanding difference is Venus's lack of control of male sexual energy. Although the snake that encircles the feet of the goddess seems quite peaceful—its "head and tail were fast combyned"—unsatisfied desire rules among her worshipers.

11

PRAISE AND DEFENSE OF THE QUEEN IN *THE FAERIE QUEENE*

Praise of the positive political power of chastity is the final step in Spenser's paradoxical defense of womankind, the feminine, and the Queen. This praise appears in Book III in the opening stanzas of cantos 2 and 4 and in Book V in the episodes narrating Britomart's visit to Isis Church, her defeat of Radigund, and Mercilla's judgment of Duessa. The stanzas in Book III mediate between Britomart, the major exemplar of female strength within the poem, and the Queen, the major exemplar of female strength in Spenser's society.[1] They indicate the superiority of the Queen's actions to those of all other women and distinguish her from Amazonian figures. The episodes in Book V also reject the Amazonian tradition; in addition, they identify the public virtue of equity with the private virtue of chastity and illustrate that legitimate female rule results in good government *because it is feminine.* Through setting the defense of the Queen in this context of paradoxical praise of the feminine and of womankind, Spenser transforms Elizabeth's female sex from the drawback, which it is for most of those who defend her right to rule, to a glory and the necessity of praising her from a handicap to a great opportunity. He does not, however, work any changes in the political position of womankind. Like all writers of paradoxical defenses, he writes political action out of the script for most women because he writes political ambition out of their character.

The Encomia of Womankind

The reader of *The Faerie Queene* first comes directly in contact with the formal praise and defense of womankind in the first three stanzas of the second canto

1. I have discussed neither Belphoebe nor Glorianna in any detail because neither one of them is set in a context that invokes the tradition of the defense of womankind. Both are defined as representative of Elizabeth alone.

of Book III. An unmistakable imitation of the encomium of women with which canto 20 of the *Orlando furioso* opens, these lines, along with those that begin Canto 4, are usually taken to indicate the general accord of Spenser's view with the optimistic humanist profeminism expressed there. They defend "the glory of women" (Durling 217), and they attempt to "redress the balance in a culture whose images of women and love, whose institutions affecting women and love were products of male imagination" (Berger, *Faerie Queene* 397). The notion of womankind celebrated in this encomium is positive as Durling and Berger state, but the praise of women's moral, intellectual, and political strengths is undercut by a bleak representation of modern times and of the political future of women that goes entirely contrary to the *Furioso* passage's optimism. The encomium of women in Book III, canto 2 deprives modern women of the hope of fame.

The *Furioso* encomium and the opening of *Faerie Queene*, canto 2 relate the history of women's history. According to the *Furioso*, accounts of ancient and of modern women are available, but the records of intermediate time have been marred by male historians. The stanzas move from positive past to negative past to triumphant present; modern women do great deeds and modern poets sing their praise. According to *The Faerie Queene*, modern writers have not broken the downward movement but rather are likely to make the situation even worse. The Narrator identifies male envy of women's accomplishments as the reason for woman's restricted social role, suggests that no amount of reeducation can eliminate this envy and the antifeminist literary and social structures that it produces, and concludes that modern women will never play a social or political role commensurate with their abilities—except, of course, for Elizabeth. She is a glorious exception to the decline caused by masculine government of time and of literary production. Finally, although the notion of womankind revealed in these stanzas is consonant with that in the *Furioso*, the political isolation of the Queen fits with the defenses written by Aylmer and his fellows.

The encomium begins with a strong humanist profeminist complaint.

> Here haue I cause, in men iust blame to find,
>   That in their proper prayse too partiall bee,
>   And not indifferent to woman kind,
>   To whom no share in armes and cheualrie
>   They do impart, ne maken memorie
>   Of their braue gestes and prowesse martiall;
>   Scarse do they spare to one or two or three,

Rowme in their writs; yet the same writing small
Does all their deeds deface, and dims their glories all.

(III.ii.1)

The assertion that many women have done deeds worthy of record and the complaint that male historians do not give women their proper share of praise is a commonplace of Italian humanist defenses and appears in the *Furioso* in the encomium in canto 20. As a commonplace, it sets up expectations about what will come next. The author of such a reproach of historians usually distinguishes himself from his predecessors by listing examples of accomplished women; Ariosto features the names of the classical women Sappho and Corinna and Camilla and Harpalyce in his first stanza. Spenser sets himself off from the mass of men by assuming a critical tone about male attempts to obscure women's glory, but he does not go on in good courtly-humanist style and correct the historical record with a series of examples proving women's share in history. He names no names.

Rather than relate the history of women's accomplishments, the poet relates the history of male authorities' repression of women each time they became noteworthy. Like all defenders of women, he turns to "true writers of histories" for information (Agrippa, *Treatise* fol. F7), but he finds that men have steadily restricted women's activities *because of* women's proven worth. Envy produces not just a lacuna in the historical record, but the circumscription of women's social role. Britomart's exploits, literally considered, are not an option for modern women.

But by record of antique times I find,
    That women wont in warres to beare most sway,
    And to all great exploits them selues inclind:
    Of which they still the girlond bore away,
    Till enuious Men fearing their rules decay,
    Gan coyne streight lawes to curb their liberty;
    Yet sith they warlike armes haue layd away:
    They haue exceld in artes and pollicy,
That now we foolish men that prayse gin eke t'enuy.

(III.ii.2)

As presented in this stanza the past provides a sad forecast of the future. Lines 1–4 evoke a Golden Age in which military achievement was the standard by which excellence was judged and assert nostalgically that women were then superior to men. Lines 5–6 describe the decline from this Golden Age caused by male envy, which suppressed female military activity. The last three lines suggest an equivalence between modern women's practice of arts and policy and ancient women's practice of arms, but their image of the present is conditional and restrictive; it contrasts with the feeling of freedom and power the first four lines evoke. There, the verbs are active and aggressive: women were wont to "beare sway," they "inclined" to "great exploits," and they "bore away" the victory. Here, their action is to lay away, a negative gesture, and to excel, a vague word with no specific relation to arts and policy. The ninth line proves the quality of female action by saying it is so good that men envy it, thus threatening that male envy will soon restrain female energy into a still narrower field. If men, whom Spenser states were physically weaker, were able to repress women's military activity when moved by envy to do so, it follows that men's envy of political accomplishments in the modern age, while certainly a tribute to women's talents, is a sign of trouble to come.[2]

As a defense of women this stanza has one striking peculiarity. It accepts the rule of men over women and the irreversible decline in women's status as facts of life; although it expresses regret for the state of things, it does not urge rebellion. This acceptance sets the poet off from the humanist tradition supporting women. Many defenders of womankind invent legendary events to account for women's low social position, as Spenser does, but they always argue that in modern times this distortion of the proper order is being or ought to be corrected. For example, in *Of the Nobilitie and Excellencye of Woman kynde*, Agrippa von Nettesheim complains that God commanded women to prophesy and preach,

> but the unworthy dealyng of the later lawe makers is so great, that breakyng goddes commaundemente, to stablysshe theyr owne traditions, they haue pronounced openlye, that women otherwyse in excellency of nature, dignitie, and honour most noble, be in condicion more vyle than all men: And thus by these lawes, the women being subdewed as it were by force of armes, are constrained to give place to men, and to obeye theyr subdewers, not by no naturall, no divyne necessitie or reason, but by custome, education, fortune, and a certayne tyrannicall occasion. (fol. G1rv)

2. In *The Feminine Reclaimed* Stevie Davies also sees a note of threat in the last line of stanza 3. "He links this [male minimization of the contributions of woman] with woman's confinement to the indoor world, from which, however, they are already showing such disconcerting signs of intellectual and political precocity that their captors are having to think up more drastic means of subjecting them" (34).

Agrippa speaks of this situation as an insupportable indignity and argues for opportunities for womankind. Like Agrippa, Spenser asserts the natural ability of women to excel in traditionally male fields, but he admits the incontestable power, if not the right, of law to restrict their actions. He makes no protest against the repression of women, no attempt to rally their forces to a renaissance.

The final stanza continues the comparison of historical and modern women; Britomart, the primary representative of the accomplishments of ancient women, is bested by Elizabeth.

> Of warlike puissaunce in ages spent,
>> Be thou faire *Britomart*, whose prayse I write,
>> But of all wisedome be thou precedent,
>> O soueraigne Queene, whose prayse I would endite,
>> Endite I would as dewtie doth excite;
>> But ah my rimes too rude and rugged arre,
>> When in so high an obiect they do lite,
>> And striuing, fit to make, I feare do marre:
>> Thy selfe thy prayses tell, and make them knowen farre.
>
>> (III.ii.3)

The comparison between Britomart and Elizabeth turns on the ambiguous phrase "be thou precedent." Although "precedent" may be read as a noun (the article "a" understood) and suggest that Elizabeth may be taken as a "model worthy of imitation," in the line as it stands "precedent" is an adjective and would seem to mean "preceding in rank or estimation."[3] This is the only meaning that works for Britomart as well: she was precedent in arms in her day as the Queen is precedent in wisdom in her day. Women will not succeed in imitating her. The sense of historical decline established in the previous stanza is not reversed. Elizabeth is simply exempted from the process by the assertion that she, unlike other women, is not threatened by the power of male envy to tarnish reputations or restrict action. "Thy selfe thy prayses tell, and make them knowen farre."

The suggestion that Elizabeth's conspicuous greatness effectively counters the effects of male envy of female accomplishments is employed by humanist

---

3. The *OED* does not recognize this meaning until 1613. For the adjective "precedent" in 1590, it offers "prededing in time" and "preceding in order." "Preceding in rank or estimation" is a logical extension of the notion that Spenser would have been capable of making.

defenders of gynecocracy to create indignation at the restrictions placed on women. George Whetstone in his *English Myrror*, states that "if the envy of men would suppresse and murther the worthiness of women, yet the divine virtues of our soveraigne Queene Elizabeth, doth and will alwaies keepe alive their divine memorie" (136). Before making this statement, Whetstone argues that women have a natural aptitude for rule, and after it he goes on to prove that laws against female government are against nature. Concerned with the general principle that women can and should rule, he presents Elizabeth as a representative of womankind; in her we can see what women are capable of. Unlike Whetstone, Spenser does not present Elizabeth as a lodestone for the "divine memorie" of ancient women or suggest that she is a force that will reverse the current trend. She is simply the best.

The rhetorical device by which Spenser introduces the topic of Elizabeth's imperviousness to male envy is the disclaimer of his own ability to praise her adequately. This topic is an integral and constant element of his praise for her. In the Proems to each of the first three books Spenser uses it as an explanation of his poetic method; his use of "colourd showes" is necessitated by his inability to represent her directly (III Proem) and his audience's inability to look on her directly (II Proem). The topic usually serves the dual purpose of praising the Queen and making the reader aware of Spenser as the poet praising her. This is especially clear in the Proem to the entire poem in which the poet appeals to Elizabeth for inspiration and guidance.

> And with them eke, O Goddesse heauenly bright,
>   Mirrour of grace and Maiestie diuine,
>   Great Lady of the greatest Isle, whose light
>   Like *Phoebus* lampe throughout the world doth shine,
>   Shed thy faire beames into my feeble eyne,
>   And raise my thoughts too humble and too vile,
>   To thinke of that true glorious type of thine,
>   The argument of mine afflicted stile:
> The which to heare, vouchsafe, O dearest dred a-while.
>   (I Proem.4)

The epithets by which Spenser describes Elizabeth in this stanza are literary rather than historical, and the scale of the comparison is divine rather than human. She is compared not with real women but with forces of nature; she is a goddess and she illuminates the world like the sun. With these Neoplatonic and Petrarchist terms, Spenser exploits the opportunities Elizabeth's sex offers for inflated praise even as he elevates her far beyond other women.

Spenser's claims of inability in this stanza are contradicted by the last line; there, he describes his poem, the work for which he has been invoking assistance, as already completed. Thomas Cain describes the complex function of the inability topos in this stanza as follows:

> The last two lines bring the paradox into the open, the eighth with its "argument of my afflicted style" still bespeaking inability and the passive poet's dependence on inspiration from the potentially creative goddess if the poem is to come into existence, while the alexandrine—"The which to heare, vouchsafe, O dearest dred a-while"—presents the poem as fait accompli and the poet as active creator, with the queen now the passive receptor. Because the queen is a goddess the poem is made possible, but the articulation of her true glorious type depends on the hymnic powers of the English Orpheus. (54)

In the encomium in Book III, the focus does not shift back to the poet. The last image is of Elizabeth independently arousing esteem for her virtues; the poet's intermediate role is ignored. The best we can say of him is that, by not attempting to praise the Queen, he is avoiding the footsteps of the males he decried in stanza 1, those who defaced the deeds of women. The omission of the usual last step of the inability topos concentrates attention on Elizabeth's superiority to the other members of her sex. The praise offered to Elizabeth, which at first seems so conventional, really operates as the last stage of Spenser's argument that she is extraordinary.

As a celebration of Elizabeth, this passage is enormously effective, but it celebrates her at the expense of contemporary womankind. Nothing in Spenser's stanzas suggests that Elizabeth can be equaled or that she is typical of her times; everything works to prove her exceptional. By treating her this way, Spenser would seem to be completely in line with Elizabeth's most conservative defender, Calvin, who allowed that her extraordinary qualities showed her to have been raised up by God to rule, but Spenser's reference to the egalitarian politics of the Golden Age and his assertion of the natural capacities of woman differentiate him from Calvin, who does not admit this potential in women. For Calvin, great women are always exceptions, and the ordinary woman does not have the natural abilities that would qualify her for rule. (See my Chapter 9.) For Spenser, the Golden Age is gone, but it did exist. As applied to women, this means that in the ancient past women developed to the fullest their innate potential for greatness, and in the modern age the times, not women, are at fault.

The representation of Elizabeth in Britomart's genealogical vision in the next canto is consistent with Spenser's syncretic position about women in this encomium. Elizabeth is the only woman mentioned in the list of descendents (as opposed to the history read by Arthur in Book II in which three women were included). She, therefore, stands out as extraordinary, one woman among many men. Her difference from the men is even more impressive, however, than her uniqueness. She brings peace through foreign conquest; they brought civil war. The description of her as stretching her white rod and smiting the "Castle" is evocative of Britomart with her lance, Venus with her boar, and (as we shall see) Isis with her crocodile and Mercilla with her rusty sword. All these women make feminine use of a masculine object, and the ascendancy of femininity over masculinity is the key to their success. The magnitude of the Queen's success is suggested in this passage by the echos of Virgil's fourth eclogue combined with the overtones of the Christian last age. Elizabeth's feminine prowess may put an end to the ravages of masculine history for all time.[4]

The compliments to the Queen in the encomium in canto 2 and in the genealogy in canto 3 depend for their success on the literal reading of Britomart's prowess, which I explained in Chapter 10. Only if Elizabeth is the same type of woman as Britomart can praise of the heroine's skill be read as praise of the Queen's abilities. Theirs is a relationship in kind as well as kin. Without the literal reading, the praise of the Queen's political skill is reduced to insubstantial flattery. But this does not mean that Britomart (and Elizabeth) is essentially the same as a man. At the beginning of canto 4 the topic of Amazonian women comes up because Britomart has just decided to go out in quest of Artegall and has put on the armor of the Saxon Queen Angela, armor with strong Amazonian connotations. Having created a dangerous aura of Amazonian potential around Britomart, the poet draws back from the action to comment on Britomart's relationship to Amazonian military women of the past; he very carefully defines Britomart's military might as having its source in feminine virtue, not in an inborn taste for violent activity or a hatred of men.

4. Fichter also sees Spenser celebrating feminine power in this passage. He goes on to argue that the prophesy suggests a course of action to Elizabeth (179). Spenser "reminds his audience that the Tudor *imperium* cannot be a perfect image of the Kingdom of God until 'melting love,' or the mercy of which Britomart speaks, has tempered force. The white rod she raises in self-defense against Spain, now a symbol of virginity and temporal power, needs to be redefined, as it will be when it appears again in Britomart's dream in Isis Church and in Mercilla's hand [in] book 5, as a symbol of chastity and equity. Tudor rule will image the Last Judgment truly only when the use of power is directed by justice, as will be the case in the Court of Mercilla, Spenser's fullest allegorical representation of Elizabeth" (180). I suggest that Book V may assist in understanding the full unfolding of this image, but that it is complete here. See my discussion below.

The passage is organized as a series of rhetorical questions comparing the present with the past and lamenting past glory. The terse questions in the opening stanza create a sense of a social crisis caused by the disjunction between ancient and modern times.

> Where is the Antique glory now become,
>> That whilome wont in women to appeare?
>> Where be the braue atchieuements doen by some?
>> Where be the battels, where the shield and speare,
>> And all the conquests, which them high did reare,
>> That matter made for famous Poets verse,
>> And boastfull men so oft abasht to heare?
>> Bene they all dead, and laid in dolefull herse?
> Or doen they onely sleepe, and shall againe reuerse?
>
>> (III.iv.1)

Because he clearly believes that women are capable of military greatness and because he expresses such passionate hope for the reawakening of feminine valor here, the poet can be placed in the same general camp as the humanist authors and the defenders of the Queen who consider such abilities to be natural. Indeed, the enthusiasm with which he recounts the shaming of male auditors by accounts of women's achievements would seem to identify him as an extreme profeminist, an antimasculinist who would restore honor to women by depriving men of it.

Yet, in the second stanza Spenser uses the list of accomplished women, one of the quintessential tools of the humanists, to achieve an effect that is the reverse of theirs. He increases the distance between ancient women and their feeble modern sisters rather than asserting modern women's potential for equal achievement; at the same time, he makes the reader (at least, this reader) feel somewhat squeamish about the extreme violence that the Amazonian women direct at male objects to produce lakes of blood.

> If they be dead, then woe is me therefore:
>> But if they sleepe, O let them soone awake:
>> For all too long I burne with enuy sore,
>> To heare the warlike feates, which *Homere* spake
>> Of bold *Penthesilee*, which made a lake
>> Of *Greekish* bloud so oft in *Troian* plaine;

> But when I read, how stout *Debora* strake
> Proud *Sisera,* and how *Camill'* hath slaine
> The huge *Orsilochus,* I swell with great disdaine.
>
> (III.iv.2)

Even Deborah is directly militant in this stanza. These valiant women are a long way from the civilizing and pacifying force that women seem to represent in the encomium in canto 2 and that Elizabeth herself embodies in the genealogy.

In order for Penthesilea, Deborah, and Camilla to demonstrate contemporary women's capacity to perform deeds worthy of fame, their names must be followed, as they are in defenses of women, by the mention of some modern women, and, as the question of the reawakening of the brave achievements of women is still open at the end of this stanza, the stanza raises the hope that the list will follow. The very women cited in the stanza create the expectation that Spenser, Elizabeth's Homer and Virgil, is going to praise the Queen herself as a modern heroine of this type. Two of the women on the list were figures for Elizabeth in contemporary writing or in *The Faerie Queene* itself: the "Amazon Penthesilea, earlier compared to Belphoebe" and "the Old Testament heroine Deborah, a favorite cult-name for Elizabeth" (Cain 123–24). Deborah is an especially important name to find here because she is the queen cited by Calvin as an example of an excellent and legitimate, divinely selected, female ruler. Consequently, even a Calvinist could celebrate Elizabeth as being in the tradition of Deborah.

Despite the expectation he develops, Spenser does not praise Elizabeth as a new Deborah in the third stanza. Instead, he compares Britomart with the ancient ladies and Elizabeth only with Britomart.

> Yet these, and all that else had puissaunce,
>   Cannot with noble *Britomart* compare,
>   Aswell for glory of great valiaunce,
>   As for pure chastitie and vertue rare,
>   That all her goodly deeds do well declare.
>   Well worthy stock, from which the branches sprong,
>   That in late yeares so faire a blossome bare,
>   As thee, O Queene, the matter of my song,
> Whose lignage from this Lady I deriue along.
>
> (III.iv.3)

This stanza is entirely different in tone and approach from the previous two. Cain explains the logical mechanism behind it: "The idea of the blossom that validates the stock rearranges categories of importance so that Britomart now derives her meaning from her offspring, an arrangement of values that descends in order of worth from Elizabeth to Britomart to [the ancients]" (124). In other words, this trick of logic makes Elizabeth superior to the greatest women of the past, and it makes her so by virtue of qualities only she among modern women can claim, her ancestry and her regal status.

Spenser does even more here than change his priorities from achievement to genealogy. He suggests a new set of values by which women may be judged. The superiority of Britomart to classical heroines does not logically resolve the initial question of whether the brave achievements of women are dead or asleep because she is an ancient woman and a fictional one; yet, the tone suggests that she solves the problem. The impatience is gone, and nonvisual, moral terms replace the brutal images that characterize the women of the second stanza. Penthesilea is "bold" and Deborah "stout"; Britomart is "noble." Penthesilea's "warlike feates" result in more than one "lake of *Greekish* bloud," and Camilla "hath slaine huge Orsilochus"; no verb of action and no violent images describe Britomart's "great valiaunce," and the "goodly deeds" she has done may owe as much to "pure chastitie and vertue rare" as to military might. The superior of the ancient heroines in their field of endeavor, she is not an Amazon, and in her balance of accomplishments and virtue she provides a transition between "antique glory" and Elizabeth.[5] She is the ideal immediately in view when the poet praises nonmilitary Elizabeth. By means of her, the Queen, none of whose "goodly deeds" is cited, holds a position superior to the greatest women of history without being the brutal kind of woman demanded by the questions raised in the first stanza.

Book V

In Book III it is possible to use the language of humanist praise and defense of womankind to connect the Queen with a tradition of female greatness and to suggest that she is superior to other women because of her "goodly deeds," while hinting that some other mysterious superiority inheres in her. In Book V

5. Fichter, too, sees that Spenser is not committed to the Amazonian type, but he argues that Britomart is Amazonian at this point (169).

there is no mystery about the source of her superiority, and the language of Aylmer, even Calvin, is heard; Elizabeth was chosen by God. This does not mean, however, that the poem's commitment to feminine virtue and to the defense of womankind has no place in Book V. The book gives affirmative answers to two of the central questions of the defenses of Elizabeth: "Are there circumstances under which a woman may legitimately hold power?" and "Can rule by a woman ever be beneficial to a nation; can a woman be a good ruler?" It bases these answers on the case developed for womankind and the feminine in Books III and IV, especially the representation of Britomart and the particular kind of lady knight she is, rather than on the exclusive principles developed by Calvin, Aylmer, and others.

The two most powerful enemies to justice in Book V are women who abuse their power: Radigund and Duessa. Each is conquered by a woman of power: Britomart and Mercilla. In each case the kind of justice represented by Artegall, the titular hero of the Book of Justice, is inadequate to the situation; he actively supports Radigund's abuse, and he wishes for revenge against Duessa. Many critics have noted that Artegall needs to be supplemented or controlled by a kind of justice learned by Britomart, embodied in Isis, and exercised by Mercilla: equity.[6] As this list shows, Spenser represents equity as a feminine virtue.[7] This is not mere sentimentality or deference to tradition; it is a logical consequence of his representation of chastity and womanhood in the earlier books. Isis and Mercilla reveal that, when given the authority it deserves, equity, like chaste female sexuality, is characterized by the power to restrain masculine force and turn it to productive use. Book V is a fulfillment of Book III; it unfolds the political benefits of chastity.

By its very nature chastity is a conservative virtue, and, in practice in Book V, the realization of the social benefits that it contributes depends on a hierarchical model of society in which the female is naturally politically inferior to the male. In the best tradition of all the defenders of womankind whose works we have examined, Spenser uses praise as a method of political containment. He represents the rejection of the Amazonian model of queenship as praiseworthy; he suggests, by means of allegory, that Elizabeth's behavior

6. For extensive treatments of equity, see Aptekar 54–57; Phillips, "Renaissance"; Knight; Kermode 49–59.

7. Spenser was not alone in his association of equity with the feminine. See Jordan, *Renaissance Feminism*, for a discussion of equity in English law and thought and of "Sidney's concern for equity as the feminine complement to justice." She notes that in Book V equity is "gendered as feminine and attributed especially to female magistrates" (236). O'Connell also stresses the "essentially feminine quality of equity" (145).

toward Mary Stuart can be read as just such a rejection of paths she herself might have chosen; thus, he simultaneously advises Elizabeth on how she ought to behave and defends his fictional world and his nation from the notion that acceptance of the legitimacy of Elizabeth's power makes an inversion of the sexual hierarchy inevitable. Only inasmuch as Elizabeth has fit and continues to fit the pattern of the virtuous woman who is raised to authority but does not seek it, is she and will she be worthy of praise.

Radigund

Radigund represents the kind of female monarch that misogynists predicted, that Aylmer defended his nation and his text against, and that even Britomart, at times, seems to be. The queen of an artificially constructed matriarchy, she subverts male authority and strength; she is politically and sexually corrupt. She makes all the men she conquers with "force or guile" dress in female clothes, perform feminine domestic occupations, and subsist on a diet of bread and water to keep them "from reuenge aduenturing" (V.iv). When Artegall makes war against her, she guilefully conquers him, keeps him prisoner, and attempts to seduce him. She is a tyrannical ruler; like a Petrarchist lover, he is "a womans slave" and "her vassall" (V.v.23). Britomart's defeat of Radigund definitively distinguishes the good powerful woman from the Amazon in both the political and the interpersonal spheres.

Artegall's capitulation to Radigund represents the danger of submitting to female authority without demanding that it have natural, legal, and divine sanctions. He conceives of his public relationship to a woman in private terms and literalizes the situation of a Petrarchist lover. When he first attacks her city, the fighting is general; at sunset when they call a temporary truce, he is winning and accomplishing the just revenge that is his goal. When Radigund's emissary brings to him the proposal that the terms of the battle be changed to single combat between the two leaders of the forces, however, he responds to the seductive atmosphere, abandons his clear advantage, and agrees, even though her terms ought to be unappealing. They make a mockery of justice because they leave the result to fortune and because they do not address the issue that prompted Artegall to fight her in the first place: the cruel, unnatural nature of her form of government.[8]

8. From Radigund's point of view her suggestion that one-to-one combat be substituted for general battle is a wise strategy; on her own she is more likely to avenge Artegall's partial victory and save her people. Nothing in the presentation of the scene encourages us to accept her point of view, however. Her mind is troubled, she seeks revenge, and her terms are unchivalric.

At the end of their duel, Artegall errs in assuming that a female opponent is necessarily a special case; he applies the doctrine of equity inappropriately. He knows the evil nature of his opponent, and in the heat of the battle he feels indignation at her "vaunting vaine"; yet, when her face is revealed, he is so touched with pity that he discards all reason and is paralyzed in front of her, as though Perseus had looked at Medusa. Unable to distinguish between women, he is willing to make exceptions of all of them on the basis of their beauty and their sex rather than on the basis of their deserts.[9] Britomart has a right to have that effect on him as she is not only a gallant knight and a good woman, but his destined bride; she demonstrates her goodness by relinquishing her authority in the course of the courtship. Radigund has no such claims to merit: she is full of unchivalric guile, and he feels no love for her.[10]

Indeed, even though Artegall does not love Radigund, troubling erotic overtones accompany the Narrator's account of the hero's assumption of female clothing and duties. A reference to Hercules stresses his erotic and unheroic aspect: when he spent time spinning and dressed as a woman he forgot war and "onely joyed in combats of sweet loue" (V v.24).[11] This suggests that infidelity to one's duty and to one's love are the inevitable results of political submission to a woman. The woman's power may include complete control of the male will.

This possibility is elevated to a political truism by the Narrator in the next stanza when he cites what happens to Artegall as exemplary of what happens when women are elevated above men:

> Such is the crueltie of womenkynd,
>> When they haue shaken off the shamefast band,
>> With which wise Nature did them strongly bynd,
>> T'obay the heasts of mans well ruling hand,
>> That then all rule and reason they withstand,
>> To purchase a licentious libertie.

9. Susanne Woods discovers that "Artegall becomes Britomart's vassal of his own free will. He becomes Radigund's slave because of her improper use of female beauty to effect political tyranny. She does not inspire with her beauty as do Britomart, the Faerie Queene, and Queen Elizabeth; she uses it to enervate her opponent" (152).

10. See Bender for a comparison of the two scenes.

11. See Aptekar, chapter 11, on the eroticism of Artegall's relationship with Radigund.

> But vertuous women wisely vnderstand,
> That they were borne to base humilitie,
> Vnlesse the heauens them lift to lawfull soueraintie.
>
> (V.v.25)

Although I once argued that "so strong is the sense of revulsion for female rule in this episode that Spenser's concession to Elizabeth's right to rule seems almost an afterthought" ("Rule Virginia" 280), I now suggest that this last line is not a "concession," but rather the encomiastic point toward which the entire episode has been moving: we must know Radigund to appreciate Elizabeth.

By this strategy Spenser emphasizes Elizabeth's divine authority. God does at times sanction female monarchs, and the validity of their governments is recognizable from their conduct. A female governor who behaves like Radigund (or Mary Stuart) is clearly not one of the chosen. Inasmuch as Elizabeth's government does not resemble Radigund's in the oppression of men and in vanity, it can be recognized as legitimate and praiseworthy.[12] Elizabeth's strength lies in her virtue, in her legitimate claim to the throne, and in her divine elevation to it; these points are made repeatedly in the formal defenses of her sovereignty (see Chapter 9). With these lines Spenser celebrates Elizabeth's position and her virtue, and the proviso is not merely an accommodation to the times.

It is also important not to allow this passage more scope than it claims as a pronouncement on womankind. The stanza is narrowly restricted to a statement of woman's place in the political hierarchy. Although the emphasis on the necessity of divine intervention to produce a queen aligns this passage with the strictest Calvinist pronouncements on gynecocracy, there is no Calvinist disdain for women present here to make it a contradiction of the proems to cantos 2 and 4 in Book III or of the characterization of Britomart. It is not antifeminist in moral or spiritual terms. It assumes that women can be virtuous and that they can recognize the claims of the political order. Force is not necessary to keep them in their subordinate position. They usually "wisely understand."

By this logic, Radigund is a necessary figure in Spenser's profeminist case as the Queen's antithesis. Given the traditional and Calvinist arguments against

---

12. Northrop suggests that God's raising of Elizabeth is an example of equity. "Spenser's contribution to the gynaecocratic controversy was to see the exceptions created by God as an instance of equity, in which the law of men's rule is put aside so that the principle of the rule of the superior will be followed by conferring sovereignty on the divinely endowed woman" (277–78).

woman rule, Spenser must admit that there can be bad female monarchs (just as there are bad male monarchs), if his praise of female monarchy is to be taken seriously instead of being discounted as mere courtier's flattery. Radigund is a cautionary figure who demonstrates that feminine qualities misused result in misrule, and she does everything that conventional wisdom said a woman monarch would do, only she does it literally: the danger of male effeminacy is realized in the dressing of male captives in female clothing and in the expectation that they will do female domestic labor. The danger that the monarch will destabilize personal sexual hierarchies as well as political ones and will become the sexual aggressor comes true in the Amazon's passion for Artegall. But the real horror of her reign is its restriction of male freedom of movement and decision. In such a realm nothing gets done. If a woman rules by taking advantage of the weaknesses of men and by appealing to their allegiance to her private person rather than to her public person, then the result is bad government.[13]

This is, of course, a typically Amazonian way of going about ruling, and Radigund shares qualities with other Amazonian figures in *The Faerie Queene*. Sexually aggressive Malecasta, for example, is comically defeated by the prior "effeminacy" of the male she believes she has conquered. The Amazonian figure with whom Radigund has the most in common, however, is Belphoebe, even though Spenser's descriptions of Belphoebe in Book III evoke the huntress Diana rather than the military Amazon. Like her, Radigund has made a lifetime commitment to carrying arms (unlike Britomart, who took them up for an express purpose) and, although she wears armor, her dress is a corrupt version of the nymph's feminine outfit (Hamilton ed., note to V.v.2–3), whereas Britomart appears to be a man. Like Belphoebe and Britomart, she conquers by her suddenly seen beauty, but like Belphoebe alone she does not relinquish government to the male. They are both feminine in appearance and masculine in conduct.

Beneath these similarities there lie profound differences, of course. Belphoebe has no interest in sex; Radigund does. Belphoebe does not rule a nation; Radigund does. These differences make it possible for Belphoebe to be a positive figure while her counterpart is negative, but they do not entirely erase the feature that the characters share: their retention of the government

13. I do not intend this interpretation to replace the readings of the episode as an allegory of Elizabeth's conflict with Mary Stuart begun by Neill, but rather to show that a more general allegory of the dangers of gynecocracy is also present. See O'Connell for an excellent recent interpretation of the episode as an allegorization of Elizabeth's relationship with Mary (140ff.). Also see Norbrook (138).

of conquered men.[14] Both are figures of the Petrarchist mistress. In the Belphoebe and Timias episode the Petrarchist problem of lack of sexual satisfaction is solved by Timias's willingness to maintain the relationship on a nonsexual plane, and the problems caused by the hierarchical reversal are avoided. Timias sacrifices his freedom to act in the political world that lies outside Belphoebe's woods, but in exchange he gets emotional satisfaction and spiritual advancement through love. Although a sense of loss in regard to Timias's heroic role in the poem permeates the episode, this solution is adequate in the domestic territory of Book IV, on the margins of the private and the public. An exception can be made for Belphoebe because she is virtuous and virginal and private; she does not rule a kingdom, just one man's heart. When her behavior is projected as a political principle in Book V, however, the result is tyranny and social chaos. The Petrarchist mistress is not a positive political model because, as public policy, restriction of the male sphere does not work.[15]

If Radigund's similarity to Belphoebe implies a criticism of Petrarchism as a model for female rule, then it may also imply criticism of Elizabeth's famed public application of Petrarchist principles, her method of rule, as opposed to her right to rule.[16] She is famous for having tempered the discomfort that courtiers felt at being ruled by a woman by presenting herself as their lady. That is, she offered them the opportunity to perceive themselves as Petrarchist lovers, ever longing, ever her vassals. Her wrath when they turned to other women for satisfaction is well known; the personal pain caused by this strategy is, of course, directly allegorized in the Belphoebe and Timias episodes.

The possibility that the Petrarchism of Radigund's queenship is a critique of Elizabeth's style is reinforced by Simon Shepherd's reading of Artegall as Raleigh and Radigund as Elizabeth in *Amazons and Warrior Women*; Book V urges Elizabeth to follow a more aggressively Protestant foreign policy and to free Raleigh to act: let him go and look what you will achieve, it says. It follows from this interpretation that the distinction between Radigund and Elizabeth in stanza 25 is not just a nod in the direction of praise, but rather a reminder

---

14. O'Connell notes the similarity of Radigund, Belphoebe, and Britomart, and suggests that they are connected with "the propaganda battle waged by supporters of Elizabeth and of Mary," but distinguishes Radigund from the others because only "she psychologically emasculates the men she encounters," as did Mary (141–42).

15. See Woods for a reading of this episode as representing Petrarchism favorably.

16. Bowman comes to a similar conclusion from a very different starting point. She argues that *Britomart* employs the same strategies to "ease Artegall's fears of her power" that the Queen used "to pacify her possibly anxious male courtiers"; yet she concludes that "when Britomart kills her [Radigund]," she rejects "the model of Elizabeth's court" (523–24).

to the Queen that she is queen by God's choice. Therefore, the episode prods her to use her men to get on with God's business (as the poet conceives of it). Her Protestant lords are her rod that will bring Europe into line. Justice is not human but divine, and she is an executor of divine justice in her international policy. She must not behave like an Amazon or Petrarchist mistress and misdirect allegiance owed to her public body to the satisfaction of her private vanity. In her relations with Artegall and in the government of her realm, Radigund is a negative exemplar of female authority; she is a "tyrannesse," as the poet says repeatedly. Elizabeth must follow another model—Mercilla—but first Radigund must be overpowered.

Before Britomart becomes the agent of Amazonian Radigund's defeat, the last traces of the Amazon in her are excised. She finishes the process of becoming Radigund's opposite: a good woman who does not hate men and who does not desire to retain political authority but who is fully capable and willing to wield it when necessary. She is neither an Amazon nor an Amoret. This characterization of Britomart is only incontrovertibly established in the representation of her meeting the challenge that Artegall's submission to Radigund presents to her.[17] Spenser first shows where Britomart stands emotionally and politically before she sets out to dispute Radigund's right to Artegall. He then represents her political education at Isis Church; finally, he shows her political act in her defeat of Radigund and her reorganization of the government.

In creating the story of Britomart's anxiety about Artegall's absence and her defeat of Radigund, Spenser makes his last use of the story of Bradamante and Ruggiero. Once again the poet's method of imitation is to take several widely separated *Orlando furioso* episodes and cross-fertilize them. In this case, the story of Bradamante's jealousy of Ruggiero's supposed engagement with Marfisa is supplemented by the story of Ruggiero's emasculating sexual captivity by Alcina; Radigund's Amazonian reign is indebted to both the story of the "donne omicide" and the establishment of female government at the end of the story of Marganorre. Once again, the political and social implications of the Ariosto stories are reversed in the Spenserian imitations, and the English poet's views of politics and gender triumph.

When Britomart receives the news of Artegall's thralldom to Radigund, she has become as helplessly feminine as Artegall. She is at home and has retired back into a traditional dependent female role of the kind revealed in Scudamour's account of his adventure at the Temple of Venus.[18] She is not wearing

---

17. For a recent reading of this episode in psychological terms, see Bowman, who argues that Britomart wants to "avoid instilling fear in the man she loves. . . . Inverting the Amazonian society enables her to respond to this dilemma" (512). Bowman finds evidence for this reading in the *Furioso*.

18. Although Spenser never says that she is at home and never gives the castle in which she waits any of the warm domestic coloring of her home in Book III, he does refer to "her bed."

armor; she considers sending someone else to look for Artegall and only daydreams of going herself (vi.6). And she indulges in jealous daydreams. After Talus tells her that Artegall is captive of a Tyranesse, she laments not "as women wont, but . . . / Like a wayward childe" (xiii.9–xiv.1). She has regressed to the girlhood she so resolutely left behind when she donned armor and set out on her quest.

Britomart's situation is evocative of Bradamante's when she learns of Ruggiero's supposed engagement to Marfisa. Like Britomart, Bradamante waits at home for the return of her lover and falls into a jealous fit when he fails to meet his appointment, but with more reason: she is told unambiguously that Ruggiero is engaged to Marfisa, even though, in fact, he merely has been delayed because he is wounded, and Marfisa is innocently nursing him. There are two major differences between these stories: Britomart is jealous without any external provocation, and yet her nightmare is true—Artegall, although technically faithful, has submitted himself to another woman's authority. Both these changes suggest an imperfect faith in the lovers. Britomart's is resolved when she seeks more information from Talus and is converted into a political as well as a personal virtue when she visits Isis Church; Artegall needs to wait for her to liberate him.

Spenser begins to establish the equation between Britomart's chaste faith and justice at Dolon's house. Dolon and his sons mistake her for Artegall not only because she is with Talus but because of "many tokens plaine," and she survives Dolon's guileful attacks because she is faithful to her mission.[19] She remains in her armor instead of relaxing and going to bed, and she resists the efforts of her own eyes to relax their vigilance, although nothing in particular has happened to put her on guard. Her conduct contrasts with her behavior at Malecasta's Castle Joyous, when her utter ignorance of guile and of her own responsibilities led her to disarm and go to bed. She is ready now as she was not then. The similarity of the situation suggests that the faith illustrated here is an aspect of the chastity illustrated there.

The role of faith in her behavior is emphasized by the poet's contrast of her with Saint Peter. She reproaches her eyes three times, stays awake, and "by Gods grace, and her good heedinesse, she was preserued" (V.vi.34). Her personal faith to her beloved takes on the aura of religious faith. Because of it, she conquers guile quite easily and arrives at Isis Church, where she encounters

---

19. Phillips sees the Dolon episode as essential to "the concept of equity exemplified in the central cantos" but he lays stress on Britomart's actions themselves and not the inner disposition they reveal. It exemplifies "the capacity to administer justice, even Justice Absolute, in a woman who will be the exception to the law against the woman ruler" ("Renaissance Concepts" 113).

equity. The only transition between the end of the bridge where she fights Dolon's sons and the entry to Isis Church is the Narrator's paean to justice. It seems that her faithful victory over guile propels her into the church, whereas Artegall's unfaithful defeat by guile propels him into Radigund's dungeon.

At the church, the identification of Britomart's chastity with faith takes on its full political significance. The statement that the female goddess Isis figures equity (V. vii. 3) sets into motion the Platonic principle that forms the basis for Sir Thomas Elyot's proof of women's capacity for government: faith is the private face of equity; equity is the essence of justice and good government; therefore, women's capacity for faith makes them capable of justice and good government. (See my Chapter 7.) Because chastity is a form of faith and faith a form of equity, Britomart's demonstration of chastity in Book III, friendship in Book IV, and justice in Book V, are all manifestations of the same virtue. This Platonic notion is an important part of Spenser's paradoxical defense of women and of gynecocracy because it values the feminine over the masculine. Woman does not ape masculinity in order to play a political role; she draws on a virtue that is inherent in her own sex and that she frequently demonstrates in private life.

Britomart's dream and the priest's interpretation of it reveal the Platonic lesson. In it, her personal sexual mission and her political function merge. Just as her initiations into sexuality and social relations were completed at the House of Busyrane and in hearing of the Temple of Venus, her initiation into politics is completed here; her prior knowledge of sexuality is applied to politics.[20] In the Garden of Adonis, the feminine tames male aggression into productive sexual activity; here Isis's rod directs the aggression of war to peaceful ends.[21] The statue of the goddess represents abstract virtue and exists in a realm outside time; her crocodile can always sleep. Britomart and her descendent Elizabeth represent virtue in this fallen world where force is necessary; they need to have relations with the savage crocodile, but, under feminine control, male aggression and sexual energy are productive of peace. The encounter between Britomart and the crocodile figures the union between feminine equity and masculine rough justice that has produced the (Protestant) lion of England that brings peace when it fights: "[he] shortly did all other beasts subdew" (viii.16). The pacific predictions of this dream come true at the end of the book when Artegall fights wars to liberate a number of

20. Roche has shown that this episode is connected with the Busyrane episode by Busiris, who is associated with Osiris (*Kindly* 81). Aptekar demonstrates the episode's closeness to emblems of marriage (99–107). Fletcher suggests that Britomart is initiated into her womanhood (268).

21. Kathleen Williams explored the relationship of Venus's Temple and Isis's (175).

monarchies, all headed by female monarchs.[22] Just war liberated by chastity-equity brings peace.

Britomart's liberation of Artegall from Radigund puts the Amazonian alternative to rest. The Amazon is conquered by the woman who fights for the good of her family and nation. Britomart's victory is marked by her lack of mercy toward the woman who humiliated Artegall and her great mercy to everyone else—the citizens of Radigund's state and Artegall himself. She cuts off Radigund's head, prevents Talus from killing any more people than he already has, and supplies Artegall with masculine attire and a lecture on the transience of fleshly force when it is not supported by virtue.[23] His virtue restored, Artegall goes on his way, no longer tempted out of his path by pity for female evildoers.

Britomart's restoration of male sovereignty undoes Artegall's misplaced equity.

> . . . she there as Princess rained,
> And changing all that forme of common weale,
> The liberty of women did repeale,
> Which they had long vsurpt; and them restoring
> To mens subiection, did true Iustice deale:
> That they as a Goddesse her adoring,
> Her wisedome did admire, and hearkned to her loring.
>   (V.vii.42)

The people's joy at their return to patriarchal order asserts the rightness of Britomart's action.

The Narrator's denomination of the restoration of hierarchy as true justice recalls his statement in the proem to the canto

> For th'heuens themselues . . .
> . . . are rul'd by righteous lore
> Of highest Ioue, who doth true iustice deale
> To his inferiour Gods, and euermore
> Therewith containes his heauenly Common-weale:
> The skill whereof to Princes hearts he doth reueale.
>   (V.vii.1)

22. "[T]he dream image of sexual *discordia concors* makes equity and the common law a fused whole of British justice" (O'Connell 145).

23. In Book III, Spenser introduces the notion that Britomart is indifferent to feminine beauty when she does not follow Florimell.

Britomart is a reigning princess, and God has revealed the secret of government to her. She is an appropriate vehicle for this revelation because of her virtue. Like Elyot's Zenobia, she takes power when a man is lacking, but in this case the appropriate man is ready to hand and so, illuminated by the wisdom of God, she relinquishes power and withdraws into private life.

Britomart's restoration of patriarchy is not a betrayal of her self-reliant conduct in the earlier books, because she has never behaved in a way that ought to lead one to believe that she would sponsor a matriarchy. Again, the contrast with Bradamante is revealing because Bradamante did establish a matriarchy after disestablishing Marganorre's cruel patriarchy. Bradamante's notion that the sexes are the same made her capable of reversing the established order. Britomart's chastity leads directly to the belief in male-headed hierarchies because it is a form of justice. She is not a humanist heroine like Bradamante, but a Protestant one.

The stern language that Spenser attributes to Britomart here and to his Narrator in the earlier passage asserting the justice of male rule with only divinely sanctioned exceptions (V.v.25) once again recalls Aylmer. The relationship of the entire episode and this stanza in particular to the contemporary English controversy about rule by women was expertly explicated by James Phillips in his pair of articles on Spenser's attitude toward female rulers. Phillips concludes:

> Because she demonstrates her ability to administer justice by forcing women into the "base humilitie" to which they were born under "mans well ruling hand," Britomart clearly identifies herself as one of those exceptional women, instruments of divine justice, whom the heavens "lift to lawfull soueraintie." The episode of Radigund and Britomart, therefore, not only exemplifies Spenser's own expressed theory of gynecocracy, but also reaffirms our conviction that his position is precisely that of the moderate Calvinists. For it is with reference to the latter that we can most consistently explain his selection of a woman to overthrow the unnatural institution of female government. ("Woman" 233–34)

On the one hand, Britomart uses her sovereignty to divest herself of power, and her action shows that proven excellence in women—even her own—does not justify reversing the natural hierarchy of the sexes; on the other hand Britomart's very capacity to overthrow Radigund and reorganize the government demonstrates the natural capacity of womankind for office, should they be called. Spenser's stress on this latter quality continues to differentiate his approach from that of the "moderate Calvinists," even while he espouses the same political doctrine. His belief that chastity has a real connection to equity explains his choice of Britomart to depose Radigund better than the more cynical motives of a "moderate Protestant" desirous of office. There is a philosophical spine to his work that is missing from the more openly opportunistic official works.

Mercilla

Mercilla's court is a fitting place to end this discussion of Spenser's defense of womankind, the feminine, and his queen because the trial of Duessa is an allegory of the legal defeat of Mary Stuart, the Catholic rival whose claim on the English throne kept alive the need to defend Elizabeth against criticism of gynecocracy for so many years after her accession. Once Mary was dead (1587), the pressing need to use biblical, legal, and historical grounds to distinguish Elizabeth from the other female claimant to the throne was greatly diminished.[24] As a result, Spenser could celebrate the capacities of womankind without appearing to support the enemy in the story of Britomart; he could celebrate the Queen's extraordinary status without becoming embroiled in the detailed evidence that proved her superiority in the encomiastic proems; and in the story of Radigund he could use Mary as a model of a kind of queenship that the Queen must always take care to renounce. The story of Mercilla is the exemplary life that completes the defense of womankind in *The Faerie Queene*. Her conduct of the trial of Duessa represents the positive alternative to the rule of Radigund; it shows how a good female ruler chosen by God disciplines her passions and wisely acts in the interests of her people.

The trial of Duessa presents the ceremonial judgment of the Amazonian model of female independence by a queen who displays none of its properties. Although she is not dressed as an Amazon, Duessa exemplifies the excesses of the Amazonian mode. She seduces Blandamour and Paridell, her male supporters, and corrupts them by offering them shadowy rewards (V.ix.41); she does not have a legitimate claim to the throne that she attempts to acquire; she is

24. Northrop distinguishes "two controversies that involved the defence of Elizabeth": "the right of women to rule" and "the justice of Elizabeth's actions as ruler" (277–78). Because it is couched in terms of defense, his discussion of the latter provides a useful supplement to my argument.

not favored by God; and she claims her sex puts her outside the law. By contrast, Mercilla is "a loiall Prince"; she has God on her side and is faithful to his law (V.ix.42). She is "the heyre of ancient kings" (V.ix.29) and exercises her legitimate power wisely; she is not a tyrannical Amazon.

Mercilla's court benefits from her feminine sex; it is not perverted by it as Malecasta's and Radigund's (and Mary Stuart's) are. It is a commonplace of criticism of this episode that, in bringing Duessa to public trial and passing judgment on her, Mercilla enforces the principle of equity, as Elizabeth did in the case of Mary.[25] She thus brings into the open and exemplifies the special political benefits of feminine virtue that the poem has been suggesting from the moment it defined chastity as an active virtue, as the capacity for justice is the supreme public expression of private virtue.

Yet, as her name suggests, Mercilla goes beyond the cardinal virtues.[26] Until this point, we have seen political Elizabeth through the prism of Britomart, and Britomart, as the poet told us in the Proem to Book III, is not one of the mirrors of the Queen. She must struggle to abolish Amazonian tendencies from herself, and she feels no mercy for her mirroring opponent; she does not think or feel beyond her assertion that Radigund is not a special case. Mercilla, the ideal representative of the alternate feminine order in power, simultaneously enforces justice and feels "the wretched plight" of her whom she must judge, unlike Artegall, who is consumed by his "zeale of Iustice" (V.ix.49). Although this capacity for mercy cannot actively intervene in the case of Duessa, it is nonetheless an all-important characteristic because it raises Mercilla's feminine Christian justice above masculine zeal and vengeance. Her mercy expresses itself in her tears, in her sheltering of Duessa from "just vengeance" (V.ix.50), in the honor she allows to Duessa's corpse, and in her conduct of cases that her subjects bring to her.

The aggressive force that Spenser associates with masculine women and with men is absent from Mercilla. The rusty sword that lies at her feet in the initial description of her (V.ix.30) is an emblem of the benefits of feminine control of government. A support of order, but not its source nor its governing principle, it now lies at rest, but it dismays the world when she draws it. Like Britomart's lance and sword, Elizabeth's white rod, the boar's tusk, and Isis's crocodile, the

---

25. See O'Connell for details of the invocation of "equitable procedure . . . in the unusual (and not notably merciful) trial of the Queen of Scots" (146); Knight (286) and Graziani (379) also note the historical invocation of the principle of equity.

26. See Stump for the case for the importance of distinguishing mercy from equity in this scene (95–96). Phillips ("Renaissance Concepts") sees this episode as belonging to the exposition of mercy, not equity. For a negative evaluation of Spenser's success in representing mercy, see O'Connell (153–54).

masculine sword, pressed into service by the feminine ruler, brings about peace.[27] In this scene, the woman ruler is the ideal ruler because her feminine qualities are what the world needs.

Because the account of Mercilla does not explicitly distinguish the rightful queen from the wrongful one on the Calvinist grounds that the former was raised by God from her natural inferior status and the latter was not (as the other moments of celebration of Elizabeth discussed in this chapter do), the defensive tone, omnipresent elsewhere, is absent here. Yet, this encomiastic representation of the Queen is an ideal, of course, and like all encomia, it serves an advisory purpose.[28] By aligning the conflict between the Amazonian and the feminine models of queenship with the conflict between Catholic and Protestant theology and politics, the narrative of Mercilla's judgment of Duessa associates the triumph of Protestantism with the defeat of autocratic female rule. Because Mercilla's treatment of Duessa is exemplary of her behavior at all times, if Elizabeth is to be Mercilla, she must imitate herself and continue her past course of action; she must not lapse into Amazonian queenship now that the need to defend herself against her Amazon rival is past.

Critics of *The Faerie Queene* frequently argue about where the allegorical core of Book V lies. Certainly, if Spenser's development of the notion of the nature of woman is taken seriously, there can be no doubt. Important as Isis Church is to Britomart's and the reader's understanding of the relationship between chastity and equity, it is Mercilla who brings the long and complex sequence to a close. In her, the positive personal, social, and political value of the feminine—which has been so carefully constructed throughout Books III, IV, and V, in such diverse episodes as the Garden of Adonis, the encounter with Malecasta, and the meeting with Dolon, to name but a few—receives its final and most showy exposition. Mercilla is the fullest fulfillment of the capacities of womankind.

Conclusion

It is not only in the interests of symmetry that I have brought the second part of this study of Renaissance defenses of and against independent women to a

27. Cheney offers a sensitive analysis of the precarious balance of action and inaction in Mercilla (166–67).

28. Goldberg offers an important corrective to the general tendency to find bland approval of the Queen's policies in this part of the poem. He stresses the contradiction and strain present in the Bonfont/Malfont episode and the trial of Duessa. Both raise questions about Spenser's relation to "the discourse of power," and the trial of Duessa lays bare the premises upon which sovereign power operates ("Poet's" 88).

close with the second installment of *The Faerie Queene,* as I ended the first with the second edition of the *Orlando furioso.* This is a logical place to conclude because in both England and Italy the terms of the discussion of woman and her social role were significantly altered by events that occurred soon after the publication of these texts: the death of the aged Queen and the deliberations of the Council of Trent. Many more books and pamphlets in praise and defense of womankind were published in both nations, but the changed political climate, the development of new rhetorical strategies and new topics, and the entry of female authors into the debate would place the books outside the scope of my study, even if it had not already grown so long that any additions would try even the kindest reader's patience.

The period I have considered forms an integral unit within the larger history of the notion of woman in European thought. Although the fundamental issue—whether the differences that are usually apparent between the sexes are physiologically or culturally caused—reappears whenever the place of woman in society becomes a question, the particular literary strategies of defense and praise that these texts use to accommodate women's newly defined capacities without disrupting traditional social and literary order make them particular to their time. They contain the textual and cultural challenge of the independent woman, even while acknowledging the positive cultural contributions that she had made in the past and was at present making.

WORKS CITED

Primary Sources

Agrippa, Henricus Cornelius von Nettesheim. *A Treatise of the Nobilitie and excellencye of woman kynde.* Trans. David Clapham. London, 1542.

———. *De Nobilitate et Praecellentia Foeminei Sexus.* 1529.

Alighieri, Dante. *Purgatorio.* Ed. Natalino Sapengo. Florence: La Nuova Italia, 1956.

Allday, John. *The Praise and Dispraise of Women.* London, 1579. [Translated from a French original.]

Anger, Jane. *Her Protection for Women.* London, 1589.

———. *Her Protection for Women* (selections). *First Feminists: British Women Writers, 1578–1799.* Ed. Moira Ferguson. Bloomington: Indiana University Press, 1985. 58–73.

———. *Her Protection for Women* (selections). *Half Humankind: Contexts and Texts of the Controversy about Women in England, 1540–1640.* Ed. Katherine Usher Henderson and Barbara F. McManus. Urbana: University of Illinois Press, 1985. 173–88.

———. *Her Protection for Women. The Women's Sharp Revenge: Five Women's Pamphlets from the Renaissance.* Ed. Simon Shepherd. New York: St. Martin's Press, 1985. 29–51.

Aquinas, Thomas. *Summa Theologica.* Trans. Fathers of the English Dominican Province. Vol. 2. New York: Benziger Bros., 1947.

Arienti, Sabadino degli. *Gynevera de le clare donne di Joanne Sabadino de li Arienti.* Ed. Corrado Ricci and Alberto Bacchi della Lega. Scelta di curiosità letterarie 223. Bologna: Romagnoli-Dall'Acqua, 1888.

Ariosto, Ludovico. *Orlando furioso.* Ed. Lanfranco Caretti. La letteratura italiana: storia e testi 19. Milan and Naples: Riccardo Ricciardi Editore, 1954.

Aristotle. *Oeconomica.* Trans. E. S. Forster. *The Works of Aristotle,* vol. 10. Ed. W. D. Ross. Oxford: Clarendon Press, 1921.

———. *The Politics.* Trans. Benjamin Jowett. Ed. Richard McKeon. New York: Random House, 1941.

———. *Rhetoric. The Rhetoric and The Poetics of Aristotle.* Trans. W. Rhys Roberts and Ingram Bywater. New York: Random House, 1954.

Aylmer, John. *An Harborowe for faithfull and trewe Subjectes agaynst the late blowne Blaste, concerninge the Gouernment of Wemen.* Strasbourg [J. Day, London], 1559.

Barberino, Andrea da. *Aspramonte.* Ed. M. Boni. Bologna: Palmaverde, 1951.

Barbero, Francesco. *De re uxoria.* La letteratura italiana: storia e testi 13. Milan and Naples:

Riccardo Ricciardi Editore, 1952. Rpt. *Prosatori Latini del quattrocento.* Vol. 1. Ed. Eugenio Garin. Turin: Einaudi, 1976. 104–37.

Bentley, Thomas. *The Monument of Matrones.* London, 1582.

Bercher, William (Barker). *A dyssputacion off the nobylytye off wymen.* London, 1559. [Borrowed without acknowledgment from Lodovico Domenichi's *La Nobiltà delle donne* and from Galeazzo Flavio Capella's *Della Eccellenza*].

Biondo, Michelangelo. *Angoscia, doglia e pena le tre furie del mondo. Trattati del cinquecento sulla donna.* Ed. Giuseppe Zonta. Scrittori d'Italia 56. Bari: Laterza, 1913.

Bisticci, Vespasiano da. *Il Libro delle lode e commendazione delle donne.* Biblioteca Riccardiana, Florence. Cod. Ricc. 2293.

———. *Il Libro delle lodi e commendazioni delle donne. Vite di Uomini illustri del secolo XV.* Vol. 3. Ed. Ludovico Frati. Collezione di opere inedite o rare 72. Bologna: Romagnoli-Dall'Acqua, 1893. 289–305.

———. "Vita di Alessandra de' Bardi." *Vite di Uomini illustri del secolo XV.* Vol. 3. Ed. Ludovico Frati. Collezione di opere inedite o rare 72. Bologna: Romagnoli-Dall'Acqua, 1893. 245–88.

Boccaccio, Giovanni. *Concerning Famous Women.* Trans. Guido A. Guarino. New Brunswick, N.J.: Rutgers University Press, 1963.

———. *De mulieribus claris.* Ed. Vittorio Zaccaria. Tutte le opere 10. Verona: Mondadori, 1970.

Boiardo, Matteo Maria. *Orlando innamorato.* Ed. Aldo Scaglione. 2 vols. 2d ed. Turin: U.T.E.T., 1963.

Bradiamonte, sorella di Rinaldo. Cantàri Cavallereschi dei secoli XV e XVI. Ed. Giorgio Barini. Collezione di opere inedite o rare 91. Bologna: Romagnoli-Dall'Acqua, 1905. 159–204.

Breton, Nicholas. "The Praise of Vertuous Ladies and Gentlewomen." *The Wil of Wit.* London, 1599.

———. "The Praise of Vertuous Ladies and Gentlewomen." *The Works in Verse and Prose of Nicholas Breton.* Ed. Alexander Grosart. 2 vols. 1879. Rpt. New York: AMS Press, 1966. II:53–60.

Bridges, John. *A defence of the Government . . .* London, 1587.

Bruni, Lionardo d'Arezzo. "De Studiis et Literis." *Vittorino da Feltre and Other Humanist Educators.* Ed. and trans. William Harrison Woodward. 1887. Rpt. New York: Teachers' College, 1963. 123–33.

Buchanan, George. *The History of Scotland.* Trans. J. Fraser. London, 1690.

Bullinger, Heinrich. *The Christen state of matrimonye.* Trans. Myles Couerdale. Antwerp, 1541.

———. *A Confutation of the Pope's Bull.* Trans. A. Golding. London, 1572.

Burdet, Robert. See Vaughan.

Calvin, John. "Letter to Sir William Cecil." Letter 15. *The Zurich Letters.* Second series. Trans. Rev. Hastings Robinson. Cambridge: Cambridge University Press, 1845.

Capella, Galeazzo Flavio. See Capra.

Capra, Galeazzo Flavio (pseud. Capella). *Della eccellenza et dignità della donna.* Rome, 1525.

———. *Della eccellenza et dignità delle donne.* Ed. Maria Luisa Doglio. Biblioteca del Cinquecento 40. Rome: Bulzoni, 1988.

Castiglione, Baldesar. *Il Libro del Cortegiano.* Ed. Bruno Maier. *Il Libro del Cortegiano con una scelta delle opere minori.* Turin: U.T.E.T., 1964.

———. *La Seconda Redazione del Cortegiano di Baldassare Castiglione.* Ed. Ghino Ghinassi. Florence: G. C. Sansoni, 1968.

Cecil, William, Baron Burghley (pseud. R. G.). *Salutem in Christo.* London, 1571.

Clapham, David. *A Treatice of the Nobiliti and excellencye of woman kynde*. London, 1542. [A translation of Heinrich Cornelius Agrippa von Nettesheim's *De Nobilitate et Praecellentia Foemenei sexus*].

Cornazzano, Antonio. *De mulieribus admirandis*. La Biblioteca Estense, Modena. Cod. Ital., J,6,21.

De Pizan, Christine. *The Book of the City of Ladies*. Trans. Earl Jeffrey Richards. New York: Persea Books, 1982.

Della Mirandola, Giovanni Pico. "Oration on the Dignity of Man." Trans. Elizabeth L. Forbes. *The Renaissance Philosophy of Man*. Ed. Ernst Cassirer, Paul Oscar Kristeller, and John Herman Randall, Jr. Chicago: University of Chicago Press, 1948. 223–54.

Domenichi, Lodovico. *La Nobiltà delle donne*. Venice, 1549.

Elizabeth I. "Tilbury Speech." *Women Writers of the Renaissance and Reformation*. Ed. Katharina M. Wilson. Athens: University of Georgia Press, 1987. 542–43.

Elyot, Sir Thomas. *The Book Named the Governor*. Ed. S. E. Lehmberg. Everyman's Library 227. London: Dent; New York: Dutton, 1962.

———. *The Defence of Good Women*. London, 1540.

———. *The Defence of Good Women*. *Vives and the Renascence Education of Women*. Ed. Foster Watson. New York: Longmans, Green and Co.; London: Edward Arnold, 1912. 211–39.

Feylde, Thomas. *A contrauersye bytwene a louer and a Jaye*. London, 1527(?).

Foresti, Giacomo Filippo (Fra Filippo da Bergamo). *De Plurimis claris selectisque mulieribus*. Ferrara, 1497.

Gibson, Anthony. *A Womans Woorth, defended*. London, 1599. [An unattributed translation of Alexandre de Pontayméri's *Paradoxe apologique*.]

Goggio. Bartolomeo. *De laudibus mulierum*. The British Library, London. MS Add. 17415.

Gosynhill, Edward. *Mulierum Paean* (selections). *Half Humankind: Contexts and Texts of the Controversy about Women in England, 1540–1640*. Ed. Katherine Usher Henderson and Barbara F. McManus. Urbana: University of Illinois Press, 1985. 157–70.

———. *The prayse of all women, called Mulierum Pean*. London, 1542.

Howard, Henry. *A dutifull defense of the lawfull regiment of women*. Pepys Library, Magdalen College, Cambridge: MS Pepys 2191; Bodleian Library, Oxford: MS Bodl. 903; and British Library, London: MS Add. 24,652.

———. *A Preservatiue against the Poison of supposed Prophesies*. London, 1583.

Hyrde, Richard (also Herde). Preface. *A Devout Treatise on the Pater Noster*. By Erasmus. Trans. Margaret Roper. London, 1525.

———. Preface. *A Devout Treatise on the Pater Noster*. By Erasmus. Trans. Margaret Roper. *Vives and the Renascence Education of Women*. Ed. Foster Watson. New York: Longmans, Green & Co.; London: Edward Arnold, 1912. 159–74.

———. Preface. *The Instruction of a Christen woman*. By Juan Luis Vives. London, 1529.

Knox, John. *The first blast of the trumpet against the monstruous regiment of women*. Geneva, 1558.

Lando, Ortensio (pseud.: Philalethe Polytopiensi Cive). *Forcianae Quaestiones*. Naples, 1535.

———. *Essortatione a gli huomini*. Brescia, 1545.

———. *La Sferza degli scrittori*. Venice, 1550.

———. *Lettere di molte valorose donne*. Venice, Giolito, 1548.

———. *Secondo libro de Paradossi*. Venice, 1544.

Leslie, John (pseud.: Morgan Philippes). *Concerning the Defence of the Honor of the Right Highe, Mightie, and Noble Princesse, Marie Queene of Scotland*. Louvain, 1571.

Lyly, John. *Euphues: The Anatomy of Wit. Euphues & His England*. Ed. Morris William Croll and Harry Clemons. London: Routledge; New York: E. P. Dutton, 1916.

Maggio, Vicentio. *Un breve trattato dell'Eccellentia delle Donne*. 1545.

More, Edward. *Defence of Women*. London, 1560.

——. *Defence of Women*. *Select Pieces of Early Popular Poetry*. Vol. 2. Ed. Edward Vernon Utterson. London, 1817. 95–140.

More, Thomas. *The Correspondence of Sir Thomas More*. Ed. Elizabeth Frances Rogers. Princeton: Princeton University Press, 1947.

——. *The Latin Epigrams of Thomas More*. Trans. and ed. Leicester Bradner and Charles Arthur Lynch. Chicago: University of Chicago Press, 1953.

——. *Latin Poems*. Ed. Clarence H. Miller. *The Complete Works of Thomas More*, vol. 3, pt. 2. New Haven: Yale University Press, 1984.

——. *St. Thomas More: Selected Letters*. Ed. Elizabeth Frances Rogers. New Haven: Yale University Press, 1961.

——. *Utopia*. Ed. Edward Surtz, S.J. *Selected Works of St. Thomas More*. New Haven: Yale University Press, 1964.

Ovid. *Metamorphoses*. London: William Heinemann; New York: G. P. Putnam's Sons, 1916.

Petrarch, Francesco. Letter 8 (V.4). *Familiarium Rerum libri*. *Prose*. Ed. Guido Martellotti. La letteratura italiana: storia e testi 7. Milan and Naples: Riccardo Ricciardi Editore, 1955. 862–71.

Petrarca, Francesco. *De Viris Illustribus*. *Prose*. Ed. Guido Martellotti. La letteratura italiana: storia e testi 7. Milan and Naples: Riccardo Ricciardi Editore, 1955. 218–67.

Pettie, George. *A Petite Pallace of Pettie his Pleasure*. London, 1576.

Piccolomini, Alessandro. *Della istitutione morale*. Venice, 1560.

——. *Oratione in lode delle donne*. *Della nobiltà et eccellenza delle donne dalla lingua francese nella italiana tradotta*. Venice, 1549.

Plato. *The Republic*. *The Dialogues of Plato*. Vol. 1. Trans. Benjamin Jowett. 1892. Rpt. New York: Random House, 1937.

Pyrrye, C. *The Praise and Dispraise of Women*. London, 1569.

R. G. See Cecil, William, Baron Burghley.

Salter, Thomas. *Mirrhor of Modestie*. London, 1579.

Scholehouse of women. London, 1541.

Scholehouse of women. *Select Pieces of Popular Poetry*. Vol. 2. Ed. Edward Vernon Utterson. London, 1817. 49–96.

Schoolhouse of women (selections). *Half Humankind: Contexts and Texts of the Controversy about Women in England, 1540–1640*. Ed. Katherine Usher Henderson and Barbara F. McManus. Urbana: University of Illinois Press, 1985. 137–55.

Smith, Henry. *A Preparatiue to Mariage*. London, 1591.

Spenser, Edmund. *The Faerie Queene*. Ed. A. C. Hamilton. Annotated English Poets Series. 1977. Rpt. London and New York: Longman, 1980.

——. *Works: a Variorum Edition*. Ed. Edwin A. Greenlaw, Frederick M. Padelford, Charles G. Osgood. Vol. 3. Baltimore: Johns Hopkins Press, 1934.

Strozzi, Agostino. *Defensio mulierum*. La Biblioteca Nazionale, Florence. MS Palat. 726. (See Zambrini.)

Tyler, Margaret. Dedication. *The First Part of the Mirrour of Princely Deedes and Knyghthood*. By Ortuñez de Calahorra. London, 1578.

Vaughan, Robert. *A Dyalogue Defensyue for Women*. London, 1542.

Vergerius, Petrus Paulus, the Elder. "De Ingenuis Moribus." *The Italian Renaissance*. Ed. Werner L. Gundersheimer. Englewood Cliffs, N.J.: Prentice-Hall, Spectrum, 1965. 25–38.

Vives, Juan Luis. *The Instruction of a Christen woman*. Trans. and preface Richard Hyrde. London, 1529.

————. *The Instruction of a Christen woman.* Trans. Richard Hyrde. London, 1541.

————. *Instruction of a Christian Woman. Vives and the Renascence Education of Women.* Ed. Foster Watson. New York: Longmans, Green & Co.; London: Edward Arnold, 1912. 29–136.

————. "The Learning of Women." *Vives and the Renascence Education of Women.* Ed. Foster Watson. New York: Longmans, Green & Co.; London: Edward Arnold, 1912. 195–210.

————. "Plan of Studies for Girls." *Vives and the Renascence Education of Women.* Ed. Foster Watson. New York: Longmans, Green & Co.; London: Edward Arnold, 1912. 137–49.

Whetstone, George. *The English Myrror.* London, 1586.

————. *An Heptameron of Civill Discourses.* London, 1582.

Xenophon. *Xenophon: Memorabilia and Oeconomicus.* Trans. E. C. Marchant. 1923. London: Heinemann; Cambridge, Mass.: Harvard University Press, 1938.

Zambrini, Francesco, ed. *La defensione delle donne d'autore anonimo: scrittura inedita del sec. xv.* Scelta delle curiosità letterarie 148. Bologna: Romagnoli, 1876. (See Strozzi.)

Secondary Sources

Adams, Robert P. *The Better Part of Valor: More, Erasmus, Colet, and Vives on Humanism, War, and Peace, 1496–1535.* Seattle: University of Washington Press, 1962.

Alpers, Paul J. *The Poetry of The Faerie Queene.* Princeton: Princeton University Press, 1967.

Andrew, Malcolm. Introduction. *Two Early Renaissance Bird Poems.* The Renaissance English Text Society and the Newberry Library. Washington, D.C.: The Folger Shakespeare Library; London and Toronto: Associated University Presses, 1984.

Aptekar, Jane. *Icons of Justice: Iconography and Thematic Imagery in Book V of The Faerie Queene.* New York: Columbia University Press, 1969.

Ascoli, Albert Russell. *Ariosto's Bitter Harmony: Crisis and Evasion in the Italian Renaissance.* Princeton: Princeton University Press, 1987.

Axton, Marie. *The Queen's Two Bodies: Drama and the Elizabethan Succession.* London: Royal Historical Society, 1977.

Battista, Giuseppa Saccaro. "La Donna, le donne nel *Cortegiano.*" *La Corte e il Cortegiano: II—Un modello europa.* Ed. Adriano Prosperi. Centro studi "Europa delle corti." Biblioteca del cinquecento 9. Rome: Bulzoni, 1980. 219–49.

Bayne, Diane Valeri. "*The Instruction of a Christian Woman:* Richard Hyrde and the Thomas More Circle." *Moreana* 45 (1975): 5–15.

Bean, John C. "Making the Daimonic Personal: Britomart and Love's Assault in *The Faerie Queene.*" *Modern Language Quarterly* 40 (1979): 237–55.

Beilin, Elaine V. *Redeeming Eve: Women Writers of the English Renaissance.* Princeton: Princeton University Press, 1987.

Bender, John B. *Spenser and Literary Pictorialism.* Princeton: Princeton University Press, 1972.

Benson, Pamela Joseph. "An Unrecognized Defender of Women in the *Orlando Furioso.*" *Italica* 57 (1980): 268–70.

————. "A Defense of the Excellence of Bradamante." *Quaderni d'italianistica* 4 (1983): 135–53.

————. "Rule Virginia: Protestant Theories of Female Regiment in *The Faerie Queene.*" *English Literary Renaissance* 15 (1985): 277–92.

Berger, Harry, Jr. "Busirane and the War Between the Sexes: An Interpretation of *The Faerie Queene* III.xi–xii." *English Literary Renaissance* 1 (1971): 99–121.

———. "The Discarding of Malbecco: Conspicuous Allusion and Cultural Exhaustion in *The Faerie Queene*, III, ix–x." *Studies in Philology* 66 (1969): 135–54.

———. "*The Faerie Queene*, Book III: A General Description." *Criticism* 11 (1969): 234–61. Rpt. *Essential Articles for the Study of Edmund Spenser.* Ed. A. C. Hamilton. Hamden, Conn.: Archon, 1972. 395–424.

Bergin, Thomas G. *Boccaccio.* New York: Viking, 1981.

Bertana, Emilio. "L'Ariosto, il matrimonio e le donne." *Miscellanea di studi critici edita in onore di Arturo Graf.* Bergamo: Istituto italiano d'arti grafiche, 1903. 161–94.

Bieman, Elizabeth. "Britomart in Book V of *The Faerie Queene.*" *University of Toronto Quarterly* 37 (1968): 156–74.

Blasucci, Luigi. "La *Commedia* come fonte linguistica e stilistica del *Furioso.*" *Studi su Dante e Ariosto.* Milan and Naples: Riccardo Ricciardi Editore, 1969. 121–62.

Bluestone, Natalie Harris. *Women and the Ideal Society: Plato's Republic and Modern Myths of Gender.* Amherst: University of Massachusetts Press, 1987.

Bowman, Mary R. " 'she there as Princess rained': Spenser's Figure of Elizabeth." *Renaissance Quarterly* 43 (1990): 509–28.

Brand, C. P. *Ludovico Ariosto: A Preface to the* Orlando Furioso. Edinburgh: Edinburgh University Press, 1974.

Brill, Lesley. " 'Battles That Need Not Be Fought': *The Faerie Queene*, III.i." *English Literary Renaissance* 5 (1975): 198–211.

———. "Chastity as Ideal Sexuality in the Third Book of *The Faerie Queene.*" *Studies in English Literature* 11 (1971): 15–26.

Cain, Thomas H. *Praise in* The Faerie Queene. Lincoln: University of Nebraska Press, 1978.

Carrara, Enrico. "Marganorre." *Annali della Scuola Normale Superiore di Pisa—Lettere*, 2d ser. 9 (1940): 1–20 and 155–82.

Cerbo, Anna. "Il *De mulieribus claris* di Giovanni Boccaccio." *Atti e memorie dell'accademia letteraria italiana*, 3d ser. 6 (1974): 51–75.

Chemello, Adriana. "Donna di Palazzo, moglie, cortigiana: ruoli e funzioni sociali della donna in alcuni trattati del cinquecento." *La Corte e il Cortegiano: I—La scena del testo.* Ed. Carlo Ossola. Centro studi "Europa delle corti." Biblioteca del cinquecento 8. Rome: Bulzoni, 1980. 113–32.

Cheney, Donald. *Spenser's Image of Nature: Wild Man and Shepherd in* The Faerie Queene. New Haven: Yale University Press, 1966.

Cian, Vittorio. Introduction. *Le Rime di Bartolomeo Cavassico.* Scelta di curiosità letterarie. Bologna: Romagnoli-Dell'Acqua, 1893.

———. Notes. *Il Cortegiano.* By Baldesar Castiglione. Florence: Sansoni, 1946.

Colie, Rosalie L. *Paradoxia Epidemica: The Renaissance Tradition of Paradox.* Princeton: Princeton University Press, 1966.

Crane, Mary Thomas. " 'Video et Taceo': Elizabeth I and the Rhetoric of Counsel." *Studies in English Literature* 28 (1987): 3–15.

Dalla Palma, Giuseppe. *Le Strutture narrative dell'* Orlando furioso. Biblioteca dell' *Archivum Romanicum* 173. Florence: Olschki Editore, 1984.

Davies, Rowena. "Britomart as 'Bona Mulier': Erasmian Influence Upon the Icon of Isis." *Notes and Queries* 32 (1985): 25–26.

Davies, Stevie. *The Feminine Reclaimed: The Idea of Woman in Spenser, Shakespeare and Milton.* Lexington: University Press of Kentucky, 1986.

De Blasi, Giorgio. "L'Ariosto e le passioni (Studio sul motivo poetico fondamentale dell *Orlando furioso*)." *Giornale storico della letteratura italiana* 129 (1952): 318–62 and 130 (1953): 178–203.

The Dictionary of National Biography. Vol. 10. London: Oxford University Press, 1921–22.

Dodge, R. E. Neil. "Spenser's Imitations from Ariosto." *PMLA* 12 (1897): 151–204.

———. "Spenser's Imitations from Ariosto—Addenda." *PMLA* 35 (1920): 91–92.

Durling, Robert M. *The Figure of the Poet in Renaissance Epic.* Cambridge, Mass.: Harvard University Press, 1965.

Elshtain, Jean Bethke. *Public Man, Private Woman: Women in Social and Political Thought.* Princeton: Princeton University Press, 1981.

Fahy, Conor. "Three Early Renaissance Treatises on Women." *Italian Studies* 11 (1956): 30–55.

Ferguson, Margaret W. *Trials of Desire: Renaissance Defenses of Poetry.* New Haven: Yale University Press, 1983.

Ferguson, Moira, ed. *First Feminists: British Women Writers, 1578–1799.* Bloomington: Indiana University Press, 1985.

Fichter, Andrew. *Poets Historical: Dynastic Epic in the Renaissance.* New Haven: Yale University Press, 1982.

Fletcher, Angus. *The Prophetic Moment: An Essay on Spenser.* Chicago: University of Chicago Press, 1971.

Floriani, Piero. *Bembo e Castiglione: studi sul classicismo del Cinquecento.* L'Analisi letteraria: Proposte e letture critiche 15. Rome: Bulzoni, 1976.

———. "Esperienza e cultura nella genesi del *Cortegiano.*" *Giornale storico della letteratura italiana* 146 (1969): 496–529.

———. "La genesi del *Cortegiano:* prospettive per una ricerca." *Belfagor* (1969): 373–85.

Fowler, Alastair. "Six Knights at Castle Joyous." *Studies in Philology* 56 (1959): 583–99.

Fox, Alistair. "Sir Thomas Elyot and the Humanist Dilemma." *Reassessing the Henrician Age: Humanism, Politics, and Reform, 1500–1550.* Ed. Alistair Fox and John Guy. Oxford: Blackwell, 1986. 52–73.

Garin, Eugenio. *L'educazione in Europa (1400–1600).* Bari: Laterza, 1957.

Ghinassi, Ghino. "Fasi dell'elaborazione del *Cortegiano.*" *Studi di filologia italiana* 25 (1967): 155–96.

Gilbert, Allan H. "Spenser's Imitations from Ariosto." *PMLA* 34 (1919): 225–32.

Goldberg, Jonathan. "The Mothers in Book III of *The Faerie Queene.*" *Texas Studies in Literature and Language* 17 (1975): 5–26.

———. "The Poet's Authority: Spenser, Jonson, and James VI and I." *Genre* 15 (1982): 81–99.

Grafton, Anthony, and Lisa Jardine. *From Humanism to the Humanities: Education and the Liberal Arts in Fifteenth- and Sixteenth-Century Europe.* Cambridge: Mass., Harvard University Press, 1986.

Gray, Hanna H. "Renaissance Humanism: The Pursuit of Eloquence." In *Renaissance Essays.* Ed. Paul O. Kristeller and Philip P. Weiner. New York: Harper and Row, Torchbook, 1968. 199–216.

Graziani, René. "Elizabeth at Isis Church." *PMLA* 79 (1964): 376–89.

Greenblatt, Stephen. *Renaissance Self-Fashioning: From More to Shakespeare.* Chicago: University of Chicago Press, 1980.

Greene, Thomas. "*Il Cortegiano* and the Choice of a Game." *Renaissance Quarterly* 32 (1979): 173–86.

———. *The Light in Troy: Imitation and Discovery in Renaissance Poetry.* New Haven: Yale University Press, 1982.

Grendler, Paul F. *Critics of the Italian World.* Madison: University of Wisconsin Press, 1969.

Griffin, Robert. *Ludovico Ariosto.* Twayne's World Authors Series 301. New York: Twayne, 1974.

Guidi, José. *Images de la femme dans la littérature italienne de la Renaissance*. Ed. André Rochon. Paris: Université de la Sorbonne Nouvelle, 1980.

Gundersheimer, Werner L. "Bartolommeo Goggio: A Feminist in Renaissance Ferrara." *Renaissance Quarterly* 33 (1980): 175–200.

———, ed. *The Italian Renaissance*. Englewood Cliffs, N.J.: Prentice-Hall, 1965.

———. "Towards a Reinterpretation of the Renaissance in Ferrara." *Bibliothèque d'Humanisme et Renaissance* 30 (1968): 267–81.

———. "Women, Learning, and Power; Eleanora of Aragon and the Court of Ferrara." *Beyond Their Sex: Learned Women of the European Past*. Ed. Patricia H. Labalme. New York: New York University Press, 1980. 43–65.

Haller, William, and Malleville Haller. "The Puritan Art of Love." *Huntington Library Quarterly* 5 (1941–42): 235–72.

Hannay, Margaret P., ed. *Silent But for the Word: Tudor Women as Patrons, Translators, and Writers of Religious Works*. Kent, Ohio: Kent State University Press, 1985.

Heisch, Allison. "Queen Elizabeth I and the Persistence of Patriarchy." *Feminist Review* 2 (1988): 45–56.

Henderson, Katherine Usher, and Barbara F. McManus. *Half Humankind: Contexts and Texts of the Controversy about Women in England, 1540–1640*. Urbana: University of Illinois Press, 1985.

Henze, Catherine. "Author and Source of 'A Dyalogue Defensyue for Women.' " *Notes and Queries* 23 (1976): 537–39.

Hill, Iris T. "Britomart and 'Be bold, Be not too bold.' " *ELH* 38 (1971): 129–46.

Hull, Suzanne W. *Chaste, Silent, & Obedient: English Books for Women, 1475–1640*. San Marino, Calif.: Huntington Library, 1982.

Jardine, Lisa. "Isotta Nogarola: Women Humanists—Education for what?" *History of Education* 12 (1983): 231–44.

———. *Still Harping on Daughters: Women and Drama in the Age of Shakespeare*. Sussex: The Harvester Press; New Jersey: Barnes and Noble Books, 1983.

Jones, Ann Rosalind. "City Women and Their Audiences: Louise Labé and Veronica Franco." *Rewriting the Renaissance*. Ed. Margaret W. Ferguson, Maureen Quilligan, and Nancy J. Vickers. Chicago: University of Chicago Press, 1986. 229–316.

Jones, Judith P., and Sherianne Sellers Seibel. "Thomas More's Feminism: To Reform or Re-Form." *Quincentennial Essays on St. Thomas More*. Ed. Michael J. Moore. Boone, N.C.: Albion, 1978. 67–77.

Jordan, Constance. "Boccaccio's In-famous Women: Gender and Civic Virtue in the *De mulieribus claris*." *Ambiguous Realities: Women in the Middle Ages and Renaissance*. Ed. Carole Levin and Jeanie Watson. Detroit: Wayne State University Press, 1987. 25–47.

———. "Feminism and the Humanists: The Case for Sir Thomas Elyot's *Defense of Good Women*." *Rewriting the Renaissance*. Ed. Margaret W. Ferguson, Maureen Quilligan, and Nancy J. Vickers. Chicago: University of Chicago Press, 1986. 242–58.

———. *Renaissance Feminism: Literary Texts and Political Models*. Ithaca: Cornell University Press, 1990.

———. "Woman's Rule in Sixteenth-Century British Political Thought." *Renaissance Quarterly* 40 (1987): 421–51.

Jvanoff, Nicola. "Le *Roland Furieux* et la querelle des femmes au XVIe siècle." *Revue du seizième siècle* 19 (1932–33): 262–72.

Kahin, Helen Andrews. "Jane Anger and John Lyly." *Modern Language Quarterly* 8 (1947): 31–35.

Kantorowicz, Ernst H. *The King's Two Bodies: A Study in Medieval Political Theology*. Princeton: Princeton University Press, 1957.

Kaufman, Gloria. "Juan Luis Vives on the Education of Women." *Signs* 3 (1978): 891–96.

Kelly, Joan (Gadol). "Did Women Have a Renaissance?" *Becoming Visible: Women in European History*. Ed. Renate Bridenthal and Claudia Koonz. Boston: Houghton Mifflin, 1977. 137–64. Reprinted in Kelly, *Women, History, and Theory*. 19–50.

Kelly, Joan. *Women, History, and Theory: The Essays of Joan Kelly*. Women in Culture and Society Series. Ed. Catharine R. Stimpson. Chicago: University of Chicago Press, 1984.

Kelso, Ruth. *Doctrine for the Lady of the Renaissance*. Urbana: University of Illinois Press, 1956.

Kermode, Frank. *Shakespeare, Spenser, Donne*. New York: Viking, 1971.

Khanna, Lee Cullen. "Images of Women in Thomas More's Poetry." *Quincentennial Essays on St. Thomas More*. Ed. Michael J. Moore. Boone, N.C.: Albion, 1978. 78–88.

King, John N. "The Godly Woman in Elizabethan Iconography." *Renaissance Quarterly* 38 (1985): 41–84.

King, Margaret Leah. "Book-Lined Cells: Women and Humanism in the Early Italian Renaissance." *Beyond Their Sex: Learned Women of the European Past*. Ed. Patricia A. Labalme. New York: New York University Press, 1980. 66–90.

———. "Thwarted Ambitions: Six Learned Women of the Italian Renaissance." *Soundings* 59 (1976): 280–304.

———, and Albert Rabil, Jr., eds. *Her Immaculate Hand: Selected Works By and About Women Humanists of Quattrocento Italy*. Medieval and Renaissance Texts and Studies 20. Binghamton, N.Y.: MRTS, 1983.

Kittay, Eva Feder, and Diana T. Meyers, eds. *Women and Moral Theory*. Totowa, N.J.: Rowman & Littlefield, 1987.

Kleinbaum, Abby Wettan. *The War Against the Amazons*. New York: New Press–McGraw Hill, c. 1983.

Knight, W. Nicholas. "The Narrative Unity of Book V of *The Faerie Queene*: 'That Part of Justice Which Is Equity.' " *Review of English Studies* 21 (1970): 267–94.

Kristeller, Paul Oskar. "Learned Women of Early Modern Italy: Humanists and University Scholars." *Beyond Their Sex: Learned Women of the European Past*. Ed. Patricia H. Labalme. New York: New York University Press, 1980. 91–116.

Lanham, Richard A. "The Literal Britomart." *Modern Language Quarterly* 28 (1967): 426–45.

———. *The Motives of Eloquence: Literary Rhetoric in the Renaissance*. New Haven: Yale University Press, 1976.

Lehmberg, Stanford E. *Sir Thomas Elyot: Tudor Humanist*. Austin: University of Texas Press, 1960.

Levi, Ezio. "*L'Orlando Furioso* come epopea nuziale." *Archivium Romanicum* 17 (1933): 459–96.

Levin, Carole. "John Foxe and the Responsibilities of Queenship." *Women in the Middle Ages and the Renaissance*. Ed. Mary Beth Rose. Syracuse, N.Y.: Syracuse University Press, 1986.

Lewis, C. S. *Studies in Medieval and Renaissance Literature*. Ed. W. Hooper. Cambridge: Cambridge University Press, 1966.

Luzio, Alessandro, and Rudolfo Renier. "La coltura e le relazioni letterarie di Isabella d'Este Gonzaga. 5. Gruppo emiliano." *Il Giornale storico della letteratura italiana* 38 (1901): 41–70.

McMurphy, Susannah J. *Spenser's Use of Ariosto for Allegory*. Folcroft, Pa.: Folcroft Press, 1969.

Maclean, Ian. *The Renaissance Notion of Woman: A Study in the Fortunes of Scholasticism and*

Medical Science in European Intellectual Life. Cambridge Monographs on the History of Medicine. Cambridge: Cambridge University Press, 1980.

———. *Woman Triumphant: Feminism in French Literature, 1610–52.* Oxford: Oxford University Press, 1977.

Major, John M. *Sir Thomas Elyot and Renaissance Humanism.* Lincoln: University of Nebraska Press, 1964.

Marinelli, Peter V. *Ariosto and Boiardo: The Origins of* Orlando Furioso. Columbia: University of Missouri Press, 1987.

Marius, Richard. *Thomas More: A Biography.* New York: Knopf, 1984.

Miskimin, Alice. "Britomart's Crocodile and the Legends of Chastity." *Journal of English and Germanic Philology* 77 (1987): 17–36.

Molinaro, Julius A. "Sin and Punishment in the *Orlando furioso.*" *Modern Language Notes* 89 (1974): 35–46.

Momigliano, Attilio. *Saggio su* l'Orlando furioso. Bari: Laterza, 1928.

Montrose, Louis Adrian. "The Elizabethan Subject and the Spenserian Text." *Literary Theory/Renaissance Texts.* Ed. Patricia Parker and David Quint. Baltimore: The Johns Hopkins University Press, 1986. 303–40.

———. " 'Shaping Fantasies': Figurations of Gender and Power in Elizabethan Culture." *Representations* 1 (1983): 61–94.

Moore, Michael J., ed. *Quincentennial Essays on St. Thomas More.* Boone, N.C.: Albion, 1978.

Negri, Renzo. *Interpretazione dell'* Orlando furioso. Milan: Mazorati, 1971.

Neill, Kerby. "Spenser on the Regiment of Women: A Note on *The Faerie Queene,* V,v,25." *Studies in Philology* 34 (1937): 134–37.

Nohrnberg, James. *The Analogy of the* Faerie Queene. Princeton: Princeton University Press, 1976.

Norbrook, David. *Poetry and Politics in the English Renaissance.* London: Routledge & Kegan Paul, 1984.

Northrup, Douglas A. "Spenser's Defense of Elizabeth." *University of Toronto Quarterly* 38 (1969): 277–94.

O'Connell, Michael. *Mirror and Veil: The Historical Dimension of Spenser's* Faerie Queene. Chapel Hill: University of North Carolina Press, 1977.

Padoan, G. "Orlando Furioso e la crisi del Rinascimento." *Ariosto 1974 in America.* Ed. Aldo Scaglione. Atti del Congresso Ariostesco, Dicembre 1974, Casa Italiana della Columbia University. Ravenna: Longo Editore, 1976. 1–29.

Phillips, James E. "The Background of Spenser's Attitude Toward Women Rulers." *Huntington Library Quarterly* 5 (1941): 5–32.

———. "Renaissance Concepts of Justice and the Structure of *The Faerie Queene,* Book V." *Huntington Library Quarterly* 33 (1970): 103–20.

———. "The Woman Ruler in Spenser's *Faerie Queene.*" *Huntington Library Quarterly* 5 (1941): 211–34.

Piromalli, Antonio. *Motivi e forme della poesia di Ludovico Ariosto.* Messina and Florence: D'Anna, 1954.

Quilligan, Maureen. *Milton's Spenser: The Politics of Reading.* Ithaca: Cornell University Press, 1983.

Rajna, Pio. *Le Fonti Dell'*Orlando Furioso. Ed. Francesco Mazzoni. Florence: Sansoni, 1975.

Robinson, Forrest G. *The Shape of Things Known: Sidney's "Apology" in Its Philosophical Tradition.* Cambridge, Mass.: Harvard University Press, 1972.

Robinson, Lillian. *Monstrous Regiment: The Lady Knight in Sixteenth Century Epic.* New York: Garland: 1985.

Roche, Thomas P., Jr. "Ariosto's Marfisa or Camilla Domesticated." *Modern Language Notes* 103 (1988): 113–33.

———. *The Kindly Flame: A Study of the Third and Fourth Books of Spenser's* The Faerie Queene. Princeton: Princeton University Press, 1964.

Roper, William. *The Life of Sir Thomas More.* Ed. Richard S. Sylvester and Davis P. Harding. New Haven: Yale University Press, 1962.

Rose, Mark. *Heroic Love: Studies in Sidney and Spenser.* Cambridge, Mass: Harvard University Press, 1968.

Saccone, Eduardo. *Il soggetto del* furioso *e altri saggi tra quattro e cinquecento.* Le forme del Significato 1. Naples: Liguori Editore, 1974.

Sanesi, Ireneo. "Gl'epistolari del Cinquecento." *Giornale storico della letteratura italiana* 24 (1984): 1–32.

Santoro, Mario. *L'Anello d'Angelica: Nuovi saggi ariosteschi.* Naples: Federico & Ardia, 1983.

———. "Rinaldo ebbe il consenso universale." *Letture Ariostesche.* Naples: Liguori Editore, 1973. 83–133.

Schleiner, Winfried. "*Divina virago:* Queen Elizabeth as an Amazon." *Studies in Philology* 75 (1978): 163–80.

Shemek, Deanna. "Of Women, Knights, Arms, and Love: The *Querelle des Femmes* in Ariosto's Poem." *Modern Language Notes* 104 (1989): 68–97.

Shepherd, Simon. *Amazons and Warrior Women: Varieties of Feminism in Seventeenth-Century Drama.* New York: St. Martin's Press, 1981.

———, ed. *The Women's Sharp Revenge: Five Women's Pamphlets from the Renaissance.* New York: St. Martin's Press, 1985.

Silberman, Lauren. "Spenser and Ariosto: Funny Peril and Comic Chaos." *Comparative Literature Studies* 25 (1988): 23–34.

Stapleton, Thomas. *The Life and Illustrious Martyrdom of Sir Thomas More.* Trans. Philip E. Hallett. London, 1929.

Stump, Donald V. "Isis versus Mercilla: The Allegorical Shrines in Spenser's Legend of Justice." *Spenser Studies* 3 (1982): 87–98.

Thickstun, Margaret Olafson. *Fictions of the Feminine: Puritan Doctrine and the Representation of Women.* Ithaca: Cornell University Press, 1988.

Tomalin, Margaret. *The Fortunes of the Warrior Heroine in Italian Literature.* Ravenna: Longo Editore, 1982.

Tonkin, Humphrey. "Spenser's Garden of Adonis and Britomart's Quest." *PMLA* 88 (1973): 408–17.

Torretta, Laura. "Il *Liber de claris mulieribus* di Giovanni Boccaccio." *Giornale storico della letteratura italiana* 39 (1901): 252–73 and 40 (1902): 35–65.

Trafton, Dain A. "Politics and the Praise of Women: Political Doctrine in the *Courtier's* Third Book." *Castiglione: The Ideal and the Real in Renaissance Culture.* Ed. Robert W. Hanning and David Rosand. New Haven: Yale University Press, 1983. 29–44.

Turchi, Marcello. *Ariosto o della liberazione fantastica.* Ravenna: Longo Editore, 1969.

Utley, Francis. *The Crooked Rib; An Analytical Index to the Argument about Women in English and Scots Literature to the End of the Year 1568.* 1944. Rpt. New York: Octagon Books, 1970.

Valesio, Paolo. "Genealogy of a Staged Scene (*Orlando Furioso,* V)." *Yale Italian Studies* 1 (1980): 5–31.

Verbrugge, Rita. "Margaret More Roper's Personal Expression in the *Devout Treatise Upon the Pater Noster.*" *Silent But for the Word.* Ed. Margaret P. Hannay. Kent, Ohio: Kent State University Press, 1985. 30–42.

Wayne, Valerie. "Some Sad Sentence: Vives' *Instruction of a Christian Woman.*" *Silent But for the Word.* Ed. Margaret P. Hannay. Kent, Ohio: Kent State University Press, 1985. 15–29.

Weaver, Elissa B. "Lettura dell'intreccio dell'*Orlando furioso:* Il caso delle tre pazzie d'amore."
    Strumenti critici 11 (1977): 384–406.
Wernham, R. B. *Before the Armada: The Emergence of the English Nation, 1485–1588.* New
    York: Harcourt, Brace, and World, 1966.
White, Beatrice. "Three Rare Books about Women." *Huntington Library Bulletin* 2 (1931):
    165–71.
Wiggins, Peter DeSa. *Figures in Ariosto's Tapestry.* Baltimore: The Johns Hopkins University
    Press, 1986.
———. "Spenser's Anxiety." *Modern Language Notes* 103 (1988): 75–86.
Williams, Kathleen. *Spenser's* The Faerie Queene: *The World of Glass.* Berkeley and Los
    Angeles: University of California Press, 1966.
Woodbridge, Linda. *Women and the English Renaissance: Literature and the Nature of Woman-
    kind, 1540–1620.* Urbana: University of Illinois Press, 1984.
Woods, Susanne. "Spenser and the Problem of Women's Rule." *Huntington Library Quarterly*
    48 (1985): 140–58.
Wright, Louis B. *Middle-Class Culture in Elizabethan England.* Chapel Hill: University of
    North Carolina Press, 1935.
Zaccaria, Vittorio, ed. Introduction and Notes. *De mulieribus claris.* By Giovanni Boccaccio.
    Tutte le Opere 10. Verona: Mondadori, 1970.
Zancan, Marina. "La donna nel *Cortegiano* di B. Castiglione. Le funzioni del femminile
    nell'immagine di corte." *Nel Cerchio della Luna: Figure di donna in alcuni testi del* XVI
    secolo. Ed. Marina Zancan. Venice: Marsilio, 1983. 13–56.
Zonta, Giuseppe, ed. *Trattati del' 500 sulla donna.* Scrittori d'Italia 56. Bari: Laterza, 1913.

INDEX